Economics

STUDIES IN HUMAN CAPITAL

ECONOMISTS OF THE TWENTIETH CENTURY

Geneal Editors: Mark Perlman, *University Professor of Economics, University of Pittsburgh* and Mark Blaug, *Professor Emeritus, University of London, Consultant Professor, University of Buckingham and Visiting Professor, University of Exeter*

This innovative series comprises specially invited collections of articles and papers by economists whose work has made an important contribution to economics in the late twentieth century.

The proliferation of new journals and the ever-increasing number of new articles make it difficult for even the most assiduous economist to keep track of all the important recent advances. By focusing on those economists whose work is generally recognized to be at the forefront of the discipline, the series will be an essential reference point for the different specialisms included.

A list of published and future titles in this series is printed at the end of this volume.

Studies in Human Capital

Collected Essays of Jacob Mincer,
Volume 1

Jacob Mincer

Columbia University and
National Bureau of Economic Research

Edward Elgar

Published by
Edward Elgar Publishing Limited
Gower House
Croft Road
Aldershot
Hants GU11 3HR
England

Edward Elgar Publishing Company
Old Post Road
Brookfield
Vermont 05036
USA

A CIP catalogue record for this book is available from the British Library

Library of Congress Cataloging-in-Publication Data
Mincer, Jacob, 1920–
    Studies in human capital/Jacob Mincer.
        p.   cm. — (Economists of the twentieth century) (The
    Collected essays of Jacob Mincer: v. 1)
      Includes index.
      1. Human capital. I. Title. II. Series. III. Series: Mincer,
    Jacob, 1920– Essays. Selections; v. 1.
    HD4904.7.M56 1993 vol. 1
    330.12 s—dc20
    [330.12]   92–21974
                                                                     CIP

ISBN 1 85278 579 9

Printed in Great Britain at the University Press, Cambridge

Contents

Chapter references

1   Originally published in *The Journal of Political Economy*, vol. 66 (1958), pp. 281–302.
2   Originally published in *The Journal of Economic Literature*, vol. 8 (1970), pp. 1–26.
3   Originally published in *Economic Dimensions of Education*, Washington, DC: National Academy of Education, 1979.
4   Originally published in *The Journal of Political Economy*, vol. 70 (1962), part 2, pp. 50–79.
5   Originally published in *Studies in Labor Markets*, ed. S. Rosen, Chicago: University of Chicago Press, pp. 21–63 (B. Jovanovic, coauthor).
6   Originally published in *Research in Labor Economics*, vol. 8 (1986), part A, pp. 171–97.
7   Previously unpublished National Bureau of Economic Research (NBER) Working Paper no. 3838, revised 1991.
8   Previously unpublished National Bureau of Economic Research (NBER) Working Paper, revised 1988.
9   A paper presented at *Conference on Job Training*, 1988, Madison, Wisconsin; revised version published in *Market Failure in Job Training?* ed. J.H.H. Ritzen and D. Stern, Springer Verlag, 1991.
10 Originally published in *Economics of Education Review*, vol. 3 (1984), pp. 195–205.
11 Originally published in *Journal of the Japanese and International Economies*, vol. 2 (1988), pp. 97–133 (Y. Higuchi, coauthor).
12 Previously unpublished. Presented at Conference on Economic Growth, 1989, SUNY, Buffalo.
13 Previously unpublished. Presented at Conference on Research and Development, 1991, Jerusalem; National Bureau of Economic Research (NBER) Working Paper no. 3581.

Acknowledgements

For support and encouragement over many years I am grateful to the National Bureau of Economic Research, the National Science Foundation, the Sloan Foundation, and the Spencer Foundation. Thanks also to the National Center for Education and Employment for supporting much of my work since 1985 at Columbia's Teachers College.

I am deeply indebted for intellectual stimulation to generations of students and colleagues, especially participants in the Columbia Economics Department Labor Workshop.

Special thanks to the Columbia University Seminars for lively discussions and for assistance in the preparation of this volume.

Introduction

Throughout the years a large part of my research effort has centred on human capital and its effects in the labour market. Starting with my 1957 doctoral dissertation on 'Investment in Human Capital and the Personal Income Distribution', and continuing to the present, successive articles have added chapters to an unwritten book produced over a working life of more than three decades. Each study raised new questions to be answered by the next work, with similar effect. This unfinished book is now put together here roughly in the same order it evolved, as a logical and almost chronological succession of research efforts.

The collection is presented in a series of three topics: (1) effects of human capital on earnings, (2) effects of human capital on wage growth, labor turnover, and unemployment, and (3) effects of technology on the demand for human capital. The effects of human capital on earnings (Part 1) is the oldest and still the central topic of research in the field. Work on the effects of human capital on individual wage growth, turnover, and unemployment (Part 2) is more recent. It was stimulated by the growth of large micro-data panels, and by the appearance of empirical information on job training activities. While the first two topics deal with the effects of a given supply (distribution) of human capital on labor market outcomes, the last one (Part 3) focuses on factors affecting the demand for human capital. This most recent work puts human capital into the context of economic growth, with the emphasis on growth affecting human capital formation and utilization rather than the converse. Of course, each direction of causality is important, but is dealt with in different fields. The link analyzed here is of major interest to labor economists. Changes in demand for human capital generate changes in the wage structure to which supply adjusts over time. Going in the other direction, human capital as a causal factor is, of course, a major topic in the study of economic growth.[1]

The distinction between human capital as a factor in economic growth and as a factor in the distribution of (labor) income, or wage structure, appeared at the very beginning of modern developments in the late 1950s.[2] Each development appeared as a response to empirical findings that became available in the 1950s: growth theories had to face up to the finding that the observed growth of conventionally measured inputs of labor and capital was far smaller than the growth of output in the US and in other countries over long periods of time. Technical change, quality of capital and 'quality' of labor, another term for human capital, had to be implicated in the large growth residual.[3] At the same time, data on personal income distribution, which began to appear in great detail in micro-data (e.g., the US Current Population Survey), showed that the variance of labor incomes, rather than the 'functional' differences between returns to labor and to capital, represented the major component of personal income inequality. Here, human capital analysis could illuminate important aspects of the wage structure, such as the sizable wage differentials by education and age, both indicative of accumulated skill or 'labor quality'.

I have used interchangeably the terms skill, labor quality, and human capital. Accumulated skill is, indeed, a commonly used definition of human capital. Irving Fisher (1930) defined capital as any asset that gives rise to an income stream. Accumulated human work capacity qualifies as a capital asset in the same sense as physical capital even if it cannot be bought and sold (it is, of course, rented), and even though investments in such capital often involve non-market activities, such as education.

When wages are viewed as the rental price of a unit of human capital, differences in accumulated human capital can account for a great deal of wage heterogeneity. The traditional measurement of labour input in terms of 'man-hours' is clearly inadequate. The shift of focus from homogeneity to labor heterogeneity, and from short run wage and employment decisions to long-run investment decisions are the major contributions of human capital theory to labor economics.

Human capital analysis does not represent a revolution in economic theory, even if it is a major redirection in labor economics and in related fields. The concept of human capital is ancient and has been eloquently stated and elucidated by Adam Smith. However, its analytical power becomes implicit in Fisher's definition of capital, and explicit in the rigorous and elegant treatment of Gary Becker (1964). Individual acquisitions of earnings power (human capital) are subject to optimization, given costs of and returns to such investments. As returns accrue over a long period, capital theoretic present values or rates of return become the decision variables. Both costs of and gains from these investments are, in large measure, implicit in the wage structure. Responses of the multitudes of individuals to these incentives generate tendencies toward market equilibria both in the distribution of human capital across persons and in the wage distributions. These distributions, in turn, change in response to shifts in demands for and supplies of human capital.

As a guide to the topics covered in the present collection and to the human capital literature in general, it is useful to note that the various categories of human capital investments can be described in a life-cycle chronology. Resources in child care and child development represent preschool investment.[4] These overlap and are followed by investments in formal school education. Investments in job training and learning, job search and labor mobility, and in work effort occur during the working life, while investments in health[5] and other maintenance activities continue throughout life. The reference to maintenance activities reminds us that the concept of depreciation, the distinction between gross and net investment, is relevant in human capital as in other capital theory applications.

The selection of topics presented here centers around consequences and determinants of investments in school education and of labor market investments such as job training and labor mobility. As indicated above, these are not the only components of human capital investments, but they are of major importance in labor economics. Human capital investments in children, especially as they affect and are affected by labor supply of the family, is a topic included in the companion volume of Studies in Labor Supply.

Human capital and earnings

The first three articles in this volume focus on the effects of human capital on earnings. This is the initial, and it continues to be the major, subject of research in the economic analysis of education and of job training. The first article, 'Investment in Human Capital and Personal Income Distribution', is a shortened version of my doctoral thesis under the same title, presented in 1957 at Columbia University. Its main interest is historical, as the initial attempt to analyze the distribution of labor incomes by means of a single model of economic choice. This was a contrast to proliferating sociological models emphasizing 'class', probabilistic models emphasizing 'chance', biological models emphasizing 'ability' distributions, or purely statistical descriptions of the observed distributions.

The choice refers to training differing primarily in the length of time it requires. Since the time spent in training constitutes a postponement of earnings, rational occupational choice means an equalization of present values of lifetime earnings at the time the choice is made. Interoccupational wage differentials arise therefore as a function of differences in training, prior to employment. Intraoccupational wage differences arise when the concept of investment in human capital is extended to include experience on the job.

Two basic empirical implications of this model are: (a) the greater the amount of human capital the higher the wage level and the larger the investments the steeper the 'wage profile', that is the increase in wages over the working life; (b) absolute differences in length of training translate into percent differences in wages. Together these propositions can account for a number of observed patterns in the wage distribution, such as (i) aggregate positive skewness, (ii) larger wage dispersion at higher occupational levels and at older ages, among others.

The insights this work yielded concerning the skill structure of wages took the form of qualitative empirical predictions of distributional patterns of wages. It did not focus on parametric analysis, such as calculations of rates of return or of investment volumes in dollar terms. Quantitative estimates had to await further developments in human capital analysis. A comprehensive theory that made this possible found its expression in Gary Becker's classic *Human Capital* (1964). A part of the analysis was first presented at a National Bureau of Economic Research (NBER) conference in 1961, together with an application in which I estimated costs of and returns to job training as distinguished from the formal educational system. This paper is reprinted here in Part 2.

Armed with a fruitful theory and the newly available computers to handle massive micro-data, the time was ripe to develop theoretically based approaches to empirical parametric analyses of human capital investments and of their effects on wage structures and wage distributions. This was in large measure accomplished in my 1974 book, *Schooling, Experience, and Earnings*, especially in the form of the now ubiquitous 'human capital earnings function'. The book, and a large literature following it, demonstrate the usefulness of the approach in estimating costs, returns, and rates of return to capital investments in school and in the labor market, as well as in estimating parameters of wage structures, including wage distributions. The extent to which accumulated human capital investments can account for these parameters appears to be considerable.

The second article in the present collection was published in 1970 as a survey of research on the distribution of labor incomes guided by the human capital approach. A large part of it was a preview of my progress in work on the earnings function and of its potential application to wage distributions. This was preceded by a history of theoretical approaches to the analyses of income distributions, and to the works in human capital by Becker, Ben-Porath, and Chiswick that led to the formulations and empirical applications later published in my 1974 book.

In contrast to my initial work, the 1974 book relaxes a number of assumptions, allowing for preexisting inequalities that generate distributions of labor incomes as returns to investments in human capital including a distribution of individual rates of return that enters the residual in earnings. However, the inequalities in abilities and opportunities are not explicitly modelled in the book. This was accomplished by Gary Becker in his famous Woytinsky Lecture (1967) which became a chapter in the second edition of his Human Capital (1975).[6]

In the latter part of the article, I describe Becker's approach and some of its empirical applications. It is worth noting at this point that, although my analysis in the 1974 book uses a 'reduced form' rather than a 'simultaneous equations' approach, the findings and their interpretation have remained robust.[7]

The analysis and findings in my 1974 book and in other research carried out up to the late 1970s is described in a largely non-technical manner in the next selection, in the article 'Human Capital and Earnings'. After an analysis of costs and returns to school education, the earnings profile, that is the growth of wages with work experience, is analyzed as a consequence of the allocation of investments over time at school and in the labor market. The analysis leads to a derivation of the earnings function. Coefficients of the earnings function are estimates of rates of return and of volumes of schooling and of post-school investments. The form of the earnings function is subject to choice in two respects: (a) it can be fitted either to dollar earnings or to the natural logarithms of earnings. In part, this choice depends on whether the focus of interest is on absolute or relative inequalities. If dollar earnings are analyzed, investment variables (schooling and experience) must also be expressed in dollar terms. If investments are recorded in units of time-years of schooling and years of experience, clearly a more convenient formulation – the dependent variable, earnings – must be expressed in logarithms. (b) The form of the experience term in the function depends on the assumed time pattern of post-school investments. There is no guidance from theory here, except that the successive installments of investment must decline after full-time entry into continuous employment. A given form of the investment–time profile implies a particular form of the earnings profile. To take the two simplest forms, a linear investment decline implies a parabolic experience function, while an exponential decline of investments gives rise to a Gompertz function. It should be clear that neither the semi-log form of the function nor the quadratic form of the experience term are inherent in the human capital earnings function. Their general use is simply a matter of convenience and consistency, bolstered by findings that the statistical fit these forms exhibit was not inferior to alternative forms.[8]

Prior to the appearance of the earnings function, rates of return to education were calculated by equating the present values of the earnings profiles for (homogeneous, or otherwise statistically 'standardized') workers who differed in education. This procedure assumed that not merely the level of the earnings profile but also its shape was determined by education. The assumption is incorrect, if job training (or more generally, post-school investments) is not rigidly tied to schooling, and if the rate of return to training differs from the rate of return to schooling. The regression procedure for the earnings function relaxes these assumptions, and separates the estimates of rates of return to schooling from rates of return on other investments. The coefficients of the schooling variables estimate the rate of return to schooling without further correction, if opportunity costs are the only costs of schooling or if direct costs (tuition) roughly equal student earnings and subsidies. Otherwise, the length of schooling completed must be corrected by a $(1 + k)$ multiplicative factor, where k is the ratio of direct (tuition) costs minus student earnings and subsidies to forgone earnings.

Another distinction that was only briefly discussed in the book is between earnings and wage rates. Which of these does human capital analysis illuminate most directly? Wage rates represent a payoff to human capital per unit of time. However, earnings are a product of wage rates and of time (hours per week, weeks per year) spent in employment. Employment periods are outcomes of worker labor supply and of demand preferences of employers. Both are related to wage rates and to human capital investments. Still the connection is not rigid, so that the earnings function is best handled as a wage function, while earnings analyses require an additional analysis of the effects of human capital on labor supply and labor demand. These effects are positive for the following reasons: (a) an increase in human capital increases the wage rate, but need not increase wealth, or not nearly as much, if the rate of return is not exorbitantly high (relative to returns on alternative investments). If so, with no effect or a minor wealth effect, increased wages induce an increased labor supply; (b) if human capital investments on the job are shared by employers and workers, both prefer stable employment to turnover.

As a result, both employment and wage rates increase with levels of human capital, and rates of return appear to be somewhat larger in earnings than in wage rates.

Labor market investments in human capital, and their implications for wage growth, labor mobility, and unemployment

In analyzing the wage structure, it is important to distinguish *levels* of lifetime earnings achieved by individuals from *shapes* of wage profiles, that is, of the course of wages over the working life. Educational attainment at school that precedes full-time entry into the labor market affects levels of lifetime earnings but not shapes of the wage profiles. The latter are affected by time-patterns of human capital investments in job training, learning, and job mobility during the working life. A great deal of statistical information is available for the calculation of costs, returns, and rates of return to school education, and such estimates are now standard practice in a large research industry. In contrast, only fragmentary information is available for comparable estimates of job training investments, and even less existed prior to the 1970s. In the absence of usable information on costs, one possible, albeit heroic, procedure was to estimate returns to post-school investments (which include job training) as a sum of annual increments in wages over the working life, and to capitalize those by an internal rate derived as a rate of return to education. This procedure was presented in the 1962 article 'On the Job Training: Costs, Returns, and Some Implications'. The conclusion, clearly very tentative, was that job training investments were a very large component of total investment in human capital in the US in 1939, 1949, and 1958. In terms of estimated dollar costs it amounted to over a half of total costs (including opportunity costs) of school education.

There are at least two reasons for believing that these estimates of volumes of job training investments are overestimates: (a) all of wage growth across experience levels was viewed as returns to job training, including gains to inter-firm job mobility which ought to be netted out as they are returns to investment in job search; (b) if the rate of return to job training exceeds that on schooling, as is plausible, the capitalization procedure overstates the volumes of investment by roughly the same (percentage) excess.

All the studies in this part of the collection deal with job training investments and their consequences. One of the important consequences is labor mobility behaviour, a connection suggested by the theory of human capital (Becker, 1975) in which job-specific investments are distinguished from general investments. Skills acquired in general training are fully portable from firm to firm. They therefore do not affect labor mobility. However, firm-specific skills are less useful in other firms. Separations from such jobs (firms, industries) are discouraged because they result in some capital losses to workers and to employers who tend to share in such investments according to the theory.

A major purpose of the articles in Part 2 is to explore empirically the implications of human capital behaviour for both the interpersonal and life-cycle structure of interfirm labor mobility. Research in labor mobility, a major topic in labor economics, had been stagnating, following an early literature in which results appeared to be mixed. In it, wage gains as well as losses appeared to be associated with mobility and even where gains were likely, immobility appeared to persist.[9] Economic rationality did not seem to fit mobility behavior. The apparent ambiguity in these findings is reconcilable in the human capital approach: as a response to perceived gains in wages, mobility promotes individual wage growth, but to the extent that on-the-job investments contain elements of specificity, wage growth is associated with attachment to the firm rather than with mobility.

Emphasis on inter-firm job mobility required a reformulation of the earnings function, by segmentation of work experience into successive firm tenures.[10] This reformulation and a number of insights into empirical findings so obtained are first presented in the joint article with Jovanovic (Chapter 5). Note that in this study, as in all preceding (and some subsequent) ones, job training is still a latent (unobserved) variable, but observed wage growth in the firm, and over experience as well as sequences of job separations, are perceived as consequences of job training. Even when job training magnitudes are measurable, the relative magnitudes of general (transferable) and specific components of training are not known (or knowable?). A working assumption which obviates this problem is that, at the firm level, training, even when largely transferable to other firms, necessarily contains some elements of firm specificity. As the greatest opportunities for training are likely to exist in firms in which training processes are closely related to and integrated with their production processes, we may infer that there is a positive relation between amounts of general and specific training received in firms. Hence, the hypothesis that the more training workers acquire, the steeper their wage growth within and across firm, *and* the stronger their attachment to the firms in which they train or continue to learn.

In this hypothesis, the inverse relation between wage growth and labor turnover is indirect, not causal; both wage growth and labor turnover are affected by human capital investments on the job. The dual effects of human capital should be distinguished from direct effects of wage growth on turnover, which are envisaged in work-incentives models (Lazear, 1979), or in selectivity in hiring models (Salop and Salop, 1976). In these models individual growth in wages in the firm is not related to job training. Only direct observations of training and its effects utilized in the last two papers of this section permit the human capital explanation to be distinguished from the other explanations.

In the absence of direct observations on training, 'Labor Mobility and Wages' falls back on the dual effects of human capital which produce the inverse relation between wage growth in the firm and turnover. Here the wage function is reformulated to distinguish tenure profiles from experience profiles of wages. The empirical findings show that the pace of wage growth in the firm is positively related to the duration of tenure as well as to slopes of the experience profiles of wages. The interpretation relies on latent training which inherently contains some degree of firm specificity.

Since specificity implies a sharing of training costs and returns by workers and firms, the predicted reduction in turnover associated with steeper wage profiles should and does show up both in quits and in layoffs. It appears that informal seniority rules prevail even in non-unionized labor markets as a result of human capital processes.

Further applications of the dual effects of human capital investments hypothesis are explored in 'Wage Changes in Job Changes' and in 'Education and Unemployment'. The purpose of the former study is to distinguish and analyze wage growth across firms due to job mobility from wage growth within firms due to training. But as we have already seen, moving and training are related: here we find that movers have lower wages than observationally comparable stayers, both in the old and in the new job, though the discrepancy is reduced by moving. The positive wage gain, most evident in quits, is largely due to the fact that movers have weaker wage growth on the job than stayers. Movers experiencing layoffs have a similar history to those who quit, but a lesser, and often negative, gain in moving. The distinction between on-the-job and off-the-job search explains the difference in mobility wage gains between quits and layoffs.

Another finding is the decline of wage gains with age and with tenure. This is again explainable in human capital terms: the payoff horizon to general (transferable) training is the remaining working life which diminishes over time, so general training diminishes as well. However, the payoff period to firm-specific training is expected tenure which, if anything, is likely to increase with age, until a decade or so before retirement. It is likely to increase because of the informational purposes of frequent job shopping in early years, and the growing costs of moving in later years.

Wage gains diminish as the degree of firm specificity increases following successful job shopping, especially as separations become more exogenous, later reflecting family and other life-cycle circumstances.[11] Beyond that, increasing difficulties of job-finding at later ages, as evidenced by an increasing duration of unemployment, result in declining wage gains, according to a job-search model. The reluctance of firms to hire older workers, which accounts for these difficulties, is in part attributable to human capital considerations: firms' perception of greater costs and smaller returns to investments in older workers discourages their hiring.

The article 'Education and Unemployment' extends the labor-market consequences of human-capital investments from job separations and wage growth to unemployment associated with job separations. In particular, it relates such unemployment to workers' educational attainment, and interprets this ubiquitously found negative relation in human capital terms. This relation is not direct, but in large part due to the positive relation between education and job training which apparently stems from a complementarity: school learning enhances learning on the job. As a result, more-educated workers experience lesser turnover, which creates fewer episodes of unemployment. It is this reduction in the unemployment *incidence*, rather than the minor reduction in the *duration* of unemployment, that is responsible for the observed relation between education and unemployment rates. It is shown in turn that the lesser unemployment incidence of the more-educated workers is, in about equal measure, due to their greater attachment to the firms employing them and to a lesser risk of becoming unemployed when separating. This lesser risk is, most likely, due to greater investment in market information and less costly on-the-job search of educated workers, and to greater intensity of search by firms to fill the more-costly skilled vacancies.

Just as differential unemployment by education is, in large part, attributable to the lesser turnover at higher levels of education, the decline of unemployment with advancing age (experience) is also explained by declining turnover over the working life. As described before, the increasing degree of specific training and increasing costs of moving are responsible for the declining separations. The resulting decline in the incidence of unemployment dominates the increase in the duration of unemployment for most of the working life. Consequently, the unemployment rates decline as workers age.[12]

The next article is the first to draw on explicit statistical information on job training, available in the Panel Study of Income Dynamics (PSID) data for selected years. Similar information, equally fragmentary, has become available also in other data sets.[13]

The emergence of job training as an observable has the potential of filling some important gaps in the empirical analyses of human capital investments, in their measurement, and in their consequences for wage growth and labor mobility. This dual-effects hypothesis can now be replaced by verified empirical relations between training and wage growth, and between training and turnover. This is the major purpose of the article 'Job Training, Wage Growth, and Labor Turnover'. Using information on timing and duration of job training in panels of PSID men (1968–87) I find negative effects of training on both quits and layoffs and positive effects of training on wage growth in the firm and over longer periods. The longer period effects are due both to substantial transferability of training across firms, and to persistence of training across firms among workers who engage in training. Wages of trainees grow 4–6 per cent faster per year over periods of training compared to other workers or periods. Growth associated with training is steeper at younger ages. Mobility wage gains contribute more to the wage profiles of unskilled than of skilled workers, but differences in slopes remain. These findings, which bring the latent variable training into empirical light, justify its use as an underpinning of the wage growth–turnover relation and of its applications described in the preceding three papers.

The availability of direct information on job training in recent data panels, though far from adequate, made it feasible to attempt once again estimates of investment volumes and of rates of return to job training. Empirically grounded direct estimates are clearly preferable to the highly indirect procedure of 30 years ago as reported in the first article (1962) in this Part. In addition, some information is now also available on employer investments in training of workers. Interest in the now feasible 'direct' estimates and in comparisons of them with the old 'indirect' estimates motivates the last paper in this section, entitled 'Job Training: Costs, Returns, and Wage Profiles'.

Costs of job training in the economy were estimated for 1976 and 1987 using three entirely different methods: (a) in the 'direct' method, time (hours) spent in training per year was valued at wage rates prior to training, or of comparable non-trainees; (b) a second method uses information on costs of formal training programs and on time spent in them, and inflates the cost to a total training level, using information on time spent in all training, including informal training which is the bulk; (c) the third method is the 'indirect' one which uses wage profiles, as in the old (1962) paper, but with wage gains due to mobility netted out. The direct estimates (a) and (b) are rather close and add up to over a half of the total costs of schooling. The indirect estimate (c) exceeds the former two by about one-third. This suggests that human capital investments can account for about 75 per cent of the growth of the (cross-sectional) wage profiles, leaving a minor role to other, not mutually exclusive, explanations.

Another objective of the study was to estimate profitabilities of job training in terms of rates of return. With estimates of costs of training and associated wage growth over the duration of training, rates of return can be computed. Since estimates of costs and returns differ in the several available data sets, a range of estimates was provided. This range of estimates seems to exceed the magnitude of rates of return usually observed for schooling investments. Given the data on workers' firm tenure, it appears also that training remains profitable to firms, even in the face of average worker mobility.

The estimated rates of return may suggest under-investment in training relative to that in schooling. However, the lower rates to schooling may in part represent a compensation for lifetime consumption benefits of education. Other qualifications, such as the trade-off between training and

mobility, need to be investigated before concluding that there is a significant under-investment in training in the US. On the other hand, the
complementarity between schooling and training may well imply potential
under-investment in training: if school quality in the US has, indeed,
become deficient at least at the pre-college level, as the clamor for reform
asserts, improvements in the quality of schooling could increase the profitability and the utilization of training.

Economic growth, technology, and the demand for human capital
The four articles in Part III initiate an exploration of sources of changes in
demand for human capital and of consequences of these changes for the
labor market. Industry demand for skilled, educated labor increases either
because demand for its services and products increases, or because its
productivity grows as a result of capital accumulation or of technological
change. The growth of demand for human capital may therefore be
viewed as a concomitant of economic growth. This is not to deny a major
role of the supply of human capital as a source or *cause* of economic
growth, an important focus of research in growth economics since mid-
century. The demand for human capital as an *effect* of growth, is of
primary interest to labor economists who focus on skill differentiation in
the labor market. An overview of the role of human capital both as
condition and consequence of economic growth is provided in the article
'Human Capital and Economic Growth'. The article also brings out the
role of human capital as a link between economic growth and the 'demographic transition'. As a result of this link, contrary to Malthus, economic
growth has not been eliminated by population growth.

When human capital is viewed as a factor of production, in addition to
physical capital and 'raw' or unskilled labor, a hypothesis of complementarity between physical and human capital produces growth of demand
for human capital as a consequence of physical capital accumulation. The
latter raises the marginal product of human capital more so than that of
raw labor producing wage (profitability) incentives for the conversion of
labor into human capital by means of education and training.

However, the accumulation of physical capital is not exogenous.
Indeed, the demand for both physical and human capital responds to
opportunities for profit which emerge from cost-reducing and product-
innovating changes in technology, to the extent that they are capital-
rather than labor-using.

A secular growth of demand for human capital, resulting from skill-
biased technological change or from physical-human capital complementarities is a plausible answer to the apparent puzzle, that of observed
small, if any, secular changes in rates of return to education in the face of

continuous upward trends in education. Except for the agricultural context,[14] this hypothesis has not been subjected to empirical verification.

Thanks to the availability of rich micro-data sets and of some indexes of technological change at the sectoral level, it became possible to test the hypothesis that the pace of technological change affects the demand for human capital in US data covering the past three decades. The empirical analysis is described in 'Human Capital Responses to Technological Change in the Labor Market'. According to the findings, (a) the utilization of better-educated workers and the incidence of training is greater in technologically progressive sectors than in others; (b) educational (relative) wage differentials are wider in progressive sectors, especially in the short run; (c) wage profiles are steeper in progressive sectors where profitability of training and of experience is greater; (d) separation rates and unemployment rates are lower in the progressive sectors, after a short initial period following the increase in the pace of technology. The utilization and wage effects are interpretable by skill-based technology. The interpretation of turnover and unemployment responses requires the previously used hypothesis of the existence of (some degree) of firm specificity in training investments which are necessitated by changing technology.

The next paper (with Higuchi), 'Wage Structures and Labor Turnover in the United States and in Japan', is an application of the hypothesis which relates (inversely) turnover to the steepness of the wage profile. The relation is ascribed to training processes which are stimulated by the pace of technological change, as shown in the previous paper.

The remarkably low turnover rate in Japan, viewed as 'lifetime employment', is frequently described as a reflection of a culture which puts great emphasis on group loyalty. Yet, in the same culture, turnover rates were a great deal higher prior to the Second War. The difference is the remarkably rapid technological progress in Japan since 1950. The technological catch-up required sizable investments in human capital in schools and in enterprises. The phenomenal growth of educational attainment in Japan in recent decades is well known. The even more intense effort to adapt, train, and retrain workers for continuous rapid technological changes is not directly visible in available data. However, effects of training on wage growth and turnover are visible in a negative relation between the two within industrial sectors observed in Japan and in the US. In both countries industries with more rapid productivity growth had both steeper individual wage profiles and lower turnover rates. Indeed, using the parameters of those relations, a rate of productivity growth in Japan that was four times that in the US in the 1960–80 period, predicted rather well the over three-fold steeper wage profiles and the less than one-third frequency of firm separations in Japan. Somewhat weaker but quite pronounced differences of the same sort were observed in a comparison of American and Japanese plants in the US, that is, in the same cultural environment. Here the much larger investments in training and screening of workers in the Japanese plants was directly observable.

The last two cross-sectional studies which show a positive association between the pace of technology in a sector (measured by proxies) and indices of relative demand for human capital do not by themselves establish a causal relation nor the directions of causality, which was articulated in the hypothesis of skill-biased technological change. For the interpretation to be more compelling, the analysis must be cast in a time-series format. That format would also show whether inferences based on sectors hold up in the aggregate – a notion that is often misleading.

The time-series analysis of annual aggregates over a recent 25-year period is provided in the last paper, 'Human Capital, Technology, and the Wage Structure'. The study focuses on rather dramatic changes in wage differentials by education and by experience during that period. Both wage differentials are indicators of the payoffs to skill, or of rates of return on human capital investments. Fluctuations in them are outcomes of changes in relative supplies of educated and experienced workers, and relative demands for them. Both relative supply and relative demand variables are brought to bear in equations which 'explain' the series of wage differentials. The findings substantially confirm the cross-sectional results: net of the relative supply variables which have the proper effects, the strongest factor is a relative demand variable represented by R&D (research and development) expenditures. Other findings were:

- Capital-skill complementarity appears to be at work alongside skill-biased technological change, when expenditures on new equipment per worker represent the relevant capital intensity. It is not clear, however, whether the skill bias of new equipment represents anything different than the effect of new technology.
- The observed steepening of experience profiles of wages is explained, in part, by changes in relative demographic supplies (cohort effects), and in part by the growing profitability of human capital which extends to that acquired on the job. Evidence appears in the significance of profitability variables or in demand factors underlying them, given the relative demographic supplies in the wage profile equations.
- The technological demand index which widens wage differentials by education also widens unemployment differentials by education. This finding represents additional evidence in favor of technology as a factor in shifting the demand for human capital.

This completes the overview of articles selected for the present volume. I hope that these studies provide a relatively clear picture of the wide-ranging power of the human-capital perspective to provide an understanding of the meaning of heterogeneity of labor and of its consequences for a variety of labor market phenomena. By paying attention to the simple facts that labor is not homogeneous and that work and employment decisions are not instantaneous but future-oriented, labor economics has initiated a fruitful interplay of theory and facts leading to rich insights into economic and social behavior of workers and firms.

A survey of my work on human capital would be incomplete without a recognition and an appreciation of the intellectual sources that influenced both the direction and nature of the evolving work. At the very start, the work of Friedman and Kuznets (1945) provided the theoretical principle for analyzing skill differentials. A strong inspiration for the use of theory in the manner of 'Occam's razor' to illuminate often opaque and unruly empirical materials was provided at the same time by Friedman's 'Theory of the Consumption Function' (1957). The conviction that a theory is worth having and using only if it provides empirically corroborated insights into the actual economy was inculcated in me by these works and by George Stigler's lectures at Columbia before that.

At the time I was working on my doctoral thesis, I was not aware of the work initiated at the University of Chicago by T.W. Schultz on the effects of human capital investments on economic growth. Only when I arrived at Chicago as a Post-doctoral Fellow did I realize that our efforts represented a division of labor: I was exploring the role of human capital in the income (wage) distribution while he looked at effects in economic growth. The more-direct influences on me at the University of Chicago were the labor economists H. Gregg Lewis and Albert Rees. Lewis, who is rightly considered to be the father of modern labor economics, convinced me that my work touched on a central topic in labour economics, a field which he urged me to cultivate even though I did not study it as a graduate student. Paradoxically, this ignorance may have been an advantage at the time. This is not to disparage the work of labor economists prior to mid-century. It is easier to fit their work now into a systematic corpus of analysis developed since that time, and to properly appreciate their contributions.

As the reader of this introduction will surmise, the greatest influence on my thinking and evolving work was my professional and personal friendship with Gary Becker. As colleagues at Columbia University we discovered a close methodological and substantive kinship about thinking and work in economics: I shared the view that economic reasoning is also applicable to non-market transactions and that invocation of changes in taste as a primary explanatory variable is an admission of an economists's defeat. Also, that the principle of Occam's razor should be extended from minimizing the number of assumptions to maximizing the number of explained facts, especially if these facts appear to be otherwise unrelated. The forum of the Columbia Labor Workshop, where the interplay of theory and fact kept opening up new horizons, was especially inspiring. The inspiration was infectious to a generation of students who, with others elsewhere, helped to stimulate, create, and systematize many of the topics comprising modern labor economics.

Notes

1. A revived focus on human capital in growth theory is apparent in a lively new literature of the past few years. A call for this emphasis goes back three decades, with T.W. Schultz's 1960 AEA Presidential address (published 1961) and his other works.
2. The work of Friedman and Kuznets (1945) is a modern precursor in the analysis of wage structures, exemplifying the human capital approach in analyzing incomes in independent professional practice.
3. According to the most recent work of Jorgenson and Fraumeni (1990), barely one half of US economic growth is explainable by conventional measures of physical capital and labor hours. Their estimates of the growth of quality of labor and of capital when added to the conventional measures explain 80% of the growth of output (value added) or about 60% of the 'growth residual' over the period 1947–85.
4. See Leibowitz (1974).
5. See Grossman (1972).
6. In Becker's formulation the earnings function is viewed as a 'reduced form' resulting from two simultaneous structural relations: demand functions (*Di*) which relate individual investments to marginal rates of return on them, and supply functions (*Si*) which relate the obtainable volume of funds for such investment purposes to their marginal interest costs. Given the distributions and shapes of the demand and supply curves across individuals, the amounts individuals invest, their marginal and average returns, and therefore their earnings are simultaneously and optimally determined by the intersection of the individual demand and supply curves.
7. For a fine survey and an interesting theoretical speculation concerning this robustness, see Willis (1986).
8. The semi-log form appears to be superior to the arithmetic form, according to Heckman and Polachek (1972). The Gompertz experience function fits somewhat better than the quadratic in 1960 Census Data analyzed in my book, and a quartic polynomial fits better more recent data analyzed by Murphy and Welch (1991). These forms do not apply to earnings of intermittent workers. See Mincer and Polachek (1974).
9. See the review by Parnes (1970).
10. A segmentation of intervals of market and non-market participation was earlier applied to the study of women's wages in Mincer and Polachek (1974).
11. See Bartel and Borjas (1981).
12. For a detailed analysis, see Leighton and Mincer (1982).
13. See Table 8.1 in the article for coverage and concepts.
14. See Welch (1970) and Schultz (1975).

References

Bartel, Ann and George Borjas (1981), 'Wage Growth and Job Turnover', in *Studies in Labor Markets*, ed. S. Rosen, Chicago: University of Chicago Press.
Becker, Gary (1964), *Human Capital*, New York: Columbia University Press; 2nd edn, Chicago: Chicago University Press, 1975.

Ben-Porath, Yoram (1967), 'The Production of Human Capital and the Life-Cycle of Earning', *Journal of Political Economy*, August.

Chiswick, Barry (1974), *Income Inequality*, New York: Columbia University Press.

Fisher, Irving (1930), *The Theory of Interest*, London: Macmillan.

Friedman, Milton (1957), *A Theory of the Consumption Function*, New York: Columbia University Press.

Friedman, Milton and Simon Kuznets (1945), *Income from Independent Professional Practice*, New York: Columbia University Press.

Grossman, Michael (1972), 'On the Concept of Health Capital and the Demand for Health', *Journal of Political Economy*, March.

Heckman, James and Solomon Polachek (1972), 'The Functional Form of the Income-Schooling Relation', NBER Report; reprinted in *Journal of the American Statistical Association*, June 1974.

Jorgenson, Dale and Barbara Fraumeni (1990), 'Investment in Education and U.S. Economic Growth', in *The U.S. Savings Challenge*, Westview, Conn.: Westview Press.

Lazear, Edward (1979), 'Why is There Mandatory Retirement?', *Journal of Political Economy*, September.

Leibowitz, Arlene (1974), 'Home Investments in Children', *Journal of Political Economy*, March.

Leighton, Linda and Jacob Mincer (1982), 'Labor Turnover and Youth Employment', in *The Youth Employment Problem*, ed. R. Freeman and D. Wise, Chicago: University of Chicago Press.

Mincer, Jacob (1974), *Schooling, Experience and Earnings*, New York: Columbia University Press.

Mincer, Jacob and Solomon Polachek (1974), 'Family Investment in Human Capital: Earnings of Women', *Journal of Political Economy*, part 2, March/April.

Murphy, Kevin and Finis Welch (1991), 'Empirical Earnings Profiles', *Journal of Labor Economics*, January.

Parnes, Herbert (1970), 'Labor Force Participation and Labor Mobility', *Review of Industrial Relations Research*, vol. 1.

Salop, Joan and Steven Salop (1976), 'Self-Selection and Turnover in the Labor Market', *Quarterly Journal of Economics*, November.

Schultz, Theodore W. (1961) 'Investment in Human Capital', *American Economic Review*, March.

Schultz, Theordore W. (1975), The Value of the Ability to Deal with Disequilibria', *Journal of Economic Literature*, September.

Welch, Finis (1970), 'Education in Production', *Journal of Political Economy*, January.

Willis, Robert (1986) 'Wage Determinants: Human Capital Earnings Functions', in *Handbook of Labor Economics*, ed. O. Ashenfelter and R. Layard, Amsterdam: North Holland.

PART I

HUMAN CAPITAL
AND EARNINGS

1 Investment in human capital and personal income distribution*

1. Introduction

Economists have long theorized about the nature or causes of inequality in personal incomes. In contrast, the vigorous development of empirical research in the field of personal income distribution is of recent origin. Moreover, the emphasis of contemporary research has almost completely shifted from the study of the causes of inequality to the study of the facts and of their consequences for various aspects of economic activity, particularly consumer behavior.

However, the facts of income inequality do not speak for themselves in statistical frequency distributions. The facts must be recognized in the statistical constructs and interpreted from them. Perhaps the most important conclusion to be drawn from research into the influence of income distribution on consumption is that the effects of inequality depend upon its causes.[1] Thus factors associated with observed inequality must be taken into account before the data can be put to any use.

Since income inequality is observable in terms of the shapes or parameters of statistical frequency distributions, theories of the determinants of personal income distribution, if they are to be operational, must predict features of the observable statistical constructs.

Probably the oldest theory of this type is the one that relates the distribution of income to the distribution of individual abilities.[2] A special form of this theory can be attributed to Galton, who claimed that 'natural abilities' follow the Gaussian normal law of error. This, it appeared to Galton, was a simple consequence of Quetelet's findings that various proportions of the human body are normally distributed. A seemingly natural corollary of this logic was the hypothesis of a normal distribution of incomes. Although the invention of intelligence quotients appeared to confirm conclusions derived by a *non sequitur*, the hypothesis of a normal distribution of incomes was definitively shattered by Pareto's famous empirical 'law' of incomes.

For a long time this refutation of a logically weak hypothesis was considered to present a strange puzzle. Pigou termed it a paradox:[3] How can one reconcile the normal distribution of abilities with a sharply

*This chapter was first published in the *Journal of Political Economy*, vol. 66 (1958), pp. 281–302.

skewed distribution of incomes? This became the central question around which thinking on the subject subsequently revolved.

One answer, of comparatively recent origin, is that the abilities relevant to earning power should not be identified with IQs. Indeed, relevant abilities are likely not to be normally distributed, as IQs are, but to be distributed in a way resembling the distribution of income.[4] This amounts to saying that income distributions should not be deduced from psychological data on distributions of abilities but, conversely, that the latter, which are not observable, should be inferred from the former, which are. This reversal of independent and dependent variables may be of interest to psychologists, but income analysts are not left with much more than a tautology.

A more general and traditional answer, given by Pigou himself, is that income-determining factors other than ability intervene to distort the relation between ability and income. Thus, given a definition of the former independent of income, the relation between the two can be discerned only in subgroups homogeneous with respect to all other factors. Ability is relegated to a residual role, and the emphasis is shifted to other factors. Pigou pointed to the distribution of property as the most important of the other factors. This position resolves the paradox, but it is not a theory of income distribution until the other factors are built into models with predictive properties.

Curiously enough, the one factor consistently selected for such constructive purposes in the recent literature is 'chance', a concept as difficult to define as 'ability'. The earliest and basic version of the stochastic models is that of Gibrat.[5] Its logical construction is as follows: Start with some distribution of income, with mean M_0 and variance V_0, and let individual incomes be subjected to a random increase or decrease over time as a result of 'chance' or 'luck'. Let the variance of the annual changes in income in year t be v_t, and let those changes be uncorrelated with the levels of income on which they impinge. Then the variance of the income distribution at time $(t + n)$ will be

$$V_n = V_0 + \sum_{t=1}^{n} v_t.$$

With n increasing without bounds, any v_t becomes very small in comparison with $\sum_t v_t$, and similarly V_0 becomes small in comparison with V_n. Under these conditions, probability theory guarantees that in time the distribution of income will approach normality, regardless of the form of the initial distribution.

Personal income distributions are not normally or symmetrically distributed, but the distribution of logarithms of income is rather symmetric and in a rough way approximates normality. The process of 'random shock' just described generates a log-normal distribution if applied to the logarithms of income rather than to income itself. Thus the proper assumption to be made is that the random shock consists of relative or percentage, rather than absolute, income changes, which are independent of income levels. This is Gibrat's 'law of proportionate effect'.

Kalecki has pointed out a serious defect in Gibrat's approach.[6] The model implies that, as time goes by, aggregate income inequality increases because each subsequent random shock adds a term to the sum on the right side of the expression

$$V_n = V_0 + \sum_{t=1}^{n} v_t.$$

This, however, is empirically false.

Subsequent models correct this defect in either of two ways. One is to postulate a negative correlation between the size of the random shock and the level of income, to be interpreted as a decreasing likelihood of large negative changes with a decreasing level of income.[7] This restriction assures constancy of the variance of the distribution. Another way is to apply the random shock, without restriction, separately to age cohorts throughout their life-histories.[8] The income variance increases with time for each age cohort but, given a stable population, the aggregate variance remains unchanged.

Unless we assign specific interpretations to the 'chance' factor, it is difficult to see how the stochastic models increase our understanding of the processes underlying the formation of personal income distributions. If the 'chance' factor is to be understood as a net effect of all kinds of causes, this approach is an admission of defeat in the efforts to gain insight into systematic factors affecting the distribution of income. Moreover, the operational scope of the stochastic models has not kept pace with the increasing empirical knowledge about the multidimensional structure of the personal income distribution. With few exceptions,[9] the sole purpose of the models is to rationalize a presumed mathematical form of the aggregate.

From the economist's point of view, perhaps the most unsatisfactory feature of the stochastic models, which they share with most other models of personal income distribution, is that they shed no light on the economics of the distribution process. Non-economic factors undoubtedly play an important role in the distribution of incomes. Yet, unless one denies the relevance of rational optimizing behaviour to economic activity in general, it is difficult to see how the factor of individual choice can be disregarded in analyzing personal income distribution, which can scarcely be independent of economic activity.

The starting point of an economic analysis of personal income distribution must be an exploration of the implications of the theory of rational choice. In a recent article[10] Friedman has pointed out two ways in which individual choice can affect the personal income distribution. One, around which Friedman built his model, is related to differences in tastes for risk and hence to choices among alternatives differing in the probability distribution of income they promise. Friedman has shown that such a model is, no less than the others, capable of reproducing the more outstanding features of the aggregative distribution of income. The other, and more familiar, implication of rational choice is the formation of income differences that are required to compensate for various advantages and disadvantages attached to the receipt of the incomes. This principle, so eloquently stated by Adam Smith, has become a 'commonplace of economics'.[11]

What follows is an attempt to cast one important aspect of this compensation principle into an operational model that provides insights into some features of the aggregate personal income distribution and into a number of decompositions of it which recent empirical research has made accessible. The aspect chosen concerns differences in training among members of the labor force.

2.   A simple model

Assume that all individuals have identical abilities and equal opportunities to enter any occupation. Occupations differ, however, in the amount of training they require. Training takes time, and each additional year of it postpones the individual's earnings for another year, generally reducing the span of his earning life. For convenience, assume that a year of training reduces earning life by exactly one year.[12] If individuals with different amounts of training are to be compensated for the costs of training, the present values of life-earnings must be equalized at the time a choice of occupation is made. If we add a provisional assumption that the flow of income receipts is steady during the working life, it is possible to estimate the extent of compensatory income differences due to differences in the cost of training.[13]

The cost of training depends upon the length of the training period in two ways. First and foremost is the deferral of earnings for the period of training; second is the cost of educational services and equipment, such as tuition and books, but not living expenses.

For simplicity, consider the case in which expenses for educational services are zero. Let

l = length of working life plus length of training, for all persons = length of working life of persons without training,
a_n = annual earnings of individuals with n years of training,
V_n = the present value of their life-earnings at start of training,
r = the rate at which future earnings are discounted,
t = 0,1,2, ... , l-time, in years,
d = difference in the amount of training, in years, and
e = base of natural logarithms.

Then

$$V_n = a_n \sum_{t=n+1}^{l} \left(\frac{1}{1+r}\right)^t,$$

when the discounting process is discrete. And, more conveniently, when the process is continuous,

$$V_n = a_n \int_n^l (e^{-rt})dt = \frac{a_n}{r}(e^{-rn} - e^{-rl}).$$

Similarly, the present value of life-earnings of individuals with $(n - d)$ years of training is

$$V_{n-d} = \frac{a_{n-d}}{r}(e^{-r(n-d)} - e^{-rl}).$$

The ratio, $k_{n,n-d}$, of annual earnings of persons differing by d years of training is found by equating $V_n = V_{n-d}$:

$$k_{n,n-d} = \frac{a_n}{a_{n-d}} = \frac{e^{-r(n-d)} - e^{-rl}}{e^{-rn} - e^{-rl}} = \frac{e^{r(l+d-n)} - 1}{e^{r(l-n)} - 1}.$$

It is easily seen that $k_{n,n-d}$ is (a) larger than unity; (b) a positive function of r; and (c) a negative function of l. In other words, as would be expected, (a) people with more training command higher annual pay; (b) the difference between earnings of persons differing by d years of training is larger, the higher the rate at which future income is discounted, that is, the greater the sacrifice involved in the act of income postponement; (c) the difference is larger, the shorter the general span of working life, since the costs of training must be recouped over a *relatively* shorter period.

These conclusions are quite obvious. Less obvious is the finding that $k_{n,n-d}$ is a positive function of n (d fixed); that is, the relative income differences between, for example, persons with ten years and eight years of training are larger than those between individuals with four and two years of training, respectively. Hence the ratio of annual earnings of persons differing by a fixed amount of schooling (d) is at least as great as

$$k_{d,0} = \frac{e^{rl} - 1}{e^{r(l-d)} - 1},$$

the ratio of earnings of persons with d years of training to those of persons with no training. However, since the change in $k_{n,n-d}$ with a change in n is negligible,[14] it can be, for all practical purposes, treated as a constant k.

This result can be summarized in the following statement: annual earnings corresponding to various levels of training differing by the same amount (d) differ, not by an additive constant, but by a multiplicative factor (k).

This important conclusion remains basically unchanged when, in addition to the cost of income postponement, expenses of training are taken into account. The additional cost element naturally widens the compensatory differences in earnings particularly at the upper educational levels, where such costs are sizable.[15]

It is, of course, the purpose of the model to make the distribution of annual earnings a sole function of the distribution of training among members of the labor force. It follows from what we have just shown that this function is of a very simple form: given the distribution of training, the multiplicative constant k serves as a 'conversion factor' which translates it into a distribution of earnings. In order, therefore, to make statements about the theoretical distribution of earnings, we must first consider the distribution of training within the universe of this model.

Under the most stringent assumptions of identical abilities and equal access to training, the distribution of occupational choice, defined as choice of particular lengths of training, would become a matter of tastes, specifically those concerning the different activities in the different occupations and time preferences. It is not clear what form the distribution of training would assume in this conjectural state of affairs, even with the usual assumption of a symmetric, or normal, distribution of tastes.

Suppose, for the sake of argument, that the resulting distribution of training is symmetric. The point which this model brings home is that, even in that case, the annual distribution of earnings will depart from symmetry in the direction of positive skewness.

As we have seen, the annual earnings corresponding to various levels of training differing by the same length of time differ by a multiplicative factor k. Were this factor constant for all levels of training, a normal distribution of absolute time differences in training would reflect itself in a normal distribution of percentage differences in annual earnings, that is, in the familiar, positively skewed logarithmic-normal income distribution. Strictly speaking, the model implies that the factor k increases somewhat with the level of training, so that even the logarithms of income would be slightly skewed.

Formally, the existence of positive skewness introduced by compensatory income differences due to differences in training can be shown, and its extent can be estimated, in a rather simple way.

Let the quartile deviation in the symmetric distribution of training be d years, and let Y be the first quartile income, Q_1. It follows from the previous argument that the median, Q_2, equals Y times k^d and the third quartile, Q_3, equals Y times k^{2d}.

Hence Bowley's measure of skewness[16] is

$$Sk = \frac{(Q_3 - Q_2) - (Q_2 - Q_1)}{Q_3 - Q_1} = \frac{k^{2d} - 2k^d + 1}{k^{2d} - 1} = \frac{(k^d - 1)^2}{k^{2d} - 1}$$
$$= \frac{k^d - 1}{k^d + 1} > 0.$$

Since k is greater than 1, Sk must be positive.

If we now relax the assumption of identical abilities, a positive correlation between the amount of training and some ability traits is plausible. Given freedom of choice, persons with greater learning capacity are more likely than others to embark on prolonged training. In so far as earnings are positively related to such qualities, aggregative skewness is augmented.

But whether or not the distribution of training depends on distributions of abilities,[17] the mere existence of dispersion in the amount of training implies that aggregative skewness is greater than it would be in its absence. In particular, even if it were true that abilities are distributed in a way which, *ceteris paribus*, implies a symmetric distribution of earnings, positive skewness would appear in that distribution as soon as choice of training was admitted into the model. Thus Pigou's paradox would persist even in the absence of the institutional factors that he invoked to explain it.

Extension of the model
Primarily for mathematical convenience, I have expressed differences in training in terms of definite time periods spent on formal schooling. However, the process of learning a trade or profession does not end with the completion of school. Experience on the job is often the most essential part of the learning process.

Just as formal training can be measured by the length of time spent at school, the other part of the training process – experience – can be introduced into the theoretical model in terms of the amount of time spent on the job. When this is done, 'intra-occupational' patterns of income variation, previously abstracted from, must emerge. By definition, the amount of formal training is the same for each member of an occupation. However, the productive efficiency or quality of performance on the job is a function of formal training plus experience, both measured in time units; hence it is a function of age. We are thus forced to relax another assumption, previously adopted for convenience, namely, that earnings are of the same size in each period of an individual's earning life.

Clearly, as more skill and experience are acquired with passage of time, earnings rise. In later years ageing often brings about a deterioration of productive performance and hence a decline in earnings, particularly in jobs where physical effort or motor skill is involved. Thus, in general, the 'life-cycle' of earnings exhibits an inverted U-shaped pattern of growth and decline typical of many other growth curves.

We have already seen that differences in formal training result in compensatory differences in *levels* of earnings as between different 'occupations', the latter defined in terms of length of formal training. This compensatory principle must, of course, also remain valid when life-paths of earnings are sloped. An important new question arises: what specific assumption is to be made about differences between these slopes in the different occupations, since these in turn imply differences in the *dispersion* of earnings within the occupational groups?

Casual observation suggests that patterns of age-changes in productive performance differ among occupations as well as among individuals. The exploration of such differences is a well-established subject of study in developmental psychology. A survey of broad, rather tentative findings in this field indicates that (a) growth in productive performance is more pronounced and prolonged in jobs of higher levels of skill and complexity; (b) growth is less pronounced and decline sets in earlier in manual work than in other pursuits; and (c) the more capable and the more-educated individuals tend to grow faster and longer than others in the performance of the same task.[18]

These findings suggest that experience influences productivity more strongly in jobs that normally require more training. The steeper growth of performance throughout the span of working life in occupations with higher levels of training implies that the growth of earnings is also greater.

These considerations point to the replacement of the previous assumption of horizontal life-paths of earnings with the assumption that the slopes of time-paths of earnings vary directly with the amount of formal training, that is, with 'occupational rank'.

Implications

In brief, we are led to the following conclusion: differences in training result in differences in levels of earnings among 'occupations' as well as in differences in slopes of life-paths of earnings among occupations. The differences are systematic: the higher the 'occupational rank', the higher the level of earnings and the steeper the life-path of earnings.

Two implications of basic importance for empirical investigation follow immediately from these findings:

(a)   Since, under our assumptions, intraoccupational differentials are a function of age only, the statement that life-paths of earnings are steeper for the more highly trained groups of workers means that income differences between any two members of such a group differing in age are greater than income differences between their contemporaries in an occupational group requiring less training.

In itself, this conclusion does not necessarily imply a systematic difference in income dispersion within the two groups. It points to age distributions within the respective groups as another factor that must be considered. Clearly, if one group consists of members with very similar ages and in another there is a wide range of ages, there may be less income dispersion in the first group, even though its life-path of earnings may be steeper than that of the second group.

Observe, however, that such a phenomenon is in part ruled out by our previous assumptions. Membership in an occupational group was defined by the number of years of the individual's formal training, which is determined once for all by the calculus of occupational choice (the equalization of present values) *before* entry into the labor force. In other words, if we define 'vertical occupational mobility' as the movement from a group with, say, $n - d$ years of training to a group with n years of training, this is, by definition, impossible after the training period is over. If, in addition, secular occupational shifts are abstracted from, occupational distribution must be alike in all age groups after all training periods are over; *a fortiori*, age distributions must be alike in all occupational groups.[19] With this qualification, the direct translation of slopes of life-paths of earnings into patterns of income dispersion is achieved: dispersion must increase with 'occupational rank'.

(b)   Now consider income recipients classified into separate age groups. In our model, income differences within each age group are due to differences in the occupational characteristics of its members. The income differences corresponding to those occupational categories, however, increase with age. Life-patterns of earnings are not parallel; their diver-

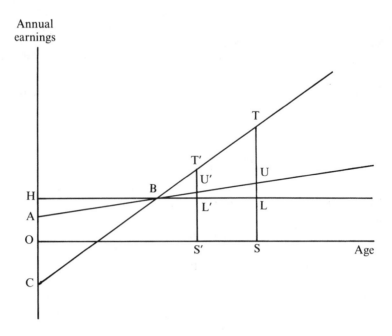

*Figure 1.1   Hypothetical life-paths of earnings in occupations differing in
the amount of training they require*

gence becomes more pronounced with added years of experience, so that
income dispersion increases as we move from younger to older age groups.

Both statements can be made stronger by specifying that they apply not
only to absolute but also to relative dispersion. The former follows directly from the model. If we now include in the assumption about the
slopes of life-paths of earnings in various 'occupations' the observation
that these slopes are negligible or even negative in occupations requiring
little or no formal training, as in many manual jobs, then the two propositions must also apply to relative dispersion.

The argument underlying these propositions can be presented quite
simply with the help of a geometric illustration as in Figure 1.1. For
convenience, divide the labor force into two broad groups of 'occupations', those requiring very little training, characterized by a practically
flat life-pattern of earnings (*ABU*), and those requiring a considerable
amount of training, with a pronounced positive slope of life path (*CBT*).
First, we may note that absolute differences in earnings are small within
untrained groups (life-path *ABU*), but they become pronounced in groups

with higher levels of training (*CBT*). These differences (absolute dispersion) may be measured by the slopes of the paths or by the segments *UL* and *TL*, respectively. Income levels are represented by the heights *US* and *TS*, respectively. Clearly $UL/US < TL/TS$. That is, relative dispersion increases with 'occupational rank'. Secondly, the ratio TS/US increases with age: $TS/US > T'S'/U'S'$. That is, percentage differences and hence the relative dispersion of earnings increase as we move from a younger to an older 'occupation-mix'.

We may now return to the aggregative income distribution and explore the implications for the total of the hypothesis about patterns of income in component groups.

First, it is obvious that the addition of 'intra-occupational' differences to the 'inter-occupational' differences increases aggregate inequality. Moreover, 'inter-occupational' differences themselves must increase: the present value of a life-flow of income of given size is smaller, the steeper the positive slope of the age–income relation. Hence the equalization of present values requires larger 'inter-occupational' differences in income than those derived on the assumption of horizontal income flows in all 'occupations'.

Finally, it can be shown that the conclusions about 'intra-occupational' patterns of income dispersion reinforce the implication of aggregative positive skewness reached on the basis of 'interoccupational' differences alone (in the simple model). This finding provides an answer to an important question frequently raised in discussions of personal income distribution.

Before invoking the distribution of property as a decisive explanation of positive income skewness, Pigou considered the possibility that positive skewness of the income distribution may arise from merging of a number of homogeneous, non-skewed subgroups into a non-homogeneous, positively skewed total.[20] Recently, H. P. Miller has offered evidence to suggest that 'the skewness of income distributions is largely due to merging several symmetrical distributions which differ primarily with respect to level and dispersion.'[21] He found that there is considerably more symmetry in component income distributions than in the aggregate. For example, the distributions for sets of the three broad occupational groups of employed males, 'blue-collar workers', 'white-collar workers', and professionals, managers, and proprietors, had less skewness when considered separately than in the aggregate.

Pigou's hunch about the anatomy of personal income distributions, even when confirmed by Miller's empirical investigations, however, cannot explain the phenomenon of aggregative positive skewness. It leaves unanswered the basic question why a merger of relatively symmetric distributions should result in a positively skewed aggregate. Clearly, without further specifications, a merger of component symmetric distributions could very well produce a negatively skewed or a symmetric aggregate.[22]

My model provides specifications which insure that a merger produces positive skewness in the aggregate. The aggregative skewness was already implied by the simple model. In that form, however, income dispersion within occupations was implicitly assumed to be zero. But if its existence is admitted, patterns of 'intra-occupational' dispersion might easily affect the aggregative, positive skewness previously derived. This would be the case, for example, if dispersion within less trained groups were systematically and considerably greater than that within more highly trained groups. Geometrically, this would mean shortening the right tail of the aggregative income distribution and extending the left tail: a change in the direction of negative skewness. However, this contingency is ruled out by my findings about component groups. In fact, I have derived patterns of 'intra-occupational' dispersion that are exactly the opposite of those given in the preceding extreme example. This positive relation between income levels and income dispersion in component groups reinforces the effect of intergroup ('interoccupational') skewness to produce an even greater positive skewness in the aggregate.

Theoretical concepts and their empirical counterparts

Ultimately, it is the degree of conformity of empirical observations with the conclusions suggested by the model that establishes its usefulness. We must note, however, that properties of the income structure specified by the model do not in themselves constitute a 'prediction' about the empirical income distribution. The validity of such an interpretation depends on the way in which theoretical concepts like training, income, and life-paths of income are translated into empirically identifiable, measurable counterparts.

The translation is necessarily imperfect, in the sense that an exact empirical representation of theoretical concepts is seldom possible, available, or even desirable. For example, the relevant income differences in a given annual income distribution are those among individuals differing in age and not those due to the aging of the same individuals. While the theoretical concepts of training and compensation thus involve a longitudinal view of individual income, they must be brought to bear on cross-sectional data.

The discrepancy between the dynamic concept and the cross-sectional measure is, however, not so serious as it would seem. Abstraction from secular trends in income imparts a downward bias to the slopes of life-paths of income. On the other hand, cyclical and seasonal forces impinging on the economy are largely eliminated by the cross-sectional 'life-path'. In this respect, it fits the theoretical construct in which these disturbances are removed by assumption. Moreover, the relevant income expectations are likely to be shaped by the contemporary cross-sectional picture.

Another translation problem that bears directly on the selection of data is presented by the concept of training. It will be recalled that I have subdivided this concept into 'formal training', defined by the time spent primarily in preparation for the job, and informal training or experience on the job. Given the former, the latter is conveniently measured by age. The identification of experience with age should not create much difficulty, since the existence of central tendencies is to be expected in the timing of both training and entry into the labor force.

More difficulty arises in measuring 'formal training'. Years of school completed as reported by the census do not, unfortunately, include time spent in vocational, trade, and business schools, not to speak of apprenticeships and various forms of on-the-job training programs.[23] Moreover, the schooling classification is of limited usefulness, since it is rarely cross-classified with other relevant characteristics of the population.

A meaningful, though not easily quantifiable, indicator of 'formal training' is occupational status. We can think of the set of occupations among which the labor force is divided as constituting a hierarchy ranging from occupations requiring little training up to highly specialized occupations whose practice presupposes a great deal of investment in human capital. If we can order occupational groups in such a 'vertical' way, we can use their ranks as indexes of the amount of formal training.

Despite the shortcomings of the educational classification and the difficulties in occupational ranking, I have used both education and occupation to measure the amount of formal training.

For defining units of income and income recipients, it is clear that earnings rather than total incomes and persons rather than families correspond to the theoretical concepts. It is also desirable to restrict the income recipients to persons between the ages of 25 and 65 years, so as to include all training groups after most have entered the labor force and before a sizable number have retired. Furthermore, in order to avoid variations in income introduced by variation in man-hours or weeks of work during the year – a factor about which the model is silent – either earnings of full-year workers or hourly rates should be studied.

Unfortunately, data fulfilling all these requirements are practically non-existent. I was forced, therefore, to use data with varying definitions of income and income recipient. The extent to which the measures deviate from the requirements must be kept in mind as possible sources of discrepancy between theory and fact.

Life-paths of income

Available data on the variation of earnings and incomes by age within broad population groups classified by educational and occupational status indicate rather clearly that earnings are not only higher but also increase more rapidly with age (or decline more slowly after the peak of earnings is reached) in the more highly trained groups than in the less-trained ones. A statistical study of the 1939 and 1949 income data provided by the decennial censuses of population reveals that the income differential between young men and those who have reached the age of peak income is much greater for college graduates than for men with less schooling.[24] According to the same study, similar differentials are found when racial groups or sex groups are viewed separately. They exist in incomes from all sources as well as in wage and salary earnings. The same differentials persist in incomes of spending units classified by the schooling of the head.[25]

When occupation, rather than education, is used as a classificatory principle, the occupational groups must be ranked with respect to the amount of training they presuppose. With broad occupational groups, the vertical ordering from unskilled to highly skilled groups as shown in census tabulations is reasonably appropriate for our purposes. By and large, skill is an end-product of training, and the occupational ranks roughly follow the levels of education and of earnings in the groups.

The positive association between occupational rank, level of earnings, and the amount of age change in earnings stands out very clearly in figures of earnings of employed males in the United States.[26] Similar differences in occupational life-paths of income can be found in a number of other sets of empirical data.[27]

Aggregative skewness

Ability to explain the existence of aggregate skewness is a preliminary test that any theory of personal income distribution must meet. The usefulness of my approach does not end with meeting this test, which can be and has been met in so many other ways. Its main merit lies in the guidance it provides for interpreting disaggregations of income distributions. Even on the aggregate level, however, the model not only indicates the existence of positive skewness but enables us to gain a rough impression of the quantitative importance of the set of factors on which we have focused.

An estimate of the extent of aggregative skewness and dispersion which is ascribable to differences in training and experience was obtained in the following fashion.

Hypothetical coefficients of relative dispersion and skewness were calculated that would obtain if differences in earnings were exclusively of a compensatory nature.[28] These are shown in row *a* of Table 1.2 under the assumption of a uniform flow of earnings during the working life, in row *b* under the assumption that the shapes of the 1949 cross-sectional life-paths (as shown in Figure 1.2) constitute the expectation which is discounted.[29] These theoretical coefficients were then compared with corresponding coefficients calculated from the actual distribution of earnings of fully employed workers in 1949 (Table 1.1). From the comparison in Table 1.2 it appears that when age variation of earnings is abstracted from (row *a*), the training factor 'explains' about a third of the existing dispersion and skewness; when age variation is introduced (row *b*), the theoretical dispersion is increased only slightly, but the extent of skewness 'accounted for' by the theory is increased considerably.

Age and income dispersion
A striking demonstration of the increase in income dispersion with age when the aggregate of spending units is partitioned into age groups is provided in a recent study based on 1948 data compiled by the Federal Reserve Board's annual Survey of Consumer Finances. The systematic positive relation between age and family income inequality is reflected in a consistent and pronounced drift of Lorenz curves away from the line of equality with increase in age.[30] According to the author, 'this relation between the degree of income concentration and age is one of the most interesting and perhaps important findings of the study'. That this relation between income inequality is just as pronounced in incomes of persons as in those of families is seen in Figure 1.3. The same phenomenon appears in a variety of data differing in time, place, and definition of income or recipient unit.[31]

Education and income dispersion
When income recipients are classified by educational background, that is, by years of schooling as defined in the census, the expected increase in income dispersion with level of training appears as shown in Figure 1.4.[32]

Occupation and income dispersion
Let us now turn to an occupational classification of income recipients. Figure 1.5 presents Lorenz curves of earnings of male workers in several broad occupational groups in the United States in 1953.[33] These conform to theoretical expectations in so far as income inequality within professional and managerial groups is greater than within clerical and skilled manual workers. Unskilled workers, however, show a greater inequality than the other groups, particularly at the lower ranges of the distribution. This partial discrepancy between theory and fact appears in most data

Table 1.1 Wage and salary income of male workers in the experienced civilian labor force who worked 50–52 weeks in 1949

Income brackets ($000s)	0–0.5	0.5–1	1–1.5	1.5–2	2–2.5	2.5–3	3–3.5	3.5–4	4–4.5	4.5–5	5–6	6–7	7–10	10 or more
Per cent distribution	1.8	2.7	4.8	7.7	14.0	15.0	18.0	11.9	8.2	4.5	5.6	2.3	2.0	1.4

Source: Occupational Characteristics (Census Special Rept. P–E no 1B), Table 23, p. 245.

Table 1.2   Actual and theoretical coefficients of dispersion and skewness

			All workers (1)	Full-time workers (2)	(3)
Coefficient of dispersion $\dfrac{Q_{95} - Q_5}{Q_{50}}$	Theoretical*	(a)	0.43	0.43	0.43
		(b)	0.48	0.48	0.48
	Actual†		1.68	1.45	1.36
Coefficient of skewness $\dfrac{(Q_{95} - Q_{50}) - (Q_{50} - Q_5)}{Q_{95} - Q_5}$	Theoretical*	(a)	0.11	0.11	0.11
		(b)	0.22	0.22	0.22
	Actual†		0.24	0.39	0.39

* The measures of dispersion and skewness are based on differences between the 5th and 95th percentiles in the distribution of training. These measures are more sensitive and of greater interest in our context than the standard ones based on quartiles. Differences between the 5th and 95th percentiles in the educational distribution of the male US population amounted to 14–16 years of schooling, according to the 1950 Census (Vol. II, Part I: *U.S. Summary*, Table 115, p. 236). A more appropriate estimate is that of 11 years obtained from occupational data (see n. 12 above) as the difference between the length of working life of professional and technical groups and the least-trained laborers, which is interpreted as the number of years of income postponement. These occupational groups are approximately coextensive with the lowest and highest deciles of the occupational distribution; hence the 5th and 95th percentiles used in my measures correspond to their median positions. Since the highest schooling classification in the census data is 16 years or more, the lowest for our purposes is 5–7 years, and the middle figure is 12. Income figures by age for these three training levels were shown in Figure 1.2. The discount rate was conservatively put at 4 per cent and the length of working life of unskilled workers at 51 years (cf. n. 12).

† Actual measures are computed from the distribution in Table 1.1. Unfortunately, that distribution includes males who worked part-time (though during the full period). This factor tends to impart a downward bias to 'actual' skewness. A rough correction for this bias is achieved by eliminating all earnings below $1500 (col. 2) and below $2000 (col. 3), even though this may result in an upward bias.

that include all workers regardless of the length of their employment during the year. I have shown elsewhere[34] that the variation in man-hours introduced by the inclusion of part-period and part-time workers is bound to create an 'excess' income dispersion (relative to the theory) at the lower levels of the occupational and educational classifications. The more effective the exclusion of part-year incomes from the annual distributions of the groups under study, the more closely do the results conform to theoretical predictions.

Some doubts about the meaningfulness of the findings for occupational groups presented in Figure 1.5 are raised by the heterogeneity of these

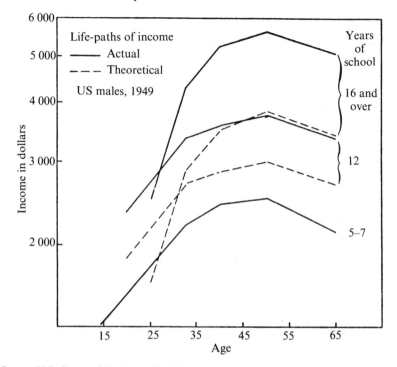

Source: *U.S. Census of Population* (1950), Ser. P-E, no. 5-B: *Education*, Tables, 12, 13

Figure 1.2   Actual and theoretical life-paths of income, US males, 1949

broad occupational groups. In each such group income dispersion might be largely a product of concealed inter-occupational income differences among more detailed and homogeneous occupations included in the broad classification. The problem may be rephrased in the following terms: does the hypothesized relation between occupational rank and intra-occupational dispersion, which seems to exist in broad occupational groups, also hold true for more detailed occupations?

An attempt to answer such a question involves breaking down the broad occupational groups into more detailed component occupations and studying their income distributions. Fortunately, a recent census monograph breaks down the large groups into 118 more detailed occupations and gives income distributions and measures of income dispersion for each of the component groups.[35] The data are suitable for our purposes, since they separate wage and salary incomes of full-period[36] workers from those of all workers.

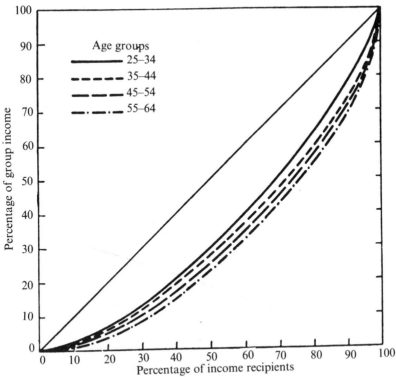

Source: U.S. Census Bureau, *Current Population Reports, Consumer Income,* Ser. P-60, no. 16, Table 3, p. 13

Figure 1.3 Lorenz curves of 1953 income of males, by age, United States

Using income shares of top quintiles of workers in each detailed occupation as a measure of intra-group inequality, we can examine the existence of a relation between such inequality and the occupational rank of the groups. One way of doing this is to inquire whether most detailed occupations in the 'top' broad groups (professional, managerial) tend to have larger quintile shares than occupations in the intermediate groups, and so on. Table 1.3 indicates a positive answer in terms of median shares and mid-ranges of shares for component occupations within the broad groups. Thus when the shares of top quintiles are arrayed in order of increasing size for the 28 subgroups of 'craftsmen and foremen', the median (quintile) share is 30.2, and the 14 central subgroups have quintile shares running from 28.0 to 31.4 per cent of the aggregate income of the sub-group. As is seen, the medians follow the occupational rank, However, the wide mid-range for clerical workers deprives the median of that

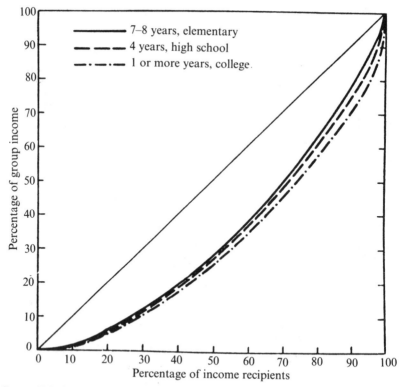

Source: U.S. Census, *Current Population Reports*, Ser. P-60, no. 3, Table 13, p. 22

Figure 1.4 Education and income inequality, United States, 1946 (urban males, 25–65 years old)

group of much significance, since it indicates an absence of central tendency.

An alternative approach to the study of the relation between occupational rank and income inequality in detailed occupational groups is to rank these groups independently instead of fitting them into the broad ranks, as in Table 1.3. However, with over a hundred occupations, ranking by the amount of training or skill is a formidable task. Direct information about the ranking criterion is not available in any quantitative form, and, with so many groups, 'common sense' will not lead different investigators to the same results.

One 'objective', though indirect, ranking procedure is implicit in the theoretical model. In the model, differences in levels of earnings in the hierarchy of occupations are due to differences in training required by them. Thus, within the framework of the model, the statement that the

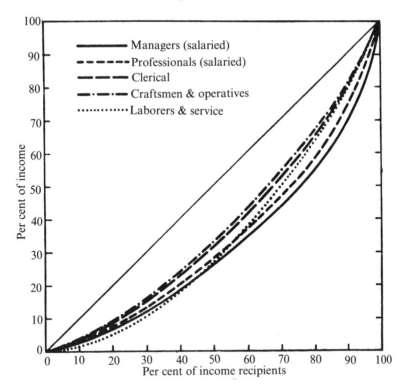

Legend:
——— Managers (salaried)
------- Professionals (salaried)
— — — Clerical
—·—·— Craftsmen & operatives
············· Laborers & service

Y-axis: Per cent of income
X-axis: Per cent of income recipients

Source: U.S. Census Bureau, *Current Population Reports, Consumer Income,* Ser. P-60, no. 16, Table 5, p. 16.

Figure 1.5   Wage and salary incomes of employed males, non-farm, United States, 1953 (14 years of age and over)

amount of intra-occupational dispersion is positively related to occupational rank can be replaced by an equivalent one, namely, that dispersion is positively related to levels of earnings in the occupational groups.

Thus we could, in effect, use average earnings of groups as indicators of their occupational rank and correlate those with the shares of top quintiles in the respective occupations. In reality, of course, the simplifying assumption that levels of earnings reflect occupational rank (training) *exclusively* is untenable. Many other factors, compensatory or not, influence these levels, especially in the short run, and more so when small differences in levels are distinguished. Yet, despite the impossibility of identifying and eliminating all such disturbing factors from the data, when this procedure was followed, a positive correlation coefficient of $r = +0.77$ was obtained.[37] 'Occupational rank', in our sense, is a factor that cannot be

Table 1.3   Income inequality in detailed occupations and occupational status, US, 1949 (male full-year wage and salary workers)

Group	Professional and managerial	Clerical and sales	Craftsmen	Operatives	Laborers and service
Median quintile share	38.2	35.6	30.2	29.6	28.7
Midrange of quintile shares	35.8–44.2	26.3–42.8	29.1–32.7	28.0–31.4	28.0–30.9

† Weeks worked, as defined in the 1950 population Census, includes all weeks in 1949 during which any work was performed. Persons who did any amount of work during each of 50 weeks in 1949 were counted as full-year workers. The variation in man-hours due to the sizable proportion of part-time workers in many occupations obscures the relation we are studying. No direct information is available on the extent of part-time work in the detailed occupations. Frequency distribution of earnings provided in Miller, op. cit., Table C-2, pp. 179–81, were used to exclude 12 occupations in which more than 10 per cent of workers earned less than $1000, working 50 weeks or more in 1949. Such low earnings in groups of male, non-farm, full-period workers can only be a reflection of part-time work or of income received to a large extent in a non-monetary form. The excluded occupations are: clergymen; musicians and music teachers; messengers; newsboys; attendants; private household workers; charmen; janitors and porters; service workers (n.e.c.); fishermen and oystermen; lumbermen, raftsmen, and woodchoppers; laborers in wood production; and laborers in wholesale and retail trade.

Source: Miller, *Income of the American People*, Table C-5, pp. 193–6.

dismissed in studies of income inequality within component population groups.

Mixed component groups

When the aggregate income distribution is broken down by any criterion other than occupation or age, it yields component groups which generally differ in occupational composition and age distribution. When such differences in composition are pronounced, the findings that the more highly trained workers are characterized by both higher income levels and greater income inequality can be utilized to predict the rank order of income inequalities of the component groups.

Let each component group consist of several occupational strata. It can be shown that inequality in a component group is a 'weighted' sum of the inequalities within strata, with 'weights' reflecting the relative sizes and relative income levels of the strata.[38] Therefore, the larger the proportion[39] of 'top' occupational strata, such as professionals and managers, in a group, the larger the income dispersion in the group. Geometrically speaking, a greater weight attached to upper occupational groups extends the right-hand tail of the income distribution of the occupation-mix.

Distributions by industry

When the distribution of wages and salaries is disaggregated by industrial origin, the component distributions of earnings must, to some extent, reflect differences in the occupational compositions of the various industries. Such differences exist, no matter what boundaries are imposed on the concept of industry.

From the point of view of organization of the production process, an industry is a particular combination of factors of production. When labor is subdivided by occupations differing in training and skill, it can be viewed as a set of distinct factors of production differing in the extent of capital accumulated in them. As with non-human capital, some industries have high 'capital ratios', others low ones, the state of the arts in each industry being what it is. Given full utilization of labor (that is, abstracting from variations due to part-period earnings), we should expect a greater dispersion of earnings in industries with relatively many professional and managerial workers than in those with relatively few.

That the occupational composition, or what may be called the average level of human capital, is an important factor in determining the extent of intra-industry income dispersion is evident on several levels of aggregation:

Table 1.4 presents data on income inequality and the occupational composition within ten major industrial groups. The occupational composition is that of 1950 as reported in the census. The inequality measure, the income share of the top quintile of workers, refers to wages and salaries in 1949 and total money incomes in 1953 and 1954. In all three years inequality is positively associated with the proportion of highly trained occupations (professional, technical, and managerial): the coefficient of rank correlation is $+0.85$ in 1949, $+0.93$ in 1953, and $+0.80$ in 1954.

At a more detailed level of aggregation,[40] the role played by occupational composition in creating patterns of intra-industry wage and salary differentials, while obscured by many other factors, is still unmistakable. When the occupational factor represented by the proportion of professional and managerial workers[41] in 75 census intermediate industry groups[42] in 1949 is correlated with income shares of top quintiles of workers in those industries in that year, the correlation coefficient is $+0.72$.

Table 1.4   Occupational composition and income inequality in industries,
US male workers, ten broad industry groups, 1949, 1953, 1954

Industry	Proportion of 'top' occupations (1)	Share of top quintile		
		1949 (2)	1953 (3)	1954 (4)
Mining	6.7	36.5	34.4	38.7
Construction	7.7	39.1	39.3	41.4
Manufacturing	10.0	38.0	37.4	38.1
Transportation	9.0	34.4	34.8	37.2
Wholesale trade	17.5	43.1	46.8	44.8
Retail trade	15.6	41.6	43.5	46.3
Finance and insurance	25.9	45.4	47.0	48.0
Entertainment and recreation	40.2	52.6	59.5	n.a.
Business service	12.8	41.8	44.6	45.3
Professional service	60.0	42.8	47.7	50.8

Sources: Col. 1: *Occupational Characteristics* (Census Special Rept P-E, No. 1B), Table 134, p. 290; Col. 2: H. P. Miller, 'Changes in the Industrial Distribution of Wages in the US, 1939–1949,' *Conference on Research in Income and Wealth*, (National Bureau of Economic Research, 1956), Appendix Table B-3; Col. 3: *Census Current Population Reports*, P-60, no. 16, Table 6, p. 18; Col. 4: *Census Current Population Reports*, P-60, no. 19, Table 6, p. 18.

Color, sex, family status, and city size[43]
When members of the labor force are classified by color, sex, family status, or city size, the resulting groups exhibit pronounced differences in occupational and age characteristics. As before, differences in the training-mix produce predictable patterns of income inequality. Roughly speaking, the greater the average amount of training in the group, the greater the inequality in its income distribution.

Thus earnings of full-year employed non-white workers show less inequality than those of similar white workers; earnings of female workers are less dispersed than earnings of male workers, when part-period earnings are excluded; earnings of male full-period workers who are heads of families are more unequal than those of single men; and, finally, income inequality increases with city size.[44]

3. Summary
The implications for income distributions of individual differences in investment in human capital have been derived in a theoretical model in which the process of investment is subject to free choice. The choice refers

to training differing primarily in the length of time it requires. Since the time spent in training constitutes a postponement of earnings to a later age, the assumption of rational choice means an equalization of present values of life-earnings at the time the choice is made. As Adam Smith observed, this equalization implies higher annual pay in occupations that require more training.

Inter-occupational differentials are therefore a function of differences in training. According to the model, this function is of a very simple form and can be summarized in the principle that absolute differences in the length of training result in percentage differences in annual earnings. It follows that, as long as the distribution of training is not substantially negatively skewed, the distribution of earnings must be positively skewed.

Intra-occupational differences arise when the concept of investment in human capital is extended to include experience on the job. Age measures both the process of acquiring experience and biological growth and decline. The growth of experience and hence of productivity is reflected in increasing earnings with age, up to a point when biological decline begins to affect productivity adversely. The important difference among occupational groups is that, on the whole, increases in productivity with age are more pronounced, and declines are less pronounced, in jobs requiring greater amounts of training.

When the positive relation between investment in human capital and the growth of productivity is incorporated in the model, the following results are produced: first, interoccupational differences increase, because the present value of a life-flow of income of given size is smaller, the steeper the positive slope and the later the peak of the age-income curve. Secondly, because of the increasing age gradient, intra-occupational dispersion must increase with 'occupational rank'. In other words, 'vertical' occupational groupings exhibit a positive correlation between income levels and income dispersion. This correlation, even when restricted to absolute dispersion, once more introduces positive skewness in the aggregative distribution. Thus the skewness is due to patterns of interoccupational as well as intra-occupational income differences. Moreover, the increasing divergence with age of life-paths of earnings among different occupations implies that inequality of income within age groups increases with age. Finally, any decomposition of the aggregate by criteria other than age, education, and occupation produces groups which constitute training and age 'mixes'. The previous conclusions imply that income dispersion in such groups must be positively related to the average amount of investment in human capital in them. Breakdowns by industry, color, sex, and city size were analyzed in these terms. As we have seen, the empirical evidence is clearly consistent with all the implications of the model about the effects of education, occupation, and age on patterns of personal income distribution.

It is useful, in conclusion, to point out some limitations of the present study so as to avoid possible misinterpretations. In terms of predictive power, the limitations are quite obvious. The model predicts the existence of empirical regularities such as aggregative skewness and ordinal patterns of dispersion in some broad classifications of income. It was not adapted to predict absolute or even relative magnitudes of parameters in the component distributions. It does not tell, therefore, how much of the observed sizes of parameters or of the difference between parameters of relevant components is accounted for by the factors built into the model.

Regarding the distinction between compensatory and restrictive income differences, it was shown that, even under perfectly free choice, differences in training would produce a number of features of the frequency distributions of income which are actually observed. This does not mean, however, that these features are a reflection of such compensatory income differences exclusively.

Interoccupational differences in income levels are not entirely compensatory, once a distribution of 'abilities' is introduced. If there is some degree of positive association between ability and choice of longer training, the compensatory differences are augmented by a differential ascribable to ability alone. The financial outlays incurred in training increase the compensatory differences in a way that magnifies dispersion and particularly skewness in the aggregative distribution. They may, indeed, increase the differences beyond the amount necessary for equalization of present values by sharply restricting supply. Finally, when incomes rather than earnings are considered, the positive association of property incomes with occupational level and age magnifies income differences in a way which is likely to accentuate the empirical regularities implied by the training factor alone.

It is thus the consensus of all the factors just listed that produces the empirical results. The purely compensatory factor around which the model is built was chosen for its inherent significance, its analytical convenience, and the theoretical interest attaching to the result that even perfect equality of ability and opportunity implies neither income equality nor symmetry[45] in the income distribution.

Notes

1. This is brought out in the distinction between the 'permanent' and the 'transitory' components of income as applied to the analysis of consumption in Milton Friedman, *A Theory of the Consumption Function*, Princeton, N.J.: Princeton University Press, 1957.

2. A more detailed review of these theories can be found in H. Staehle, 'Ability, Wages, and Income', *Review of Economics and Statistics*, vol. xxv (February 1943), pp. 77–87.
3. A. C. Pigou, *The Economics of Welfare*, London: Macmillan, 1932, p. 648.
4. C. Burt, 'Ability and Income', *British Journal of Educational Psychology*, xiii (June 1943), pp. 95ff.; A. D. Roy, 'The Distribution of Earnings and of Individual Output', *Economic Journal*, vol. lx (September 1950), pp. 489–505. For the origin of the hypothesis see C.H. Boissevain, 'Distribution of Abilities Depending on Two or More Independent Factors', *Metron*, vol. xiii (December 1939), pp. 49–58.
5. R. Gibrat, *Les Inégalités économiques*, Paris: Sirey, 1931.
6. M. Kalecki, 'On the Gibrat Distribution', *Econometrica*, vol. xiii (April 1945), pp. 161–70.
7. Ibid.; see also D.G. Champernowne, 'A Model of Income Distribution', *Economic Journal*, vol. lxiii (June 1953), pp. 318–51.
8. R. S. G. Rutherford, 'Income Distributions: a New Model', *Econometrica*, vol. xviii (July 1955), pp. 425–40.
9. Ibid.
10. M. Friedman, 'Choice, Chance, and the Personal Distribution of Income', *Journal of Political Economy*, vol. lxi (August 1953), pp. 277–90.
11. Thus termed by J. R. Hicks in *The Theory of Wages*, New York: P. Smith Co., 1941, p. 3.
12. According to a recent study, the average length of working life in eight broad occupational groups is as follows:

Occupation	Mean no. years in labor force
Professional and technical workers	40
Managers and officials	41
Craftsmen and foremen	44
Operatives and kindred workers	45
Clerical and sales workers	47
Non-farm laborers	51
Service workers	52

Similar patterns were observed in 1930, 1940 and 1950. Commenting on the findings, the authors of the study observe: 'In general men spend, on the average, fewer years in what may be termed the better jobs. The three occupations with the shortest working life are those in which greater training, education and experience are required. These are also the jobs which in general afford larger earnings. Clearly the men in the better jobs – as measured by earnings and education – spend a shorter period of their lives in the working force' (A. J. Jaffe and R. O. Carleton, *Occupational Mobility in the United States, 1930–1960*, New York: King's Crown Press, 1954, p. 50).

13. With minor exceptions, the procedure is basically a generalization of the one used by Friedman and Kuznets in *Income from Independent Professional Practice*, New York: National Bureau of Economic Research, 1945, pp. 142–51.
14. Assuming the values of r and l to be in a rather wide neighbourhood of 0.04 and 50, respectively.
15. The percentage increase in relative income differences between persons with (n) and ($n - d$) years of training resulting from the introduction of schooling expenses can be measured by the ratio of annual schooling expenses to annual earnings in groups with ($n - d$) years of training.

For example, if average earnings of high-school graduates are $4000 and the annual expenses of a college education are $1000, then to the compensatory income differences due to the deferral of income for 4 years ($k^4 - 1$) we must add $(1000/4000)$ ($k^4 - 1$) to compensate for the cost of tuition. This increases the differences by 25 per cent (see my unpublished PhD dissertation, 'A Study of Personal Income Distribution', Columbia University, 1957, ch. ii, note 2).

16. By the same procedure, a simple measure of relative dispersion is

$$\frac{Q_3 - Q_1}{Q_2} = \frac{k^{2d} - 1}{k^d} = k^d - \frac{1}{k^d}.$$

17. Differences in abilities introduce additional dispersion into the income distribution. In particular, any degree of positive correlation between ability and differences in training magnifies the extent of 'interoccupational' income differences.
18. See Mincer, 'Study of Personal Income Distribution', ch. ii, note 1.
19. Actually, the assumptions need not be so rigid, as a certain amount of dissimilarity in age distributions will not affect the systematic effects of differences in the steepness of life-paths on intra-group dispersion. Indeed, 1950 Census data indicate that the dissimilarity is rather small among broad occupational groups when comparisons are restricted to the ages between 25 and 65:

Percentage distribution of ages by occupation, US male wage and salary earners, 1950

| | Age groups | | | | |
Occupation	25–35	35–45	45–55	55–65	Total
Professional and managerial	30.6	31.1	23.8	14.5	100.0
Clerical and sales	35.8	28.0	21.8	14.4	100.0
Craftsmen and foremen	29.9	30.0	24.1	16.0	100.0
Operatives and service	33.8	29.8	21.6	14.8	100.0
Non-farm laborers	32.4	28.2	22.7	16.7	100.0

*Source: Occupational Characteristics (Census Special Rept P-E, No. 1B), Table 5, pp. 53–59.

20. Pigou, *Economics of Welfare*, p. 246. Other writers have followed Pigou along these lines.
21. H. P. Miller, 'Elements of Symmetry in the Skewed Income Curve', *Journal of the American Statistical Association* (March 1955), pp. 55–71.
22. For a formal statement and discussion of the necessary and sufficient conditions for positive skewness see Mincer, 'Study of Personal Income Distribution', ch. ii, note 4.
23. *U.S. Census of Population 1950*, vol. II: *Characteristics of the Population*, part I: *U.S. Summary*, Introduction, pp. 44–6.
24. H. P. Miller, *Income of the American People*, New York: John Wiley, 1955, pp. 65–8.
25. *Federal Reserve Bulletin*, XLI (June 1955), p. 615, Supplementary Table 3.
26. Miller, *Income of the American People*, Table 24, p. 54.
27. See H.F. Lydall, 'The Life Cycle in Income, Saving, and Asset Ownership', *Econometrica*, April 1955, pp. 131–50; *BLS Bulletin 643*, p. 55; M. Leven, *The Income Structure of the U.S.* (New York: Brookings Institution, 1938), pp. 50–156; Friedman and Kuznets, *op. cit.*, p. 247; and *Survey of Current Business*, April 1944, Table 4, p. 19, and July 1951, Table 8, p. 15.
28. See formulae on p. 9.
29. The dashed lines in Figure 1.2 were obtained by shifting the upper two solid lines downward to the level at which all present values were equalized (at age fourteen). For purposes of discounting, the lowest income path was extrapolated back to age fourteen,

the middle one to age nineteen. The use of income rather then earnings figures may bias the slopes upward; abstraction from similar trends in education and earnings may impart a counteracting bias. The procedure is clearly to be viewed as groping for some orders of magnitude rather than as estimating in any more rigorous sense of the word.

30. J. Fisher, 'Income, Spending, and Saving Patterns of Consumer Units in Different Age Groups', *Studies in Income and Wealth*, vol. xv (New York: National Bureau of Economic Research, 1952), p. 83.
31. See Mincer, 'Study of Personal Income Distribution', pp. 79–81.
32. The same mean ($12,000) was assigned to the upper, open-ended class in the three distributions. Consequently, inequality of groups with greater education is underestimated relative to the others. For additional empirical instances of the relation between education and income inequality see Mincer, ibid., pp. 81–5.
33. For comparable information about intra-occupational income dispersion for various dates, places, and definitions see ibid., Table III—8, p. 87.
34. Ibid., pp. 66–70, and *passim*.
35. Miller, *Income of the American People*, Table C-5, pp. 193–6.
36. Persons working 50 weeks or more in 1949.
37. After excluding the twelve occupations listed in the note to Table 1.3.
38. For a mathematical formulation see Mincer, 'Study of Personal Income Distribution', ch. iv, notes 1–3.
39. Up to a point, depending on the number and sizes of parameters distinguished in the group (see ibid.).
40. Miller's study quoted in Table 1.4 contains further breakdowns of the census wage and salary statistics into 91 intermediate industry groups. These are subdivided into 117 more detailed industries. The study provides frequency distributions of 1949 wages and salaries as well as corresponding means, medians, quartiles, and income shares of quintiles for each industry. The recipient units are males, fourteen years of age and over, including part-period and part-time workers (Miller, 'Changes in the Industrial Distribution of Wages in the US, 1939–1949', *Conference on Research in Income and Wealth*, National Bureau of Economic Research, 1956, Appendix Tables B-1 and B-3).
41. Proportions were computed from *Occupational Characteristics* (Census Special Rept. P-E, No. 1B), Table 134, p. 290.
42. These contained over 90 per cent of all male wage and salary workers. The exclusion of 16 industries from the correlation is the result of a crude, but conservative, attempt to eliminate part-period workers from the distributions: industries with over 20 per cent of workers receiving less than $1000 during the year were excluded as being too strongly affected by the part-period income variable. These were agriculture, forestry, fisheries, lumber and wood, printing and publishing, foodstores, five-and-ten-cent stores, gasoline service stations, drugstores, eating and drinking places, retail florists, private households, hotels and lodgings, dress and shoe repair, theaters and motion pictures, and miscellaneous entertainment.
43. For statistical details and sources see Mincer, 'Study of Personal Income Distribution', pp. 109–27.
44. The same explanation holds for the systematic increase in income levels with city size, which is a more familiar phenomenon. The increase in income level with city size is more apparent in the statistics that do not separate full-period from part-period workers. The greater proportion of part-period workers in smaller communities accentuates the differences in income levels, while it obscures the differences in income variances.
45. In this connection, recall the statement of Allyn Young to the effect that it is not income inequality but skewness that is a symptom of the distortion (in a normative sense) of the income scheme of society (Allyn Young, 'Do the Statistics of the Concentration of Wealth in the United States Mean What They Are Commonly Assumed To Mean?', *Journal of the American Statistical Association*, March 1917, pp. 471–84).

2 The distribution of labor incomes: a survey*

Empirical knowledge about income distribution has grown during the past two decades at a rate much greater than that of any other comparable period. The stock of information on individual incomes increased enormously with the appearance of the 1950 and 1960 Population Censuses and Bureau of Labor Statistics (BLS) Surveys of Consumer Expenditures, the periodic Current Population Surveys of the Census Bureau, and the Michigan Surveys of Consumer Finances, to mention only the most important sources. At the same time, high-speed electronic computers made possible the processing and statistical analyses of these massive collections of individual observations.

While traditional and mainly speculative preoccupations with factor shares, ability vectors, and stochastic processes continued in evidence, the dominant form of research was empirical. A still modest but significant change in emphasis is emerging in recent empirical work: beyond the usual and necessary efforts to summarize, measure, and occasionally interpret the bewildering varieties of statistical frequency distributions of income, some of the new studies attempt multivariate statistical analysis of 'causal' factors associated with size of individual income.

Parallel conceptual developments are more general and more striking. Interest has shifted from the consumption function and its role in short-run fluctuations in income and employment to the production function as a key concept in the study of economic growth. The focus on income as a determinant of consumption behavior is giving way to an interest in income as a dependent variable. Thus the analysis of causes of income variation in the aggregate and among individuals is returning to the mainstream of theoretical and empirical research. One impressive outgrowth of this shift is the rapidly developing literature on human capital. The human capital approach is intimately related to the study of income distribution: costs and returns to investments in human capital are measured in the first instance by earnings differentials. Consequently, there is a growing recognition of the importance of investment in people as an underlying principle in theoretical and empirical analysis of income distributions.

*This chapter was first published in the *Journal of Economic Literature*, vol. 8 (1970), pp. 1–26.

This review concentrates largely on the emerging human capital approach to the analysis of personal income size distribution. This approach is no reflection on the actual or potential value of alternative approaches to the subject. Fortunately, the field of income size distribution is already blessed by a number of excellent surveys containing detailed summaries of past and recent work. The surveys usually appear as necessary background to the author's own contribution and represent valiant efforts at an orderly exposition of a field which lacks conceptual unity.[1] Since they contain rather full accounts of a wide spectrum of analyses and findings, however disparate and fragmentary, the present rather specialized exposition should be viewed as a complementary rather than competing effort. Nevertheless, the traditional interest in the role of chance, ability, and opportunity will not be neglected.

In the distribution of income, as in all statistical distributions, the most dramatic cases are those at the tails. Some readers will be disappointed that no mention is made here of 'the super-rich who own America' or of the many poor who are not even in the labor force. The present survey is limited to earnings of labor. Even within this narrow compass of the survey, a variety of topics are omitted. To the extent that the omissions cannot be blamed on the limitations of the literature, separate surveys are called for.

The traditional approaches centering on differences in opportunity, ability, and chance, are briefly reviewed in the next few pages. This review serves both as contrasting and complementary background to the human-capital approach. Following the introductory review, the survey is devoted to an exposition of the development and application of the human-capital model as an instrument of analysis of income distribution. The order of the exposition is both chronological and methodological. Starting with the simplest 'schooling model' (section 1) which relates earnings to schooling we move to the more general formulation of the relation between earnings and human capital investments (section 2) of which schooling is only a part. Continuing investments which follow the completion of schooling and their effects on working life 'earnings profiles' of individuals are the subject of special attention in section 3. The implications of individual differences in self-investments and in rates of return on them are individual differences in levels and shapes of earnings profiles. These implications, it is shown, can yield an understanding of the characteristic shapes and of comparative magnitudes of parameters of observed statistical distributions of earnings in the aggregate and in component schooling and age groups. Following the review of such 'qualitative' analysis, section 4 describes econometric attempts to answer the question: how much of the observed inequality in earnings is attributable to individual differences in the sizes of human capital investments? The correlation between investments and earnings is interpreted in section 5 in terms of the interplay of factors which influence human capital investment decisions. In the last few sections there is a discussion of distinctions between long- and short-run income inequality, of transformations of personal into family distributions of earnings, and of some research agenda.

1.   Traditional approaches

In the literature which dates back to Ricardo, the major *economic* approach to income distribution is the functional or factor-share approach. In the past, this approach was motivated by an identification of the trinity of factors of production with corresponding and distinct social classes. The approach continues to flourish in the literature despite the blurring of such social class identifications and despite the recognition that under modern conditions the variance in labor incomes is the dominant component of total income inequality. Remote links exist between the functional and the size distribution of total incomes, but this approach does not address itself to the distribution of labor incomes.[2]

To be sure, the heterogeneity of rewards to individual workers did not escape the attention of classical economists. Their comments are summed up in two famous principles: first, Smith's compensatory principle is conditional on the strength of competitive forces in the labor market. Labor mobility produces earnings differentials which tend to equalize 'net advantages and disadvantages' of work. Secondly, Mill's and Cairnes' doctrine of 'noncompeting groups' proclaims in effect the absence of labor mobility resulting in real income differences, produced and perpetuated by socially, legally, and culturally imposed and inherited stratifications.

A great deal of research on labor markets is directed toward the assessment of the relative validity of the two principles. Though this research is abundant, as is the passion surrounding it, it is often vague. In a recent summary, Reder (1962) concludes that evidence favors the competitive hypothesis, at least in so far as long-run differences in average occupational and industrial wages are concerned. Wage differentials which compensate for differences in risk and in the cost of living have also been noted as illustrations of compensatory differentials. Indeed, Friedman (1953) has shown that risk-taking behaviour can produce an overall pattern of income distribution which, like the observed distribution, is positively skewed and humped. Mincer (1957 and 1958) has shown that a similar shape is likely to arise in consequence of compensatory differentials due to costs of occupational training. Some of the predictions of the compensatory principle are often rejected *prima facie*: on the whole, occupations in which work is more unpleasant and unstable command lower, not higher wages. The costs of occupational training, however, can reconcile these apparent contradictions. The reconciliation requires sufficiently large training costs and a negative correlation between occupational skill and both unpleasantness and instability. Becker's theory of specific training (1964) provides a possible explanation of the latter. In occupations requiring similar training costs, compensatory differentials are more clearly observable.

The doctrine of noncompeting groups is rarely accepted in the extreme form enunciated by Mill. It usually denotes a recognition of the importance of 'institutionally' determined inequalities of opportunity. In its moderate versions this doctrine has had many adherents, but it has not produced any cumulative theoretical developments in the analysis of income distribution. It did contribute, however, by its emphasis on a variety of environmental factors, to a pragmatic statistical approach. In this spirit, such 'institutional' or 'demographic' factors as sex, age, occupation, education, location, and parental wealth have become objects of multivariate analyses of statistical associations with individual income differences (Adams, 1958; Hill, 1959; Morgan *et al.*, 1962b). It is true, of course, that without the guide of a theoretical framework, the statistical formulations and the interpretations attached to them are often insecure and ambiguous. Nevertheless, they are a welcome departure from the largely speculative, single-factor theories that have traditionally competed for attention in this field.

According to Stigler (1966), 'the major modern noncompetitive force on wages is the labor union'. Specialized research on union wage effects is voluminous[3] but rarely related to the overall pattern of income distribution. On this question Rees (1962) concludes that 'unions have probably raised many higher income workers from above the middle to a position closer to the top of the income distribution'. While this effect is not clearly described as an increase or decrease in the equality of the income distribution, 'it seems closer to the latter than to the former'.

One version of 'noncompeting groups' which has been elevated to a theory of income distribution is the view that worker differences in productivity, and hence in earnings, are due to differential abilities. Starting with Galton (1869) this idea has fascinated geneticists, psychologists, statisticians, and economists. Referring to the alleged normal distribution of intelligence, Pigou (1920) dramatized the issue by posing the question: if capacities are normally distributed, why is this not true of earnings?

One answer, stated by Reder (1968), is that the distribution of capacities is not the same as the distribution of marginal productivities. The transformation of the former into the latter depends on cooperating factors and on the form of the production function of services which these capacities help to produce. Another response is to question any arbitrary definition of relevant abilities, to the point of denying the possibility of measuring earning capacity independently of earnings.

Indeed, recent research is now attempting to infer the distribution of abilities from the distribution of earnings. And because variables such as education, age, and location also affect earnings, the distribution of abilities is studied in earnings distributions of homogeneous groups of workers (Roy, 1950; Bjerke, 1969). Thus the relevance of ability theories is reduced to residual variations in income distribution, after the systematic factors have been netted out. This orientation is, however, too narrow because it ignores the interaction between ability and the systematic variables. A possible link is restored on theoretical grounds in Becker's recent formulation of the human capital model (1967). But in this formulation, to be discussed later, the role of abilities is neither exclusive nor dominant.

2.   Mathematical models of chance and ability

It may seem paradoxical that one of the most popular approaches to the analysis of income distribution singles out residual variation, or 'chance', as the principal source of income inequality. Actually the 'chance' factor is not conceived as a residual, but as a substitute for, or net effect, of all kinds of causes which are too numerous and obscure to be treated explicitly. This is the standard rationale of applied probability models. As we are increasing our insights into the subject, the need for such models is decreasing together with the size of the residual variation which is left over.

The basic stochastic model dates back to Gibrat (1931): starting with some initial distribution, individuals are subjected to the play of 'chance'. If they experience increases or decreases in income unrelated to income levels, the central limit theorem guarantees that, in time, the distribution of income will approach normality, regardless of the form of the initial distribution. If this specification of 'random shock' applies to percentage rather than absolute changes, the process converges to a log-normal distribution. The latter has been observed to fit aggregate distributions of income better than the normal distribution, hence the name 'law of proportionate effect'.

The model recently received a number of interesting elaborations. Champernowne (1953) has shown that when certain assumptions are introduced about the distribution of the proportionate random shock, the income distribution converges to a Pareto distribution.

Aitchison and Brown (1957) have shown that even if the law of proportionate effect produced a log-normal distribution only within homogeneous subgroups ('trades'), the aggregate distribution would remain log-normal so long as variances in the component distributions are of the same size and the means of the components are log-normally distributed.

Since income at any time is portrayed as a sum of uncorrelated random shocks in all previous periods, the implication of these models is that the variance of income must grow over time.[4] Yet empirical observations of aggregate income inequality remain relatively stable. In his model, Rutherford (1955) turns this apparent defect into a virtue. He applies the random shock to age cohorts. The income variance must increase with age for each age cohort, but given a relatively stable age distribution, the aggregate variance does not change much. Rutherford also observes that the observed distributions do not fit the log-normal distribution very well: a graph of the cumulative distribution on log-normal probability paper is more akin to an S-curve (the distribution is 'leptokurtic') than to a straight line. This, Rutherford shows, will result from aggregation when population frequencies decline with age (exponentially in his formulation). If, in addition, income grows with age, the implied positive correlation between means and variances by age groups will impart (additional) positive skewness to the aggregate.[5] Among the several stochastic models, Rutherford's is the richest in empirical predictions, providing a standard which a substantive economic model should match.

Mandelbrot (1960) substitutes an additive process for the multiplicative (proportionate) random shock. He notes that the characteristic shape of the aggregate income distribution remains similar when the empirical definition of income is varied (wages and salaries, self-employment, taxable income, etc.). If the differences in the definitions of income are due to alternative inclusions or exclusions of additive components, this is precisely the condition under which a Pareto–Levy distribution arises. This distribution is rather realistic: two-tailed, positively skewed, with a Pareto upper tail. Mathematically, the result is generated by the repeated application of a weighted sum of independent random elements.

In a subsequent paper, Mandelbrot (1962) provides another interpretation of such a process. Abilities can be factor-analytically represented as weighted sums of uncorrelated components. The distribution of weights determines the specific mathematical function within the general family of distribution functions. The effective distributions are in turn produced by a selection process, in which component abilities required by particular jobs are matched with abilities that different individuals will supply in combinations reflecting their comparative advantage.[6]

The alternative application of the same mathematical argument to stochastic and to ability models is not new. It was, in fact, the way ability theorists tried to find an answer to Pigou's question of whether a skewed distribution of earnings can be associated with an allegedly normal distribution of abilities. The argument, originating with Boissevain (1939), runs as follows: earnings are proportional to ability. But ability is a multidimensional concept. If component abilities combine multiplicatively, as 'random shock' does in stochastic models, the resulting implications are: symmetric distributions of component abilities produce positively skewed aggregates, hence earnings. If the component abilities are positively intercorrelated, skewness is augmented. And if the variances of the components are unequal, humpedness (leptokurtosis) will result (Roy, 1950).

Roy studied distributions of physical output (piecework) in samples of homogeneous workers. Results were mixed, though positive skewness was encountered more often than symmetry or negative skewness. Similar results were found for wages of homogeneous groups of workers by Bjerke (1969).

Lydall (1968) argues that if the random shock models are accepted, ability models must be applied only to new entrants into the labor force. Lydall accepts the view of ability as a multiplicative combination of components, but rejects the 'random shock' hypotheses. He replaces the latter by psychological findings to the effect that abilities and their variances grow with age – at least up to middle age. Thereafter, levels decline, though variances do not. The empirical implications are clearly similar to Rutherford's and quite realistic. But Lydall's restoration of ability from the more modest residual role assigned to it by Roy and Bjerke to a dominant place in the overall distribution verges on the tautological: stating facts about distributions of productivities comes dangerously close to stating facts about distributions of earnings. Both sets of facts require explanation.

The attention paid to the mathematical random shock and ability models is perhaps undeserved. The models seem rather superficial in focusing on an unexplained category and in the single-minded objective of theoretically reproducing a presumed mathematical form of the aggregative distribution. Still, an acquaintance with these models may be useful. Residual distributions may be best treated in a probabilistic fashion. More instructive is the explicit treatment and the demonstrated flexibility of the mathematical structure of the arguments. As we shall see, similar structures reappear in very different substantive models, thereby assuring at least as much explanatory power as the just described models are capable of producing.

3.   The human-capital approach

1.   The schooling model

Common to the mathematical models described in the previous section is the view that the distribution of earnings is unaffected by individual choice. The exogenous variables have economic effects, but do not pertain to economic behavior.

In contrast, human-capital models single out individual investment behaviour as a basic factor in the heterogeneity of labor incomes. Indeed, the first model of this kind (Mincer, 1957 and 1958) starts by assuming a complete absence of environmental inequalities. These assumptions are not inherent in the human capital approach and have been relaxed. They were initially imposed in order to reveal the effects of individual choice unhindered by the non-competitive forces which are so prominent in the traditional literature.

The model takes the length of training as the basic source of heterogeneity of labor incomes. Training raises productivity, but the time spent in training necessitates postponement of earnings to a later age. Individuals undertake various amounts of training in the expectation that their occupational incomes in the future will be sufficiently large to compensate for the cost of training. For simplicity, the cost of training is restricted to forgone earnings, the dominant component of private training costs. In a competitive equilibrium, the distribution of earnings is such that the present values of future earnings, discounted at the market rate of interest, are equalized at the time training begins.

The model is formulated in terms of training periods which are completed before earnings begin. It, therefore, applies strictly to schooling rather than to all occupational training. Assume that no further investments in human capital are undertaken by individuals after completion of their schooling, and that the flow of their earnings is constant throughout their working lives. Then, the equalization of present values of earnings for individuals with s_1 and s_2 years of schooling, and with n_1 and n_2 years of working life, results in the following ratio of annual earnings:[7]

$$k_{2,1} = \frac{E_{s2}}{E_{s1}} = \frac{e^{-rs1}(1 - e^{-rn1})}{e^{-rs2}(1 - e^{-rn2})} \tag{2.1}$$

Here r stands for the market discount rate or for the internal rate of return on the differential investment which it must equal, E is annual earnings, and e is the base of natural logarithms. If n_1 and n_2 are large, k approaches the value $e^{r(s2-s1)}$. More compactly, putting $s_2 = s$, $s_1 = 0$, $k_s \rightarrow e^{rs}$. Alternatively, when $n_1 = n_2 = n$, regardless of the length of working life, $k_s = e^{rs}$, exactly. These formulations, incidentally, highlight the principle that it is not the shorter pay-off period of the more educated, but the postponement of earnings that is the basic cause of differentials in earnings. Empirically, both formulations are roughly correct,[8] so that (2.1) can be written:

$$\lg E_s = \lg E_0 + rs \tag{2.1a}$$

If the competitive assumptions are relaxed, internal rates of return cannot be equated with the market rate of interest and generally differ among individuals.

(2.1a) can remain serviceable, however, with r interpreted as a group average internal rate of return on schooling, while individual differences in r and in $\lg E_0$ are impounded in a statistical residual.

Relation (2.1) makes percentage differentials in earnings a linear function of time spent at school. This transformation is one source of the tendency toward positive skewness in the distribution of earnings: for a symmetric distribution of years of schooling would imply a positively skewed distribution of earnings. Indeed, unless the distribution of schooling is highly negatively skewed, a positive skew will be imparted to the distribution of earnings.[9]

Relation (2.1) also implies that relative dispersion and skewness in the distribution of earnings are greater the larger the absolute dispersion in the distribution of schooling. Earnings inequality and skewness are also greater the higher the rate of return.[10] If, for example, barriers to investment in schooling produce a higher rate of return to schooling, greater inequality will result.

The model does not predict the shape of the distribution of schooling. Empirical schooling distributions are more likely to be positively skewed when the average level of schooling is low. In the United States the distribution has even become negatively skewed in the most recent cohorts, though not in the aggregate. Even in the recent cohorts, the negative skewness in schooling is not sufficient to create a negatively skewed distribution of earnings.

Chiswick (1967) applied model (2.1a) to a comparative analysis of income inequality among different regions in the US and a few other countries. Regressions of (log) earnings of males over 25 years of age on their schooling in each of the regions do, indeed, show that inequality (variance of logs) and skewness (measured by the third moment in the distribution of log-earnings) are larger the greater the variance in the distribution of schooling and the higher the rate of return as estimated by the size of the regression slope in (2.1a). These factors jointly explain over a third of the differences in inequality among regions, and the rate of return is apparently the more important factor. Lydall (1968), who did not employ the rate of return as an explicit variable, also found that the dispersion in the distribution of schooling is a significant factor in explaining differences in the inequality of employment incomes within a wider set of countries.

Within a region, however, the explanatory power of the schooling model is quite low, R^2s running a little over 10 per cent in the various states in 1959, and less than 10 per cent in the regression based on individual observations of the 1960 Census 1: 1000 sample.[11] Moreover, the regression slope which serves as an estimate of the rate of return to investment in schooling is from a half to two-thirds the size of the rates of return calculated directly (cf. Hansen, 1963; Becker, 1964; Hanoch, 1965). Evidently, the residuals in that regression are very large and related to the schooling variable. That is to say, the schooling model, which says something about differences in earnings among schooling *groups*, is a rather blunt instrument when applied to the whole distribution of individual earnings.

Equation (2.1a) was applied by Lydall (1968) and Mincer (1969) to grouped data (mean earnings of males classified by schooling). Logs of earnings yield a better fit than dollar earnings.[12] The slope remains low as in Chiswick's regressions. However, when average earnings of all individuals in a schooling group are replaced by earnings of individuals who have the same amount of labor force experience, measured by years elapsed since completion of schooling,[13] not only does the statistical fit improve, but the slope rises to a level within the range of the rates of return directly estimated.

2.   The general earnings function

The need to incorporate post-school investments such as 'experience' into the earnings model is evident. Developments in that direction were facilitated by Becker's (1964) formulation of a general earnings function within the context of a comprehensive theory of investment in human capital. Earnings of individual i in period j is expressed as a sum of the returns on all his previous net investments and the earnings from his 'original' endowment (ibid., equation 33). Earnings are 'gross' if current investments are included in the concept, 'net' if not included. The gross earnings function is:

$$E_{ji} = X_{ji} + \sum_{t=0}^{j-1} r_{ti}C_{ti} \qquad (2.2a)$$

and the net earnings function:

$$Y_{ji} = X_{ji} + \sum_{t=0}^{j-1} r_{ti} C_{ti} - C_{ji} \qquad (2.2b)$$

Here C_{ji} are net investment costs of person i in period j and X_{ji} is the 'raw' earnings stream that would obtain without investments. An additional subscript may be added if it is desired to distinguish between different forms of investments (e.g., training, migration, recreation). The average rate of return may differ among persons, periods, and investments.

The schooling model (2.1a) can be shown to be a special case of (2.2): if investments are restricted to time costs of schooling: $(C_t = E_t)$, if the rate of return is the same in all periods and for all individuals, $(r_{ti} = r)$, and if $X_{ji} = E_0$ is fixed and the same for all. Substituting in (2b):

$$E_{j>s} = E_0 + r \sum_{t=1}^{s} E_{t-1} = E_0(1 + r)^s \qquad (2.1b)$$

This is the discrete form of equation (2.1a).

The general implication of equations (2.2) is that the distribution of earnings depends not only on the distribution of investment costs C_i, but also on the distribution of the rates of return r_i, and the correlation between these parameters. The distribution of original capacities X_i is also relevant, but we take these as given. For fixed X and r, the distribution of earnings would be of the exact same form as the distribution of investment costs, while for fixed X and C, earnings would vary as does r_i, which can in that case be interpreted as an index of 'ability'. Several specific conclusions are:

(a)   Even if rates of return r_i and investment costs C_i were symmetric and uncorrelated, the distribution of earnings, at least in so far as the component of returns $r \sum C$ is concerned, would be positively skewed – another application of a multiplicative mathematical structure, familiar from the models of ability and chance. The skewness would be strengthened, if a positive correlation between r_i and C_i can be assumed.
(b)   Consequently, the larger the accumulated human capital component $r \sum C$ in earnings, the more skewed is the distribution of earnings likely to be. Thus skilled workers are expected to have a more skewed earnings distribution than unskilled workers.
(c)   During the investment period, defined by positive net investments, the subtraction of current investment costs C_j in (2.2b) weakens the importance of $r \sum C$, more so at younger than at older ages, since $r \sum C$ cumulates with age. Positive skewness, therefore, increases with age.

Though empirically confirmed, these implications are theoretically conditional on a zero or positive correlation[14] between r_i and C_i. It is tempting to postulate a positive correlation between the two, based on the greater incentive to invest of more able people. Becker's later work (1967), how-ever, suggests that the correlation across individuals is not necessarily positive, though it would be under conditions of equality of opportunity, as he defines it.

(d)   Compared to the special case (2.1a), the implications about earnings inequality are now broadened to include the effects of average levels of investment and dispersion in rates of return among individuals. Chiswick (1968) illustrates these effects when he introduces dispersion in r in the schooling model, while assuming no correlation between rates of return r_i, and years of schooling s_i: from $\lg E_i = \lg E_0 + r_i s_i$, it follows[15] that:

$$\sigma^2(\lg E_i) = \bar{r}^2\sigma^2(s) + \bar{s}^2\sigma^2(r) + \sigma^2(s)\sigma^2(r) \tag{2.3}$$

In other words, inequality in earnings is large not only when r and $\sigma(s)$ are large, as we have already learned, but also when $\sigma(r)$ and the average level of schooling $\bar{s}$ are large.

Several recent studies have found a negative correlation between aver-age income and income inequality by states in the US, and between average levels of schooling $\bar{s}$ and income inequality. Chiswick (1968) shows that this is no contradiction of (2.3): the *partial* correlation is positive, once $\bar{r}$ and $\sigma(s)$ are held constant.[16]

Note that in (2.3),

$$\sigma^2(\lg E) = \bar{s}^2\sigma^2(r), \text{ for fixed } s,$$

and

$$\sigma^2(\lg E) = \bar{r}^2\sigma^2(s), \text{ for fixed } r.$$

If r_i can be taken as an index of individual ability, the interpretation is: (a) individual differences in ability create greater relative (and absolute) differences in earnings at higher levels of schooling; and (b) differences in schooling create greater differences in earnings at higher levels of ability.

3.   The life-cycle of earnings: optimization, and levels of earnings by schooling and age

Variation of earnings over the life cycle is an important source of income inequality. This variation was disregarded in the schooling model, but it can be analyzed by means of earnings function (2.2): A specification of changes in C_{ti} over the life cycle traces out the 'age profile' of earnings of individual i.

Generally speaking, the fact that age–earnings profiles slope upward over a large part of the life cycle is a consequence of the tendency to invest in human capital at young ages. According to Becker (1964 and 1967) this tendency is due to the following incentives: (a) with finite lifetimes, later investments produce returns over a shorter period, so total benefits are smaller; (b) to the extent that investments in human capital are profitable, their postponement reduces the present value of net gains; and (c) a person's time is an important input in his investment, but the consequence of human capital accumulation is an increase in the value of his time. Investments at later periods are more costly, because forgone earnings (per hour) increase. The incentive to shift from learning to earning activities follows, except in the special or temporary cases when productivity in learning grows as fast or faster than productivity in earning.

Should we then not expect an early and quick accumulation of all the desired human capital even before individuals begin their working life? The answer of human capital theory to this question is twofold. Investments are spread out over time, because the marginal cost curve of producing them is upward-sloping within each period. They decline over time both because marginal benefits decline and because the marginal cost curve shifts upward.

Specifically, the argument (Ben-Porath, 1967; Becker, 1967) visualizes the individuals as firms which produce additions (Q) to their own human capital stock (H), by combining their human capital with their own time (T) and with other market resources (R) in a production function:

$$Q = f(H,T,R) \qquad (2.4)$$

Attempts to increase Q within a given period run into diminishing returns: costs rise with the speed of production. Thus the marginal cost curve in Figure 2.1 is upward sloping.

The marginal revenue of adding a unit of Q to the capital stock is the discounted flow of future increases in earning power. For reasons indicated, the benefits of later investments decline. The MR curve slides downward with increasing age, tracing out a declining pattern of investment over the life-cycle.

The decline is reinforced if MC shifts to the left with increasing age. As already mentioned, this is not a logical necessity, but will happen if the increasing cost of time – greater earning power in the market – is not matched by increased efficiency of the larger stock in producing additional human capital. A recent attempt by Ben-Porath (1968) to test this 'neutrality' empirically, suggests that investments decline over the life-cycle faster than would be predicted by the mere downward slope of MR on a fixed MC in Figure 2.1.

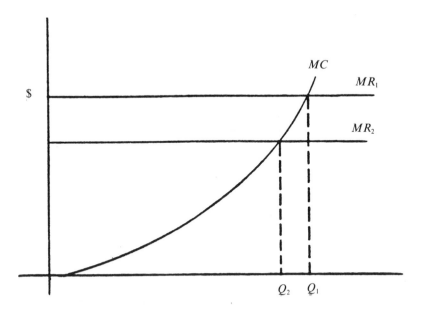

Figure 2.1

Investments, however, need not decline throughout the life-cycle. Ben-Porath (1967) has shown that the optimization process may lead to an increase in investment during the early stages, because of 'corner solutions': The initial stock (H) may be so small that even an input of all the available time, other resources not being highly substitutable, produces less than the optimal amount of output. As the stock increases, investment output will increase for a while until optimum is reached with an input of less than the total available time. At this point investments and time devoted to them begin to decline. The initial period of complete specialization in the production of human capital may be identified with the period of schooling, though more rigorously by the absence of earnings.

The optimization process described above applies explicitly (Ben-Porath, 1967) to gross investments in human capital. Note, however, that the predicted decline in gross investment applies *a fortiori* to net investment, if depreciation increases with age. This would be true, even if the depreciation rate were constant.

The implications of this analysis for age variations in earnings can now be spelled out in terms of earnings model (2.2):

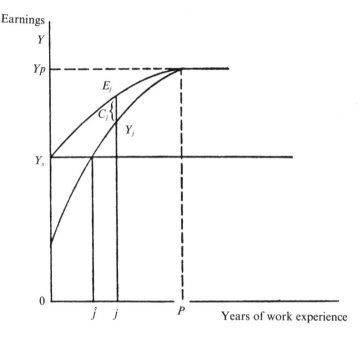

Figure 2.2   Earnings profiles

$$\frac{dE_j}{d_j} = r_jC_j > 0, \text{ when } C_j > 0, \tag{2.5a}$$

and

$$\frac{d^2E_j}{d_j^2} = r_j\frac{dC_j}{d_j} < 0, \text{ since } \frac{dC_j}{d_j} < 0. \tag{2.6}$$

The simplifying assumptions here are:

$$\frac{dX_j}{d_j} = 0, \text{ and } \frac{dr_j}{d_j} = 0.$$

Their relaxation is not likely to change the conclusions.[17] Gross earnings slope upward in a concave fashion during the post-school net investment period after labor force activities begin to dominate. The profile of net earnings, which is better approximated by observed earnings, has a steeper slope, and peaks and declines somewhat later than gross earnings.[18] Its shape is also concave – at least eventually.

Figure 2.2 indicates the shapes of gross earnings E_j and of net earnings

Y_j during the post-school investment period OP. $\hat{j}$ is the year of 'overtaking' when $Y_j = Y_s$ earnings obtainable without post-school investment.

With the same initial earnings capacity, individuals who invest more have steeper slopes, at time j, than those who invest less, provided their average rate of return r is not excessively smaller. This is the basic explanation for the fanning out of earnings profiles with age and for increases of variances of earnings with age, so long as individuals with different investments in human capital comprise the earnings distribution.[19] This conclusion holds strictly for gross earnings. Net earnings would initially be lower for those who invest more, later surpassing those of the smaller investors. The variance of observed earnings might, therefore, initially decline with age. However, the time $(\hat{j})$ it would take for a trained person to overtake an untrained is rather short:

Let $Y_{j1} = X_j$, and

$$Y_{j2} = X_j + r_j \sum_{i=0}^{j-1} C_i - C_j$$

Then $Y_{j1} = Y_{j2}$, when

$$r_j \sum C - C_j = 0, \text{ or } \frac{C_j}{\sum\limits_0^{j-1} C_i} = r_j$$

If C_j were all the same, the time of overtaking $\hat{j} = 1/r_j$. Since $C_{j-1} < C_j$, $\hat{j} < 1/r$, less than a decade, if $r = 10\%$.

Although reversals of dollar variances have not been observed, they have been observed in relative variances (Morgan, 1962; Mincer, 1969). The analysis of relative variances suggests that attention be paid to logarithmic rather than to dollar profiles of earnings. A logarithmic version of the earnings function (2.2) was used in the special case of the schooling model (2.1a). This model can be expanded to cover post-school investments by means of the following device (Becker and Chiswick, 1966): let k_j be the ratio of investment costs C_j to gross earnings E_j in period j. This ratio can be viewed as the fraction of time (or a 'time equivalent', if investment costs include direct outlays as well as time costs) the worker devotes to the improvement of his earning power. His net earnings in year j are, therefore, smaller by this fraction than they would be if he did not invest during that year.

$$C_j = k_j E_j, \text{ and } E_j = E_{j-1} + rC_{j-1} = E_{j-1}(1 + rk_{j-1})$$

By recursion, therefore:

$$E_j = E_0 \prod_{i=0}^{j-1} (1 + r_i k_i)$$

and, assuming $k \leq 1$, r relatively small, this can be expressed:

$$\lg E_j = \lg E_0 + \sum_{i=0}^{j-1} r_i i_i \qquad (2.7)$$

Since net earnings $Y_j = E_j(1 - k_j)$:

$$\lg Y_j = \lg E_0 + \sum_{i=0}^{j-1} r_i k_i + \lg(1 - k_j) \qquad (2.7b)$$

Assuming, as in the schooling model, that $k_i = 1$ during the school years:

$$\lg E_j = \lg E_0 + rs + \sum_{i=s+1}^{j-1} r_i k_i \qquad (2.7c)$$

Let

$$P_j = \sum_{i=s+1}^{j-1} k_i,$$

the cumulative 'time' expended on the post-school investments and assume r_j the same for all j. Then:

$$\lg E_j = \lg E_0 + r_s s + r_j P_j \qquad (2.7d)$$

If $r_s = r_j$, this last expression is basically the same as the schooling model (2.1a). The total 'time' spent investing ($s + P_j$) replaces the time spent in schooling (s), and (P_j) is the number of 'years' devoted to net post-school investments.[20]

The shape of the logarithmic earnings profile is upward-sloping, as long as $k_j > 0$, and concave, *a fortiori*, if the dollar profile is upward sloping and concave. If individuals who accumulate more human capital spend more time accumulating it, logarithmic age profiles also fan out and produce the observed increase of log-variance with age. If years of schooling are viewed as indicators of total 'time' an individual intends to invest over his lifetime, age-profiles of upper schooling groups will typically grow faster, percentagewise, than those of lower schooling groups, in given age intervals.

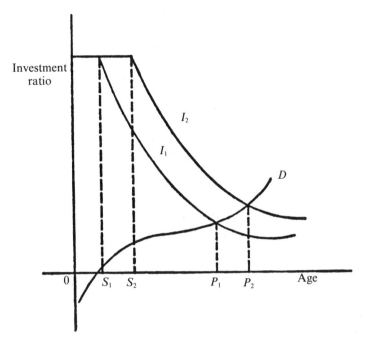

Figure 2.3

Summing up the implications: (a) at given ages, earnings profiles grow faster (in dollars and percentages) at higher levels of human capital investments; (b) dollar and log-variances of earnings increase with age. These implications have been repeatedly verified in empirical studies (Kravis, 1962; Lydall, 1968; Mincer, 1957; Morgan, 1962b).

The special assumptions and some additional implications of the human capital model which underlie the preceding discussion can be clarified by Figure 2.3.

In Figure 2.3 I is gross investment in human capital measured as a fraction of obtainable earnings, and D is the fraction by which such earnings are diminished as a result of depreciation. The net investment fraction is $k = I - D$, at each age. If retirement were compulsory and investment had no effect on non-market productivities, gross investment would terminate at retirement age. Otherwise, as is assumed in the diagram, gross investment remains positive throughout the expected life span. Retirement here can be viewed as endogenous, its timing being related to the decline in earning power, that is to the time at which depreciation outstrips gross investment.[21]

Depreciation is portrayed as a function of age, initially negative (appreciation), rising slowly and accelerating at later ages. The diagram shows age profiles of investment of two individuals: assuming the same life span, it is plausible that $I_2 > I_1$ at each age. Consequently, net investment $k_2 > k_1$ at each age. The empirical implication, it will be recalled, is that earnings of the larger investor grow faster, relatively and absolutely, at given ages. An additional implication shown by the diagram is that earnings of the larger investor decline later in life: the more educated retire at a somewhat older age, though they do not necessarily have a longer working life, since it begins after a longer schooling period.

In the diagram the schooling period $s_2 > s_1$, and this is an indication that total 'time' invested of individual (2) is larger. It does not follow, however, that individuals who have more schooling also spend more 'time' in post-school investment. In the special case of parallel investment profiles illustrated in the diagram, the larger investor spends no more 'time' in post-school investment than the smaller investor. If the investment ratio of the larger investor declines faster, the smaller investor may experience faster growing earnings in the age interval S_1P_1 than the larger investor does in the corresponding age interval S_2P_2. But so long as the age-investment profile I_2 is above I_1, dollar investments are larger at each year of experience,[22] hence the dollar *experience* profile of earnings of the large investor must be steeper.

Empirical evidence does show that earnings of the more-educated peak later, grow faster in dollar terms at given years of age as well as at given years of labor force experience, grow also relatively faster (in logs) at given ages, but no faster[23] at given years of experience. Across schooling groups, these findings reflect a positive correlation in the dollar volumes of schooling and post-school investment, and a negligible correlation between time equivalents of these investments.

4.   *Dispersion and skewness of earnings*

School is a convenient empirical indicator of investment in human capital. However, differences in investment behaviour among individuals with the same number of years of schooling are ignored (averaged) in the observable typical earning profile of such a group.

This average conceals individual differences in the quality of schooling and in post-school investments. These considerations suggest that even if investments ceased after completion of schooling, a dispersion in earnings would be observed reflecting schooling quality, as well as individual ability and other residual factors. The fact of post-school investments, however, means that even within a schooling group, the variance of earnings changes with age. The nature of these changes is predictable, given the correlations between schooling and post-school investments. If these correlations are positive in dollar terms within schooling groups, as they were observed across schooling groups, dollar variance tends to increase with age monotonically. If they are negligible in time equivalent terms, logarithmic variances tend to decline during the first decade of experience and increase thereafter. Empirical observation of variation of earnings within schooling groups shows dollar variances increasing strongly with age, but somewhat less clear U-shaped patterns of relative variances (Mincer, 1969).

It will be recalled that Lydall (1968) explains the age patterns of earnings and of earnings inequality as a reflection of growth of abilities with age and experience, as observed by developmental psychologists. This, however, need not be viewed as an alternative interpretation, unless the observed patterns of age changes in productivity are somehow intrinsic to the individuals. Psychologists do note that it is difficult to isolate intrinsic age patterns in productivity from age-changes affected by the individuals' adaptation, such as training or health care, that is, investments in human capital. To the extent that adaptation is important, the analysis of human-capital investment behaviour contributes to the understanding of the observed 'learning curves'.[24] Of course, the converse may also be true.

The psychological data to which Lydall refers may simply reflect effects of differential training on productivity, a major focus of the human-capital model. The data may also show differential growth in productivity even without differential training (investments) among the individuals. But this possibility is also implicit in the human-capital model, so long as the existence of investment is not denied. For simplicity, look at gross earnings in equation (2.2):

$$E_{ji} = X_i + r_i \sum_j C_{ji}$$

Assume that intrinsic dispersion $\sigma^2(X_i)$ does not change with age. For given levels of investment C_i, r_i the average rate of return can be viewed as an index of ability. Assume $\sigma^2(r_i) > 0$. The variance of earnings will grow with age only when $C_{ji} > 0$, even if $\sigma^2(C_{ji}) = 0$. This is most simply shown by neglecting the X_i term.

$$\sigma^2(E_{ji}) = \left(\sum_j C_j \right)^2 \sigma^2(r_i)$$

Since the first term on the right hand side increases with j, the variance rises with age. A similar monotonic growth of relative variances can be derived from the logarithmic formulation (equation 2.7).

A general approach is to assume both $\sigma^2(C_{ij}) > 0$ and $\sigma^2(r_i) > 0$. The empirical implications are basically the same as before, except for the conclusion (previously shown in equation 2.3) that, at given years of experience, earnings inequality should increase with level of schooling.

Let us once again summarize the important, though not unconditional, predictions of the human capital analyses:

Inequality
(a)   Relative and dollar dispersions are positively related to rates of return and to the dispersion in the distribution of schooling.
(b)   Dollar dispersion increases with schooling and experience. Relative dispersion increases with experience, though initial reversals are plausible.
(c)   The relation between level of schooling and relative dispersion is complex: it is likely to be positive at given experience intervals but it need not be in the aggregate.[25]

2.   *Skewness*   There are several distinct, but not mutually exclusive explanations:

(a)   the distribution of schooling is roughly symmetric. This creates a tendency toward positive skewness of earnings. More specifically, if symmetry is assumed in investments measured in time equivalents, as well as in 'raw earnings' X_i, two implications follow: dollar skewness tends to be positive, but logarithmic skewness negative. Moreover, when subgroups are distinguished by average level of investment (such as by schooling and experience), positive dollar skewness tends to be larger and negative log-skewness smaller the higher the schooling or experience level.
(b)   Interaction of ability and investment: even if the distribution of dollar investments C_i, and of average rates of return r_i, were symmetric, but r_i and C_i not excessively negatively correlated, earnings would be positively skewed.
(c)   Dollar variances increase with age and with schooling. The resulting positive correlation between means and variances of component distribution is sufficient to create aggregate positive skewness. It also creates humpedness (leptokurtosis) in the shape of the aggregate distribution, as both Rutherford's (1955) and Hill's (1959) mathematics prove in a different context.[26]

Note, in conclusion, that the predicted phenomena are relatively well-established features of empirical earnings distributions.

Even in terms of the qualitative implications reported thus far, the predictive range of the human-capital model clearly exceeds that of the random-shock models. The stochastic models say nothing about age and experience profiles of earnings. They do little more then predict a monotonic growth of variances with age. Distinctions between aggregates and components, or between absolute and relative parameters, are outside the reach of these models.

5. Quantitative accounting of earnings inequality: the correlation between earnings and investment in human capital

The human-capital model provides interpretations for a large variety of qualitative features of observed distributions of earnings. Major interest, however, attaches to the quantitative dimension of earnings inequality. Can the model help in measuring the extent to which observed inequality in earnings can be attributed to individual differences in investment?

By definition of the earnings function (2.2), if investment costs and average rates of return were available for each worker, all of the inequality, except a random component, would be accounted for. Comprehensive information on individual investments is almost entirely restricted to schooling, measured in years. Information on post-school investments, except perhaps for medical care, is available only in a highly fragmentary fashion.

As already mentioned, the heroic statistical specification of the schooling model (2.1a) yields very low explanatory power and biased estimates of rates of return. This may be due to the exclusion of post-school investments. In principle, their inclusion can be accomplished by the expanded model in equation (2.7).

$$\lg Y_{ij} = \lg Y_0 + r_s s_i + \sum_{i=1}^{j-1} r_t k_{it} + \lg(1 - k_{ij}) + u_{ij} \qquad (2.7)$$

Even if information on post-school investments k_{ij} were available, individual rates of return could not be directly observed. The residual u_{ij} would therefore contain differentials in school quality not measured by years, as well as individual differences in average rates of return. Note that the rates of return to schooling r_s and to post-schooling investment r_j are allowed to differ. The partial coefficient r_s measures the rate of return to schooling alone, a concept not measured in the usual calculations.[27] Its estimate in (2.7) is unbiased, as it applies to schooling, net of post-school investments.

Of course, neither k_{ij} nor even typical k_{js} within groups are observable. However, the effects of the latter on earnings could be estimated by expressing k_j as a declining function of j, as optimization theory suggests. A statistical function would be:

$$\lg Y_{ij} = \lg Y_0 + r_s s_i + f(r_j, k_j) + v_{ij} \tag{2.8}$$

Compared to residual u in (2.7) residual v in (2.8) is augmented by individual variation in post-school investments as well as by errors in using a functional form $f(r_j, k_j)$. To that extent (2.8) understates the explanatory power of the investment variables s_i and k_{ij}.

The functional form of the investment profile in (2.8) must be fitted by experiment, since there is no theory to specify it. It can be shown that a linearly declining net investment profile yields a parabolic earnings profile in logs (Mincer, 1969; Johnson, 1969).

If $k_j = k_0 - (k_0/T)j$, where k_0 = investment ratio at the start of work experience, T = span of investment period. Then:

$$\lg Y_j = \lg Y_0 + r_s s + rk_0 j - \frac{rk_0}{2T} j^2 + \lg \left(1 - k_0 + \frac{k_0}{T} j\right) + v \tag{2.8a}$$

If investment k_j declines exponentially:

$$k_j = k_0 e^{-\beta j}$$

Then:

$$\lg Y_j = \lg Y_0 + r_s s + \frac{rk_0}{\beta} (1 - e^{-\beta j}) + \lg (1 - k_0 e^{-\beta j}) + v \tag{2.8b}$$

$\lg E_j$ is the same, except that it excludes the term before the residual v.

In this case, the earnings function E_j is a familiar growth curve, known as the Gompertz curve.[28]

Some experiments with individual observations of the 1:1000 US Census Sample of 1960 indicate that the Gompertz curve fits somewhat better than the parabola, when the distribution is restricted to about 40 years of experience in each schooling group.[29] The results of applying this equation to the individual annual earnings of white, urban males are: (a) a coefficient of determination of 35 per cent. (The coefficient rises to 55 per cent when weeks worked (in logs) are included in the regression); (b) an estimate of the rate of return to schooling above 10 per cent, and not clearly different from the rate of return to post-school investment.[30]

Even with the use of only two variables, years of schooling and of experience, the explanatory power of specification (2.8) compares quite favorably with results of statistical studies of comparable microeconomic data which employ a large number of explanatory variables on a more or less *ad hoc* basis.

Adams (1958) found a coefficient of determination of 43 per cent in an analysis of earnings of white males in 1949 reported in the Michigan Survey. In addition to education and a parabolic age variable, his explanatory factors included geographic region, city size, employment status, and occupation. Hill (1959) achieved a correlation of about the same magnitude in an analysis of a 1953 sample of male full-time wages and salaries in Britain. His variables included age, occupation, region, and industry. Morgan *et al.* (1962b) explain 34 per cent of the variance of wage rates of family heads in the 1959 Michigan Survey by regression on education, age, occupation, city size, geographic mobility, employment status, as well as indexes of ability and motivation. Hanoch (1965) gets a similar coefficient of determination for 1959 annual earnings of males in the Census 1:1000 sample, using schooling, age, race, location, marital status, weeks worked, family size, and industry.

To repeat, in the statistical regression based on (2.8) a third of earnings inequality is attributable to schooling, measured in years, and to *average* (within schooling groups) variation of post-school investment with age. The remainder contains individual differences in post-school investment, in quality of schooling, in ability, and in other 'transitory' income variations. Because the first two are components of human capital investment, regressions based on (2.8) understate the explanatory power of human capital investments.

One indirect procedure (Mincer, 1969) makes it possible to include the additional contribution of individual variation in post-school investment that regression (2.8) does not capture. Recall that at a relatively early stage of work experience ($\hat{\jmath}$ in Figure 2.2) each investor reaches the 'overtaking point': this is the level of earnings (Y_s in Figure 2.2) a worker would receive if he ceased investing after completion of schooling. Net earnings of individuals at that stage of their careers are not affected by their post-school investments. Consider the distribution of earnings of individuals observed only in the 'overtaking' period: denote $\sigma^2(u')$ the residual variance from the regression of log-earnings at overtaking on years of schooling. On the assumption of homoscedasticity, $\sigma^2(u')$ is an estimate of the residual variance in the expanded, but not directly observable, regression model (2.7). Therefore, the ratio of $\sigma^2(u')$ to aggregate earnings inequality $\sigma^2(\lg Y_{ijs})$, subtracted from unity, is an estimate of R^2, the proportion of total earnings inequality attributable to measured variation in schooling (in years only) and in post-school investments. Several variants of this procedure applied to earnings of white, urban males in 1959 yield estimated R^2 ranging from a half to two thirds, with lower coefficients for all annual earnings and higher for full-period earnings.[31]

6.   *Ability, opportunity, and investment*

Do we necessarily expect a strong correlation between investments in human capital and earnings? The answer to this question is neither obvious nor invariant. Not surprisingly, a better understanding of the relation between investment and earnings requires an understanding of the factors determining investment.

Becker's recent work (1967) treats this problem in a conventional and highly illuminating demand–supply framework. The analysis yields insights into the meaning of gross and partial correlations between investment and earnings, suggests approaches to the question whether the inequality in earnings is due mainly to inequality in opportunities or in abilities, and clarifies some of the normative issues that arise in the context of income distribution.

In effect, the investment–earnings relation is viewed as a 'reduced form' resulting from two simultaneous structural relations: demand functions (D_i) relate individual investments to marginal rates of return on them, and supply functions (S_i) relate the obtainable volume of funds for such investment purposes to their marginal 'interest' costs.

The amounts individuals invest, their marginal and average returns, and therefore their earnings are simultaneously and optimally determined by the intersections of the D_i and S_i curves, as shown in Figure 2.4. Here DC is total investment (in dollars). Earnings are given by the area under the demand curve ODPC, that is by $\bar{r}C$, where $\bar{r}$ is the average height of the relevant segment of the demand curve.

The downward slope in the demand curves represents diminishing returns to self-investments. Presumably, limitations of human capacity, the 'fixed human body', produce this effect. Differences in levels of demand curves represent individual differences in productivities, or abilities. On the supply side, curves are upward-sloping to represent the increasing difficulty of financing investments of increasing size. There are differences among individuals in the costs of the same volume of investment: for example, students differ in family wealth and in costs and availabilities of loans and of scholarships. These differences are represented by the dispersion in levels of supply curves.

It is important to note that the dispersions in D_i and in S_i can be viewed as broadly corresponding to inequalities of ability and of opportunity, respectively, and that some of the factors involved are not independent: tastes and motivation can be reflected in greater productivity (higher level of D) as well as in greater willingness to reduce consumption in order to finance investment (lower S). Discrimination can be reflected both in lower D and in higher S. More important, some of the dispersion in demand curves represents differences in opportunity disguised as differ-

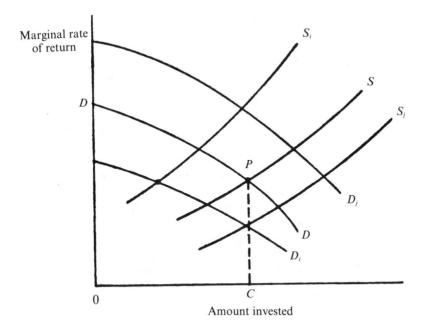

Figure 2.4

ences in ability: the importance of the home environment and of social contacts is unlikely to have been isolated and 'costed' as a component of investment. It is none the less true that social policy can more easily affect the dispersion in supply curves than that in the demand curves. With fixed demand curves, an evolutionary or political change in the distribution of opportunities will alter the distribution of average rates of return, thereby affecting the distribution of earnings as well as the correlation between investment and earnings.

Among the possible configurations of the distributional equilibrium in Figure 2.3, three special cases are of particular interest: (a) equality of opportunity: this is defined by a common supply curve for all individuals. Here investments, marginal (and average) rates, and earnings are all positively related; (b) equality of ability: this is defined by a common demand curve. Here investment and earnings are positively related, but investment and rates of return are negatively correlated; (c) a perfect positive correlation between ability and opportunity:[32] individuals with greater productivity have lower costs in financing their investments. Again investment and earnings are positively related, but investment and rates of return can relate positively or negatively.

Each of these and only these conditions yield a perfect correlation between investments and earnings. If both inequalities of ability and of opportunity are sizable, a substantial correlation between investment and earnings must reflect primarily a strong correlation between ability and opportunity.[33] Otherwise, there is a range of intersection points at the same levels of investment, creating residual dispersion in the regression of earnings on investments. If, in addition, the scatter of equilibrium points in Figure 2.4 has a downward slope, as is suggested by findings that rates of return are, on the average, higher at lower levels of schooling (Hansen, 1963; Becker, 1964; Hanoch, 1965), the inference is that inequalities in opportunity are larger than inequalities in ability.

Statistical studies of factors associated with earnings often include indicators of investment such as schooling and age, as well as of ability, such as IQ scores, and/or of opportunity such as family background or wealth. The structural model proposed by Becker can be helpful in interpreting some of the findings resulting from such studies. For example, the less accurate the measurement of investment, the stronger the positive correlation between ability and opportunity at measured levels of investment. The more precise the measurement of investment, the more negative this correlation becomes. Hence appropriate additional ability variables should remain significant in the earnings regressions, even net of investment. However, opportunity indicators may lose their significance or become 'perverse', as the measurement of investment is improved.

One interesting insight is relevant to empirical studies which infer distributions of ability from distributions of earnings. The distribution of ability is not observable: it is given by the heights of the demand curves at fixed levels of investment. This distribution cannot be equated with the conditional distributions of earnings at fixed levels of investment. Only a subset of the ability distribution is reflected in a conditional earnings distribution, and the ability subsets observable at different levels of investment are not comparable. What is more important, given the distribution of abilities (a fixed set of D curves), the conditional distributions of earnings change with a change in opportunities. For example, if inequality of opportunity (dispersion in S) diminishes, the conditional variance in earnings diminishes as well. But this is not to be interpreted as an equalization of abilities. Such a change, incidentally, gives rise to an increased correlation between investment and earnings. These are two sides of the same story, and not competing hypotheses in explaining the change.

There are some interesting insights into normative questions, such as: under what conditions does more equal opportunity or greater productive efficiency increase the equality of earnings? An efficient distribution of earnings is one in which marginal rates of return on human capital investments are the same for all individuals. Hence, given a dispersion of ability, equality of opportunity does not suffice to bring about maximum product, unless the common supply curve is horizontal – no segmentation in the capital market. Note, however, that maximum efficiency can also be achieved with highly unequal opportunity, when a perfect correlation of ability and opportunity yields a horizontal locus of intersections of S and D curves in Figure 2.4. An increased equality of opportunity (without change in the slopes of the S-curves) may, therefore, mean decreased efficiency. It will, to be sure, reduce the inequality of earnings. On the other hand, increased efficiency resulting from flattened S curves, without a change in their dispersion, increases the inequality of earnings.

Perfect equality of opportunity and maximum efficiency would characterize a meritocratic society. Such a society, which many consider attractive, is quite consistent with large earnings inequalities, all of which depend on differences in ability. If abilities are believed to be invariant and inherited, this vision becomes rather less attractive. However, technical and cultural changes and associated uncertainties would continue to reshuffle abilities and earnings, providing safeguards against a new type of caste system.

Even if some objectives are ultimately inconsistent with one another, this need not be true about improvements in conditions which are not generally optimal. For example, if inequality of opportunity dominates, and if the correlation between ability and opportunity is far from perfect, a reduction in inequality of opportunity is likely to lead to greater efficiency and greater equality in earnings. If it is also true that the rate of return on investments in human capital is, on the average, higher than on other forms of capital, a greater aggregate investment in human capital will also produce greater efficiency and greater equality.

7. *Long and short-run inequality*

Once ability and opportunity are introduced as determinants of investment, earnings differentials can no longer be considered as wholly compensatory. Rents or 'profits' from investment in human capital arise as the differences between returns ($\bar{r} C$), where $\bar{r}$ is the average rate of return, and repayment costs ($\bar{\imath} C$), where $\bar{\imath}$ is the average interest cost. They appear in Figure 2.4 as differences between the areas under the individual demand and supply curves. Barring some perverse configurations of the curves, it is easily seen that the size of profits is positively correlated with earnings as well as with investments. The present value of profits is $PV_i = 1/r_i \, (\bar{r}_i - \bar{\imath}_i)C_i$, where r_i is the discount factor. Present values also tend to correlate positively both with earnings and with investment. It is interesting to observe that (relative) inequality in profits may or may not be smaller than the inequality in current earnings. In the special case when the curves have a constant and common elasticity, Becker shows that factors determining this 'ultimate' inequality are exactly the same as those determining the inequality in current earnings.

If the distinction between the long and short run is defined in terms of length of the accounting period, observed earnings inequality tends to diminish as the accounting period is lengthened. The major components of individual income variation which average out in this process are: the longer-run age profile of earnings, and the short-run cyclical and random fluctuations. If age variation in earnings over the working life is attributable to the life-cycle allocation of net post-school investments, the inequality of earnings among individuals, in which this variation is eliminated, would be given by the variance of earnings at the 'overtaking' stage of experience. A comparison of the variance in earnings of individuals with about a decade of labor force experience with the aggregate variance shows the former to be about 25 per cent smaller than the latter.[34]

Estimates of the contribution of short-run temporal fluctuations in earnings to the overall variance in earnings are comparable in size to the age effects (Krayis, 1962; Hanoch, 1965; Mincer, 1969). In a procedure[35] which smooths out both short-run and life-cycle variation, Summers (1956) found earnings inequality reduced by over a half.

Short-run variation in earnings is the exclusive focus of random shock theories of income distribution. It will be recalled that these models generally predict increasing variances of earnings with age as well as certain specific mathematical forms of the earnings distribution. The greater predictive power of the human-capital model was pointed out before. Where the two models yield similar predictions, they interpret the empirical phenomena differently. Thus, the stochastic models interpret temporal variation in income as a matter of chance. In contrast, human capital models view much of the temporal variation as a systematic and persistent consequence of cumulative investment behavior. Discrimination between the two views can be sought in so-called panel correlations of earnings of the same cohort in two different time periods. The random shock models predict a fixed rate of decay in the coefficients of determination, as the interval between the two time periods is lengthened. It also predicts a fixed correlation for a fixed size interval, regardless of the life-cycle stage. Accumulating empirical evidence (Friedman, 1957; Hill, 1959; Kravis, 1962; Mincer, 1969) indicates, however, that the decay in panel correlations is weak and decelerating with span. It also shows weak correlations in intervals bracketing the 'overtaking' age, and strong correlations afterward (Mincer, 1962b, 1969). Both phenomena are consistent with human-capital analysis, particularly when it is remembered that observed earnings are net rather than gross of investment.

The finding that the systematic (investment) component may account for a large part of the temporal variation in earnings does not preclude a residual random component; panel correlations are certainly less than unity. But even the residual component need not have the stochastic properties specified in the random shock models. Instead of being independent of the previous level of income, thereby creating an explosive variance, the random 'transitory' component may be unrelated to a latent, 'permanent' level of income, so that the variance does not change much over time, if at all. Under this formulation, introduced by Friedman (1957), the contribution of the short-run fluctuation to total income inequality was estimated from income and consumption data to be as much as 30 per cent. This figure is roughly comparable to the contribution of the dispersion in weeks worked during the year to annual earnings inequality.[36]

The short-run, within-year, and cyclical variation in earnings reflects in large part labor turnover, job and labor force mobility, unemployment and illness. In many ways, not as yet fully worked out, economic theory (Becker, 1964; Reder, 1969) predicts that the incidence of the employment phenomena is inversely related to age (experience) and to the level of human capital. The greater average departure from full-period work the larger the added dispersion in earnings introduced by it. For these reasons variances of earnings are augmented at low levels of skill and early stages of experience. The short-run component is, therefore, a force in the direction of negative skewness (Staehle, 1943; Morgan, 1962a; Kravis, 1962).

These amendments work in the opposite direction to some of the predictions of human-capital models in which the short-run component of earnings was ignored. Since earnings are a product of wage rates and of 'hours' of work, the degree to which these amendments tend to obscure effects previously implied depends on the size of the inequality (log variance) in 'hours' relative to the inequality in wage rates.

8.   Female and family earnings distribution

The relative contribution of employment ('hours') dispersion to earnings inequality is not small in population groups with full and permanent labor force attachment, but can be quite substantial in groups whose attachment is, on the average, weak. Men and women (particularly married men and married women) exemplify these differences in labor force behaviour. The distribution of earnings of all adult males is, therefore, roughly similar to the distribution of earnings of full-period male workers. For women, however, the all-earnings distribution is quite different from the full-period earnings distribution. Thus the inequality in annual earnings of all women workers is larger than the inequality in the comparable male distribution, while the opposite is true of full time earnings (Woytinsky, 1953).

Some of the differences between earnings distributions of males and females are explainable by the effects of labor supply behavior on human capital investment decisions. Individuals who expect to spend only a part of their adult lives in the labor force have weaker incentives to invest in forms of human capital which primarily enhance market productivities than persons whose expected labor force attachment is permanent. Women are likely to invest less than men in vocational aspects of education and particularly in on-the-job training. This is reflected in the comparative (to males) structure of their full-time earnings by flatter age–earnings profiles, smaller variances within school and age classes, and a lesser aggregate inequality of earnings (Mincer, 1957).

One important aspect of income distribution, not yet discussed, is the definition of the recipient unit. Analyses of consumption behavior and notions of economic welfare are more closely linked to family rather than to personal distributions of income. From this point of view *sums* of male and female earnings are of greater interest than the differences.

As a matter of arithmetic, dollar dispersion in family earnings is a positive function of the variances in earnings of family members and of the correlation between these earnings. For relative dispersion the relevant correlation is between levels and shares.[37] The sign and size of these intra-family correlations depend, in part, on labor supply functions. In standard economic theory the amount of time a person allocates to money earning activity is positively related to his money earning power (wage rate), and negatively to his total real (family) income. The positive correlation between earning powers of husbands and wives is therefore a factor which increases the variance of family earnings relative to the variance of husband's earnings. However, the income effect is a force which tends to reduce the variance of family earnings. The empirical results are: a larger dollar variance and a somewhat smaller relative variance in family earnings than in husbands' earnings (Mincer, 1960, 1969). The results are entirely consistent with parameters of market labor supply functions that have been estimated for married women (Mincer, 1960, 1962a; Cain, 1966).

It should be noted that these findings have been observed in data which include property income in family income. Because of the well-known under-reporting of non-employment incomes, it cannot be concluded that total family income, correctly measured, would behave similarly. Nor can we conclude that real family income patterns are similar to the observed money income distributions. Indeed, the partial labor force attachment of wives is largely the obverse of the importance of their non-money contributions to real family income.

4. In lieu of a conclusion

The relative success of the human-capital model in explaining a variety of features in the observed distribution of earnings is actually something of a surprise. This is because the model does not directly apply to cross-sections. The theory deals with lifetime behavior of individuals, not with differences among individuals of different ages. There are special cases where the distinction between longitudinal (cohort) analysis and contemporaneous (cross-section) analysis would not matter. These are the cases of a stationary economy, or of an economy in which changes are 'neutral' with respect to categories entering the human capital model. In the more general case, however, modifications introduced by secular change should be taken into account when the models are applied to cross-section.

There are a few recent empirical studies of moving cross-sections of income (Miller, 1960; Brady, 1965; David, 1969; Mincer, 1969). Abstracting from cyclical and other fluctuations in the economy, the findings confirm some of the qualitative features of cross-sections: concave age profiles of income; differential age profiles by occupation or education; and variances (in dollars or logs) increasing with age. There are severe data limitations in this area, but it deserves a great deal of research: cohort analyses should help not only in a better understanding of the cross-section, but also in providing insights into secular changes in income distribution.

Another very important issue to which occasional allusions were made in the survey is the distinction between effects of human capital investments on productivity and on the allocation of time to earning activity. Over a period of time, earnings are a product of hourly wage rates and hours worked during the period. The latter are affected by human capital investments as well as the former, in a number of ways. The theory of the effects of worker and employer human capital investments on labor mobility and employment distributions (Becker, 1964) can be elaborated and applied to sort out the effects in observed earnings distribution. For sex, age, occupation, and industry comparisons of earnings, the employment effects are clearly a basic research need.

At a deeper level, there is no shortage of positive and normative questions about investment in human capital as a dependent variable. But this takes us beyond the scope of an already overlong survey.

Notes

1. The most thorough treatments are in Reder (1969); Bjerke (1969); Lydall (1968, ch. 2); Schultz (1965); and Kravis (1962, ch. 6). The monographs of Kravis, Bjerke, and Lydall are products of original empirical research. They contain useful data and analyses of income distributions in the US (Kravis), Denmark (Bjerke), and a set of international comparisons (Lydall).

2. Half a century ago Dalton (1920) complained that the emphasis of economists on the functional distribution of income in effect largely relegates the personal distribution of incomes, 'a problem of more direct and obvious interest', to the status of a residual to be studied, if at all, 'by plodding statistical investigations, which professors of economic theory were content to leave to lesser men'.

    Garvy (1952), who quoted Dalton several decades later, saw little progress in the meantime: he points out that the American Economic Association's volume on *Readings in the Theory of Income Distribution* (1946) contains only one article on income size distribution (Bowman, 1945).

    Garvy's remark can now be updated with reference to the International Economic Association's recent volume on *The Distribution of National Income* (1968). It contains only one paper exclusively devoted to the analysis of income size distribution (Reder, 1968).

3. For a basic reference and analysis see Lewis (1963).

4. If Y is income and E the 'random shock',

$$Y_t = Y_0 + \sum_{i=1}^{t} E_i$$

    and $\sigma^2(Y_t) = \sigma^2(Y_0) + t\sigma^2(E)$, assuming $\sigma^2(E_i)$ same for all i.

5. Such a correlation in subsets of a distribution is easily visualized as stretching the right tail of the distribution.

6. This rough sketch does not do justice to Mandelbrot's sophisticated analysis. His approach, incidentally, represents a solution to a scheme of income distribution proposed by Tinbergen (1956). For a more detailed discussion see Bjerke (1969).

7. Using continuous discounting, the present value for s and n is:

$$V_s = E_s \int_s^{n+s} e^{-rt} dt = \frac{1}{r} E_s e^{-rs}(1 - e^{-rn})$$

    $k_{2,1}$ is obtained by equating $V_{s_2} = V_{s_1}$

8. Recent data suggest that the differences in lengths of working lives are rather small.

9. Positive skewness in earnings obtains so long as

$$1 - \frac{d_u}{d_l} < rd_l,$$

    where d is the interval (in years) between the median and a symmetric percentile (u—upper, l—lower) (Mincer 1969).

10. This is apparent by taking variances across individuals in eq. (2.1a) and by varying r in the expression in note 9.

11. The state R^2s are higher partly because they are derived from data grouped by income brackets.

12. An error crept into Lydall's test. While the equation (p. 90) properly relates log-earnings to years of schooling, the statistical test (p. 95) relates log-earnings to logs of years of schooling. The proper form is, therefore, mistakenly rejected (Lydall, 1968).

13. Standardization by age improves the regressions only slightly (Chiswick, 1967).

14. Strictly speaking, a small negative correlation need not be ruled out. Also, the term X_{ji} and its correlation with the other terms of (2.2b) are disregarded.

15. By a theorem of L. Goodman (1960).
16. Of course, this finding does not explain the negative correlation between level and inequality of income by region. Chiswick (1968) provides some interesting conjectures on this matter.
17. Cf. note 24 for empirical statements about the constancy of X_j throughout most of the working life.
18. From (2.2b):

$$\frac{dY_j}{dj} = rC_j - \frac{dC_j}{dj} > \frac{dE_j}{dj}$$

19. Assuming that the ranking of investments across individuals is roughly the same in the different periods.
20. If on-the-job training is the bulk of it, this formulation provides a method of measuring on-the-job training in the same time units as schooling. In Mincer (1962b) all net post-school investments were interpreted as on-the-job training.
21. For this to be valid, the substitution effect must dominate in the relevant supply of labor function. Cf. Lewis (1957). At a deeper level, the lifespan itself is endogenous, since it can be lengthened by investment. An illuminating analysis of this problem is contained in Grossman (1969).
22. The experience scale is not given by age, but by years spent in the labor force, assumed to start at completion of schooling.
23. In most data the logarithmic *age profiles* of annual earnings of various school groups are clearly divergent (fan out). In US data, the logarithmic *experience profiles* of annual earnings are convergent. Interestingly, the convergence vanishes in estimated hourly earnings data (based on Fuchs, 1967).
24. In this connection note the following statement in a recent survey of developmental psychology (Birren, 1968): 'Except for individuals with cumulative injuries or problems of health, worker performance up to age 60 should be little influenced by physiological changes in aging', and, 'at the present time there is little evidence to suggest that there is an intrinsic age difference in learning capacity over the employed years, i.e., up to age 60.'
25. Empirical findings are mixed, often showing a U-shaped relation. This may be due in part to less rapidly growing experience profiles in the higher schooling groups, and to differential age distributions, a consequence of strong educational trends.
26. It is interesting to recall at this point that in puzzling over the paradox of presumably symmetric abilities but skewed earnings, Pigou proposed the possibility that aggregate skewness might result from a merger of homogeneous, symmetric components. H. P. Miller (1955) offered some rather weak evidence in support of this hunch, but no explanation why the merger should produce positive skewness.
27. They measure rates of return to the mix of incremental schooling and of post-school investment.
28. An interesting implication of the Gompertz experience profile is that human capital accumulates at a rate proportional to the percentage gap between the current and eventual peak level. It can also be shown that (cf Eisner and Strotz, 1963) this pattern of capital accumulation arises as an optimal life-time distribution when the cost function of producing human capital is quadratic (in logs). In an analysis of optimal time-distribution of investments specific to firms, Rosen (1969) derives the same Gompertz formula for 'age-progress curves' of firms.
29. Johnson (1969) applied the parabolic fit (2.8a) to grouped earnings profiles estimated by Hanoch (1965), Johnson interprets the k coefficient as gross, not net investment. This enables him to estimate an assumed fixed depreciation rate. Its estimate was about 6% per year.
    A similar procedure applied to the micro-data yields a very small difference in explanatory power, and a very small estimated depreciation rate, whether the parabola

or Gompertz are used. However, in contrast to Johnson's work, these experiments (Mincer, 1969) excluded individuals past age 65.

30. If correct, this suggests that there is little error in calling the directly calculated rates by the name 'rates of return to schooling'.
31. The estimated R^2 is an underestimate, because variation in the quality of schooling is still left in the residual. The variation is not negligible. Judging by figures quoted by Becker (1964), the coefficient of variation in expenditures on a college education in New York state alone was no less than the coefficient of variation in the national aggregate distribution of years of schooling.
32. A negative correlation is conceivable, but not plausible.
33. An interesting and important research question is, to what extent does this correlation reflect motivation and encouragement of abler individuals which is independent of family background and wealth, or links between parental wealth, environment, and ability? Social mobility is furthered by the former and inhibited by the latter.
34. Note that this method of eliminating age variation in earnings is not quite the same as an extension of the accounting period to cover all of the working life.
35. Summers estimated lifetime average annual distributions from panels of 500 spending units, separated by one year. The estimates are based on parameters of first-order difference equations, separate for each of ten year age intervals. The estimates for a 40-year period were not very sensitive to assumed initial distributions.
36. However, the two components of income variation are not coextensive. Some of the employment variation is 'permanent', and some of the age variation is discounted by consumers.
37. Let $Y_F = Y_H + Y_W = Y_H(1 + R_W)$, where $R_W = Y_W/Y_H$. Then

$$\sigma^2(Y_F) = \sigma^2(Y_H) + \sigma^2(Y_W) + 2 \text{ Cov } (Y_H, Y_W)$$

and

$$\sigma^2(\lg Y_F) = \sigma^2(\lg Y_H) + \sigma^2 \lg (1 + R_W) + 2 \text{ Cov } [\lg Y_H, \lg(1 + R_W)]$$

References

Adams, F. G. (1958), 'The Size of Individual Incomes: Socio-economic Variables and Chance Variation', *Review of Economic Statistics*, Nov.
Aitchison, J. and J. A. C. Brown (1957), *The Lognormal Distribution*, Cambridge: Cambridge University Press.
Becker, G. S. (1964), *Human Capital*, New York: Columbia University Press for NBER.
Becker, G. S. (1967), 'Human Capital and the Personal Distribution of Income', *W. S. Woytinsky Lecture no. 1*, University of Michigan.
Becker, G. S. and B. R. Chiswick (1966), 'Education and the Distribution of Earnings', *American Economic Review*, May.
Ben-Porath, Y. (1967), 'The Production of Human Capital and the Life-Cycle of Earnings', *Journal of Political Economy*, August.
Ben-Porath, Y. (1968), 'The Production of Human Capital Over Time', paper presented at NBER *Conference on Research in Income and Wealth*, Nov.
Birren, J. E. (1968), 'Psychological Aspects of Aging', in *International Encyclopedia of the Social Sciences*, vol. 1.
Bjerke, K. (1969), *Income and Wage Distributions*, Copenhagen.
Boissevain, C. H. (1939), 'Distribution of Abilities Depending Upon Two or More Independent Factors', *Metron*.
Bowman, M. J. (1945), 'A Graphical Analysis of Personal Income Distribution in the United States', *American Economic Review*, Sept.
Brady, D. S. (1965), *Age and Income Distribution*, Washington, D.C.: Social Security Administration, Research no. 8.

Cain, G. G. (1966), *Married Women in the Labor Force*, Chicago: University of Chicago Press.

Champernowne, D. G. (1953), 'A Model of Income Distribution', *Economic Journal*.

Chiswick, B. R. (1967), 'Human Capital and Personal Income Distribution by Region', unpublished PhD dissertation, Columbia University.

Chiswick, B. R. (1968), 'The Average Level of Schooling and the Intra-Regional Inequality of Income: a Clarification', *American Economic Review*, June.

Dalton, H. (1920), *Some Aspects of the Inequality of Incomes in Modern Communities*, London: G. Routledge.

David, M. (1969), 'Time-series versus Cross-section Lifetime Earnings Patterns in Different Occupational Groups', paper no. 6941, *Social Systems Research Institute*, University of Wisconsin, August.

Eisner, R. and R. H. Strotz, (1963), 'Determinants of Business Investment', in *Impacts of Monetary Policy*, by the Commission on Money and Credit, Englewood Cliffs, N.J.: Prentice-Hall.

Friedman, M. (1953), 'Choice, Chance and the Personal Distribution of Income', *Journal of Political Economy*, August.

Friedman, M. (1957), *A Theory of the Consumption Function*, Princeton, N.J.: Princeton University Press.

Fuchs, V. R. (1967), 'Differentials in Hourly Earnings by Region and City Size', Occasional Paper 101, NBER.

Galton, F. (1869), *Hereditary Genius*, London: Macmillan.

Garvy, G. (1952), 'Inequality of Income: Causes and Measurement', *Studies in Income and Wealth*, vol. 15.

Gibrat, R. (1931), *Les Inégalités Économiques*, Paris: Sirey.

Goodman, L. (1960), 'On the Exact Variance of Products', *Journal of the American Statistical Association*, December 1960.

Grossman, M. (1969), 'The Demand for Health', unpublished PhD dissertation, Columbia University.

Hanoch, G. (1965) 'Personal Earnings and Investment in Schooling', unpublished PhD dissertation, University of Chicago.

Hansen, W. L. (1963), 'Total and Private Rates of Return to Investment in Schooling', *Journal of Political Economy*, April.

Hill, T. P. (1959) 'An analysis of the Distribution of Wages and Salaries in Great Britain', *Econometrica*.

Johnson, T. (1969) 'Returns from Investment in Schooling and On-the-Job Training', unpublished PhD dissertation, North Carolina State University at Raleigh.

Kravis, I. (1962), *The Structure of Income*, Philadelphia: University of Pennsylvania Press.

Lewis, H. G. (1957), 'Hours of Work and Hours of Leisure', *Proceedings of the Industrial and Labor Relations Association*.

Lewis, H. G. (1963), *Unionism and Relative Wages in the United States*, Chicago: University of Chicago Press.

Lydall, H. (1968), *The Structure of Earnings*, Oxford: Oxford University Press.

Mandelbrot, B. (1960), 'The Pareto–Levy Law and the Distribution of Income', *International Economic Review*, May.

Mandelbrot, B. (1962), 'Paretian Distributions and Income Maximization', *Quarterly Journal of Economics*, Feb.

Miller, H. P. (1955), 'Elements of Symmetry in the Skewed Income Curve', *Journal of the American Statistical Association*, March.

Miller, H. P. (1960), 'Annual and Lifetime Income in Relation to Education, 1939–59', *American Economic Review*, Dec.

Mincer, J. (1957), 'A Study of Personal Income Distribution', unpublished PhD dissertation, Columbia University.

Mincer, J. (1958), 'Investment in Human Capital and Personal Income Distribution', *Journal of Political Economy*, August. (Chapter 1 of this volume.)

Mincer, J. (1960) 'Labor Supply, Family Income, and Consumption', *American Economic Review*, May.

Mincer, J. (1962a), 'Labor Force Participation of Married Women', in *Aspects of Labor Economics* (Chapter 1 of Volume 2), Princeton, N.J.: Princeton University Press for NBER

Mincer, J. (1962b), 'On the Job Training: Costs, Returns, and Some Implications', *Journal of Political Economy*, Supplement, October. (Chapter 4 of this volume.)

Mincer, J. (1969), 'Schooling, Age, and Earnings', in *Human Capital and Personal Income Distribution*, NBER.

Morgan, J. N. (1962a), *Income and Welfare in the United States*, New York: McGraw-Hill.

Morgan, J. N. *et al.* (1962b), 'The Anatomy of Income Distribution', *Review of Economic Statistics*, August.

Pigou, A. C. (1920), *The Economics of Welfare*, London: Macmillan.

Reder, M. W. (1962), 'Wage Structure Theory and Measurement', in *Aspects of Labor Economics*, Princeton, N.J.: Princeton University Press for NBER.

Reder, M. W. (1968), 'The Size Distribution of Earnings', in *The Distribution of the National Income*, International Economic Association, New York: St Martins Press.

Reder, M. W. (1969), 'A Partial Survey of the Theory of Income Size Distribution', in *Six Papers on the Size Distribution of Income and Wealth*, ed. Lee Soltow, New York: Columbia University Press for NBER.

Rees, A. (1962), *The Economics of Trade Unions*, Chicago; University of Chicago Press.

Rosen, S. (1969), 'The Supply of Human Capital', NBER, *mimeo*.

Roy, A. D. (1950), 'The Distribution of Earnings and of Individual Output', *Economic Journal.*, Sept.

Rutherford, R. S. G. (1955), 'Income Distributions: a New Model', *Econometrics*, July.

Schultz, T. P. (1965), *Personal Income Distribution Statistics of the United States*, prepared for the Joint Economic Committee of Congress.

Staehle, H. (1943), 'Ability, Wages, and Income', *Review of Economic Statistics*, Feb.

Stigler, G. J. (1966), *The Theory of Price*, 3rd edn, London: Macmillan.

Summers, R. (1956), *An Econometric Investigation of the Size Distribution of Lifetime Average Annual Income*, Technical Report no. 31, Stanford University.

Tinbergen, J. (1956), 'On the Theory of Income Distribution', *Weltwirtschaftliches Archiv*.

Woytinsky, W. S. (1953), *Employment and Wages in the United States*, Twentieth Century Fund.

3   Human capital and earnings*

Human capital is an old concept but a relatively new research area in economics. The central idea is that human capacities are in large part acquired or developed through informal and formal education at home and at school, and through training, experience, and mobility in the labor market. These activities are costly, as they involve direct expenses and earnings or consumption forgone by students, by trainees, and by workers in the process of labor mobility. Since benefits derived from these activities accrue mainly in the future and are for the most part quite durable, the costly acquisition of human capacities is an act of investment. Deterioration of health and erosion or obsolescence of skills represent depreciation of human capital which is offset, though not indefinitely, by maintenance activities such as the production of health or retraining.

As Adam Smith pointed out long ago, the notions involved in investments in human resources are basically the same as the concepts in the economics of physical capital investments. It follows that the standard tools of economic analysis can be applied to a wide range of human activities whether or not the activities take on forms of explicit market transactions. This realization is a welcome step toward the obliteration of traditional boundaries among the several fields of behavioral science. In the field of education, as in other fields, such steps have been taken only very recently. Whether it was intellectual fear of economic reductionism or emotional resentment against treating labor 'as machine' that inhibited progress, the emergence of modern analytical and econometric research in human capital is not more than two decades old. But its growth into a veritable avalanche can be seen in the exploding volume of bibliographical references.

The sprawling research literature has rapidly outgrown the capacity of a single individual to comprehend and to survey it. My task is somewhat more manageable, since this survey is restricted to studies of effects of human capital on earnings. Note, however, that the concept of human capital is broader than school education and cannot be reduced to the latter for analytical purposes: since schooling is one among several and related forms of human capital, its effects cannot be isolated when these other forms are ignored.

*This chapter was first published in *Economic Dimensions of Education*, Washington, D.C.: National Academy of Education, 1979.

The general categories of human capital investments can be described in a life-cycle chronology. Resources in child care and child development represent pre-school investments. These overlap and are followed by investments in formal school education. Investments in labor market mobility, job choice, job training, and work effort occur during the working life, while investments in health and other maintenance activities continue throughout life.

1. School Education

Initially, investment in school education received almost exclusive attention from human-capital analysts. While economists since Smith have recognized the importance of education as a type of private or social investment, only recently have economists undertaken rigorous conceptual and statistical examination of the evidence on costs, benefits, and rates of return to education.

The costs of education borne by the student or his parents consist not merely of tuition and other school expenditures but also of forgone earnings – the loss of what the student could have earned if he had spent the school years in gainful employment. Beyond early schooling, forgone earnings are the largest component (over one-half) of schooling costs.

Investors in schooling envisage flows of earnings in the labor market that correspond to each schooling level. The discounted difference between the future flows with and without additional schooling – namely, the present value of the return on the additional investment in schooling – represents the gain or loss on the investment. Gains induce further schooling and losses discourage it. Of course, the discounted difference between the future flows (the gain or the loss) depends on the size of the relevant discount rate: the interest rate at which the individual can borrow or which he can earn elsewhere on the funds he would invest in education. Unfortunately, such individual discount rates are not observable.

An alternative way to represent this decision-making process is to calculate the internal rate of return on the investment – that hypothetical rate of interest which will make the profit equal to zero and, thus, the investment just about worthwhile. Further schooling is encouraged if the internal rate of return on schooling exceeds the rate of alternative investments. This method is more useful, since internal rates of return can be calculated given estimates of costs and of typical earnings streams.

Comparison of rates of return to education with rates of return on other (say, in business capital) investments not only can explain flows into the respective fields, but also can indicate the desirability of existing allocations or changes in relative allocations of investments from society's point of view – provided estimates of social costs and social returns can be formed.

It is understood, of course, that relevant concepts of costs and benefits are real, that is, not restricted to pecuniary terms: education itself may be desirable for its own sake and it may enhance future enjoyment of life, apart from the monetary gain. Since people differ in these attitudes and perceptions, different monetary gains (or losses) for different individuals may correspond to the same real rate of return.

More generally, variation in observed individual monetary returns to educational investments is partly due to individual differences, not only in nonpecuniary aspects of education (consumption components), but also in efficiency in absorbing education, and to individual differences in discount rates. These in turn result from differences in preferences between the present and the future and from differential access to financing of such investments.

But why do employers pay higher wages to the more-educated workers, on average? Evidently, the value productivity of the better-educated worker is seen and experienced as higher than that of the less-educated worker. Now, an increased supply of educated workers reduces the marginal value product, while increased wage differentials induce a greater supply. Hence, relative supplies are stabilized at levels at which the wage differential translates into rates of return comparable to those on alternative human or non-human investments. Increases in demand favoring more-educated workers raise the rate of return on schooling, inducing growth of enrollments until the increased return has been eliminated by the increased supply of the more-educated workers. This appears to be the history of US education in the past three decades, at least up to 1970.

Initially, analyses of effects of education on earnings were carried out by estimating direct and forgone costs of a given increment of schooling and discounting the differentials between earnings profiles of workers with the higher and lower levels of schooling. These procedures, utilizing decennial census data on annual earnings, produced a variety of estimates. Most estimates showed rates of return comparable to rates on business investments, though higher at lower levels of schooling, and rather stable between 1950 and 1970. The rates were permanently higher prior to World War II and have temporarily declined in the 1970s (Becker, 1975; Chiswick and Mincer, 1972; Freeman, 1976).

The calculations that are available do not include nonpecuniary or 'consumption components' of costs or of returns. To the extent that these are positive and important in the benefits of schooling (an assumption dear to the hearts of educators), the rates are underestimated, though the pattern of their historical changes need not be affected. Distinctions are also made between private and social rates. In calculating private rates, costs and returns to students and their families are computed from after-tax data, and schooling costs do not include public financing of schools. In contrast, the calculation of social cost is based on before-tax earnings, and school costs are the total costs of the relevant school system (per student) regardless of the source of financing. The difficulty in calculating true social rates of return is the problem of measuring externalities. To the extent that the gain to society exceeds the sum of gains to students, social returns are underestimated. Again, an assumption of public policy dear to educators, though less readily accepted today than in the past by policy-makers, is that such educational externalities are substantial and positive. This is an important, if almost unverifiable, economic justification of public support to education, though it is hardly an explanation of the public ownership of schools.

2.   Earnings profiles

An important source of earnings differentials among people who have completed the same level of education is age or amount of time already spent in employment. The discounting of earnings differentials among 'typical' earnings profiles for the purpose of estimating the profitability of schooling assumes, in effect, that human capital investments cease with the termination of schooling. This assumption is not valid theoretically or empirically. The profiles do not automatically follow a particular level of schooling. Their shapes differ among people even at the same level of schooling and they are subject to explanation by the same human-capital framework in which investments continue in the labor market after completion of schooling. Indeed, the major reorientation that human-capital analysis has provided for labor economists is the shift of focus from analysis of current earnings of groups to complete lifetime earnings profiles.

The analysis of the earnings profile is the starting point of the human-capital study of earnings. According to this approach, earnings at any time are seen as a return on the skill level – the human-capital stock embodied in the person and accumulated by him up to this time. Since the size of this capital stock grows over the life cycle by means of investment and declines because of depreciation and obsolescence, earnings change correspondingly. Specifically, the average level of the earnings profile depends on total investments (plus endowment), the slope (rate of growth) depends on investment prior to the observed period, and the rate of change (deceleration) in growth reflects the rate of decline of investments over the life cycle.

An average age profile of earnings shows rapid growth during the first decade of working life, lesser growth subsequently, and a leveling in the third and fourth decades. Such profiles are descriptive of earnings of homogeneous groups (for example, male workers with a fixed level of education), net of general economic fluctuations and trends over time. Approximations to such profiles are observable in cross-section data, which show earnings of persons of given education levels who differ in age.

In longitudinal data that have recently become available, we can observe individual earnings histories. The average longitudinal profile in a homogeneous group is affected by trends and cycles in the economy, but to the extent that those can be isolated, it bears a general similarity to the synthetic cross-sectional construct.

Why do earnings grow over the life-cycle in a decelerating fashion? According to human-capital theory, the life-cycle growth of earnings reflects the rate of accumulation of personal investments (this is why economy-wide and random changes should be excluded). This self-investment can be analyzed as an optimizing decision of the individual:[1] Briefly, rational allocation requires that much of the investments in the person be concentrated at younger ages. The investments may increase initially, but continue at a diminishing rate through the rest of the working life. If it pays to invest early, why don't people undertake all their planned investments at an early age? The basic answer is that the cost of producing a unit of human capital is greater the shorter the time period of its production. The solution is to stagger investments over time and to decrease each dose in the time sequence. Investments diminish over time because, first, benefits decline as the pay-off period (remaining working life) shortens and secondly, the opportunity cost of time, which is an input in the learning process, is likely to rise over the working life. While gross investment proceeds at a slackening rate throughout working life, net investments (gross minus depreciation) vanish or turn negative earlier. This occurs when depreciation (including obsolescence) begins to outstrip maintenance, a progression which eventually brings about retirement.

An alternative interpretation of the earnings profile is that it is an intrinsic age phenomenon; initial productivity growth corresponds to inherent biological and psychological maturation, while later stability and decline are due to first stable then declining physical and intellectual vigor. In the perspective of human capital this view is incomplete since it explains the earnings profile solely by a life-cycle pattern of the depreciation rate, seen as negative in early years, zero in middle life, and positive in later years. There is evidence, moreover, that indicates that this inherent age-depreciation factor affects earnings only to a minor degree, except at teenage and in the near or post-retirement years. In data in which age and length of work experience are statistically separable, levels and shapes of earnings curves are mainly a function of experience rather than of age. In addition, earnings profiles differ by occupation, sex, and other characteristics in systematic ways that cannot be attributable to aging.

One may also interpret the shape of the earnings profile as a 'learning curve', or a reflection of growth of skills with age and experience known as 'learning by doing'. This view is not at all inconsistent with the human-capital investment interpretation, as long as opportunities for learning are not costless. If more learning, and hence a more steeply rising wage, is available in some jobs compared with others, all qualified workers would gravitate to such jobs if learning were thought to be costless. In consequence, entry wage levels in such jobs would be reduced relative to entry wages elsewhere for workers of the same quality, thereby creating opportunity investment costs in moving to such jobs. Thus, it is not merely training on the job (formal or informal), but also the processes of occupational choice that give rise to investments beyond schooling. Similarly, geographic mobility and other labor turnover in search of higher real earnings represent investments in human capital. Job mobility of this sort declines over the working life for the same reasons that the training investments do, and reinforces the general concave shape of the earnings profile while imposing occasional discrete jumps corresponding to job turnover. It is not surprising, therefore, to find that individual longitudinal earnings profiles appear rather unstable, while they are considerably smoother and characteristically shaped when earnings of homogeneous groups are averaged.

3. Earnings function[2]

The earnings function is a mathematical and econometric specification of the earnings profile. A simple recursion produces the basic accounting equation of the earnings function: Let 'earnings capacity' in the time period t be the amount of earnings E_t (in dollars) that could be observed if there were no investments in t. Given investments C_t, however, observed earnings

$$Y_t = E_t - C_t. \tag{3.1}$$

Earning capacity grows over time as a result of investment: At time t earning capacity E_t exceeds E_{t-1} by the return on investments incurred in $(t-1)$. Thus,

$$E_t = E_{t-1} + r_{t-1}C_{t-1} \tag{3.2}$$

where r_{t-1} is the rate of return on the investments in $(t-1)$. By recursion:

$$E_t = E_0 + \sum_{j=0}^{t-1} r_j C_j, \qquad (3.3)$$

so that

$$Y_t = E_0 + \sum_{j=0}^{t-1} r_j C_j - C_t. \qquad (3.4)$$

In principle, the rates of return r may differ among periods, forms of investment, and persons. We do, however, suppress the subscripts whenever convenient. E_0 is 'original' earnings capacity: if it originates at age 0 we can view it as a return on the person's genetic endowment and state of health at birth. If the starting point is after completion of schooling at entry to the labor force, E_0 is a mixture of genetic and environmental influences, the latter including parental investments of time, money, and effort, as well as schooling investments.

Data on the individual installments of investments are not easily observable, except for formal schooling and training programs, which are only a part of the story. Even so, it is years of school attainment and not dollar costs for which data are abundant. For this reason alone, it is preferable to express the right-hand variables in the earnings function in terms of 'time spent in investment' rather than in dollar magnitudes. This is accomplished by viewing the ratio of investment expenditure to gross earnings as a time-equivalent amount of investment:

Define

$$k_t = \frac{C_t}{E_t}. \qquad (3.5)$$

If t is a given year and $k_t = 20$ per cent, this means that 20 per cent of the year's gross earnings was spent in investment. If the costs of investments are exclusively time costs, i.e., earnings forgone, then k does in fact represent the fraction of the year spent in investment activities.

Substituting equations 3.5 in equation 3.2, we have

$$E_t = E_{t-1}(1 + rk_{t-1}), \qquad (3.6)$$

and by recursion

$$E_t = E_0(1 + rk_0)(1 + rk_1) \dots (1 + rk_{t-1}).$$

With rk a relatively small number, a logarithmic approximation is appropriate, and

$$\ln E_t = \ln E_0 + r \sum_{j=0}^{t-1} k_j. \tag{3.7}$$

Some investments are in the form of schooling; others take the form of pre-school care, job training, job mobility, medical care, acquisition of information, and so forth. At this stage of development of the earnings functions, the k-terms have been segregated into two categories, namely, schooling and postschool investments.

Thus equation 3.7 can be written:

$$\ln E_t = \ln E_0 + r_s \sum_{i=0}^{s-1} k_i + r_p \sum_{j=0}^{t-1} k_j \tag{3.8}$$

where i runs over years of schooling and j over years of post-school experience. The investment ratios are represented by k_i during the school period and by k_j thereafter. The subscripts at r_s and r_p indicate that, in principle, the rates of return on schooling may differ from the rates of return on post-school investment.

Equations 3.1 and 3.8 are specified in terms of net investment ratios (k). Net investments can be decomposed into gross investment and depreciation as follows: Let C^*_{t-1} be the dollar amount of gross investment in period $t - 1$, δ_{t-1} the depreciation rate of the stock of human capital, hence of earnings E_{t-1} during that period, and $k^*_t = C^*_t/E_t$ the gross investment ratio. Then

$$E_t = E_{t-1} + rC^*_{t-1} - \delta_{t-1}E_{t-1}$$

and

$$\frac{E_t}{E_{t-1}} = 1 + rk^*_{t-1} - \delta_{t-1} = 1 + rk_{t-1},$$

by equation 3.7. Therefore, $rk_t = rk^*_t - \delta_t$, and the function of equation 3.8 can be written:

$$\ln E_t = \ln E_0 + \sum_{i=0}^{s-1} (r_s k^*_i - \delta_i) + \sum_{j=0}^{t-1} (r_p k^*_j - \delta_j). \tag{3.9}$$

The earnings function of equation 3.8 or 3.9 must be adapted for empirical purposes in at least two respects.

First, the dependent variable, E_t, 'earnings capacity', is the earnings figure that would be observed if the individual stopped investing in himself in period t. Continued investment means, however, that 'net' earnings (Y_t) are smaller than E_t by the amount invested, C. For practical purposes, I equate observed earnings with 'net earnings'.[3]

Since $Y_t = E_t(1 - k_t)$, the earnings functions can be written:

$$\ln Y_t = \ln E_t + \ln(1 - k_t), \tag{3.10}$$

substituting the appropriate expressions from equation 3.8 or 3.9 for $\ln E_t$.

Next, the investment ratios k_t or k^*_t have to be given empirical content. In the schooling stage, $k^*_i = C^*_i/E_i$, where C^*_i are forgone earnings (E_i), plus tuition and cost-of-living differential attributable to schooling, minus student earnings and student aid. Without knowing the C^*_i for each individual, we know that k^*_i is not far from unity during school years, and this is a convenient approximation.[4] In the post-school stage, we have only the theoretical hypothesis that k_j declines after completion of schooling, when it was close to unity. Positive earnings upon entry into the labor force mean that $k^*_j < 1$, and since C^*_j eventually declines to zero, so must k^*_j. Note that a monotonic decline of k^*_j is not inconsistent with an initial constancy or even increase in C^*_j. This means that concavity of logarithmic earnings profiles is not inconsistent with initial linearity or even convexity of dollar earnings profiles.

My own experiments with specifying k or k^* as functions of time proved that the simplest linear specifications fit as well as other forms. Recalling that $k^*_t = 1$ and putting $k^*_j = k^*_0 - (k^*_0/T^*)t$, when T^* is the length of working life, we get:

$$\ln Y_t = \ln E_0 + (r_s - \delta_s)s + (r_p k^*_0 - \delta_p)t \tag{3.11}$$
$$- \frac{r_p k_0^*}{2T^*} t^2 + \ln(1 - k^*_t).$$

Alternatively, in terms of net investment:

$$\ln Y_t = \ln E_0 + r_s s + r_p k_0 t - \frac{r_p k_0}{2T} t^2 + \ln(1 - k_t). \tag{3.12}$$

Here T is the period of positive net investment, so that $T < T^*$. Thus the peak of earning capacity when depreciation nullifies or outstrips gross investment is reached sometime before the end of working life.

For the purposes of econometric estimation, the term $\ln(1 - k_t)$ may be approximated by one or more terms. With a one-term approximation and a linearly declining profile of investment ratios, Equation 3.12 becomes:

$$\ln Y_t = (\ln E_0 - k_0) + r_s s + (r_p k_0 + \frac{k_0}{T})t - \frac{r_p k_0}{2T}t^2. \qquad (3.12a)$$

The timing of the peak of observed earnings, obtained from $(d \ln Y_t)/dt = 0$ is $t_p = T + (1/r_p)$. Therefore, $T < t_p < T^*$: observed earnings reach a peak sometime (perhaps a decade) after net investment has declined to zero but before gross investment ceases.

Hours of work appear to decline in the last decade of working life, according to available data. If capacity rather than observed wage rates are important in labor supply behaviour, hours would decline before the peaking of wage rates is observed, while the end of working life (retirement) is likely to be linked to the cessation of gross investment (T^*).

Equation 3.12 permits a separate estimate of effect of schooling r_s, but r_p and k_0 cannot be separately estimated. Estimates of the post-school investment profile can be obtained if it is assumed that r_s and r_p are the same.

We have not, as yet, distinguished between earnings and wage rates. Information on hours of work during the year permits this distinction. More interestingly, when such information exists for prior years, as in recently available longitudinal data, it is possible to separate the estimates of the post-school investment profile given by k_0 and T from the rate of return, r_p, on these investments.[5]

As was noted, the investment ratio k_t is equivalent to the fraction of time at work devoted to investment in further progress of the worker. If all persons worked the same number of hours during the year and over the years, equation 3.10 would estimate both annual earnings and wage rates. Otherwise, a fixed ratio k_t across individuals implies that people who work less invest correspondingly less. This is a plausible assumption within the theory, suggesting that opportunities as well as incentives to learn on the job are directly related to the amount of time spent at work. If people differ systematically in average annual hours they devote to the labor market, then an earnings function for wage rates must be distinguished from annual earnings equations. The derivation is as follows.

Let λ be the ratio of actual (annual) hours worked by person i to standard hours (say, 2000 per year – the base is arbitrary), and let E_t^f be the full-time earning capacity and Y_t^f be observed full-time earnings (a fixed multiple of the wage rate per hour). Then

$$C_t = k_t E_t = \lambda_t k_t E_t^f, \qquad (3.13)$$

so that

$$E_t^f = E_{t-1}^f (1 + r\lambda_t k_t). \qquad (3.14)$$

Recursion of equation 3.14 leads to:

$$\ln E_t^f = \ln E_0^f + \sum_{j=0}^{t-1} r_j \lambda_j k_j. \qquad (3.15)$$

After the summation (integration in the continuous case) and substitution of $Y_t^f = E_t^f(1 - k_t)$,

$$\ln Y_t^f = \ln E_0^f + r_s s + r k_0(\lambda t) - \frac{1}{2} r \frac{k_0}{T} (\lambda t^2) + \ln(1 - k_t).$$

With a linear approximation for the last term on the right:

$$\ln Y_t^f = \ln Y_0^f + r_s s + r k_0(\lambda t) - \frac{1}{2} r \frac{k_0}{T} (\lambda t^2) + \frac{k_0}{T} t_i. \qquad (3.16)$$

This is an equation for full-time earnings or wage rates. Since annual earnings are a product of wage rates and hours, the annual earnings equation (in logarithms) contains an additional term, $\ln \lambda_t$. Here λ_t refers to the current period t, while in the wage rate equation, λ is an average over the past excluding the current period t.

$$\ln Y_t = \ln Y_0^f + r_s s_i + r_p k_0 (\lambda_i t_i) - \frac{1}{2} r_p \frac{k_0}{T} (\lambda_i t^2) + \frac{k_0}{T} t_i + \ln \lambda_t. \qquad (3.17)$$

Since individual differences in levels of schooling s, work time λ, and elapsed years of working life t are observable, equations 3.16 and 3.17 can be statistically estimated in the cross-section (with historical information on λ). In contrast to equations 3.11 and 3.12, all parameters can be estimated: these are averages of rates of return to schooling (r_s), to post-school investment (r_p), linear investment profiles $k_t = k_0 - (k_0/T)t$, and the net investment period T.

There are several merits in using earnings functions of types 3.12 and 3.16 relative to the calculations of costs and returns to schooling as differentials between earnings profiles of two schooling groups:

(a) The earnings function permits an estimate of the effect of schooling on earnings (coefficient r_s) uncontaminated by and separately from estimates of effects and volumes (in dollars or time-equivalents) of post-school investments. The association between the schooling and post-schooling investment is another relation that can be ascertained.

(b)   It sheds light on the role of age in the earnings profile: age can represent a depreciation factor, but it is not a good measure of accumulated post-school investments. The latter are better indexed by actual experience in the labor market: earnings rise rapidly during the early decade of work experience. At the same age, less-educated workers are higher on their experience profile than the more educated workers are on theirs. Consequently, the differentials in earnings, that is, returns to schooling, in samples of young workers may be severely underestimated, and this is more generally true when age rather than experience is the variable used (as in most *ad hoc* analyses) in the earnings function. Age is an especially poor substitute for experience in the analysis of earnings of women, whose labor-market experience is often discontinuous. The earnings function, however, can be adapted to discontinuous work histories as well (cf. Mincer and Polachek, 1974).

4.   Some empirical findings of research with earnings functions
Earnings of men
Multiple regressions of the functional form of equation 3.12 run on large samples of the Decennial US Census, as well as on other sample data, provide the following estimates:

(a)   The average rate of return to *schooling* varies between 7 per cent and 11 per cent in various bodies of data. It showed no time trend between 1949 and 1969, but there was a significant (about one-third) drop in the rate between 1939 and 1949. Some indication of decline appears in the 1970s, based on fragmentary data (Freeman, 1976). The rate itself is higher at lower levels of schooling in the analysis of annual earnings but does not differ much by level of schooling in wage-rate comparisons.

(b)   The rate of return to *post-school* investments (r_p) and the average magnitudes of those investments are estimable by the regression form of equation 3.14. Estimated from the *Michigan Income Dynamics* data (Hanushek and Quigley, 1976), r_p was about 13 per cent at each education level, while the intercept of the investment profile was about 25 per cent on the average – lower (17 per cent) at elementary-school levels and higher (32 per cent) at college and beyond. With the net investment period T estimated at about 20 years and an assumed linear decline in the investment ratio, it would appear that men spend an equivalent of three years at work in activities promoting their advancement. In terms of opportunity cost, however, these job investments are not much less than the costs of schooling, since forgone earnings are much smaller at school ages.

(c)   The two variables, schooling and work experience, account for a third of the variance in wage rates. This is a significant insight into the structure of earnings, especially when it is realized that individual differences such as the quality of schooling, the differential rates of skill accumulation on the job or through job mobility, and 'home investments' of parents in children are not captured by these few crude variables. Annual earnings is a product of wage rates and hours per year. When hours worked (or even only weeks worked) during the particular year are taken into account, the equation consisting of these easily available variables explained as much as half of the variation in earnings among men in the 1960 Census.

It is true, of course, that schooling and years of work experience are rather obvious determinants of wage rates and that (current) hours of work are an arithmetical factor in annual earnings. Their inclusion in earnings equations does not require analytical models such as human-capital theory. The model, however, does provide guidance for the specification of these variables and of the equation form in ways that provide interesting interpretations. Some of the contributions of the human-capital model to the analyses of earnings, as distinguished from *ad hoc* analyses with the same variables, are the following:

(a)   The coefficients of the function represent estimates of (average) rates of return and of volumes of investment in schooling and after schooling. It appears that rates of return are somewhat higher in post-school activities and that the total volume of investment is somewhat larger in schooling. Since the calculations are based on monetary values, one reason why the rate on schooling investments is less than that on job training is that schools are more likely to produce non-pecuniary returns, that is, 'consumption' or cultural gains, in addition to monetary gains.

(b)   The relation between schooling and post-school investment can be observed and interpreted. In dollar terms, the relation is positive: more-educated people invest more in the labor market. One interpretation is that the ability and opportunity factors that induce individuals to have more schooling also affect their post-school investment behavior. The correlation is far from strict: abilities and opportunities change over the life cycle and there is a fair amount of substitution between the two forms of skill accumulation. Another interpretation of the same phenomenon is that schooling improves the efficiency with which people can absorb learning on the job, thereby leading to greater job investments. This hypothesis has not been tested on an individual level, but it is consistent, in a dynamic context, with evidence on the 'worker allocative effect' propounded by Schultz (1975) and Welch (1970). Their proposition that education promotes the adjustment to technological change has been documented, mainly in studies of agricultural production activities.

(c)   The simple correlation between schooling and earnings is quite weak. In the Census data, previously referred to, the simple coefficient of determination between earnings and years of schooling for the whole sample was merely 7 per cent. Even multiple coefficients of determination, after a number of other variables are added, remain relatively small, as in Jencks (1972). Standardizing for effects of age doubles the coefficient in age groups 35–44, but the coefficients decline below and above these ages.

The proper standardization suggested by the human-capital framework is not by age but by experience. The R^2 by years of experience is a much more substantial 30 per cent during the first decade of working life, with a gradual decay thereafter. The decay is due to the fact that, although positively correlated, post-school investments are not perfectly correlated with schooling investments at the individual level. The decay in the correlation does not set in until the second decade of work experience, because schooling differentials in earnings during the initial years of experience are attenuated by the greater incidence of post-school investment at higher levels of schooling. The experience structure of the education–earnings relation which the human capital theory makes intelligible is confounded in age classifications that tend to produce downward biases in studies restricted to limited age groups (see the review by M. J. Bowman, 1976).

Employment effects

The more-educated and experienced workers enjoy larger annual earnings than their less-skilled fellows for two reasons: their wage rates per hour are higher and the amount of time they spend in gainful employment during the year is greater. The relative importance of employment compared with wage rates is greater at lower levels of schooling and at older ages. At lower levels of schooling the effects of education and of job experience are about equally divided between gains in wage rates and gains in employment stability. In contrast, the effects of higher levels of education are due largely to gains in pay rates.

The relation between human-capital accumulation and employment is mutual in the post-school stage. The more stable the employment and the more time spent at work, the greater both the opportunities and the incentives for further job investments. Conversely, the greater the earning power (in part due to past investments in human capital), the greater the payoff from additional work. This last statement must be qualified, however, by the opposite effects of resultant increases in income or wealth which are likely to increase the demand for consumption time or leisure. It can be shown, however, that so long as the rate of return on schooling investments is not exorbitant, human capital investments increase wealth less than they increase wage rates. Positive effects of wage rates on time at work are therefore likely to dominate in a cross-section of workers differing in education.

Induced labor-supply behavior may explain in part why hours of work and labor-force participation increase with education. Other factors that help to account for the observed positive correlation between education and employment are health differentials and differences on the demand side:

(a) There is some evidence that physical capital is more easily substitutable for unskilled than for skilled labor. If fluctuations in output are produced with relatively fixed physical capital, the employment of unskilled labor must fluctuate more than that of skilled labor.

(b) Employers invest resources in the training and experience of their employees to the extent that the resulting increases in worker productivity are more effective in their firms than elsewhere. To guard against capital losses in such investments, firms tend to minimize layoffs of their 'specifically' trained workers. In so far as these 'specific' job investments are related to educational attainments of workers, they are a factor in the unemployment differentials observed by education. As mentioned before, worker self-investments appear to increase with levels of schooling. Employers, in turn, tend to invest more in the more educated workers, either because job specificity is more likely in more complex jobs or because they think education confers greater capacity and motivation for training.

(c) A variety of institutional factors may account for differences in unemployment and labor-force participation among educational groups. Minimum wages on the demand side and income maintenance programs on the supply side tend to price low-quality labor out of the market. Consequently, inexperienced and uneducated workers with submarginal market productivities are frequently unemployed or withdraw from the labor market into welfare.

Earnings and employment of women

In the United States the educational attainment of women is not very different from the attainment of men, except for still sizable differences in higher and professional education. Wages of women are, on the average, 30–40 per cent lower than wages of men and the differences are even larger on an annual basis. The comparison of sex differentials in earnings provides a major illustration of the difficulty of understanding the effects of education when other investments in human capital are disregarded.

Even today, after a long and upward trend in the market employment of women, their average labor force rate is about 50 per cent. This, of course, does not mean that one-half of all women work all the time and the other half never works. Rather, it represents a spectrum of full-time and life-long work behavior of some and intermittent or part-time participation of others. According to Census (National Longitudinal Surveys – NLS) data, less than 50 per cent of married women worked in 1966, but close to 90 per cent worked sometime since they left school. More than half of the working women dropped out of the labor force when the first child was born and large numbers returned after the youngest child reached school age. In contrast, women without husbands and without children spent close to 90 per cent of their working lives in the labor market.

The lesser amount and often discontinuous pattern of women's market work reduce both their incentives and opportunities, as well as the incentives of employers to invest in furthering women's skills in the market place. Consequently, the growth of wages with age is much smaller for women. Even if wages of women grew at the same rate as wages of men in intervals of work activity, the overall growth would be half as large for women since they work, on the average, half the time. However, expectations of discontinuity (or uncertainty about it) reduce investment incentives even further while the actual periods of withdrawal from market work tend to erode acquired skills. Thus, average wage growth in women's earnings profiles is less than half the wage growth of men. Note that the widely held view of wage discrimination against women refers to differences in wage *levels*, while the human-capital hypothesis implies differences in wage *growth* resulting from differences in work experience. In principle, the two hypotheses are not mutually exclusive, but the literature on sex differentials in wages contains as yet little or no attempt to identify distinct implications of each of these hypotheses.

The empirical analysis of data containing earnings and work and family histories of women is consistent with human capital hypotheses. We observe that although starting wages of men and women (with the same educational qualifications) do not differ much, they grow apart over the subsequent decades. However, the profiles of women who work continuously are much closer to those of men.

An adaptation of the earnings function to deal with discontinuous work experience has made it possible (Mincer and Polachek, 1974) to decompose the human capital factors involved. Rates of return to school education do not appear to differ between the sexes. Lesser work participation implies both a lesser payoff and lesser costs (forgone earnings). Close to half of the differences in wages emerging two decades following school were due to shorter accumulated work experience and to depreciation resulting from long gaps (usually when children were small) in participation. The estimated depreciation rate increased with level of schooling. This phenomenon counteracts the higher labor-force rate of more-educated women in the combined effects on wage rates.

The fact that labor-force rates of women increase with education is of special interest. Though similar in direction to the behavior of men, education-associated differences in employment are much stronger among women than among men. The higher market earning power of the more-educated women induces families to substitute, to some extent, purchasable goods or services for their work in the household. This kind of substitution is stronger than the substitution between market work and leisure which are still the more typical alternatives for men. Indeed, the strong substitution response to the growing wages (and education) in women's allocation of time between market and home is the basic factor in the historical growth of the female labor force (Mincer, 1962).

Although more-educated women generally spend more time in the labor market, they are more likely to reduce their market work to take care of their children, particularly when they are of pre-school age. The opportunity cost of shifting from market to home as measured by the forgone market earnings is much greater for the more-educated women. Maternal withdrawal from the labor market represents one component of the parental investments in the human capital of their children. It may contribute to the explanation of the importance of family background in children's school performance and of the positive correlation between the educational attainment of children and of their parents, particularly the mother. Whether such pre-school investments have an effect on the children's earnings, beyond affecting their education, is a question that is answered negatively in much of the current research, but it is far from settled. In any case, the greater earnings – and presumably also the consumption capacities of children – may be viewed in the family context as a part of the return on the education of mothers. If so, the profitability of educating women is understated when inferred from their earnings alone.

An important consequence of the higher opportunity cost per unit of time spent in child care by more-educated mothers is the reduction of total time so spent. This is accomplished largely by a reduction in the number of children. The strong inverse relation between education of mother and number of children is repeatedly documented. Taken together, it appears that growth of wages and of education is, in part at least, responsible for the major social trends of our time, such as the growing market employment of women (with all that this implies for the family), declines in fertility, and increases in human-capital investments (especially education) in the resultant smaller number of children per family.

5. Human capital and the income distribution
Shape of the distribution
There are several prominent features of the statistical distribution of earnings that are repeatedly observed in temporally and regionally differing data. Aggregate skewness and the growth of inequality with age are the best known. Other features are less familiar, and perhaps less stable. These characteristic patterns have puzzled observers ever since statistical data have become available. Largely non-economic hypotheses ranging from genetic configurations to chance ('random shock') income fluctuations have been proposed to explain the shapes of income distributions.

In the human-capital framework, most of these features can be explained by the correlation between the stock of human capital at any stage of the life-cycle and the volume of subsequent investment. This correlation is understandable if incentives and opportunities for self-investment tend to persist over long periods of life. One example of this correlation, mentioned before, is the steeper growth of earnings with experience at higher levels of schooling. The statistical consequence is that earnings profiles 'fan out'; hence, variances of earnings increase with experience and with age. Similarly, because the dispersion of schooling costs increases with the level of schooling, variances of earnings increase with levels of schooling. The resulting positive correlation between means and variances in age and schooling subgroups of the earnings distribution is a sufficient condition for the appearance of positive skewness in the aggregate.

This factor is independent of (and, in a way, more basic than) the shape of the distribution of schooling which may itself contribute to positive skewness in earnings. Since the earnings function relates years of schooling linearly to logarithms of earnings, even a symmetric distribution of years of schooling must result in a positively skewed distribution of earnings. When the overall level of schooling is less, the distribution of years of schooling tends to be positively skewed. It becomes symmetric as average attainment rises. In the United States, skewness in the distribution of schooling has turned negative in the younger cohorts. So the shape of the distribution of schooling (measured by years) is no longer an important factor in explaining the persistence of positive skewness in the distribution of earnings in the US. As the level of schooling in the US is among the highest anywhere, the findings of aggregate skewness in earnings in most other countries are not surprising.

Education and income inequality
According to the earnings function of equation 3.12, the relative (logarithmic) variance of earnings is a positive function of the variance in years of schooling, in year-equivalents of other investments, of the size and variance of the rates of return, and of the covariances between rates and volumes of investment. Using these parameters as well as variances in the distribution of employment, Chiswick (1974) was able to explain over 85 per cent of the interregional differences in relative earnings inequality.

Using the same approach, Chiswick and Mincer (1972) studied annual changes in inequality among US males (ages 25–64) between 1939 and 1969. Again, over 85 per cent of the annual variation was explained by these parameters, even though no long-term trend was observed after 1949. There was a strong decline in inequality between 1939 and 1949 which was attributable in part to the decline in unemployment and in part to a sizable reduction (about one-third) in the rate of return to education.

Many observers are puzzled by findings that the inequality of earnings has not narrowed in the postwar era despite the large increases in mean education levels and despite the narrowing of educational disparities in years of schooling during this period. A sensitivity analysis (Chiswick and Mincer, 1972) of the estimated parameters of the earnings functions suggests that even large changes (in standard deviation units) in the distribution of schooling and of age have minor effects on annual earnings inequality. The strongest effects are produced by changes in rates of return. Indeed, economic theory predicts that increases in educational investments should lower the rate of return on the investment and narrow the income differentials. This did not happen. A reasonable hypothesis, not fully documented, is that the supply of educated labor grew largely in response to growing demands, leaving rates of return roughly stable. Prior to the Second World War, low family incomes hampered investments in education and inhibited such supply responses. Consequently, the rate of return was and remained (too) high, until the postwar affluence and subsidies to education spurred a boom in enrollments.

6.   School quality

The measurement of school education by the number of years spent at school is excessively crude for much the same reason that the measurement of work experience ('post-school investments') is merely by elapsed years of working age. The problem of measuring school quality has been attacked in several ways: by using school expenditures per student, salaries or other characteristics of teachers, and various ratings of schools as indicators of quality. Inclusion of such data in the earnings function reveals positive effects on earnings of greater resources per student, superior teachers, or higher ratings of schools. Johnson and Stafford (1973) find that a 10 per cent increase in school expenditures per student increases the annual return to schooling by close to 2 per cent; Wachtel (1974) found similarly strong effects in data in which student test scores were available as well; the correlation between school quality measures and student test scores was also quite high. Wise (1975) also found strong effects of school quality on earnings and even on rates of advancement of workers in a large firm.

Since better students and better schools tend to select one another, a clear analytical separation of student ability from school quality cannot be achieved in aggregated data such as school districts, counties, or states (Coleman *et al.*, 1966; Johnson and Stafford, 1973). Micro-data based on individual students do show the separate effects more convincingly (cf. Wachtel, 1974, 1975; Solmon, 1973; Taubman, 1976a, 1976b; Hauser and Sewell, 1975).

7.   Ability, opportunity, and income

The main subject of the initial work in human capital has been an elucidation of costs and returns to education and other investments in human capital, including the estimates of private and social rates of return to such investments. Subsequently, human-capital theory has been widely applied to the study of the structure of earnings, by schooling, labor market experience, occupation, sex, region, and so forth. In this analysis the distribution of earnings is viewed as a direct reflection of the distribution of accumulated stocks of human capital among members of the labor force. The appropriate qualifications, if the reader needs to be reminded, are that this statement refers, first, to real wages, so that non-pecuniary aspects of work may be reflected in compensatory money wage differences and, secondly, to equilibrium tendencies, since in the short run wages may deviate from the norm because demand has changed and supply has not yet adjusted.

Granted that the distribution of human capital among persons affects the distribution of their earnings, what are the reasons for differences among persons in the distribution of human capital? This is an interesting and important question. In terms of economic analysis generally applied to investment behavior, the volume of individual investments in human capital is determined on the demand side by the productivity of such investments and on the supply side by their cost. The equilibrium amount of investment is attained when an additional unit of investment, say, an additional year of schooling, brings about an expected increase in real income that is just equal to the increase in cost.[6] From the individual's point of view, this is the best he can do, given his abilities and his financial circumstances.

In principle, such constrained optima exist either because of diminishing returns on the demand side, where additional gains in income diminish as investment increases, or because of a rising supply price, i.e., the marginal costs of the investment rise as more is invested. Although the volume of accumulated human capital, together with the (marginal) rate of return on it, determines income, all three are simultaneously determined by the more-fundamental forces of demand for and supply of human capital. In substantive terms, individual demand for human capital depends on the efficiency with which the person can put it to use, while individual supply depends on the terms of financing the costs of such investment. Thus, personal ability and investment financing opportunity are the ultimate determinants of earnings, but the proximate cause or instrumentality by which earnings capacity is achieved is the accumulated human capital.

If equality of opportunity (defined by equal terms of access to capital funds) prevailed, income differentials would still exist because more-able persons would have incentives to invest more. Conversely, even if all people were (potentially) equally able, differential opportunities, due either to differences in inherited wealth or to other constraints, would result in differences in investments and therefore in earnings.

Given upward-sloping supply curves and downward-sloping demand curves, equality of opportunity (a common supply curve) implies a positive correlation between volumes of individual investments and (marginal) rates of return, while equal efficiency or ability implies a negative correlation. In US data, the correlation between educational attainment and rates of return is negative and close to zero, suggesting that inequality of opportunity is at least as important as the inequality of abilities in creating the existing inequality in earnings (Mincer, 1970).

A great deal of research by economists and sociologists is devoted currently to the elucidation of the role of ability and opportunity in earnings. These factors may influence earnings directly or indirectly via schooling and other human capital acquisitions. Repeated observations of a positive correlation between educational attainment, socio-economic background, and assorted measures of ability are not surprising in light of the economic analysis of human capital investment behavior. But they are also a basis for questioning the association between education and earnings. Is it not plausible that more-educated people could earn more because of their ability and background in any case, rather than as a result of the schooling process? In less-extreme form, the question is: how biased are the estimates of the effects of education on earnings by the omission of the ability and family background variables?

In the human-capital approach, ability plays a double role: as the initial endowment that exists prior to investments but also as an interactive factor or efficiency parameter because more-able persons receive a higher rate of return on the same investment. Denison (1962) conjectured that ability accounts for about 40 per cent of the effects of education on earnings. Becker (1975) argued that the opportunity costs of college graduates are understated when measured by typical earnings of high school graduates, if the latter are less able than typical college graduates. The adjustment, using fragmentary evidence on IQ, was not sizable. Since that time much greater attention has been devoted to this adjustment problem in econometric studies. Most of them conclude that the true effect of schooling on earnings is major and the correction for ability bias is minor (Welch, 1974).

Aside from problems related to the variety of ability measures (from IQ to AFQT), there is the question of the age at which the measure was taken. As is well known, these measures grow over time with age and with education. Griliches and Mason (1972) estimated that the coefficient of schooling is reduced by 7–10 per cent if IQ measured prior to high school is included, while if IQ of adults is used the downward bias in the schooling coefficient is exaggerated by almost 100 per cent.

Unless what is meant is racial discrimination, class collusion, or nepotism, it is more difficult to visualize the nature of the direct effect of opportunity or socio-economic background on earnings.[7] The indirect effects may run via genetic inheritance, which would be manifested in the ability traits already discussed, or in the quality of the early environment including purposive investment by parents in the early human capital stock of their children. Most of the studies that include family background variables in the earnings equations report small effects, net of human capital variables like schooling and experience. On the other hand, the background variables, which usually include parental occupation, education, and number of siblings, are shown to be significant predictors of the child's educational attainment. As an example, Corcoran, Jencks, and Olneck (1976) report a study of several large bodies of data in which they found strong family background effects on children's education and test scores, but no effects on their earnings, once education and test scores are controlled.

The Griliches–Mason work (1972) previously noted shows the importance of the indirect effect in another way. Their measure of schooling is partitioned into schooling completed prior to serving in the armed forces and subsequent schooling. By controlling for background variables, the early schooling coefficient is reduced by 25 per cent, but the post-armed-service schooling effect shows a negligible reduction.

In a more recent study (1976) of young men, Griliches finds that parental background and region of origin account for about a quarter of the variance of measured IQ. Together with IQ they account for about a half of the variance of schooling. Later ability (at survey) is affected about equally by schooling and by early ability (IQ), as well as by parental background. Working through the recursive equations system, Griliches concludes that the relation between education and earnings is not spurious. There remains an important and sizable effect of schooling on wages, net of family background and of measured IQ. At the same time, the ultimate effect of background variables on earnings is quite attenuated. As an illustration, the estimated equations system implies that two young men who are one standard deviation apart on each of the family variables and on IQ would find themselves about 0.75 and 0.4 of a standard deviation apart on schooling and wages, respectively. This is a rather strong regression toward the mean, with important implications for income mobility.

Other studies find lower coefficients of schooling and larger effects of ability and of family background. Some of these findings are, in part, biased by the use of age standardizations. In the Hauser–Sewell (1975) study, which covered no more than eight years of early work experience, the effects of schooling appeared to be negligible. In a recent extension of that study in which the panel was updated to 14 years, Hauser and Daymont (1976) replace age by experience in their equation and find in consequence that the schooling coefficient doubled in size (to 9–10 per cent), while the ability-background bias was reduced to about 15 per cent of the schooling coefficient. These findings approximate the results reported by Griliches and summarized for other studies by Welch (1974).

Perhaps the major problem with the background factors is the difficulty of measurement. IQ or other scores do not really measure the ability to earn, nor does father's occupation or other available family data fully capture the degree of financing or market opportunity. An indirect approach is to analyze earnings of siblings, presumably because the intra-family variation is less affected by ability differences. Of course, intrafamily analyses reduce not only variations in ability but also in other advantages or disadvantages provided by the family background.

An example of this work is a variance component model of data for young men (Chamberlain and Griliches, 1975). Ability is viewed as an unobserved factor with a common family component. In this sample, exclusion of 'ability' did not appear to bias estimated effects of schooling on earnings. Taubman (1976) carries the intrafamily approach to its logical extreme by analyzing earnings of identical and fraternal twins. A basic assumption in the analysis of twins is that identical twins differ from each other environmentally as much as fraternal twins do, while the variance in genotype is clearly much greater among fraternal twins. Consequently, the genetic effects can be isolated in statistical analyses involving both sets of twins. Taubman concludes that genetics could account for 20–40 per cent, and common family environment for 8–15%, of the variance in earnings. Both account for about 70 per cent of the variance in schooling, but differences in the schooling of twins have very small effects on their earnings.

Goldberger (1976) has expressed doubt about the statistical identification of parameters in the twin data: his analysis raises strong objections to the assumption of equal environmental correlation. Griliches (1977), as well as Welch (1974), maintain a methodologically pessimistic view to the effect that measurement errors become increasingly mischievous as the models become increasingly complex, putting an insupportable burden on the data. The more refined the data or the more variables included in the analysis, the smaller the intragroup variance. The relative importance of the same measurement error in the smaller variance can become overwhelming.

A substantive comment on the intrafamily analyses emerges from the recent work of Becker and Tomes (1976). Granted that ability, motivation, and family background are much less variable among siblings than in the whole population, it is not the variation in such characteristics but the covariation with amounts invested in human capital that is the source of possible bias in estimates. For example, if parents tend to provide more education to the more able or motivated of their children, intrafamily effects may not be reduced relative to those across the whole population. Conversely, if similar education is provided to less- and more-able children, the within-family relation between education and earnings may well appear to be tenuous, especially in the presence of measurement error.

Imprecise measurement is not restricted to the determinants of earnings. Earnings themselves are not fully measured by paid-out money wages. The missing components are so-called fringe benefits, some of which are deferred payments such as pensions or contributions to medical insurance, while others are in the form of various perquisites or comfortable working conditions. The demand for deferred payments and fringe benefits is a positive function of income for two reasons. First is the usual income effect on consumption, and second is the effect of the increasing marginal tax rate as income rises. Indeed, calculations of the value of fringe benefits and of deferred payments show that these components of wages increase more than in proportion to the currently received wage. Consequently, omission of these 'wage supplements' creates *downward* biases on the measured effects of human capital investments.

In a recent study of two national sample data sets in which information on wage supplements and fringe benefits was available, Duncan (1976) found that the schooling coefficient increased as much as 20 per cent when the 'non-wage' variables were added to the earnings measure. The increased return to education was sustained even when measures of ability, motivation, and family background were taken into account. Indeed, the upward correction of the schooling coefficient due to the omission of wage supplements and fringe benefits was at least as great as the alleged bias due to omission of background variables in a single-equation education-earnings function.

I think it is fair to say, based on the preponderant evidence thus far, that employers pay for characteristics and efforts of the workers, not of their parents. The economic analysis of human capital investment decisions suggests that the effects of background variables are *indirect* by influencing the accumulation of human capital. Since the latter is commonly measured only crudely by years of schooling and by years of work experience, the relatively small direct (net) effects of background variables that remain might well disappear with the introduction of more-refined measures of human capital.

8. Some critique and response

Accepting the reality of an education–income relationship, some critics question the interpretation that schools contribute anything to individual marketable (especially cognitive) skills. These critics do not believe that wage differentials shed any light on productivity differences. Actually, research on production functions by Griliches (1963, 1967) and others has shown that not only differences in wage rates but also differences in productivity are related to differences in the education of the labor force across states, regions, or enterprises. The potential contribution of education to aggregate economic growth is not merely a conjecture. But these findings tend to be ignored by critics.

Other critics claim that it is not cognitive knowledge but socialization that schools accomplish (Gintis, 1971). Still others assert that schools serve as a filter to sort differences in ability that exist independently of schooling – this is the so-called screening hypothesis. Although these views about the content of the contribution of education appear provocative, they do not conflict with the fundamental notion of human capital – of forgoing current income for increased future earnings. For this general concept, it does not matter whether the increased marketability produced by schools is due to their affective, informational, or cognitive function.

In principle, indeed, schools are institutions with all of these purposes, and the search for student talent by the school and by the student is an activity no less important than the search for any other scarce natural resource. It is true that the private return from the production and dissemination of information may exceed the social return. But the empirical magnitude of this differential is likely to be exaggerated.

The productivity and screening functions of schooling are not mutually exclusive in a world of imperfect information, given that ability is an input in the educational process. The controversy, if any, concerns the *relative* importance of the productivity and screening functions of schooling in affecting earnings. Unless screening is a deliberate device for monopolization, its effect on earnings can be neither major nor durable, once the productivity of the worker can be directly observed. Moreover, the characteristics for which schooling serves as a screen should be discoverable by means of direct interviewing and testing much more cheaply than by expenditures of many years and tens of thousands of dollars on an average education. Markets for testing would surely spring up if such tremendous savings were possible; their absence is a strong argument against a 'pure' screening hypothesis.

Even the proponents of screening as the major function of schooling do not maintain that the screen is permanent. If it were, the correlation of schooling with earnings would be fixed at all levels of work experience. This is obviously false, as was already indicated. Individual correlations between schooling and earnings decay over time, while differential job turnover and advancement within jobs create huge variances in wage levels and wage progressions among individuals possessing identical 'screens'.

The validation of positive effects of education on income has led to careless claims about the marketability of schooling. If what is being done at school matters, it cannot be merely a question of how many years a student spends there, but how these years are spent. Let us also not forget that the estimated rates of return suggest a reasonable investment, even purely in market terms, only *on average*. The dispersion in the rate means that a sizable proportion of below-average students may do better with other investments, unless they are the ones who weigh the non-pecuniary benefits more heavily.

It also appears that the economics of education, or its misinterpretation, has led to exaggerated hopes for the achievement of egalitarianism. Superficially, it would seem that an expansion of schooling and reduction in the variance should reduce income inequality. Since World War II, education has been expanded and democratized throughout the Western world with rather small effects on income inequality. The expected effects did not materialize simply because an expansion in the supply of educated labor will not lead to a reduction in the rate of return, and hence a reduction in inequality, unless the demand for educated labor is increasing at a less than comparable rate. In view of the positive relation between rates of return to education and rates of growth of economies or regions, as shown in the research of Schultz (1975) and Welch (1970), growth in the postwar period has been biased in favor of skills.

It appears that a slowdown in population and economic growth has reduced the demand for education in recent years. Whether the drop in demand for educated labor is a short-run or long-run phenomenon (cf. Freeman, 1976), I rather doubt that the social benefits of a reduced variance in income will outweigh the problems that even a transitory cohort of unemployed intelligentsia can create. I say transitory, because economic analysis assures us that supply adjusts to demand on the downswing as well as on the upswing, so a new, lower equilibrium is looming – witness the declining enrollments in response (in part) to the lessened profitability of education.

The expectation that education will reduce the cross-sectional variance in US incomes is probably misplaced. Rather, the traditional egalitarian effects of education should be viewed in terms of social mobility. Both the proponents of education as a tool of egalitarianism and their radical critics appear to underestimate the degree of social mobility that did occur and the role of the schooling system as a source of social mobility (Blau and Duncan, 1967) for individuals and for successive waves of immigrant groups in US history (Chiswick, 1976).

The economists' inquiries into market productivity and into the informational and distributional effects of education may hearten or discourage educators and policymakers. But they should not obscure the central role of education in society. Education is neither a panacea nor a conspiracy. It is and will remain the basic enterprise for the transmission and growth of human culture.

Notes

1. This approach was pioneered by Becker (1967) and Ben-Porath (1967).
2. This section is based on Mincer (1970, 1974).
3. Note that observed earnings, as they are usually reported in statistical accounts, would equal 'net' earnings, if C_t consisted only of opportunity costs. Since direct expenditures are not usually 'netted out', observed earnings overstate net earnings somewhat. Given the importance of opportunity costs in human capital investments, observed earnings more closely approximate the 'net' than the 'gross' concept.
4. It appears from 1960 US data on college students that, on the average, student earnings plus scholarship roughly paid for tuition. Even if true on the average, this assumption is worth relaxing when data are available, as has been done in the recent work by Solmon (1973); Wachtel (1973); Johnson and Stafford (1973); and Leibowitz (1974). The correction for quality requires relaxing the assumption that $k_i = 1$ during school years. This requires expenditure data that differ among schools for the numerator of k_i. Of course, expenditure data do not fully capture quality, particularly in the public school system. Still, accounting for variation in expenditures among schools was significant in the empirical analyses in the references cited above. See the section on school quality.
5. The procedure derives from an idea suggested by E. A. Hanushek and J. M. Quigley (1976).
6. This approach is spelled out in Becker (1967).
7. Direct effects in consumption and on property income via gifts and bequests are, of course, observable.

References

Becker, G. S. (1967), *Human Capital and the Personal Distribution of Income*, Ann Arbor, University of Michigan.

Becker, G. S. (1975), *Human Capital*, 2nd edn, New York: National Bureau of Economic Research (NBER).

Becker, G. S. and N. Tomes (1976), 'Child Endowments and the Quantity and Quality of Children', *Journal of Political Economy*, vol. 84, no. 4, pp. S143–S162.

Ben-Porath, Y. (1967), 'The Production of Human Capital and the Life-cycle of Earnings', *Journal of Political Economy*, vol. 75, no. 4, pp. 352–65.

Blau, P. M. and O. D. Duncan (1967), *The American Occupational Structure*, New York: John Wiley.

Bowman, M. J. (1976), 'Through Education to Earnings?', *Proceedings of the National Academy of Education*, vol. 3, pp. 221–92.

Chamberlain, G. and Z. Griliches (1975), 'Ability, Schooling and the Economic Success of Brothers', *International Economic Review*, vol. 16, no. 2, pp. 422–50.

Chiswick, B. R. (1974), *Income Inequality*, New York: NBER.

Chiswick, B. R. (1976), *The Americanization of Earnings*, unpublished manuscript.

Chiswick, B. R. and J. Mincer (1972), 'Time Series in Personal Income Inequality in the U.S. since 1939', *Journal of Political Economy*, vol. 80, no. 3, part 2, S34–S66.

Coleman, J. S., E. Q. Campbell, C. J. Hobson, J. Mc Partland, A. M. Mood, F. D. Weinfeld and R. L. York (1966), *Equality of Educational Opportunity*, Washington, D.C.: US Department of Health, Education, and Welfare, Government Printing Office.

Corcoran, M., C. Jencks and M. Olneck (1976), 'The Effects of Family Background on Earnings', *American Economic Review, Proceedings*, vol. 66, no. 2, pp. 430–35.

Denison, E. F. (1962), *Sources of Economic Growth in the U.S.*, New York: Committee for Economic Development.

Duncan, G. J. (1976), 'Earnings Function and Nonpecuniary Benefits', *Journal of Human Resources*, vol. 11, no. 4, pp. 462–83.

Freeman, R. B. (1976), *The Overeducated American*, New York: Academic Press.

Gintis, H. (1971), 'Education, Technology and Productivity', *American Economic Review, Proceedings*, vol. 61, no. 2, pp. 266–9.

Goldberger, A. S. (1976), *Twin Methods: A Skeptical View*, paper presented at the Conference of the Mathematical Social Science Board, May.

Griliches, Z. (1963), 'The Sources of Measured Productivity Growth', *Journal of Political Economy*, vol. 71, no. 4, pp. 331–6.

Griliches, Z. (1967), 'Production Functions in Manufacturing', in M. Brown (ed.), *Theory and Empirical Analysis of Production (Studies in Income and Wealth*, vol. 31), New York: Columbia University Press, for NBER.

Griliches, Z. (1976), 'Wages of Very Young Men', *Journal of Political Economy*, vol. 84, no. 4 part 2, pp. S69–S86.

Griliches, Z. (1977), 'Estimating the Returns to Schooling', *Econometrica*, vol. 45, no. 1, pp. 1–22.

Griliches, Z. and W. Mason (1972), 'Education, Income and Ability', *Journal of Political Economy*, vol. 80, no. 3, part 2, pp. S74–S103.

Hanoch, G. (1967), 'An Economic Analysis of Earnings and Schooling', *Journal of Human Resources*, vol. 2, no. 3, pp. 310–29.

Hansen, W. L. (1963), 'Total and Private Rates of Return to Investments in Education', *Journal of Political Economy*, vol. 71, no. 1, pp. 128–40.

Hanushek, E. and J. Quigley (1976), '*Explicit Tests of the Human Capital Model* (Working Paper 767), New Haven, Conn.: Yale University.

Hauser, R. and T. Daymont (1976), *Schooling, Ability and Earnings* (CDE Working Paper 76–19), Madison: University of Wisconsin.

Hauser, R. and W. Sewell. (1975), *Education, Occupation and Earnings*, New York: Academic Press.

Jencks, C. *et al.* (1972), *Inequality*, New York: Basic Books.

Johnson, G. E. and F. Stafford (1973), 'Social Returns to Quantity and Quality of Schooling', *Journal of Human Resources*, vol. 8, no. 2, pp. 139–55.

Leibowitz, A. (1974), 'Home Investments in Children', *Journal of Political Economy*, vol. 82, no. 2, part 2, pp. S111–S131.

Mincer, J. (1962), 'Labor Force Participation of Married Women', in *Aspects of Labor Economics*, Princeton: Princeton University Press, for NBER. (Chapter 1 of Volume 2.)

Mincer, J. (1970), 'The Distribution of Labor Incomes: a Survey', *Journal of Economic Literature*, vol. 8, no.1, pp. 1–26. (Chapter 2 of this volume.)

Mincer, J. (1974), *Schooling, Experience and Earnings*, New York: Columbia University Press, for NBER.

Mincer, J. and S. Polachek (1974), 'Earnings of Women', *Journal of Political Economy*, vol. 82, no. 2, part 2, pp. S76–S108.

Schultz, T. W. (1975), 'The Value of the Ability to Deal with Disequilibria', *Journal of Economic Literature*, vol. 13, no. 3, pp. 827–46.

Solmon, L. (1973), 'Schooling and Subsequent Success', in L. Solmon and P. Taubman (eds), *Does college matter?*, New York: Academic Press.

Solmon, L. and P. Taubman (eds) (1973), *Does College Matter?*, New York: Academic Press.

Spence, M. (1974), *Market Signalling*, Cambridge, Mass.: Harvard University Press.

Taubman, P. (1976a), *Sources of Income Inequality*, New York: North Holland.

Taubman, P. (1976b), 'The Determinants of Earnings: Genetics, Family and Other Environments', *American Economic Review*, vol. 66, pp. 858–70.

Wachtel, P. (1974), *The Effect of School Quality on Achievement, Attainment and Earnings*, New York: New York University.

Wachtel, P. (1975), 'The Returns to Investment in Education: another view', in F. T. Juster (ed.), *Education, Income, and Human Behavior*, New York: McGraw-Hill.

Welch, F. (1970), 'Education in Production', *Journal of Political Economy*, vol. 78, no. 1, pp. 35–59.

Welch, F. (1974), 'Relationships between Income and Schooling', *Review of Research in Education*, vol. 2, pp. 179–201.

Wise, D. (1975), 'Academic Achievement and Job Performance', *American Economic Review*, vol. 65, no. 3, pp. 350–66.

PART II

HUMAN CAPITAL WAGE GROWTH, LABOUR TURNOVER, AND UNEMPLOYMENT

4 On-the-job training: costs, returns, and some implications*

Introduction

In the context of the economist's concern with education as a process of investment in manpower, it is important to be reminded that formal school instruction is neither an exclusive nor a sufficient method of training the labor force. Graduation from some level of schooling does not signify the completion of a training process. It is usually the end of a more general and preparatory stage, and the beginning of a more specialized and often prolonged process of acquisition of occupational skill, after entry into the labor force. This second stage, training on the job, ranges from formally organized activities such as apprenticeships and other training programs[1] to the informal processes of learning from experience. Indeed, historically, skills have been acquired mainly by experience on the job. The vast schooling system and the delayed entry into the labor force are distinctly modern phenomena.

As history suggests, it is useful to view the two broad classes of training not only as a sequence of stages but also as alternatives or substitutes. In many cases, the same degree of occupational skill can be achieved by 'shortening' formal schooling and 'lengthening' on-the-job training or by the reverse. The degree of substitutability between the two will, of course, vary among jobs and over time with changes in technology.

When training is viewed as a process of capital formation in people, three major empirical questions may be raised for economic analysis: (a) How large is the allocation of resources to the training process? (b) What is the rate of return on this form of investment? (c) How useful is knowledge about such investments in explaining particular features of labor-force behaviour?

Recently flourishing research in these areas provides some tentative answers.[2] T. W. Schultz estimated the amount and growth of resources devoted by the economy to formal education. G. S. Becker estimated the rate of return to training at higher levels of education. In his National Bureau of Economic Research (NBER) study, now in progress, Becker outlines the capital-theoretical approach to investment in people and shows it to be a tool of great analytical power and of extensive empirical relevance.

*This chapter was first published in the *Journal of Political Economy*, vol. 70 (1962), part 2, pp. 50–79.

My first task in this paper is to estimate the amount of investment in on-the-job training. The estimates are indirect, and the concept of on-the-job training rather broad, but I am hopeful that results are at least suggestive of the orders of magnitude involved. The estimates and a discussion of their limitations are given in the first section of the paper. In the second section I attempt to estimate rates of return on some particular forms of on-the-job training, such as apprenticeships and medical specialization. The results are then compared with the rates of return on investment which includes both components: formal education and on-the-job training. In consequence, some tentative inferences are formulated about the separate components. In the final section of the paper I consider some preliminary empirical implications of my results. In particular, differentials in on-the-job training are related to income and employment differentials among population subgroups, classified by levels of education, occupation, sex, and race. The observed behaviour patterns seem largely consistent with the investment hypothesis underlying this study, though it was not possible in this preliminary empirical exploration to control for all other important factors at play.

1. Estimates of costs of on-the-job training

For the purpose of this paper, the term 'training' denotes investment in acquisition of skill or in improvement of worker productivity. The concept, therefore, includes schooling and training obtained on the job. The latter, under this definition, is a much broader concept than what is conveyed by the common usage of the word 'on-the-job training'. It includes formal and informal training programs in a job situation, as well as what is called 'learning from experience'.

The method of estimating the volume of investment in on-the-job training, which is described in this section, treats 'learning from experience' as an investment in the same sense as are the more obvious forms of on-the-job training, such as, say, apprenticeship programs. Put in simple terms, an individual takes a job with an initially lower pay than he could otherwise get because he knows that he will benefit from the experience gained in the job taken.[3] In this sense, the opportunity to learn from experience involves an investment cost which is captured in the estimation method.

While data are much more scarce and the arithmetic is more arduous, calculation of on-the-job training costs is guided by the same theoretical principles[4] as the calculation of schooling costs. Costs of schooling consist of direct outlays (private tuition and public support), and of indirect, 'invisible' opportunity costs, such as forgone earnings of students resulting from the necessary reduction of their labor-force activities while at

school. Once the direct outlays are known, it is possible to infer the costs
of an increment of schooling from comparative data on earnings of two
sets of individuals: students, and people similar to them with respect to
previous educational attainment, age, sex, ability, except that they are
'economically active' in the labor force and do not engage in additional
schooling. In empirical work these conditions are approximated as well as
data permit.

According to the available calculations,[5] forgone earnings constitute
over half of total costs of schooling and about 75 per cent of the costs
borne by students. Forgone earnings bulk even more in the costs borne by
trainees on the job. Indeed, nowadays it is difficult to think of any
important direct payments by trainees, though in the past it was not
uncommon for apprentices to pay their masters for the training. This does
not mean, however, that no direct outlays are incurred in the training of
workers on the job. Firms do spend sizable sums to finance apprenticeships and other training programs: equipment must be purchased and
instructors paid. These sums presumably appear in accounts of firms as
costs of training workers, though such data are rarely available.

Should all or a part of *firm outlays* be added to the sum of *forgone
earnings of workers* to arrive at a total figure of costs of on-the-job
training, indirect and direct? The answer is no, if *all* of the firm outlays are
currently charged to the worker in the form of a reduction in wages. In this
case the worker buys training services from the firm. The cost of the
purchase is simply part of his forgone earnings – the other part being the
difference between the actual marginal product of the trainee and the
larger amount he could produce if he did not engage in training. Adding
firm outlays in this case would constitute double counting.

It is likely, however, that some fraction of firm outlays is not charged
currently to the workers but recouped by the firm at a later date.[6] The part
of firm outlays which is not matched by current reductions in wages of
trainees should be added to forgone earnings of workers. Unfortunately, it
is impossible to estimate how large a fraction of firm outlays are costs
borne by the firm. Worse yet, data on costs of training (whether borne by
firms or workers) are not only scarce but, in principle, highly unreliable.
Such items as loss of production by experienced workers who are helping
the trainees or wear and tear of equipment do not show up in any entry as
direct costs of training. Rather, they are likely to be hidden in the wage
and depreciation costs. Even if all costs of training were borne by firms, so
that they would also pay all the foregone earnings of workers, only a
fraction of costs would be revealed by accounting data. I conclude that an
attempt to gauge costs of on-the-job training in the economy by account-

ing data of firms, even if they were made available, would lead to severe underestimates.

On the other hand, working with earnings data of workers to estimate their forgone earnings also leads to an underestimate, to the extent that some training costs are borne by firms. The calculation reported below is an estimate of forgone earnings of workers, using Census income data rather than firm accounting data. At least, in terms of population coverage, this is a complete calculation of what probably is the more important component of on-the-job training costs. The alternative procedure, of using firm data, is practically ruled out because of the meager supply of information, aside from the serious conceptual inadequacies. However, some attempt is made to supplement the estimates obtained from workers' income data with fragmentary estimates of firm costs.

A direct computation of forgone earnings of workers engaged in on-the-job training would be possible if data were available on their earnings during and after the period of training, and on earnings of a comparison group of workers who have the same amount of formal schooling and are otherwise similar to the trainees, but do not receive any on-the-job training. Presumably, the latter would have a flatter age–earnings profile than the former. That is, trainees would initially receive lower earnings than those not training, the difference representing costs of training. At a later age, earnings of trainees would rise above earnings of the untrained, the difference constituting a return on the investment. Unfortunately, it is impossible to classify workers empirically into such comparison groups.[7] Given the group, say, of all male college graduates, there is no readily available statistic which would provide information on differential amounts of on-the-job training received by subgroups, and no income data are provided by such subclassifications. Even the fragmentary information on apprenticeships does not satisfy these requirements.

Fortunately, an alternative procedure based on Becker's theoretical analysis of investment in people[8] permits utilization of the comprehensive income data available in the United States Censuses. The procedure consists of a comparison of two average income streams of workers differing by levels of schooling, such as male college graduates and high-school graduates.

Taking this comparison as an example, the procedure involves year-by-year estimation of training costs which a high-school graduate must incur in order to acquire a college education and the additional amount of training on the job which is, on the average, characteristic of college graduates. Such estimates are obtained on the assumption that the rate of return is the same on each year's investment whether at school or on the job.[9] In any given year *j* after high-school graduation, those who go on to, or have graduated from, college would have earnings (Y_j) which equal the earnings of high-school graduates (X_j) plus the income earned on differential investment in training made since graduation from high school, *provided no further investment in training was incurred by them during the year j*. Costs of (incremental) training in year *j* are, therefore, measured by the difference between Y_j and X_j augmented by the (forgone) return on the previous (incremental) costs.

The procedure and the basic data utilized in it are shown in detail in the Appendix. The first step in the procedure is to compute the rate of return (r) on the investment in training by which the two groups differ. This is done by equating the sum of discounted earnings differences to zero, after direct schooling outlays are netted out of earnings.

Once the rate of return is obtained, the comparison of net earnings streams Y_j and X_j permits the following step-by-step calculation of training costs: let $j = 1$ denote the first year of additional training. Then training costs in year 1 are $C_1 = X_1 - Y_1$, the observed income differential. In year 2 the costs are $C_2 = (X_2 + ra_1C_1) - Y_2$, the observed income differential, augmented by the (forgone) return on previous costs.[10] Proceeding sequentially, training costs in any year *j* are

$$C_j = X_j + (r \sum_{i=1}^{j-1} a_i C_i) - Y_j. \tag{4.1}$$

$$\alpha_i = \frac{1}{1 - (1/1 + r)^{n-i}},$$

α is a correction factor for finite life,[11] n is the length of the working life.

Figures in Table 4.1 were computed in this fashion and cumulated over the working life. They constitute estimates of training costs: these are schooling costs before entry into the labor force and opportunity costs of on-the-job training afterward. The cumulation of annual costs over the working life stops at about 15 to 20 years after entry into the labor force, since the computed training costs decline with age after labor-force entry and become negligible, fluctuating around zero, around age 40 (see cols (4), (5), and (6) in Appendix Tables A4.5–A4.7). The decline of training with age is consistent with *a priori* expectations about investment behavior: younger people have a greater incentive to invest in themselves than older ones, because they can collect the returns for a longer time.[12]

The age–earnings profiles which are the basic data used in deriving estimates of training costs are presented in Appendix Tables A4.1–A4.4. These are before-tax incomes of United States males (wage and salary in 1939, income in 1949 and 1958), classified by age and education, and

Table 4.1 Lifetime investment in training per capita at school and on-the-job, United States males, 1939, 1949, 1958, by level of schooling (in thousands)

Educational level	Current dollars						1954 dollars*					
	Marginal cost			Total cost			Marginal cost			Total cost		
	School (1)	On-the-job (2)	Sum (3)	School (4)	On-the-job (5)	Sum (6)	School (1)	On-the-job (2)	Sum (3)	School (4)	On-the-job (5)	Sum (6)
1939												
College	4.9	3.5	8.4	7.7	7.9	15.6	9.4	6.7	16.2	14.7	15.2	29.9
High school	2.0	2.4	4.4	2.8	4.4	7.2	3.9	4.6	8.5	5.2	8.5	13.7
Elementary school	0.8	2.0	2.8	0.8	2.0	2.8	1.3	3.9	5.2	1.3	3.9	5.2
1949												
College	10.2	15.7	25.9	15.9	24.3	40.2	11.5	17.7	29.3	18.0	27.4	45.4
High school	4.1	4.7	8.8	5.7	8.6	14.2	4.6	5.3	9.9	6.4	9.7	16.0
Elementary school	1.6	3.9	5.5	1.6	3.9	5.5	1.8	4.4	6.2	1.8	4.4	6.2
1958												
College	16.4	22.5	38.9	26.0	30.7	56.7	15.3	21.2	36.5	24.1	28.8	52.9
High school	7.1	2.9	10.0	9.5	8.2	17.7	6.6	2.7	9.3	8.8	7.6	16.4
Elementary school	2.4	5.3	7.7	2.4	5.3	7.7	2.2	4.9	7.1	2.2	4.9	7.1

Source: Appendix Tables A4.1–A4.7.
*Deflated by the Bureau of Labor Statistics' Consumer Price Index.

adjusted to approximate the relevant concepts. The adjustments involve netting out direct school costs and corrections for part-time employment of students during the period of school attendance. For these purposes, and in order to separate school and on-the-job training costs, the assumption was made that people with none up to eight years of schooling enter the labor force at age 14 and have no forgone earnings while at school; high-school graduates enter the labor force at age 18, and their forgone earnings during high-school attendance are obtainable by comparison with incomes of elementary-school graduates of the same age; college students graduate at ages 22 to 23, and estimates of relevant income differentials are constructed in a similar way.

For each date and education group, year-by-year estimates of marginal costs of training were calculated by equation (4.1). An illustrative calculation is shown in Appendix Table A4.4. Detailed annual figures are shown in Tables A4.5–A4.7, columns (1), (2), and (3). The annual estimates of marginal costs are then cumulated horizontally in columns (4), (5), and (6) of Tables A4.5–A4.7, to obtain annual total costs of schooling and of on-the-job training. Summing the figures in each column yields, separately, lifetime total costs of schooling and of on-the-job training typical of groups with given levels of schooling per person. The results are presented in Table 4.1.

In reading this table it is important to distinguish between the 'marginal' and 'total' figures. The costs of attending high school, shown as marginal costs of high-school education, do not measure the total costs of schooling of the individual up to and including high school. For this purpose the costs of high-school attendance must be added to the costs of elementary-school attendance. Similarly, the costs of on-the-job training of a high-school graduate as obtained by equation (4.1) are *additional* costs over and above the costs of on-the-job training incurred by elementary-school graduates. These marginal costs (col. (2) in Table 4.1) are first differences of the total costs of on-the-job training for graduates of any particular level of schooling, shown in column (5) of Table 4.1.

The estimates of on-the-job training costs in Table 4.1 are per capita magnitudes approximating the sum of resources the average male of a given educational level may be expected to invest in training on the job during his working life. Estimates of the aggregate investment by male workers in the economy during a given year are shown in Table 4.2. They are obtained by multiplying the year-by-year costs of training, as shown in Tables A4.5–A4.7 (cols. (4), (5), and (6)), by the number of workers[13] (student enrolment during the period of schooling) in the corresponding age and educational group (cols. (7), (8), and (9)). The cross-products are

Table 4.2   Aggregate annual investment in training at school and on-the-job, United States males, 1939, 1949, 1958, by level of schooling (in $ billions)

Education level	1939			1949			1958		
	School	Job	Total	School	Job	Total	School	Job	Total
				Current dollars					
College	1.1	1.0	2.1	3.8	4.3	8.1	8.7	8.7	17.4
High school	1.8	1.4	3.2	3.4	3.8	7.2	8.4	3.8	12.2
Elementary	0.9	0.6	1.5	2.1	0.9	3.0	4.5	1.0	5.5
All levels	3.8	3.0	6.8	9.3	9.0	18.3	21.6	13.5	35.1
				1954 Dollars					
College	2.1	1.9	4.0	4.3	4.7	9.0	8.1	8.1	16.2
High school	3.5	2.7	6.2	3.8	4.2	8.0	7.8	3.5	11.3
Elementary	1.9	1.1	2.8	2.4	1.0	3.4	4.2	0.9	5.1
All levels	7.3	5.7	13.0	10.5	9.9	20.4	20.1	12.5	32.6

Source: Appendix Tables A4.1–A4.7.

then summed to obtain aggregate costs corresponding to the total cost classifications in Table 4.1, columns (3), (4), and (5).

In contrast to Tables 4.1, Table 4.2 represents actual opportunity costs in the economy, not expectations of individuals. The relative sizes of the two components of training costs, formal and on the job, are also different in the two tables. This is because the aggregative estimates in Table 4.2 depend on the age distribution of workers with given levels of educational attainment. Secular trends in population size and in educational attainments affect the relevant age distributions in a way which makes the aggregative on-the-job training costs somewhat smaller in relation to school costs than is true on the per capita basis.

Before proceeding to discussion and interpretation of the findings one must raise questions about their validity and reliability. A number of possible sources of bias are easily identified. First, the estimates of per capita training costs (Table 4.1) are based on cross-section income profiles. They, therefore, may approximate expectations of an average male of a given educational level, provided the differences between his earnings and earnings of males at the next lower educational level will change year after year in the future, precisely the way they do change in the cross-sectional comparison from one cohort to the next, one year older. If secular trends are expected to tilt both income streams upward by the same percentage, the returns (income differentials at a later stage of life) are likely to increase somewhat, with income differentials at an early stage largely unaffected. On this assumption, the procedure involves a small underestimate of the rate of return since differentials later in life are heavily discounted. In turn, this implies an understatement of costs, to the extent that costs are, in part, a positive function of the discount rate (equation (4.1)).

Another bias is introduced by using the cross-sectional patterns as approximations for the true earnings streams. This is the misreporting of years of schooling by Census respondents. According to Denison, the older the group in an education class, the larger the fraction of persons reporting a level of education higher than the one they reported at the previous Census.[14] This means that observed cross-sectional age–income profiles are biased downward at older ages in all educational groups except the lowest. The failure to tilt the income streams upward leads, as before, to an understatement of costs, mainly at the upper levels of education.

For another reason, costs were underestimated also at the lower levels of education. I compared the earnings stream of elementary-school graduates with that of persons with one to four years of schooling rather than with persons with zero schooling. The group with no schooling is small, and its composition so different from that of the other groups (it is heavily weighted with farm workers, single persons, and non-whites) that its age–earnings profile could not serve as a bench mark. To the extent that persons with zero to four years of schooling undergo some on-the-job training, which is undoubtedly true, the costs of such training have been omitted from my estimates.

An opposite bias is imparted by omission of the survival factors, as mentioned previously (n. 12). Lack of adjustment for mortality, for example, means that earnings differentials at later ages are overstated. Costs are therefore *overestimated*, because the rate of return is overestimated, though by a small amount.

The 1949 and 1958 income figures include property income in addition to labor income, and this too tends to widen differentials between profiles noticeably at later ages. This is because of a positive correlation of property income with age and with education. The result is a slight overestimate of costs by an overestimate of the rate of return.

A more serious question is posed by the assumption that differences in income streams of the groups compared are attributable to differences in training. Such an assumption disregards other factors which may affect shapes and levels of age profiles. Biases will arise if these other factors are not independent of the classificatory criteria: for example, the higher the years of schooling and the higher the age, the lower the fraction of males who are non-white. Farmers and farm laborers are disproportionately distributed in the low years of schooling and low age classes. Restriction of estimates to non-farm whites (as in 1939) avoids the distortions, but such data were not available for all the periods. It is clear, however, that, even in data which are quite homogeneous by Census criteria, certain selective or restrictive factors are not neutral with respect to the educational classification: people who undertake more training are likely to have higher intelligence quotients, higher parental income and education, more motivation and information.

The extent to which earnings of more-trained persons exceed earnings of less-trained persons is, therefore, an *overestimate* of the return on training. Part of the observed return is a return to these 'ability' factors. But, for the same reasons, the observed data are likely to underestimate the costs incurred: if more capable high-school students enter college, their forgone earnings are probably underestimated by the observed earnings of the less-capable high-school graduates who did not go on to college. It is difficult to say, *a priori*, how large such biases may be. But, if a correction for the 'ability' factor involves a decrease in return and a simultaneous increase in cost via income differentials, it is clear that the relative decline in the rate of return must be larger than the relative increase in costs.[15]

According to Becker, an adjustment for class standing of high-school graduates brings the rate of return down by about 15 per cent. If costs are underestimated, this figure measures the maximum amount of bias, when the dimension of ability which is measured by class standing is taken into account. Other factors may account for more.

Once again, the bias need not be in one direction. To the extent that the restrictive factors under discussion affect returns (earnings differentials after the training period) *without* affecting income differentials during the training period, the rate of return *and* costs are overestimated. This is because costs, as we computed them, are in part a positive function of the rate of return.

Possibly the largest source of downward bias in the estimation of costs was already mentioned: the omission of costs of training which are borne by firms. These costs do not show up in the income data at all. As a simple example, take the case of a firm which pays half the costs of training, the other half being paid by the worker. Later on, the firm captures half of the returns. Rates of return are not affected, and forgone earnings of workers are cut in half.

It is not possible to arrive at an overall notion of the direction of bias without knowing more about the magnitudes of each possible error. But, if there is some reason to believe that totals are underestimated, there are reasons to believe that the distortion is weaker when it comes to relative sizes of subtotals in the classifications of Tables 4.1 and 4.2. If ability factors bias costs in the comparison of college and high school, they have similar effects in the high school and elementary school.

The striking finding in Table 4.1 is that the opportunity costs of on-the-job training per male are almost without exception somewhat higher than costs of a comparable increment of schooling. But while per capita amounts of formal schooling (as measured by costs in constant dollars) grew between 1939 and 1958 at all levels, the corresponding quantities of on-the-job training per capita grew mainly at the higher educational levels.

On an aggregative basis (Table 4.2) on-the-job training costs were a little smaller than schooling costs in 1939 and grew at a slower rate than the former. Formal education expenditures grew rapidly at all levels during the 1939–58 period. On-the-job training expenditures grew just as fast as schooling at the highest educational level, increased before 1949 and decreased afterward at the high-school level, and continuously declined at the elementary-school level. The per capita figures (Table 4.1) indicate, however, that the decline in aggregate on-the-job training for the elementary-school class was not a result of a decline in costs per head but a decline in the number of heads. Similarly, the increase in on-the-job costs in the aggregate for the college class also consisted mainly in an increase in the number of heads rather than in training costs per head, particularly in the second decade.

One feature of the findings in Table 4.1 is worthy of closer attention: on-the-job training is a larger quantity the higher the level of education. This is not a truism as in the case of schooling, where the marginal quantities of schooling are positive by definition. There is nothing in the calculation of on-the-job training costs that would make the marginal quantities necessarily positive. In other words, the positive association between school training and on-the-job training is not definitional; it is an empirical inference from the observed income data. More training seems to involve more of both forms of training, though not in any fixed proportion. This is reasonable: school education is a prerequisite, a basis on which to build the further, more specialized training.

Some independent evidence on this positive association is provided by recent Department of Labor estimates of amounts of school and on-the-job training, both measured in school-grade equivalents, required for the acquisition of occupational skill in 4000 detailed occupations.[16] From the 4000 occupations listed in the publication, a sample of 158 occupations was selected on the basis of comparability with the 1950 Census occupational breakdown. The two measures of school and on-the-job training requirements given in rank form were correlated with coefficient +0.86.

The positive association between schooling and on-the-job training helps in understanding trends. It suggests that an expansion of education is likely to bring about an expansion of on-the-job training, a development indicated in Tables 4.1 and 4.2. To the extent that an expansion of education is induced by a decrease in its price relative to the price of on-the-job training, some substitution will take place, and education may grow at the expense of on-the-job training. Such factors, among others, may underlie the slower growth of on-the-job training than of schooling. More precisely, the data suggest slow or no growth of on-the-job training at the lower educational levels and pronounced growth at upper educational levels. This finding supports popular impressions about the changing levels of on-the-job training: a shift from apprenticeships to technicians, scientific personnel, and executive development programs. Such shifts may, in the aggregate, reflect the upward trend in supplies of labor with high levels of educational attainment and possibly some substitution phenomena at the lower levels. The questions about trends are very intriguing, but the data do not lend themselves to more than conjectures.

Turning to bodies of data other than the comprehensive income statistics, I tried to exploit them, though not very intensively, for two purposes: (a) to provide some empirical checks on the reliability of estimates based on forgone incomes of workers; (b) to form some guesses about firm costs or outlays.

(a)   On the basis of the Bureau of Labour Statistics (BLS) publication on skill requirements for 4000 occupations, Eckaus estimated the average number of college-equivalent years of on-the-job training imbedded in the labor force (including females).[17] The estimate was 1.66 and 1.72 for 1939 and 1949, respectively. But these are average quantities for the whole age distribution, figures representing a stock. We are interested in the flow of current investment in on-the-job training, and this is incurred mainly by the younger age groups. These groups have higher education levels than the labor force as a whole and are, therefore, likely to invest more also in on-the-job training. In 1949 the age group 18–29 had a median schooling of 12 years compared to a labor force median of 10 years. The discrepancy between means was even greater. Since the investment in on-the-job training is higher at higher educational levels, an upward adjustment is required. Using the ratio of medians to revise Eckaus' estimates upward, roughly in proportion, yields 1.99 and 2.06 years for 1939 and 1949 respectively.

In terms of equivalent college costs per year, 2.06 years of training would cost about $6000 per member of the labor force in 1950, according to Table 4.1. The average female invests in on-the-job training about one-tenth as much as the average male,[18] and the number of females was slightly over a third of the total labor force in the age group 18–29. Hence, the implicit cost (C) of on-the-job training incurred per male in 1949 is:

$$\$5200 = \frac{2}{3}C + \frac{1}{30}C$$

$$C = \$7500.$$

This compares with our estimates of $8600 costs of on-the-job training of male high-school graduates (Table 4.1, col. (5)), the modal group in the population. A similar calculation for 1939 yields about $3600 to be compared with our estimate $4400. Elements of subjectivity in the BLS-derived figures make the comparison difficult, but the fact that the two sets of estimates are not very far apart is encouraging.

Another piece of supplementary evidence is provided by data on the distribution of federal expenditures on the GI Bill for 1945–55. The expenditures and their distribution are given in Table 4.3. In columns (3) and (5) we compare the percentage distributions of expenditures: costs of college training of veterans during the ten-year period are compared with

Table 4.3   GI Bill expenditures, by level and type of training, 1945–55

Level of training	No of veterans (millions)	GI Bill Expenditures		All males, aggregates for 1949	
		$ Billions	Per cent	$ Billions	Per cent
	(1)	(2)	(3)	(4)	(5)
College	2.2	5.5	38.1	4.5	40.8
High school	1.4	2.2	15.3	3.3	30.0
Trade school	2.1	3.3	23.1		
On the job	2.1	3.5	24.5	3.2	29.2
Total	7.8	14.5	100.0	11.0	100.0

Source: Cols (1) and (2), President's Commission on Veterans' Pensions, *Readjustment Benefits, Staff Report* No. IX, Part B, Washington, D.C.: Government Printing Office, 12 September 1956, pp. 22–4, 30–2.

costs of college of all males in 1949; a similar comparison of veterans' costs is made with marginal costs of high school, and with total costs of on-the-job training of high-school graduates. The distributions (col. (3) and col. (5)) look reasonably comparable. The greater selectivity of veterans toward college and vocational training (trade schools and on the job) in comparison to all males is understandable in view of differences in age and in educational backgrounds already acquired.

(b)   Several recent surveys of training activities in firms have shown that such functions are carried by many firms.[19] Of course, only formally arranged programs are described in such surveys. Unfortunately, questions about costs are seldom raised in these surveys. Undoubtedly, it would be difficult to interpret the financial data, even if they were forthcoming. In only one of the recent studies were such questions asked, with these results:

> Although questions were asked concerning total expenditures for in-company education, few firms replied – perhaps the chief reason was that often the books of the firm were not kept in a manner that would make it easy to separate educational costs from other costs. Other reasons centered around questions of allocation and items to be considered as costs – the data reported are not comparable, since some of the figures include salaries and some exclude them. It is not certain that the figures reported include all in-company programs. In one case it was specifically stated that the figure reported was for one program.[20]

If the scant financial replies shown in this survey are blown up to an aggregate, the result is an estimate below $1 billion for 1957, undoubtedly a severe underestimate of even those current firm outlays which are easily identifiable. Smaller case studies indicate that firm expenditures on formal training programs must be much larger: estimates range from $85 for an operative in training[21] to over $10,000 for an executive training program.[22] According to the recent comprehensive survey of New Jersey industries made by the Bureau of Apprenticeship and Training,[23] the proportion of workers participating in formal training programs in 1959 was about 5 per cent. Of these 20 per cent enrolled in management development programs, 10 per cent in apprenticeships, 10 per cent in technical (semi-professional) training, 12 per cent in sales training, and the rest in short programs of operative training, orientation, safety, etc. Applying almost any vaguely reasonable dollar figures – from $85 per operative to a conservative $2000 per executive trainee per annum, and projecting to the aggregate labor force in recent years, yields an estimate of $2–3 billion. But this, of course, misses all costs incurred in informal training, which is the typical situation: only 16.2 per cent of firms in New Jersey had *formal* training programs.

One estimate which takes into account 'invisible' costs of firms, including costs in informal training processes, can be obtained using figures shown in a recent study of California firms by the American Management Association.[24] In this study estimates were made of costs of labor turnover to the firm. The concept of replacement cost includes hiring costs such as advertising, recruitment, interviews, and separation costs; on-the-job training costs are defined more comprehensively as 'the expense brought about by sub-standard production of new employees while learning their job assignments and becoming adjusted to their work environment; the dollar value of time spent by supervisors and other employees who assist in breaking in new employees on their job assignment, and costs of organized training programs'.[25] These training costs per worker replacement were estimated at about $230. If hiring and separation costs are included the figure doubles. Multiplying these costs of a replacement by the total number of replacements in industry in 1958[26] yields an estimate of $7 billion. Inclusion of hiring and separation costs raises the estimate to $14 billion. The assumption that all of these costs are borne by the firms is, of course, highly questionable. How much is shifted back to the trainee in the form of a wage reduction is not known. At the same time, a large part of the opportunity cost of workers – the difference between what they did produce while in training and what they could produce if they did not train – is also missed in these figures.

All these heroic attempts to estimate firm costs add up to an uncomfortable range of uncertainty when it comes to answering the question: how much of firm costs should be added to the estimates of forgone incomes of workers? It is possible that billions of dollars are involved, but it is not clear how many.

Besides firm costs two more items must be added to our estimates in Table 4.2 to get total costs of on-the-job training in the economy: training costs incurred by women and training expenditures in the Armed Forces. The latter are estimated at $1.6 billion[27] in 1959, and the former at $1.4 billion[28] in 1958. According to Table 4.2, aggregate opportunity costs of male workers were about $13.5 billion in 1958. Addition of the two items brings the figure up to $16.5 billion, more than half of the aggregate costs of schooling (males and females) in 1956.[29] The addition of possibly several billion dollars of costs borne by firms narrows the difference but may not close it. Since most of the on-the-job training costs are incurred by and spent on male workers, it is probably correct to say that, in the male half of the world, on-the-job training – measured in dollar costs – is as important as formal schooling.

2.   Estimates of rates of return

An estimate of rates of return to on-the-job training is both desirable and difficult to obtain. The rate of return computed by equating the present values of net earnings of two education groups should not be interpreted as a rate of return on schooling costs. The computed rate is some average of rates of return to schooling and to on-the-job training. The hybrid rate depends on the weights (costs) of the two training components and on the rates on each component.[30] If the rate on one component is known, the other can be approximated in a residual fashion. What is immediately important, the larger the difference between the rates of return on investment in schooling and in on-the-job training, the less accurate are the cost estimates in the preceding section, as well as the various recent estimates of rates of return on (school) education. If the rate of return on schooling exceeds the rate on on-the-job training, the estimates are on the low side.

It is not obvious, on *a priori* grounds, whether the money rate of return to on-the-job training is likely to be smaller or larger than the rate on formal education. It could be argued that non-pecuniary, 'consumption' elements may be a more important part of the real return to formal education than to on-the-job training. If so, and if this were the only difference, the money rate of return on schooling would appear smaller than the rate to on-the-job training. Larger public subsidies to formal education would also have this effect, if returns are computed on total costs (private and public). These arguments are based on an assumption of

Table 4.4 Rates of return on apprenticeship training, selected trades, 1949

| Trades | Assumptions about alternative income streams | | |
| | Operatives in same industries | Operatives with highest schooling | Assuming a 10 per cent return on additional schooling |
	(1)	(2)	(3)
Metal	16.4	10.4	9.5
Printing	16.0	12.6	9.0
Building	18.3	11.3	9.7

Source: Table A4.8.

equality of the real (pecuniary and non-pecuniary) private rate of return in both training sectors.

One could argue, however, that larger impediments to a flow of investment into formal education make for higher rates of return to schooling than to on-the-job training. Income constraints are less severe in the latter case as costs are more spread out over time. Perhaps more important is that this investment is undertaken at a later age and in the context of a concrete, existing work situation: there is much less uncertainty about future prospects, about one's own abilities and motivations, etc. These circumstances tend to produce a lower *real* rate of return to on-the-job training and may well reduce the *money* rate on it to a lower level than the money rate on formal education.

There are no comprehensive data comparable to the Census classifications by formal education level from which to compute rates to on-the-job training. The rates shown in Table 4.4 were estimated for a few selected skills for which tolerably good data are available. These refer to apprenticeship training in the several industries in which they are concentrated. All estimates are for 1949.

The rates of return on apprenticeship training were computed in three different ways providing a range of estimates, from the highest values in column (1) to the lowest in column (3) of Table 4.4. However, the lowest values (col. (3)) are conceptually the soundest. The computations involve equating to zero the present value of differentials between earnings of workers who served an apprenticeship and earnings of their assumed alternative occupational groups. During the period of training the apprentice receives an average wage W_a after which he becomes a journeyman receiving an average wage W_m. A suitable alternative occupation,[31] where almost no training is involved, is the operative, and his average wage is W_o. The annual wage differential $d = W_a - W_o$ is negative during the training period and positive afterward, $k = W_m - W_o$ assumed constant for the rest of the working life. Under these assumptions, and disregarding a negligible correction for the finiteness of working life, the rate of return (r) is easily obtainable from:[32]

$$(1 + r)^n = 1 + \frac{k}{d},$$

(4.2)

where n is the number of years of training, or length of the apprenticeship.

Estimates in column (1) of Table 4.4 are based on comparisons of earnings of apprentices, journeymen, and operatives *in the same industries*. While operatives and corresponding craftsmen had the same median schooling, the apprentices had two to three more years of schooling than the other two groups in 1949. Thus k, the difference between earnings of journeymen and operatives, is computed correctly, holding formal schooling the same. But forgone earnings of apprentices are underestimated: having more schooling than the operatives with whom they are compared, the apprentices could earn more in alternative jobs. With returns correct and costs underestimated, figures in column (1) are too high.

In column (2) this defect is corrected to a large extent. In the calculation, k is the same as before, but d was computed from a comparison of wages of apprentices with wages of operatives whose schooling levels are closer to levels of apprentices, regardless of industry attachment. As Table A4.8 shows, however, median schooling of these operatives is still about a year less than of apprentices, so rates may still be overestimated.

In column (3) the same k is used again, but the opportunity cost is computed by adding to d (as computed in col. (1)) a return on additional years of (high-school) education[34] by which apprentices exceed the operatives with whom they are compared in column (1). This brings the rates down to the levels shown in column (3).

The estimates probably suffer from several biases. Operatives have some on-the-job training, but so do craftsmen after completion of apprenticeships. If the additional training of the latter exceeds that of the former, the rates of return on apprenticeships are overestimated. On the other hand, abstraction from secular rates of growth, as in the general case,[35] may have the opposite effect. It is also possible that union restrictions on entry to apprenticeships resulted in higher returns in the several fields selected in Table 4.4 than in other kinds of on-the-job training.[36]

Table 4.5   Returns to 'Education' and to on-the-job training, 1950

| | Per cent | |
| | College level* | On-the-job training[†] |
	(1)	(2)
Total costs	11	9.0–12.7
Private costs before tax	14	
Private costs after tax	13	8.5–11.3

Source: G. S. Becker, 'Underinvestment in College Education?', *American Economic Review, Papers and Proceedings*, May 1960.
[†]Range based on columns (2) and (3) of Table 4.4, and on return to medical specialization.

For a comparison with another high level of skill, I computed rates of return on medical specialization, comparing incomes of residents and specialists (after residency) with incomes of general practitioners. The computation utilizes age–income profiles of independent medical specialists, starting with an initial period of residency, with the income profile of independent general practitioners, starting with the first year in practice. Estimates of income in money and kind of residents were obtained from American Medical Association sources;[36] earnings from 1950 Census sources.[37] The calculation on before-tax incomes showed a return of 12.7 per cent. A rough adjustment for taxes brought the rate down to 11.3 per cent. It is difficult to judge whether this is high or low in comparison with apprenticeships.[38]

Table 4.5 compares estimated rates of return on apprenticeships and on training at the college level.

Generalizing boldly, a comparison of columns (1) and (2) suggests that money rates of return (before tax) on *total costs* (public and private) are similar for school and on-the-job training. Figures in column (1) are weighted averages of returns on the two sectors; similarity of average and component means that rates on each component are alike. It does appear, however, that private rates of return are lower for the selected instances of on-the-job training than for total training at college levels. If the selected instances can be generalized, the rate of return on college education per se is somewhat underestimated by the figures in column (1). Apparently, the greater ease of investing in on-the-job training outweighs the possibly greater consumption elements in college education. Another intriguing implication is that the apparent, but not clearly documented, stability over time in the rates of return to training (both in school and on the job) may conceal a decline in the rate of return to formal education, given that investment in education seems to have grown faster than in on-the-job training, at least at the lower levels.

These conclusions are hazardous. The rates are not adjusted for ability factors. If there is a greater selectivity (based on ability) for admission into college, differences between adjusted rates in the two sectors may disappear, or reverse. But this is not at all obvious. More detailed data and intensive research are needed.

3.   On-the-job training as a factor in income and employment behavior

In the first section of this paper, the economic theory of investment in people was used to bring the very elusive process of on-the-job training under the measuring rod of money. In this section the theory will be used to produce additional measurements and to explain, in part, certain well-known but not well-understood patterns of income and employment in population subgroups. The empirical analyses sketched below are no more than preliminary, but perhaps they are sufficiently indicative.

A calculation of (marginal) on-the-job training costs per capita for female college graduates in 1949 provided two estimates: (a) $830, (b) $2160. The comparable figure for males was $15,700 (Table 4.1, col. (2)). The calculation is the same as the one underlying Table 4.1. It is based on a comparison of net earnings of college and high-school graduates, given in Table A4.9. Estimate (a) is based on earnings data adjusted for (multiplied by) labor-force rates of women in the various age groups (Table A4.9, cols (3) and (4)); estimate (b) is based on the unadjusted earnings (Table A4.9, cols (1) and (2)). The adjustment for participation rates assumes that the return on investment in training of women (at college and on the job) is obtainable only in the labor market. If it is believed that this investment in training results also in the same amount of productivity increase in the 'home industry', earnings should not be adjusted by labor-force rates. This certainly cannot be assumed of investments on the job, but may be true of schooling. The estimate (b) based on unadjusted earnings is, of course, larger. Both assumptions are extreme, and, in principle, provide limits for a correct estimate.[39]

While formal education costs are not much smaller for females than for males, investments in on-the-job training are very small, about one-tenth (taking a middle figure between the two estimates) of the amounts invested by males. The figures may not be highly reliable, but their smallness is quite reasonable, in the light of investment theory: the average female expects to spend less than half her working life in the labor force. In particular, she has a high probability of dropping out of the work force for prolonged periods of child-rearing soon after, and possibly during, the training period. It is clear that returns on prolonged on-the-job training would be small. Hence pecuniary incentives to invest in on-the-job training leading to higher levels of skill are weak. And even when a girl plans on a career, that is, expects to be permanently attached to the labor force, the opportunity for investing in on-the-job training is likely to be limited. So long as there are some elements of specificity in any training programs or promotional schemes of the firm, the employer will prefer men to women trainees, even if the latter profess occupational ambitions. This also implies that to the extent that women do obtain specific training they bear a larger fraction of the total costs of such training than men and, therefore, that the difference between on-the-job training costs (including those borne by employees) for women and those for men is even larger than is suggested by our estimate.

Some direct evidence on scant female participation in on-the-job training is provided in a recent international survey.[40] In all countries surveyed, apprenticeships are shorter for women than for men. They are half the length of male apprenticeships in the United States in bookbinding and in the garment industry, where women concentrate. In other industries, numbers of women apprentices are negligible, perhaps because of physical requirements but not because of any legal obstacles. It is interesting to find that, in contrast to other countries, applications for apprenticeships by women were quite numerous in the early postwar years in Germany and Austria. By 1949 in these countries, the number of skilled women in trades previously considered male was quite pronounced and increasing. Because of the war-caused imbalance in the sex ratio in the young age groups, unfavorable marriage prospects of young females clearly increased worker and employer expectations of their more-permanent attachment to the labor force. Larger investment in on-the-job training became economical to both parties. Aside from patriotism, such motivations may play a role in the increased labor-force rates and job-training of women during wars in all countries. And the willingness of employers to train women as well as men is enhanced by governmental subsidies of the training function.

Returning to our estimates: the small amounts of investment in on-the-job training by females were derived from female age–income profiles. This procedure is, of course, equivalent to a hypothesis which emphasizes the lack of on-the-job training as the factor responsible for both the observed flatness of females' age–income profiles and the small differential between observed incomes of women of different levels of formal education.

A recent detailed study of income differentials between males and females shows that wage rates approach equality when the detailed job

*Table 4.6   Costs per non-white male of school and on-the-job training, 1949
(in $ thousands)*

Educational level	Marginal costs		Total costs		Total costs of all United States males	
	School	On the job	School	On the job	School	On the job
College	8.05	3.98	13.20	7.87	15.9	24.3
High school	3.92	0.46	5.15	3.89	5.7	8.6
Elementary school	1.23	3.43	1.23	3.43	1.6	3.9

Source: Tables A4.10 and 4.1.

specification is identical for both sexes.[41] The rougher the occupational classification, the bigger the wage differentials at the higher skill levels. Lack of on-the-job training fits these phenomena quite well.

These same phenomena, however, are possibly attributable to differential market discrimination against women appearing at the more-skilled job levels and increasing with levels of skill. The calculation based on Table A4.5 indeed revealed a somewhat lower rate (about two percentage points) of return on total training of women than of men. The lower rate may reflect discrimination. Another explanation which is consistent with the investment hypothesis[42] is that, in view of the expected smaller rate of participation in the labor market, education of women is more strongly focused on the 'consumption' sphere, and returns are in larger part non-pecuniary than for males. Hence the apparently smaller money rate of return.

In Table 4.6 a 1949 comparison of training costs of black and white males indicates much smaller investments in on-the-job training by blacks, though the investments are not negligible. The investment in on-the-job training is also smaller in relation to investment in formal schooling, suggesting a lesser access to on-the-job training than to formal education. Again, fragmentary direct evidence abounds on the small proportions of blacks in apprenticeships and other training programs.

Conversely, the smaller amounts of on-the-job training received by blacks than by whites is an interpretation of income differentials: the relative flatness of their age–income profiles and the smaller differentials in earnings by education (even when the latter are standardized in terms of cost). The lesser on-the-job training relative to school training of blacks is an element in their occupational distribution. It creates an even lower skill concentration in the occupational distribution than would be predicted by the educational distribution. As in the sex comparison, this results in a statistical finding that the ratio of non-white to white incomes declines with increasing level of formal education.[43]

It has long been observed that at lower levels of skill and education workers are affected by a stronger incidence of unemployment than those at higher occupational and educational levels. The reasons for this phenomenon have never been clarified.

In his analysis of investment in people, Becker points out that, for a given demand situation, turnover and unemployment rates are likely to be milder under conditions of specific on-the-job training than elsewhere. Specific training is defined as an investment which increases the worker's marginal product in the firm in which he is trained more than elsewhere. According to this theory, marginal products of specifically trained workers exceed their wages, but the latter are higher than in alternative employments.[44] Hence employers have more incentive to retain such workers, and these have more incentive to remain with the firm. The differential behavior is implicit both for cross-sectional observations and for cyclical changes. In a recent study, a similar hypothesis was elaborated and put to an empirical test by Walter Oi.[45] Oi related the severity of cyclical changes (1929–33) in employment to levels of wages in a particular industry and found an inverse correlation between the two. He also correlated average wages by industry with turnover rates for a number of industries at a given time. Here again the (partial) correlation was negative. Oi interprets his results as favorable evidence for the investment hypothesis, on the assumption that wage levels (by occupation and industry) are a proxy for amounts of specific training.

This is a bold assumption. Even if cross-sectional wage differentials (by occupation and industry) represented returns to training only, these conceptually reflect returns to two forms of training: school training which is 'general', and on-the-job training which may be 'general' or 'specific'. It is not easy to see why the total return should be particularly strongly correlated with what is probably the smallest component: that part of on-the-job training which is specific. Oi did not attempt to segregate the explanatory factors into 'general' and 'specific' components of training because his data did not permit standardizations by education or by age. Without such standardizations the results are ambiguous. The wage rate reflects schooling as well as on-the-job training: a higher rate will prevail with very little on-the-job training but sufficiently more school training.

This might obscure the relation which is tested. Conversely, the lack of control for age makes for a spurious correlation between the wage rate and turnover. Larger proportions of younger people in an industry, or occupation, mean both more turnover and lower wages.

In an attempt to get a stronger test of the investment hypothesis and more insight into factors affecting turnover and unemployment, I ran a multiple regression relating a hybrid unemployment and turnover variable to average full-time incomes in 1949 of males in 87 detailed occupations, standardizing by educational level, age, and industrial distribution. The dependent variable (y) is the proportion of wage and salary workers who worked 50 to 52 weeks in 1949. This variable reflects both differential turnover and unemployment incidence among the groups, so it is well suited for the purpose.[46] The independent variables are full-time mean incomes in the occupations (X_1), median years of schooling (X_2), proportion of workers less than 25 years old (X_3), and (X_4) proportion of workers employed in durable-goods manufacturing and in construction.

The rationale for the choice of independent variables is as follows: according to the investment hypothesis, the turnover plus unemployment variable Y is a positive function of specific training costs, part of which are borne by workers, part by firms. Unfortunately, there are no data or readily available proxies for specific costs. I shall assume that such costs are positively related to the total of on-the-job training. This is a much weaker assumption than that of a positive correlation of specific training costs with wage rates.

Consider now the average wage X_1 in an occupation. This wage will tend to be higher, the higher is the average education X_2 and the greater the amount of on-the-job training in the occupation. For given values of X_2, larger X_1 will therefore tend to reflect more on-the-job training. Thus the sign of the partial regression coefficient of X_1 is expected to be positive. Conversely, for given occupational wage levels X_1, the higher the schooling X_2, the less on-the-job training in the occupation. Unless formal schooling itself has an effect on turnover and unemployment, the sign at X_2 should be negative. The two additional variables used in the regression, age, X_3 and industrial composition, X_4, standardize for factors other than training. Among persons less than 25 years of age there is more job and labor-force mobility than among older people, even when the other variables are held constant. X_4 crudely standardizes for effects of short-run demand fluctuations by industry.

Using these variables, the following regression was obtained (all variables are measured as deviations from their means; standard errors of regression coefficients are in parentheses):

$$y = 2.08X_1 + 1.86X_2 - 2.29X_3 - .74X_4$$
$$(1.04) \quad (.46) \quad (.68) \quad (.21)$$
$$R^2 = .65.$$

All variables are statistically significant. All signs, except that for X_2 conform to expectations. In particular, the positive effect of X_1 is consistent with the investment hypothesis.

Even if formal education *per se* had no effect on employment stability, the effects of on-the-job training (reflected in the coefficient at X_1) would explain the previously described systematic patterns of unemployment rates of workers classified by educational levels. As we have seen in Table 4.1, more on-the-job training is received by workers at higher educational levels.

However, in terms of the investment hypothesis, which emphasizes specific training in this context, the positive sign at X_2 is puzzling. Could it possibly reverse if the analysis were expanded to include such variables as urbanization, unionization, race, marital status? Such an expansion, if feasible, would be desirable. I experimented with inclusion of two easily accessible variables: X_5, percentage of males older than 55, and X_6, percentage of non-whites in an occupation. Neither was statistically significant. Their inclusion did not increase the correlation coefficient, nor did it affect the coefficient of X_2. The inclusion of the racial variable X_6, however, lowered the coefficient of X_1 and weakened its reliability.

Is stability of employment affected by training, regardless of whether it is general or specific, acquired at school or on the job? One could argue, to be monistic, that educational levels are more strongly correlated with specific training than is on-the-job training. For example, the employer may be using information on educational attainment as an index of capability or suitability for selection to specific on-the-job training. If so, the coefficient of education (at X_2) 'catches' more of the effects of specific training than does the coefficient at X_1. However, there may be good reasons for the behavior of X_2 other than the investment hypothesis, and it remains an open question for some significant exploration of unemployment phenomena.

Another way of discerning the effects of on-the-job training on employment stability is to compare population groups with the same amount of formal education but differing in on-the-job training. Comparisons by race and sex should serve the purpose. As we have seen (in this section and Table 4.1), the amounts invested in on-the-job training differ substantially among the groups compared within the same educational levels. It also appears that differences in amounts of on-the-job training increase with increasing educational level in both race and sex comparisons. If on-the-

Table 4.7   Black–white unemployment differentials,* by age and education, United States males, civilian labor force, 1950

Years of schooling	Age					Total
	25–29	30–34	35–44	45–54	55–64	
0	0.9	0.8	− 1.1	0.3	0.6	− 0.2
1–4	0.0	0.2	0.3	0.3	0.6	0.3
5–7	0.6	1.4	1.5	1.3	1.3	1.8
8	4.4	3.1	3.3	2.3	2.8	3.5
9–11	5.8	3.5	4.4	3.3	2.5	4.7
12	5.6	4.7	4.0	2.8	3.9	4.4
13–15	4.8	4.9	4.0	0.4	3.8	3.8
16 or more	0.0	3.0	0.9	0.8	1.7	1.2

*Black minus white unemployment rate.
Source: U.S. Census of Population, 1950, Special Reports: Education, Table 9.

job training were a major factor in explaining differentials in employment stability, the investment hypothesis would predict higher unemployment rates for blacks than for whites at each educational level and an increasing differential in rates the higher the educational level. A similar prediction would apply to the female–male comparison.

Data shown in Table 4.7 are differences between unemployment rates of black and white males classified by age and education in 1950. Black unemployment rates are higher in almost all classifications; the difference is negligible at the lowest educational levels and, generally, increases with education. The differentials remain positive, but decrease at the highest educational level. Similar patterns have been observed by Harry Gilman for an occupational breakdown of the black and white male labor force, both for cross-sectional differences and cyclical changes.[47] In the occupational breakdown, the differentials increase with skill level in the 'blue-collar' groups; differentials remain positive but the increase is halted in the 'white-collar' groups. Additional factors, such as differential industrial attachments of 'blue-collar' and 'white-collar' groups are likely to be responsible for some of the deviations from the theoretical predictions. A multivariate analysis is clearly desirable. But, by and large, even the gross comparisons suggest that the investment hypothesis is relevant in explaining differences in unemployment incidence of black and white labor.[48]

Comparison of unemployment rates of males and females, classified by education, show only small, apparently random, differences (Table 4.8).

Table 4.8   Male–female unemployment differentials,* by age and education, civilian labor force, 1950

Years of schooling	Age				
	25–29	30–34	35–44	45–54	55–64
0	2.6	−1.4	0.3	−0.4	−1.5
1–4	2.5	2.2	1.4	0.4	−1.4
5–7	0.5	1.2	0.3	0.1	−0.4
8	0.3	1.0	0.3	−0.1	−0.5
9–11	0.8	0.7	0.5	0.2	0.3
12	−0.1	0.7	0.1	−0.3	−0.6
13–15	−0.6	0.2	0.1	−0.4	−0.6
16 or more	−0.8	0.7	0.1	−0.2	−0.6

*Female minus male unemployment rate.
Source: U.S. Census of Population, 1950, Special Reports: Education, Table 9.

The levels are similar and decline with increasing education in both groups. Does this mean that formal education affects unemployment rates and on-the-job training does not? This would be, *prima facie*, inconsistent with the other findings. A multivariate analysis is needed in which the net effect of the training factor could be isolated, in order to resolve this puzzle.[49]

Summary
The empirical exploration described in this paper was designed to achieve several purposes: (a) to estimate the amount of resources invested in on-the-job training as distinguished from investments in the formal educational system; (b) to estimate rates of return on such investments; (c) to investigate the relevance of these investments to certain well-known but not well-understood patterns of income and employment behaviour of population groups.

Since the research was exploratory rather than intensive, the conclusions reached are very tentative. Briefly stated:

(a) Investment in on-the-job training is a very large component of total investment in education in the United States economy. Measured in terms of costs, it is as important as formal education for the male labor force and amounts to more than a half of total (male and female) expenditures on school education. Aggregate and per capita investments in on-the-job training have been increasing since 1939, though at a slower rate than investments in formal education. It seems, however, that on-the-job training has grown at a much faster rate at higher skill levels than at lower ones.

(b)   The rate of return on selected investments in on-the-job training, such as apprenticeships and medical specialization, was not different from the rate of return on total costs of college education, both unadjusted for ability factors. However, the private return, that is, the return on private costs seems to be higher in formal education than in on-the-job training. These findings raise questions about possible downward biases in the calculated rates of return to education.

(c)   The last section of the paper is a preliminary analysis of differential income and employment patterns of population groups, classified by education, occupation, sex, and race. The analyses are incomplete, but they suggest that new empirical knowledge about forms and amounts of investments in people can lead to a significant increase in our understanding of such major areas of economic behavior as income distribution, unemployment incidence, and labor mobility.

Empirical ventures into unexplored territory are hazardous. The margins of error are difficult to assess, and they are likely to be large. At least the findings should provoke further research. The need for more, better, and different data is evident. I hope that some guides for future research do emerge from this preliminary work.

Acknowledgements
This work was stimulated and made possible by Gary Becker's fundamental theoretical analysis of investment in human capital. H. G. Lewis contributed very thoughtful and useful comments on the first version of the paper. I am also indebted for helpful comments to T. W. Schultz, G. H. Moore, G. P. Shultz, Z. Griliches, and H. Gilman. Dave O'Neill provided highly competent research assistance. Financial support by the Carnegie Corporation of New York is gratefully acknowledged.

Notes
1.   A good sample of a growing literature on the subject includes P. H. Douglas, *American Apprenticeship and Industrial Education*, New York: Columbia University Press, 1921; United States Department of Labor, Bureau of Apprenticeship and Training, *Apprenticeships Past and Present*, Washington, 1955; *Apprentice Training*, Washington, 1956; and *Employee Training in New Jersey Industry*, Washington, 1960; National Manpower Council, *A Policy for Skilled Manpower*, New York: Columbia University Press, 1954, and *Improving the Work Skills of the Nation*, New York: Columbia University Press, 1955; H. F. Clark and H. S. Sloan, *Classrooms in the Factories*, Rutherford, N.J.: Fairleigh Dickinson College, 1958; O. N. Serbein, *Educational Activities of Business* (Washington, D.C.: American Council on Education, 1961).
2.   G. S. Becker, 'Investment in People', unpublished manuscript, National Bureau of Economic Research, 1961, and his 'Underinvestment in College Education?', *American*

Economic Review, Papers and Proceedings, May 1960; T. W. Schultz, 'Capital Formation in Education', *Journal of Political Economy*, December 1960, and his 'Investment
in Human Capital', *American Economic Review*, March 1961.

3. This proposition is sometimes questioned on the basis of casual observation. Greater
    learning from experience is characteristic of workers with greater motivation and
    ability, and their earnings at the early stages of the career may in some cases be as high
    or higher than those of other workers. But such finding that people with greater ability
    have higher productivity than others at any given stage of experience does not negate
    the existence of investment in on-the-job training, though it may bias the estimation of
    its magnitude.

4. The conceptual and mathematical frameworks are developed and stated in Becker's
    'Investment in Human Capital: A Theoretical Analysis', *Journal of Political Economy*,
    vol. 70, no. 5, part 2, Supplement, October 1962.

5. See references in n. 2.

6. Under competitive conditions, all of the firm's costs will be charged to the worker if the
    training increases his future productivity in other firms just as much as in the firm in
    which he is training. Some fraction of costs will not be charged to the worker if the
    training contains elements of specificity, that is, if it increases the worker's future
    productivity in the firm more than in other firms. For a full exposition see Becker,
    'Investment in Human Capital'.

7. One interesting exception is the information obtained from an analysis of a sample of
    more than 400 heads of households from the Consumer Union Panel, taken in 1959.
    The respondents were college-educated males who started on their first full-time job
    approximately 12 years before the survey date. The correlation between initial earnings
    of these individuals with their current earnings was used to test the existence of
    investment in on-the-job training by the predicted effects on age-earnings profiles:

    Consider Y_t, the earnings of any individual at time t, as consisting of four additive
    components: $\overline{Y}_t$, average earnings of the group; a_t, an ability component of the indivi-
    dual; c_t, the investment component (a cost if negative, return if positive); and u_t, a
    random component.

    $$Y_t = \overline{Y}_t + a_t + c_t + u_t.$$

    For simplicity assume that the components are not correlated with one another, and u is
    not correlated over time. Since $\overline{Y}_t$ is the same for all individuals in the group, the
    covariance between earnings in the first and the twelfth year is:

    $$\text{Cov}\,(Y_1,\,Y_{12}) = \text{Cov}\,(a + c + u_1,\,a_{12} + c_{12} + u_{12}) = \text{Cov}\,(a_1,\,a_{12}) + \text{Cov}\,(c_1,\,c_{12}).$$

    The correlation was found to be very close to zero. Since the covariance of the ability
    factor is surely positive (and roughly equal to the variance of the ability component of
    earnings), the second covariance must be negative and equally sizable. That is, the
    larger (more negative) the initially foregone earnings (c_1), the larger (more positive) the
    return twelve years later (c_{12}).

8. Becker, 'Investment in Human Capital'.

9. This assumption is later questioned. However, the fragmentary evidence in Sec. 2
    suggests that the assumption of equal rates is not unreasonable, when rates are com-
    puted on the sum of private and public costs of training.

10. After a year of additional training, the income alternatives of the trainee are better than
    those indicated by the age profile X_j, which assumes no additional training.

11. The correction factor α is not a sufficient correction for the effective length of the
    working life. Use of this factor alone assumes that all of a given cohort survive to a
    given age and have a 100 per cent labor-force participation rate (after schooling) to this
    age. A complete correction should take into account mortality rates and the fraction of

a cohort which is out of the labor force at each age. Adjustments for mortality and for labor-force participation were not incorporated in the estimating procedure. Neither have any significant effects on age-income profiles of males before the age of 50. The effects on income *differentials* are small. According to Becker's work the mortality adjustment results in a small reduction of the rate of return, if the same mortality table is used for all education groups. The correction factor was used in the initial set of calculations, but discarded in the final revision, as it turned out to be negligible. Leaving out all these 'survival' factors results in a small overstatement of costs, as is discussed later in the text.

12. Becker, 'Investment in Human Capital'.
13. To obtain estimates of investments by all workers, those with 'some elementary school-ing', 'some high school', and 'some college' have to be included in the calculation. It was assumed that their investment costs are halfway between investment costs of graduates at neighbouring educational levels. See notes to Appendix Tables A4.5–A4.7.
14. E. F. Denison, 'A Note on Education, Economic Growth, and Gaps in Information', *Journal of Political Economy*, vol. 70, no. 5, part 2, Supplement, October 1962.
15. The rate of return is a ratio of returns to costs, $r = k/c$. If only c were increased, with k left the same, the relative (per cent) decrease in r would equal the relative increase in c. But, since k is decreased, the relative decrease in r is stronger than the relative increase in c.
16. United States Department of Labor, Bureau of Employment Security, United States Employment Service, *Estimates of Worker Trait Requirements for 4,000 Jobs as Defined in the Dictionary of Occupational Titles* (Washington, D.C., 1956).
17. R. S. Eckaus, 'Education and Economic Growth', in *Economics of Higher Education*, ed. Selma J. Mushkin, Washington, D.C.: United States Department of Health, Education, and Welfare, 1963, Tables 1 and 2. College equivalence is implied in United States Department of Labor, Bureau of Employment Security, United States Employment Service, *Estimates of Worker Trait Requirements*, p. 111.
18. See Part 3.
19. Clark and Sloan, *Classrooms in the Factories*, Serbein, *Educational Activities of Business* and the 1960 New Jersey Survey of the Bureau of Apprenticeships and Training.
20. Serbein, *Educational Activities of Business*, pp. 9–10.
21. 'Training Manpower', *Fortune*, July 1951.
22. Clark and Sloan, *Classrooms in the Factories*, p. 3.
23. See references cited in n. 1.
24. Merchants and Manufacturers Association, *Labor Turnover: Causes, Costs and Methods of Control*, New York: MMA, (1959).
25. Ibid.
26. About 30 million, using the observed average monthly replacement rate of 4 per cent.
27. Includes military schools and training programs but excludes basic training and depreciation of equipment (estimated by R. C. Blitz, 'The Nation's Educational Out-lay', in Mushkin (ed.), *Economics of Higher Education*.
28. Based on 1949 estimates for female college graduates (see Part 3).
29. According to Schultz, the total cost of schooling was $28.7 billion in 1956 (see 'Invest-ment in Human Capital').
30. It also depends on timing. The chronologically earlier component receives greater weight (see Becker, 'Investment in Human Capital').
31. This occupation is more appropriate as an alternative, in terms of educational back-ground, than laborers. Clerical work is an alternative, but it probably contains more on-the-job training than operative jobs, which involve at most a few months of training.
32. Calculated from

$$d \cdot \sum_{i=1}^{n} \frac{1}{(1 + r)^i} = k \cdot \sum_{j=n+1}^{\infty} \frac{1}{(1 + r)^j}.$$

The assumption of infinite life creates a negligible error.

33. A 10 per cent rate was used. Higher rates would lower the figures in col. (3) even more.

34. See Part 1.

35. However, according to a recent study by H. G. Lewis, the impact of unionism on wage differentials was very small in the 1945–50 period ('Union Effects on Relative Wages', in *Aspects of Labor Economics*, National Bureau of Economic Research Conference, 1960, New York: NBER, 1960).

36. *Journal of the American Medical Association*, 22 September 1956, pp. 277ff., and 10 October 1959, pp. 665ff.

37. 'Income of Physicians', *Survey of Current Business*, July 1951.

38. The 1950 rate of return to medical specialization may have been above equilibrium. The proportion of specialists among physicians was less than half in 1950 and increased to about two-thirds by 1960 (according to *Medical Economics*, 1961). If this was a supply shift in response to a high level of demand, the rate of return on specialization should be less today than in 1950. Data from medical sources (*Physicians' Earnings and Expenses*, published by *Medical Economics*, 1961) indicate that in 1959 the money income differential between specialists and general practitioners is no larger than it was in 1949, despite the fact that the average incomes of specialists rose over 60 per cent during the period, residencies lengthened somewhat, and opportunity costs clearly increased. If the data are reliable, it would seem that rates of return today are a few percentage points lower than in 1949. Incidentally, estimates of rates of return on specialization in medicine have little bearing on the question of alleged monopoly returns in medicine. Whatever the barriers to entry into medicine, once a medical degree was obtained, institutional obstacles to specialization are weak.

39. Empirical evidence on labor-force behavior of married women is more consistent with the first than with the second assumption (see my 'Labor Force Participation of Married Women', in *Aspects of Labor Economics*).

40. 'The Apprenticeships of Women and Girls', *International Labor Review*, October 1955.

41. H. Sanborn, 'Male–Female Income Differentials', unpublished doctoral dissertation, University of Chicago, 1959.

42. Yet another explanation, suggested by Becker ('Underinvestment in College Education?') is that the personal money returns shown above understate the money returns which actually accrue to women as family members. According to this argument family income differentials are the relevant measures.

43. See M. Zeman, 'A Quantitative Analysis of White–Non-white Income Differentials in the United States', unpublished doctoral dissertation, University of Chicago, 1955.

44. Becker, 'Investment in People'.

45. 'Labor as a Quasi-fixed Factor of Production', unpublished doctoral dissertation, University of Chicago, 1961.

46. The variable is also affected by seasonality. The obvious cases where seasonality is strong had fewer than 50 per cent of workers employed year-round. To avoid arbitrariness, all occupations (more than twenty) with $y < 50$ per cent were excluded from the analysis.

47. 'Discrimination and the White–Non-white Unemployment Differentials', doctoral dissertation, University of Chicago.

48. The turnover regression analysis described before is also suggestive: once the levels of education and of on-the-job training were taken into account, the racial factor did not seem to have any discernible effects on turnover plus unemployment.

49. The prevalence of women in cyclically insensitive jobs (clerical, government, teaching, and nursing) is an obviously plausible explanation.

Appendix

Table A4.1   Net average wage and salary incomes,* by years of schooling and age, white urban males, United States, 1939 (in dollars)

Age	Years of schooling			
	16 or more	12	7–8	1–4
Less than 14[†]	− 850	− 850	− 850	− 340
14–15[‡]	− 115	− 115	281	258
16–17[‡]	− 103	− 103	352	315
18–19[‡]	− 452	481	443	373
20–21[‡]	− 400	755	579	431
22–24	1,028	947	750	503
25–29	1,661	1,244	959	648
30–34	2,395	1,606	1,179	802
35–44	3,147	2,073	1,434	916
45–54	3,483	2,286	1,570	1,018
55–64	3,147	2,105	1,439	950

*All income data are before tax.

[†]This now shows total rather than annual costs of elementary school per student.

[‡]Gross earnings of high-school and of college students were assumed to be one-quarter of earnings of elementary-school graduates and of high-school graduates, respectively.

Source: Wage and salary incomes: unpublished National Bureau of Economic Research materials of G. S. Becker, based on 1940 Population Census. Direct costs per student were derived from Tables 3, 5, and 6 in T. W. Schultz, 'Capital Formation by Education', *Journal of Political Economy*, December 1960, and from *Biennial Survey of Education in the United States, 1939–40*.

Table A4.2   Net average incomes,* by years of schooling and age, United States males, 1949 (in dollars)

Age	Years of schooling			
	16+	12	8	1–3
Less than 14†	− 1,576	− 1,576	− 1,576	− 394
14–17‡	− 205	− 205	676	670
18–19‡	− 910	1,071	1,079	720
20–21‡	− 753	1,745	1,523	952
22–24	2,284	2,356	1.929	1,192
25–29	3,441	2,975	2,341	1,474
30–34	4,846	3,576	2,680	1,667
35–44	7,085	4,055	3,029	1,814
45–54	8,116	4,689	3,247	1,990
55–64	7,655	4,548	3,010	1,892

see n. in Table A4.1. Here income includes property income.
†See n.† in Table A4.1.
‡See n.‡ in Table A4.1.
Source: Income data derived from *1950 Census of Population*, Ser. P-E, no. 5B, *Education* Tables 12 and 13 (also H. P. Miller, 'Income in Relation to Education', *American Economic Review*, December 1960, Table 1. Direct costs per student derived from T. W. Schultz, op. cit. and *Biennial Survey of Education, 1948–50*.

Table A4.3   *Net average incomes,* by years of schooling and age, United
States males, 1958 (in dollars)*

Age	Years of schooling			
	16+	12	8	0–4
Less than 14[†]	−2,400	−2,400	−2,400	−600
14–17[‡]	−224	−224	1,208	1,080
18–21[‡]	−682	2,800	1,910	1,532
22–24	3,663	3,537	2,520	1,931
25–29	5,723	4,381	3,223	2,387
30–34	7,889	5,182	3,848	2,757
35–44	10,106	6,007	4,403	3,023
45–54	11,214	6,295	4,337	3,008
55–64	10,966	6,110	3,960	2,956

See n. in Table A4.2.
[†]See n.[†] in Table A4.2.
[‡]See n.[‡]n in Table A4.2.
Source: Income data derived from the March 1959 *Current Population Survey*, and Miller,
op. cit. Direct costs per student derived from *Statistical Abstract of the United States,
1960.*

Table A4.4   Illustrative calculation of annual incremental costs of investment in schooling and in on-the-job training, male college graduates, 1939 (r = 11.0 per cent)*

Age	Net earnings of high school graduates† (1)	Net earnings of college graduates† (2)	Differentials in earnings (1−2) (3)	Returns on last year's cost $(r \cdot C_{j-1})$ (4)	Return on all previous costs $(j-1)$ $r \cdot \sum_{k=18} C_k$ (5)	Cost† at age j (3+5) (6)
18	409	−468	877			877
19	563	−437	1,000	96	96	1,096
20	717	−407	1,124	121	217	1,341
21	793	−391	1,184	148	365	1,549
22	870	870	0	170	535	535
23	947	1,028	−81	59	594	513
24	1,021	1,186	−105	56	650	485
25	1,095	1,344	−249	53	703	454
26	1,169	1,502	−333	50	753	420
27	1,244	1,661	−417	46	799	382
28	1,316	1,807	−491	42	841	350
29	1,388	1,954	−566	39	880	314
30	1,460	2,101	−641	35	915	274
31	1,533	2,248	−715	30	945	230
32	1,606	2,395	−789	25	970	181
33	1,668	2,495	−827	20	990	163
34	1,730	2,595	−865	18	1,008	143
35	1,792	2,695	−903	16	1,024	121
36	1,854	2,795	−941	13	1,037	96
37	1,916	2,895	−979	10	1,047	68
38	1,978	2,995	−1,017	7	1,054	37
39	2,041	3,096	−1,055	4	1,058	3

*Obtained by equating to zero the present value of col. (3). (3) (continued to age 65).
†Age–earnings profiles from Table A4.1, interpolated within age groups.
‡School cost for ages 18–21; on-the-job training cost thereafter.

135

Table A4.5 Estimated cost of schooling and of on-the-job training, by age and level of education, United States males, 1939

Age	Marginal costs ($) Elementary school (r = 20.9) (1)	High school (r = 12.5) (2)	College (r = 11.0) (3)	Total costs ($) Elementary school (4 = 1) (4)	High school (1 + 2) (5)	College (1 + 2 + 3) (6)	'Employment' (Thousands) Elementary school (7)	High school (8)	College (9)
14	510	0	0	510	510	510			
14	85	388	0	85	388	388			
15	98	455	0	98	455	455			
16	110	545	0	110	545	545			
17	125	643	0	125	643	643	105.7		
18	142	254	877	142	396	877	105.7		
19	133	200	1,096	133	333	1,096	193.2		
20	122	139	1,341	122	261	1,341	193.2		
21	108	148	1,549	108	256	1,549	246.1		
22	92	158	535	92	250	785	246.1	283.1	164.3
23	71	170	513	71	241	754	288.7	283.1	156.7
24	70	169	485	70	239	724	288.7	349.6	149.9
25	69	168	454	69	237	691	322.8	349.6	131.1
26	67	167	420	67	234	654	322.8	377.9	129.1
27	65	166	382	65	231	613	368.7	377.9	127.4
28	65	159	350	65	224	574	368.7	331.2	127.1
29	66	151	314	66	217	531	368.7	331.2	128.8
30	67	142	274	67	209	483	368.7	331.2	119.7
31	68	131	230	68	199	429	375.7	331.2	112.6
32	69	118	181	69	187	368	375.7	256.4	108.6
33	64	105	163	64	169	332	375.7	256.4	104.7
34	58	90	143	58	148	291	375.7	256.4	101.2
35	51	73	121	51	124	245	375.7	256.4	90.0
36	42	54	96	42	96	192	360.4	167.1	67.2
37	31	37	68	31	67	135	360.4	167.1	67.2
38	18	14	37	18	32	69	360.4	167.1	67.2
39	4		3	4	4	7	360.4	167.1	67.2
Total cost of on-the-job training				2,000	4,400	7,900			

Notes: Cols (1), (2), (3) obtained by the method represented by equation (4.1) in the text and illustrated in Table A4.4. Schooling costs are above the broken lines; on-the-job costs below it. r is the internal rate of return on the marginal costs. Columns terminate at ages when costs become zero. Thereafter they turn negative and positive for several runs; but they are small, and their sum is negligible.

Cols. (4), (5), (6) are horizontally cumulated costs (for each year of training, separately for schooling (above the broken line), and for training on the job (below the broken line). Vertical sums (rounded) of training costs in col. (4), (5), (6) are shown in the bottom row. These are entered in col. (5) of text Table 4.1. Figures in col. (2) of text Table 4.1 were first differences of figures in col. (5), not vertical sums of col. (1, 2, 3) in Tables A4.5–A4.7.

Col. (7) includes male workers with eight years of education, plus half the workers with less than eight years and half the workers with more than eight and less than twelve years of schooling.

Col. (8) includes workers who have high school education, plus half of the 'some high-school' and of 'some college' groups.

Col. (9) includes workers who have college education or more, plus half of 'some college' groups.

In principle, the employment figures (cols (7), (8), (9)) are supposed to represent numbers of workers of a given educational category by numbers of years elapsed since completion of schooling, and not by age. Clearly, all college graduates do not graduate at age 22. Very few graduate at an earlier age, but large proportions do at later ages. The number of college graduates aged 22 therefore, severely underestimates the number of persons who are in their first year after college graduation. The bias in numbers of workers, of course, reverses at later ages. However, since higher costs of on-the-job training decline with age, aggregate costs (Table 4.2) would be underestimated. This bias is roughly corrected at the college level (col. (9)) by the use of graduation rather than employment data. No such correction was made at the lower levels. Graduation at the lower levels cannot be equated with labor-force participation, and the problem of bias is less acute anyway: age dispersion at graduation and cost figures are much smaller.

Source: Cols (7), (8), (9): *1940 Census of Population, Education*, Tables 75, 76; *1950 Census of Population*, G-E, No. 5B, *Education*, Tables 75, 76; Bureau of Labor Statistics, *Special Labor Force Reports*, no. 1, February 1960, Table D; United States Department of Health, Education, and Welfare, *Earned Degrees Conferred by Higher Educational Institutions: 1948–58: Biennial Survey of Education*, before 1948.

Table A4.6 Estimated costs of schooling and of on-the-job training, by age and level of education, United States males, 1949*

Age	Marginal costs ($) Elementary school (r = 22.2)	High school (r = 11.8)	College (r = 10.6)	Total costs ($) Elementary school	High school	College	'Employment' (Thousands) Elementary school	High school	College
	(1)	(2)	(3)	(4)	(5)	(6)	(7)	(8)	(9)
14	1,182	0	0	1,182	1,182	1,182			
14	375	777	0	375	777	777			
15	382	939	0	382	939	939			
16	377	1,121	0	377	1,121	1,121	98.3		
17	401	1,309	1,881	401	1,309	1,309	98.3		
18	316	544	2,268	316	860	1,881	184.1		
19	263	538	2,778	263	801	2,268	184.1		
20	231	441	3,304	231	672	2,778	233.1		
21	202	383	1,143	202	585	3,304	233.1	425.5	
22	157	363	1,273	157	520	1,663	244.7	425.5	342.0
23	125	329	1,329	125	454	1,727	244.7	415.7	266.7
24	130	315	1,335	130	445	1,774	285.1	415.7	204.7
25	129	307	1,311	129	436	1,771	285.1	443.7	118.3
26	123	293	1,294	123	416	1,727	285.1	443.7	114.6
27	108	268	1,267	108	376	1,670	303.5	443.7	112.0
28	114	264	1,260	114	378	1,640	303.5	476.8	138.6
29	104	255	1,252	104	359	1,619	303.5	476.8	169.7
30	102	225	1,218	102	327	1,579	303.5	476.8	169.2
31	94	196	1,150	94	290	1,508	329.5	476.8	173.1
32	76	148	1,075	76	224	1,374	329.5	442.1	164.2
33	45	161	1,008	45	206	1,281	329.5	442.1	157.8
34	30	154	884	30	184	1,192	329.5	442.1	150.1
35	16	167	763	16	183	1,067	329.5	442.1	139.5
36		151	599		151	914	379.3	442.1	125.8
37		143	432		143	742		387.5	125.8
38		149	228		149	581		387.5	125.8
39		156	47		156	384		387.5	125.8
40		129	17		129	176		387.5	115.8
41		89			89	106		267.5	115.8
42		65			65	65		267.5	115.8
43		17			17	17		267.5	115.8
Total cost of on-the-job training				3,902	8,600	24,300			

*See notes to Table A4.5

137

Table A4.7 Estimated costs of schooling and of on-the-job training, by age and level of education, United States males, 1958*

Age	Marginal costs ($) Elementary school (r = 19.3)	High school (r = 15.1)	College (r = 11.5)	Total costs ($) Elementary school	High school	College	'Employment' (Thousands) Elementary school	High school	College
	(1)	(2)	(3)	(4)	(5)	(6)	(7)	(8)	(9)
14	1,800	0		1,800	1,800	1,800			
14	296	1,266	0	296	1,266	1,266			
15	314	1,538	0	314	1,538	1,538			
16	303	1,917	0	303	1,917	1,917			
17	300	2,338	0	300	2,338	2,338			
18	297	225	3,246	297	522	3,246	65.8		
19	293	224	3,776	293	517	3,776	65.8		
20	289	223	4,368	289	512	4,368	73.8		
21	284	222	5,027	284	506	5,027	73.8	361.4	
22	278	220	2,090	278	498	2,588	191.5	361.4	
23	271	217	2,001	271	488	2,489	191.5	432.3	385.7
24	262	214	1,902	262	476	2,378	182.4	432.3	360.0
25	251	211	1,891	251	462	2,353	182.4	432.3	335.3
26	237	208	1,880	237	445	2,325	182.4	432.3	285.4
27	221	204	1,660	221	425	2,085	182.4	502.1	289.0
28	202	200	1,528	202	402	1,930	254.5	502.1	304.4
29	180	195	1,367	180	375	1,752	254.5	502.1	332.7
30	161	189	1,197	161	350	1,547	254.5	502.1	387.3
31	153	183	1,149	153	336	1,485	254.5	502.1	392.2
32	144	175	1,096	144	319	1,415	254.5	502.1	359.5
33	133	165	1,037	133	298	1,335	254.5	502.1	264.2
34	120	154	971	120	274	1,245	254.5	502.1	192.2
35	104	141	898	104	245	1,143	254.5	502.1	125.9
36	85	126	815	85	211	1,026	254.5	501.6	117.1
37	63	109	719	63	172	991	254.5	501.6	114.0
38	37	89	616	37	126	742	323.5	501.6	140.6
39	6	67	501	6	73	574	323.5	501.6	171.7
40		43	423		43	466	323.5	501.6	175.6
41		16	339		16	355	323.5	501.6	165.0
42			245			246			165.0
43			144			144			165.0
44			27			27			165.0
Total cost of on-the-job training				5,300	8,200	30,700			

*See notes to Table A4.5

138

Table A4.8 Average wage and salary income and median years of schooling of apprentices, operatives, and journeymen in three industry groups, 1949

	Metal trades (4 years)*		Printing and publishing (5.5 years)*		Construction (3.8 years)*	
	Schooling	Wage ($)	Schooling	Wage ($)	Schooling	Wage ($)
Apprentices	12.2	2,480	12.2	2,525	11.8	2,576
Operatives (in same industry)	9.0	3,015	10.4	3,239	8.8	2,937
With more schooling†	11.3	3,286	11.3	3,500	11.3	3,208
Assuming a 10 per cent return on schooling‡		3,415		3,540		3,340
Journeymen	9.5	3,534	10.9	4,138	8.9	3,216

*Average length of apprenticeship.
†In industries where they are found.
‡This return is added to the wage figure in second row. k = row 5 minus row 2; d_1 = row 2 minus row 1; d_2 = row 3 minus row 1; d_3 = row 4 minus row 1.
Source: U.S. Census of Population, 1950: Special Reports, Occupational Characteristics, Tables 10 and 23.

Table A4.9   *Net average incomes of females with and without adjustment*
for labor-force participation rates, by level of education and
age, 1949 (in dollars)

Age	Unadjusted		Adjusted*	
	High school (1)	College (2)	High school (3)	College (4)
18–19	970	− 786	970	− 786
20–21	1,468	− 706	1,468	− 706
22–24	1,614	1,900	734	1,313
25–29	1,635	2,120	520	939
30–34	1,674	2,293	532	1,016
35–44	1,859	2,600	662	1,277
45–54	2,062	2,907	767	1,608
55–64	1,968	2,974	559	1,448

*Observed average incomes multiplied by labor-force rates after age 22. Rates from Gertrude Bancroft, *The American Labor Force*, New York: John Wiley, 1958, Table D, p. 62.
Source: U.S. Census of Population, 1950, Special Reports, Education, Tables 10 and 12.

Table A4.10   *Mean incomes of non-white males, by age and education*
level, United States, 1950 (in dollars)

Age	Education			
	No schooling	Elementary school	High school	College or more
18–19	570	809	809	
20–21	808	1,177	1,349	
22–24	997	1,520	1,783	1,555
25–29	1,109	1,747	2,137	2,121
30–34	1,187	1,916	2,374	2,950
35–44	1,300	2,008	2,453	3,437
45–54	1,254	2,068	2,419	3,639
55–64	1,108	1,921	2,238	3,246

Source: Computed from distributions given in *U.S. Census of Population, 1950*, Vol. IV, *Special Reports, Education*, Table 12.

5 Labor mobility and wages*

In this essay we explore the implications of human capital and search behavior for both the interpersonal and life cycle structure of interfirm labor mobility. The economic hypothesis which motivates the analysis is that individual differences in firm-specific complementarities and related skill acquisitions produce differences in mobility behavior and in the relation between job tenure, wages, and mobility. Both 'job duration dependence' and 'heterogeneity bias' are implied by this theory. Exploration of longitudinal data sets – National Longitudinal Surveys (NLS) and Michigan Income Dynamics (MID) – which contain mobility, job, and wage histories of men in the 1966–76 decade yield the following findings, among others:

(a) The initially steep and later decelerating declines of labor mobility with working age are in large part due to the similar but more steeply declining relation between mobility and length of job tenure.
(b) Given tenure levels, the probability of moving is predicted positively by the frequency of prior moves and negatively by education. The inclusion of prior moves in the regression reduces the estimated tenure slope because it helps to remove the 'heterogeneity bias' in that slope.
(c) The popular 'mover–stayer model' is rejected by the existence of tenure effects on mobility.
(d) Differences in mobility during the first decade of working life do not predict long-run differences in earnings. However, persistent movers at later stages of working life have lower wage levels and flatter life cycle wage growth.
(e) The analysis calls for a reformulation of earnings (wage) functions. Inclusion of tenure terms in the function permits separate estimates of returns to general and specific human capital after correction for heterogeneity bias. A rough estimate is that 50 per cent of lifetime wage growth is due to general (transferable) experience and 25 per cent to firm-specific experience and interfirm mobility.

Sections 1–8 contain an exposition and empirical analysis which ranges

*This chapter was written with B. Jovanovic and was first published in *Studies in Labor Markets*, ed. S. Rosen, Chicago: University of Chicago Press, pp. 21–63, 1981.
Note: MID data are better known as PSID panels.

over somewhat wider subject matter than sections 9–11 which focus on the stochastic structure of mobility processes.

1.   Introduction: renewed interest in labor mobility

Labor mobility is one of the central topics of labor economics and a long-standing subject of empirical research. Earlier studies reflected primarily a concern with the allocative efficiency of the labor market. They analyzed attitudes, job change decisions, and the direction of observed labor mobility in attempts to ascertain whether information, motivation, and behavior of workers were consistent with the postulates of economic theory.

In a comprehensive survey of this literature, Parnes (1970) concluded that the evidence on the operation of market forces was mixed, both among different studies and even within them. Although research in the 1960s was more sophisticated and utilized larger data sets than prior work, it did not provide any change in perspective.

Reviewing the more recent literature, Parsons (1978) finds promise in the emergence of theories of human capital and of search theories as tools for the analysis of labor mobility, labor turnover, and unemployment. However, applied work in search theory has, thus far, only partially touched on problems of labor mobility and of unemployment: its emphasis has been largely on conditions terminating job search, rather than on circumstances which generate it.

The reformulation of labor mobility as a human capital investment decision has been fruitfully applied to migration (Sjastaad, 1962, and other work reviewed by Greenwood, 1975). The connection between investments specific to the firm (and to larger units) and the incidence of industrial and occupational labor turnover has been elucidated in studies by Becker (1975), Oi (1961), and Parsons (1972).

The novel approaches suggested by human capital and by search theories are producing a renewed interest in the formerly stagnant field of labor mobility. A further source of interest has come from stochastic models of labor mobility. The first of these, the 'mover-stayer' model, appeared two decades ago (Blumen, Kogan, McCarthy, 1955) and they have recently reappeared in more sophisticated form (Heckman, 1977, 1978; Jovanovic, 1978b; for a review, see Singer and Spilerman, 1976).

The purpose of this essay is to explore the implications of human capital and search behavior for both the interpersonal and life-cycle structure of interfirm labor mobility. The apparent ambiguity in the relation between labor mobility and wages which characterizes much of the literature surveyed by Parnes is implicit and reconcilable in human capital analysis; as a response to perceived gains in wages, mobility promotes individual wage growth, but to the extent that on-the-job investments contain elements of specificity, mobility is a deterrent to wage growth. The study of differences in mobility behavior requires information over time; of special importance, in our approach, is information on time spent in the firm (tenure) and on the life-cycle changes in job attachments. The availability of longitudinal microdata (especially NLS and MID panels) enables us to study these phenomena.

The economic hypothesis which motivates the analysis is that individual differences in firm-specific human capital behavior lead, via wage effects, to heterogeneity in mobility behavior, and to 'tenure effects' on attachment to the firm. Implications for life-cycle mobility are then derived in the absence or presence of 'aging' (changes in mobility with age, at given tenure levels). Both 'tenure dependence' and 'heterogeneity bias' are implied by the theory. We explore data sets which contain mobility histories to ascertain the existence of these phenomena and to correct for the predictable biases. Next we investigate corresponding features of the wage structure. Labor mobility and tenure effects are introduced and tested in a reformulated earnings function in which specific and general human capital accumulation can be distinguished.

Sections 9–11 present a rigorous formulation of the structure of mobility viewed as a stochastic process.

2   Tenure, working age, and mobility: some definitions and facts

We define labor mobility as change of employer, whether or not unemployment intervenes. We exclude exits from and entries into the labor force. This exclusion is a minor one for the male labor force which we study.[1] Consequently, job separation is synonymous with job change in our data. Except for one illustration of observed differences (see Table 5.1), we do not distinguish here between separations initiated by (or reported as) quit and layoff. Geographic, industrial, and occupational mobility are components of job mobility which are included in our concept but not singled out for separate treatment.[2]

Two probabilistic relations, or time profiles, are basic in our discussion and measurement of labor mobility. (a) The 'tenure turnover profile' $S(T)$ is the relation between the probability of separating from a job in period t and the time spent in that job prior to t (current tenure T). In the language of renewal theory, $S(T)$ is the 'hazard function'. At the individual level this is a profile of 'propensity to move' conditional on tenure. Such a profile is not observable. In large homogeneous groups, that is, groups consisting of individuals with the same propensity $S(T)$, we can observe estimates of the probabilities in each period in the form of relative frequencies or separation rates conditional on tenure. (b) The relation between an indivi-

Table 5.1   Mobility by experience and tenure, pooled, 1967–73 (percent moving in a two-year period)

Experience (years)	All	0–1	1–3	3–5	5–7	7–9	9–11	11–15	15–19	19+	n
A. Separations											
0–4	0.47	0.73	0.58	0.28	0.07	0.12	0.04				2,246
5–9	0.38	0.77	0.60	0.38	0.08	0.07	0.06				1,197
25–29	0.11	0.46	0.16	0.22	0.10	0.19	0.04	0.03	0.06	0.04	441
30–34	0.11	0.40	0.20	0.15	0.10	0.16	0.12	0.04	0.06	0.06	1,499
35–39	0.12	0.51	0.19	0.19	0.11	0.08	0.08	0.06	0.04	0.04	1,998
40–44	0.12	0.43	0.20	0.10	0.10	0.11	0.13	0.05	0.05	0.06	1,542
B. Quits											
0–4	0.32	0.48	0.41	0.20	0.06	0.08	0.04				
5–9	0.25	0.48	0.42	0.26	0.06	0.05	0.07				
25–29	0.06	0.19		0.22	0.10	0.11	0.04	0.00	0.01	0.00	
30–34	0.07	0.20	0.12	0.09	0.08	0.09	0.11	0.03	0.03	0.02	
35–39	0.05	0.18	0.10	0.10	0.06	0.05	0.06	0.03	0.02	0.01	
40–44	0.05	0.13	0.09	0.03	0.07	0.06	0.07	0.03	0.04	0.02	
C. Layoffs											
0–4	0.14	0.26	0.17	0.08	0.01	0.05					
5–9	0.12	0.28	0.18	0.11	0.03	0.02					
25–29	0.05	0.27	0.16	0.00	0.00	0.08	0.00	0.02	0.03	0.01	
30–34	0.05	0.21	0.08	0.06	0.02	0.07	0.01	0.01	0.03	0.05	
35–40	0.07	0.33	0.09	0.10	0.05	0.04	0.02	0.03	0.02	0.03	
40–44	0.07	0.30	0.12	0.06	0.03	0.05	0.05	0.03	0.01	0.03	

dual's propensity to move and working age, regardless of his current tenure, is his 'experience turnover profile' $S(X)$. Again, this is observable as a relation between experience and separation rates.

The most firmly established fact about labor mobility of all kinds is that it declines with age. It declines much more sharply with length of tenure. The declines in both $S(X)$ and $S(T)$ are strongest initially and decelerate subsequently. Several tenure and age profiles of separation rates are shown in tables 5.1–5.3.

Table 5.2 shows the decline with age in the proportion of job changers (number of job changers divided by number employed) in 1961. The

Table 5.2   Job changers as percent of employed men, US, 1961

			Age			
	18–19	20–24	25–34	35–44	45–54	55–64
Percent	23.5	24.4	14.9	10.2	7.1	4.0

Source: BLS, 1963.

Table 5.3   Separation equations (1967–73)

Young men, pooled

$S(X) = 0.486 - 0.034X + 0.002X^2$ $R^2 = 0.02$
              (5.2)   (3.6)

$S(X,T) = 0.692 + 0.006X - 0.0000X^2 - 0.172T + 0.009T^2 = 0.29$
                    (1.0)   (0)   (19.7)   (16.3)

Older men, pooled

$S(X) = 0.015 + 0.0028X - 0.000X^2$ $R^2 = 0.003$
              (0.4)   (0.5)

$S(X,T) = 0.208 + 0.0035X - 0.0000X^2 - 0.024T + 0.0005T^2$ $R^2 = 0.10$
                    (0.3)   (0.2)   (6.4)   (4.1)

Source: NLS Tapes.

decline is similar when measured in terms of number of job changes rather than job changers, since a similar fraction (35%–40%) of job movers in each age group changed jobs more than once during the year (BLS, 1963, Table A).

Table 5.1 shows cross-classifications of separations, quits, and layoffs by experience and tenure in the period 1971–3 in the two NLS samples of men (young men, ages 19–29, and older men, ages 50–64, in 1971). The tenure profiles within working age (experience) classes are steeply declining and decelerating (convex). Mobility does not decline with working age at given tenure levels *within* each of the cohort age ranges. The decline *between* the young and old cohort is pronounced, but it shows mainly in quits.

The separation equations in Table 5.3, derived from NLS panel data, summarize the conclusion that *within* the two age panels declines of mobility with working age (experience), shown by $S(X)$ in Tables 5.1 and

5.2, are due to the effect of tenure which is revealed in the regression $S(X,T)$: for young men, experience effects (coefficients of X, X^2) vanish when tenure (T, T^2) is included. No experience effects are observed for older men with or without the tenure variables.[3] However, estimates of $S(X)$ and $S(X,T)$ in Michigan Income Dynamics data which cover the complete age spectrum (Table 5.5, panel C, lines 1 and 2) show that net aging effects remain even after the inclusion of tenure, although they are reduced in size and significance. In all data sets the explanatory power resides mainly in the tenure variables; mobility is convex both in tenure and in experience; and the tenure profile is much steeper than the experience profile.

3.   Wage and mobility structures: some theory

We now turn to broad theoretical considerations with which we may analyze the facts of labor mobility. Some skills acquired in a particular firm are not transferable to other firms. The acquisition of such 'specific' components of human capital by workers and the consequent wage pattern suffice to produce the tenure effects in the attachment to the firm which we observed in Tables 5.1 and 5.3. At the same time, individual differences in amounts of specific capital investment imply a heterogeneity in mobility, or in attachment to the firm (length of tenure), as well as in the strength of tenure effects, that is, in slopes of the tenure–separation probability relation.

The effects of acquiring job-specific capital on mobility may be described as follows: successful job matches eventually result in wage levels W which exceed expected alternative wages W_g. The higher the wage W the less incentive to quit, given W_g and the usual fluctuations in demand. Separations are high during the initial 'probation' period and then drop to low levels. It is reasonable to assume that a successful match is only a starting point for a continuing employment relation which often involves investments of workers and firms in worker skills, and these are partially nontransferable.[4] Employer investments involve hiring, screening, and training costs which are recouped by a wage policy such that both quits and layoffs are deterred, that is, $W_g < W < \text{VMP}$, where VMP is the worker's value of marginal product in the firm.

Define $W = W_g + W_s$, where W_g is the worker return on his general (transferable) human capital and W_s is the difference between the (higher) wage received in the firm and the opportunity wage elsewhere (also W_g). Similarly, W_e is the employer's return on the costs of investing in workers, the difference between the worker's productivity (VMP) and the wage paid to him (W). Workers are deterred from quitting, and employers from dismissing workers, because of these returns. Total separations are affected by $\Delta = (\text{VMP} - W_g) = W_s + W_e$, that is, by both components of returns to specific capital. In this paper we do not focus on the distinction between quit and layoff or consider the question whether employers and workers engage in joint or in separate optimizing behavior (but see Mortensen, 1978). Plausibly, W_s and W_e are expected to be positively related: a good match and opportunity for joint investments are recognized by both employee and employer.

The distribution of returns to specific capital (Δ) creates individual (and group) differences in tenure–turnover profiles. Tenure profiles are horizontal only when $\Delta = 0$, in which case tenure has no effect on mobility or on wages. With $\Delta > 0$, tenure profiles of specific capital do not emerge instantaneously as the worker joins the firm. Specific capital is accumulated over time, given a successful match, and the returns grow over time. Both the rate of growth of these returns and their ultimate level affect mobility: the 'tenure effect' is positively correlated with both. The convexity of the tenure–mobility profiles, and concavity of the tenure–wage profiles, are due to the eventual completion of specific capital accumulation in the firm.[5]

Thus the economics of specific human-capital information predict the coexistence of heterogeneity and of 'tenure dependence' in accounting for mobility. The two aspects of behavior are related and are not to be viewed as mutually exclusive hypotheses: persons who favor large volumes of specific capital investment exhibit relatively little mobility (except for an initial period of repeated search and occasional later moves) and strong tenure effects.[6] Low levels of specific investment behavior, whether intentional or due to inefficiency in job matching, imply high (persistent) mobility levels independent of tenure (zero or small tenure effects). If rates of decline of experience profiles of mobility reflect primarily the slopes of tenure profiles, as appears to be the case, the flat and high profiles of 'movers' and the downward-sloping profiles of 'stayers' imply a progressive divergence over the life-cycle in observed mobility behavior of a heterogeneous population.

The growing divergence of mobility rates over the working age parallels the repeatedly observed divergence of individual life cycle wage profiles (see Mincer, 1974). The human-capital model can interpret both divergences as lifetime outcomes of unchanging individual differences in abilities and opportunities. This view cautions against literal impressions that older cohorts are more heterogeneous than younger ones, or against the notion that the experience of longer tenure creates a 'reinforcement effect', that is, a desire to invest in specific capital. This is not to say, however, that such views are not valid. Habit formation and unexpected events do modify lifetime histories, but they need not be invoked in an initial analysis.

The major implication of specific capital heterogeneity for the structure of mobility is the existence of differential tenure effects. Levels of $S(T)$ are higher and slopes flatter for individuals and groups who acquire little specificity in their human capital, while steeper slopes and eventually lower levels characterize tenure functions of large specific capital investors. Empirical observations should reveal steep downward slopes in tenure–turnover profiles uncorrected for 'heterogeneity bias', as well as 'true' negative slopes after correction for bias.

A related set of predictions applies to the wage structure: a major one is the existence of tenure effects on wages which are additional to the effects of general human capital accumulation. This suggests a reformulation of the earnings function to include a tenure term. The experience and tenure coefficients should provide a decomposition of worker returns to general (transferable) and specific (nontransferable) human capital investments. As in the case of mobility, it is also necessary to attempt correction for the danger of upward biases in tenure effects which is posed by the existence of heterogeneity.

Other implications of the theory relate to the effects of age (experience) on mobility and wages $S(X)$ and $W(X)$. An interesting conclusion is that mobility declines and wages grow with age even if there are no 'aging' effects, that is, even if mobility depended only on levels of tenure and not directly on age (given tenure). Similarly, wages grow (on average) over the life cycle even if no general (experience) capital is accumulated. Also $W(X)$ should be concave if $W(T)$ is concave, and $S(X)$ convex because $S(T)$ is. Indeed, without specific capital phenomena, the convex shape of the age patterns of mobility $S(X)$ would be difficult to understand.

4.   Tenure effects on mobility in homogeneous and in heterogeneous groups

A simple heuristic model makes the notions intuitively clear:[7] The propensity to move at the individual level, or the separation rate in a homogeneous group, is a function:

$$s = f(T, X) \qquad (5.1)$$

where s is the probability of separation in period t, T is length of current employment in the firm up to time t, and X is total work experience (working age). The slope of the age (experience) profile is:

$$\frac{ds}{dX} = \left(\frac{\partial s}{\partial T} \cdot \frac{dT}{dX}\right) + \frac{\partial s}{dX} \qquad (5.2)$$

Here $\partial s/\partial T$ is the slope of the tenure profile, dT/dX is the growth of tenure with working age, and $\partial s/\partial X$ is the true age effect, if any. Note that $0 < dT/dX < 1$. Tenure would grow by the same amount as age only in the case of perfect immobility: it increases initially with age since it is necessarily short at early stages of experience. At later stages dT/dX approaches zero as T approaches the fixed value $[(1/s) - 1]$ in the case of no tenure dependence, that is, when $\partial s/\partial T = 0$. In the case of job specificity or tenure dependence, i.e., when $\partial s/\partial T < 0$, dT/dX remains positive at later ages as well.[8] A regression of T on X, not shown here, reveals a positive slope and slight concavity.

Decomposition (5.2) yields the following conclusions about the observed decline of mobility with age:

(a) Even if there were no 'age effects' ($\partial s/\partial X = 0$), mobility would decline with age, because of job specificities, that is, because mobility declines with tenure ($\partial s/\partial T < 0$). No decline would be observed if mobility were independent of tenure (see section 9, theorem 2).

(b) Again abstracting from age effects, since $dT/dX < 1$, the slope of the experience profile is less than that of the tenure profile.

(c) Convexity in the tenure profile would be reinforced or simply reflected in the age profile if dT/dX decreases over time, or is constant. Moreover, this could happen even if there is an age effect and even if the age effect were concave.

(d) Decline of mobility with age is faster the stronger the decline of mobility with tenure, apart from the pure age effect.

Up to this point the analysis applies to a homogeneous group, defined by the identical $S(X,T)$ function for each of its members. Components of life cycle mobility can be observed directly in such groups by estimation of equation (5.1). Generally, it is not possible to define homogeneous groups empirically, so that estimation of (5.1) cannot be carried out directly. If in fact individual propensities to move are not reduced by tenure, yet differ among workers, the observed group tenure profile $S(T)$ will have a downward slope, and it is likely to be convex as well, because persons with high propensities to move are more likely to separate at early levels of tenure while those with low propensities are more likely to stay on a long time. The decline in the tenure profile consequently reflects the degree of heterogeneity when measured by the variance in propensities to move, while convexity would reflect a decline in that variance, as only stayers remained in the long-tenure classes.[9]

Let us now define a heterogeneous population in consonance with specific capital heterogeneity as a collection of homogeneous subgroups among which mobility rates differ at given levels of tenure, while tenure curves $S(T)$ decline in some or most of the subgroups. By the preceding argument, any degree of specific capital heterogeneity will lend a downward bias (steeper than average slope) to the observed group tenure curve. We should note that heterogeneity biases can exist without any true tenure effects, for reasons not involving specificity. But, if the tenure effect $(\partial s/\partial T)_i$ is zero in each subgroup i, the observed population experience profile $S(X)$ will be horizontal, since its slope is an average of slopes in the subgroups. Conversely, if $(\partial s/\partial T)_i < 0$ in each or some subgroups, the observed experience profile must slope down. Thus, in the absence of age effects, the age profile of mobility $S(X)$ provides a clear test of the presence or absence of tenure effects in the group, regardless of the group's degree of heterogeneity.

As an example, the popular 'mover–stayer' model (see Blumen, Kogan, and McCarthy, 1955; Singer and Spilerman, 1976), which assumes heterogeneity and neglects tenure effects, must be rejected by the decline in the age–mobility profile, in so far as the latter is not exclusively due to pure age effects [$\partial s/\partial X < 0$ in (5.1)].

Although the decline in life cycle mobility reflects the existence and strength of tenure effects, it yields no information on the extent of heterogeneity in the population. Assessment of heterogeneity is important, however, both in its own right and as a basis for recognition and correction of bias in the estimated tenure effects.

5. Empirical mobility functions

An open-ended empirical procedure for estimating tenure effects in the presence of heterogeneity is to enter a number of variables which are likely to capture heterogeneous behavior in a regression of tenure on mobility. The tenure slope estimate in the multiple regression is reduced compared with its value when it is the only right-hand variable. The reduction measures the extent of heterogeneity bias due to these variables. This procedure was applied to the NLS data and the results are shown in Table 5.4. In addition to experience, the heterogeneity factors in the regressions were education, health, hours of work, family status variables, industry, and union membership. In terms of contribution to the adjusted coefficient of determination R^2, the last two factors were the most pronounced. The reduction in slope was about 20–30 per cent for the young men, and larger (relative to the flatter slope) for the older men. This procedure is clearly incomplete for our purposes here, although of interest in the substantive studies of particular factors.

A scheme that is more general, in the sense that it does not require an enumeration of heterogeneity factors, derives from another definition of a

Table 5.4 *Gross and net tenure–separations slope, NLS, 1967–71*

	Young men				Older men			
	1967–69		1969–71		1967–69		1969–71	
	Slope[d]	R^2	Slope	R^2	Slope	R^2	Slope	R^2
Gross Coefficient[a]	−0.1420	0.182	−0.1100	0.151	−0.028	0.12	−0.027	0.12
Net Coefficient[b]	−0.0845	0.200	−0.0847	0.165	−0.016	0.17	−0.006	0.20
Heterogeneity factors[c]		0.131		0.110		0.07		0.11

Notes
[a]Linear coefficient in the regression of separation of tenure.
[b]Partial coefficient of tenure (linear term) in the multiple regression.
[c]Regression variables other than tenure.
[d]Tenure coefficients always highly significant (t > 4).

heterogeneous population: at a given level of tenure, members of a homo-geneous group have equal probabilities of moving during the next period regardless of their past mobility, while in a heterogeneous group probabi-lities differ even at fixed current tenure. Since frequency of past mobility is an indicator of personal probability ('propensity to move'), which differs among workers, its (partial) correlation with mobility in the next period, given tenure, reveals the existence, and estimates the degree, of heteroge-neity. And to the extent that the prior mobility variable captures and therefore standardizes for differential mobility levels, its inclusion corrects the bias in the estimated tenure slope.

Information on prior mobility was available in the NLS data for young men as the number of interfirm moves (NM) between 1966 and 1971. For the older men in NLS such information was not available, but we con-structed a variable (PM) on the number of (survey to survey) periods between 1965 and 1973 during which at least one move took place.[10]

Table 5.5 presents, in successive steps, regressions for young men (panel A) in which separations (job changes) in the period 1971–3 are predicted by years of work experience (X,X^2) up to 1971; tenure (T,T^2) in 1971; and mobility prior to the current job (NM). The prior mobility variable was also interacted with experience (XNM). The same regressions (except that PM replaces NM) predict job change rates of NLS older men in 1973–5 (panel B), and of all MID men in 1975–6 (panel C).

Briefly, the findings are: inclusion of tenure (row 2) shows it to be the

Table 5.5 Mobility functions $s = f(X, T, NM, Ed)$

Constant	X	X^2	T	T^2	NM	$X \cdot NM$	Ed	R^2
A. Job change rates of young men in NLS, 1971–3 ($n = 1,595$; $\bar{s} = 0.375$)								
0.506	-0.0424	0.0020						0.023
	(3.98)	(2.44)						
0.612	-0.0064	0.0002	-0.1071	0.0057				0.124
	(0.61)	(0.24)	(10.41)	(5.73)				
0.547	-0.0034	0.0001	-0.0963	0.0051	0.0060			0.131
	(0.32)	(0.17)	(9.02)	(5.08)	(3.65)			
0.547	-0.0171	0.0003	-0.0822	0.0048		0.0035		0.141
	(1.63)	(0.36)	(7.38)	(4.72)		(5.56)		
0.850	-0.0253	0.0004	-0.0797	0.0047		0.0032	-0.0211	0.149
	(2.37)	(0.48)	(7.17)	(4.64)		(5.04)	(3.89)	
Sample means	5.05	40.72	2.82	15.75	5.17	17.28	12.54	

Constant	X	X^2	T	T^2	PM	$X \cdot PM$	Ed	R^2
B. Job change rates of older men in NLS, 1973–75 ($n = 1,282$; $\bar{s} = 0.091$)								
0.1645	-0.0063	0.0001						0.0008
	(0.16)	(0.22)						
0.5060	-0.0165	0.0002	-0.0172	0.0003				0.065
	(0.44)	(0.5)	(7.67)	(5.78)				
0.5553	-0.0282	0.0004	-0.0045	0.00009	0.0921			0.098
	(0.57)	(0.85)	(1.57)	(1.49)	(6.82)			

152

Table 5.5 Mobility functions $s = f(X, T, NM, Ed)$ concluded

Constant	X	X^2	T	T^2	X·SM	SM	Ed	R^2
0.5680	-0.0275 (0.76)	0.0004 (0.79)	-0.0049 (1.72)	0.0001 (1.64)		0.0024 (6.77)		0.098
0.7551	-0.0344 (0.93)	0.0005 (0.93)	-0.0052 (1.82)	0.0001 (1.75)	(0.79)	0.0024 (6.62)	-0.0026 (0.79)	0.098
Sample mean 38.09		1464.78	16.42	415.26	0.5226	19.89	11.67	

C. Job change rates of all ages, MID, 1975–6 ($\bar{s} = 0.116$; $n = 1,562$)

Constant	X	X^2	T	T^2	X·SM	SM	Ed	R^2
0.2285	-0.0099 (4.08)	0.0001 (2.61)						0.027
0.2402	-0.0054 (2.11)	0.00009 (1.66)	-0.0149 (4.35)	0.0004 (3.09)				0.043
0.2014	-0.0063 (2.46)	0.0001 (1.95)	-0.0097 (2.71)	0.0002 (1.91)		0.2300 (5.01)		0.058
0.2329	-0.0078 (2.92)	0.0001 (2.16)	-0.0107 (2.91)	0.0003 (2.25)	0.0112 (3.09)			0.049
0.3484	-0.0062 (2.42)	0.00008 (1.43)	-0.0099 (2.82)	0.0002 (2.05)		0.2175 (4.74)	-0.0105 (3.46)	0.066
Sample mean 18.71		516.37	7.26	113.38	1.27	0.095	12.64	

Note: X = years of work experience; T = years of tenure on the current job; Ed = years of schooling, NM = number of interfirm moves in the period 1966–71 of young men in NLS. Adjusted to length of period if experience started after 1966; PM = number of 2-year periods between 1965 and 1973 during which job change occurred among older men in NLS; SM = number of annual periods between 1968 and 1975 during which a job change occurred among men in MID. Adjusted work experience started after 1968; w = logarithm of hourly wage; $\bar{w}$ = mean of w; $\bar{s}$ = mean rate of job change (over a 2-year period in NLS, annual in MID); n = sample size; R^2 = adjusted coefficient of determination, t = statistics in parentheses.

153

variable which is responsible for the gross age decline in separations among young NLS men (row 1, panel A). Looking at rows 1 and 2 of panel B, we find that the older NLS men show neither gross nor net age (experience) effects. While net age effects are absent within the limited age ranges in the NLS data (young $\leq$ 29, old $\geq$ 50), they are reduced (going from row 1 to row 2 in panel C) but remain significant in the MID regressions which cover the whole, age spectrum. The absence of gross age effects (row 1, panel B) in the older cohort reflects very small tenure effects (slopes) at this stage. This is consistent with a strong convexity of tenure (and age) profiles over the long run. The comparable tenure slopes are much steeper for the young because they are dominated in regressions by early tenure levels. Indeed, in a subsample of older men whose tenure does not exceed eight years (not shown here), the tenure slopes are quite as steep as those of young men. Thus, the differences between the young and the old need not be interpreted as a change in the mobility structure.

The inclusion of prior mobility variables shows the existence of heterogeneity in mobility behavior; the variable is a strong predictor of mobility in the next period given experience and tenure at the beginning of the period. Persons who moved more frequently prior to the current job are more likely to leave the job earlier than others. Prior mobility appears to be a stronger predictor at older than at younger ages. When converted into an elasticity, prior mobility is also several times larger in the older group. Evidently, repeated mobility at an advanced age represents persistent mobility, suggesting little stake in job tenure or lack of opportunity, while repeated mobility at young ages does not have the same connotation. We tried to test the proposition that prior mobility at older ages is a better index of heterogeneity *within* each of the panels: the experience–prior mobility interaction variable, shown in row 4 of each panel, with positive and significant. Incidentally, the existence of this interaction implies that age (experience) profiles of mobility are not only higher but also flatter for movers (PM large) than for stayers (PM small), as we theorized in section 3.

The introduction of the prior mobility variable was designed to separate 'movers' from 'stayers'. If effective, such 'standardization' should reduce the tenure slope in the regression. Tenure slopes are indeed reduced in row 3 and below in all three data panels. The reduction is small among the young and large among the old, as would be expected since PM is a stronger indicator of persistent mobility at older ages. The average reduction in the linear tenure term at mid-experience levels (MID) is about one-third. That is, heterogeneity biases the steepness of tenure-turnover profile upward by about 50 per cent, on average. The education variable shown in the last rows of Table 5.5 appears to predict some reductions in mobility at given levels of initial mobility, but has no additional predictive power among the old.

6. Net age effects on mobility

Although they do not appear in the NLS regression of Table 5.5, age effects (coefficients of experience $\partial s/\partial X$) on mobility are present in the MID regressions in panel C and were seen in the decline of mobility rates at fixed levels of tenure when the older cohort was compared with the younger (Table 5.1). The economics of this downward shift in tenure curves may be found in the more traditional aspects of labor mobility; job change is a response to higher wage levels beckoning elsewhere as well as a search for specific investment opportunities.

For a given wage gain, the supply response would diminish with working age (at given levels of tenure), since the payoff period declines. Such effects, however, would not become pronounced until late in the working life, especially in view of positive and not negligible discounting. Emphasis on the effect of finite life (working age) on expected returns cannot produce a convex experience–turnover profile, nor can it rationalize the fact that the observed net age declines ($\partial s/\partial X$) occur relatively early in the working life (see rows 3 to 5, panel C). However, the gain from mobility may decline early in the life cycle not because of the declining payoff period but because of rising costs: in particular, costs of geographic mobility rise with family size and the presence of school-age children.

Age effects are, indeed, more important in migration than in local job mobility. The decline in migration with age is steeper than the decline in local job mobility: one-third of young compared to less than 10 per cent of older job changers migrate. But the greater costs of migration include also costs due to locational specificities which exist in addition to job specificity, so stronger 'pure aging' is not the only reason for a sharper age decline in migration than in local job mobility: tenure effects which reflect both job and location specificities are, indeed, sharper for migrants.

Another set of age factors, unrelated to location, may operate in the early years of work experience: the range of quality of jobs and of the job match cannot be ascertained by mere search, and some knowledge must be acquired by actual experimentation. Also, job training and opportunities for investment in general human capital may present themselves sequentially in different firms. Beyond the first decade of working life, we may expect that human capital investors who eventually find a reasonably compatible workplace develop a strong attachment to the job.

7. Tenure and mobility effects in the wage function

Specific capital investments imply tenure effects on wages which cause the tenure effects in mobility. Wage heterogeneity due to differential specificities similarly produces some of the heterogeneity in mobility. Consequently, we should observe tenure effects in addition to general work-experience effects in wage functions. Moreover, these effects may be exaggerated in empirical estimates in view of interpersonal diversity in specific investment behavior.

Information on job mobility can and should be built into the standard earnings function. The inclusion of the tenure variable should capture returns to specific (nontransferable) capital accumulation, permitting the experience term to measure returns to general (transferable) capital accumulation. Information on prior mobility should also be used in correcting for heterogeneity bias. The explanatory power of the enriched wage function ought to be enhanced.

The coefficients of experience (X) in the standard wage function, which includes only education in addition to the experience terms, reflect a gross effect dw/dX which is a mixture of returns to general and specific capital:

$$\frac{dw}{dX} = \left(\frac{\partial w}{\partial t} \cdot \frac{dT}{dX}\right) + \frac{\partial w}{\partial X} \tag{5.2a}$$

The standard wage function has an upward-sloping and concave experience profile (the concavity is more pronounced when $w = \log$ wage) in cross-sections and in longitudinal data.[11] Its slope has been derived in human capital theory and in econometric studies. In view of (5.2a), it is incorrect to interpret the coefficients of experience dw/dX as measures of returns to general human capital stocks. Such returns are measured by $\partial w/\partial X$, that is, by coefficients of experience *when tenure is included in the wage function.* Clearly dw/dX overstates $\partial w/\partial X$ if specific capital is of any importance. The experience coefficients in the earnings function which omits tenure is an upward-biased measure of returns to general human capital accumulated on the job.

It is interesting to note, according to (5.2a), that even if no general capital were accumulated in the work career, wages would still rise over the life cycle, and, as a group average, the wage profile would tend to be concave so long as the tenure wage profile is concave and dT/dX does not increase over the life cycle.

Wage functions with tenure variables $w(X,T)$ can be estimated in homogeneous groups without bias (homogeneity defined as the same tenure wage profile), but no such groups can be defined *a priori*: in the presence of heterogeneity, the tenure coefficient is likely to be exaggerated, as in the case of mobility, and corrections need to be devised. More precisely, the bias arises because greater specificity produces larger discrepancies between the marginal product in the firm and the opportunity wage $\Delta = $ VMP $- W_g = W_s + W_e$, where W_s is the specific return to the worker, and W_e to the employer, and Δ as well as W_s differ among workers and firms. Δ affects the length of tenure. It is plausible for W_s and W_e to be positively correlated, because a fruitful match has to be recognized as such by both parties. Therefore W_s is a good index of Δ, and the tenure–wage coefficient which attempts to measure W_s is likely to be correlated with expected tenure (see discussion of theorem 3, section 10 below). Heterogeneity in W_s is thus likely to produce an upward bias in the estimates of tenure effects of wages, that is, of returns to specific worker investments. An additional source of bias could result from a positive correlation between general and specific investments; here steeper tenure–wage curves would start at higher levels. To the extent that general returns to capital (W_g) are not fully measured (standardized) by regression variables, the bias will arise.

Of course, positive tenure coefficients need not reflect wage growth in the firm. Higher wage levels (not growing with tenure) for the same labor in some firms also create incentives to stay there longer. Although transitional, this relation is likely to be widespread in a dynamic economy as an equilibrating phenomenon. Such supply adjustments to shifting demands are most likely to involve younger people whose mobility is less costly especially in terms of specific capital losses. Note that in this case prior mobility is not a good index of wage heterogeneity. Similar and more long-lasting effects can be created by above-equilibrium union wages and nepotism.

Can information on prior mobility be used in the wage function as an index of relevant heterogeneity, that is, of individual differences in W_s and consequently in the wage–tenure coefficient? The answer is less clear in the wage equation than in the mobility equation. Positive serial correlation in mobility makes the link between length of tenure and mobility almost definitional whatever the source of heterogeneity in mobility. The problem for the wage equation is that bias in the tenure coefficient is only in part due to heterogeneity in specific capital, and the latter is responsible for only a part of the heterogeneity in mobility. Thus prior mobility may be a weak instrument for elimination of heterogeneity bias. Its role in wage formation is nevertheless of interest to our study.

Table 5.6 presents wage functions of the younger and older NLS men, and of all men in MID. The independent variables are the same as in the mobility functions in Table 5.5; the dependent variable is the logarithmic wage.[12] Row 1 is the 'standard' wage function where the independent

Table 5.6 *Wage functions*

A. Wages functions of young men, NLS, 1971 ($\bar{w}_{71} = 1.28$; $n = 1,442$)

Constant	Ed	X	X²	T	T²	NM	X·NM	R²
-0.0311	0.0847	0.0658	-0.0022					0.194
	(17.93)	(7.36)	(3.23)					
0.0021	0.0079	0.0433	-0.0011	0.0702	-0.0052			0.229
	(16.50)	(4.70)	(1.52)	(7.27)	(5.24)			
0.0026	0.0779	0.0432	-0.0011	0.0702	-0.0052	-0.00003		0.229
	(16.47)	(4.69)	(1.53)	(6.99)	(5.17)	(0.03)		
-0.0343	0.0790	0.0401	-0.0010	0.0780	-0.0055		0.0011	0.231
	(16.64)	(4.29)	(1.46)	(7.49)	(5.49)		(1.98)	
Sample mean	12.52	4.97	39.94	2.78	15.06	5.29	17.48	

B. Wage functions of older men, NLS, 1973 ($\bar{w}_{73} = 1.59$; $n = 982$)

Constant	Ed	X	X²	T	T²	PM	X·PM	R²
0.6733	0.0696	0.0113	-0.0002					0.175
	(10.37)	(0.14)	(0.22)					
0.5359	0.0683	0.0130	-0.0002	0.0136	-0.0002			0.199
	(10.19)	(0.17)	(0.24)	(2.99)	(1.58)			
0.6105	0.0666	0.0157	-0.0003	0.0067	-0.00006	-0.0482		0.202
	(9.88)	(0.2)	(0.3)	(1.09)	(0.4)	(1.8)		
0.5996	0.0668	0.0146	-0.0003	0.0080	-0.00009		-0.0011	0.201
	(9.90)	(0.2)	(0.28)	(1.32)	(0.57)		(1.52)	

Table 5.6 *Wage functions concluded*

Constant	Ed	X	X²	T	T²	PM	X·PM	R²
Sample mean	11.58	38.05	1462.28	15.23	367.19	0.573	21.83	

C. Wage functions of all ages, MID, 1975–6 ($\bar{w}_{75} = 1.69$; $n = 1,560$)

Constant	Ed	X	X²	T	T²	SM	X·SM	R²
0.2437	0.0741	0.0467	−0.0007					0.263
	(17.45)	(14.07)	(9.56)					
0.2351	0.0732	0.0372	−0.0006	0.0305	−0.0007			0.295
	(17.57)	(10.70)	(8.08)	(6.59)	(4.25)			
0.2791	0.0722	0.0378	−0.0006	0.0264	−0.0006	−0.1842		0.298
	(17.33)	(10.91)	(8.32)	(5.44)	(3.49)	(2.94)		
0.2541	0.0725	0.0404	−0.0007	0.0249	−0.0006		−0.0150	0.299
	(17.43)	(11.15)	(8.55)	(5.01)	(3.39)		(3.04)	
Sample mean	12.63	18.72	516.96	7.27	113.53	0.094	1.26	

Note: Regression variables as in Table 5.5.

variables are education and experience. In the next row the tenure terms are added. In the third row we add the prior mobility variable, and in the last row we observe its interaction with experience.

In the young men's panel (A), the introduction of tenure reduces the experience coefficients. At this stage (on average, five years of experience), wages grow 6.6 per cent per year of experience (row 1); 4.3 per cent as returns to general post-school human capital accumulation (row 2); and the remaining 2.3 per cent owing to specific capital accumulation. The tenure coefficients are large and significant. Prior mobility is not related to current wages and does not affect the tenure coefficients. The coefficient of the interaction variable (XNM) is positive but quite small, and its introduction raises the tenure coefficient slightly. Apparently, differences in early mobility of young men are not indicative of future differences in specific capital investments, nor do they capture differences in wage levels which are positively related to the length of current tenure.

In the wage function for NLS older men (panel B), the experience profile is a plateau, but tenure slopes are positive (and concave) though much flatter than for young men.[13] Still, the observed tenure effect is biased upward. Introduction of prior mobility cuts the linear term in half and reduces its significance. We may conclude that repeated mobility at an advanced stage of the life cycle is an indicator of persistent turnover, denoting little investment in specific capital. The mobility variable has a negative effect, showing that frequent movers have lower wages than stayers, given education, experience, and current tenure. This is in contrast to the young whose past mobility did not imply a downward selection. We may conclude that intensive early mobility – about a half of the first decade in our NLS data – is not necessarily an inverse index of longer-run tendencies to acquire specific capital or an index of inability to acquire a good job match. It may even be a positive index of efficiency in making wage gains by moving across firms or of greater intensity of search for an optimal career.

Taken together the findings in both NLS panels (A and B) show that tenure effects on wages are significant, reflecting the firm-specific component of wage progress on the job. This component accounts for about one-third of wage growth per year in the early part of working life. At young ages, past mobility does not clearly distinguish tendencies toward firm-specific human capital behavior. It does so, however, at older ages. At that stage lesser specific investments also result in lower wages, apparently as a result of slower growth over the past decades.[14]

The age function in the MID panel (C), which covers all working ages, indicates that on average (and in mid-career) the firm-specific component accounts for 20–25 per cent of wage growth per year (difference between the X-coefficients in rows 1 and 2). Prior mobility is negatively related to wages. The interaction term is also negative suggesting that men who continue to be frequent movers in the third decade of their working lives have both lower wages and flatter experience profiles of wages. The inclusion of prior mobility variables reduces the tenure slope by close to 20 per cent. Thus, heterogeneity biases the tenure–wage slope coefficient upward by about 25 per cent, half as much as it biased the tenure-mobility slope (panel C of Table 5.5).

8.   Tenure, experience, and mobility: additional remarks

We used the generalized term 'specific human-capital behavior' to cover both the informational aspect of job matching and the theory of specific human-capital investment. The former is a necessary condition for the latter, and both are required for completeness.

There is another and popular view that the reality of tenure effects on mobility and on wages is largely institutional. The effects we analyzed are seen as 'seniority rights' which include job security, pension rights, vacations, and seniority-based pay and promotion advantages. But the distinction is superficial. The 'rights' themselves may well derive from human capital specificities in the presence or absence of formal, especially union, regulations. Indeed, recent research shows that tenure turnover profiles decline and tenure wage profiles grow as much and more (!) in the non-union as in the union sector.[15]

In the past, experience coefficients dw/dX were sometimes crudely interpreted as returns to on-the-job general investments. In the wage function which includes tenure, the experience coefficients $\partial w/\partial X$ effectively segregate returns to general human capital investments, but they contain both returns to on-the-job general investment and across-jobs wage gains due to mobility (but not to tenure). These across-jobs wage changes are positive in purposive quits especially in migration, but are often negative when job change results from layoff, 'exogenous' quit, and job dissatisfaction (Bartel and Borjas, 1981).

Over the life cycle, the effects of mobility on wages become increasingly less favorable, at least as measured by money wages. Quits, migration, and occupational upgrading predominate in mobility of the young, but they become relatively unimportant at older ages. Since the frequency of job change declines over the life-cycle for reasons already spelled out, the mobility component of wage growth declines over the life-cycle as a result of declines both in the size and in the frequency of wage gains across firms. This is another aspect of the well-known concavity of the experience profile of wages.

Some models elevate the across-firm wage change to a single explanation of the typical concave life-cycle wage profile: the worker is envisaged as moving up a fixed offer-wage distribution over his lifetime. Successful on-the-job search results in across-jobs wage growth. With a fixed offer-wage distribution, turnover declines with labor market experience. Thus older workers have a higher wage and a smaller probability of future separation.[16]

Although they produce concavity in the wage profiles, such models are quite inadequate as major explanations of magnitudes of wage growth over the life cycle (dw/dX). In a calculation based on the Coleman–Rossi data, Bartel (1975) shows that no more than 25 per cent of personal wage growth can be attributed to across-firms wage changes during the first 15 years of work experience, when mobility is most pronounced. The models, therefore, neglect the bulk of the phenomenon they are trying to explain. Moreover, concavity in the wage profile does not require job mobility, in human capital theory, or in fact: Borjas (1978a) found the typically pronounced concavity in wage profiles of NLS workers who spent all of their working life in a single firm.

Although crude, our estimates of tenure and experience wage effects suggest that about 25 per cent of life-cycle wage growth, which abstracts from economy-wide changes, is due to specific capital investment. Taken together, the estimates provide a complete though very rough decomposition of lifetime wage growth: about 25 per cent of it is due to interfirm mobility; another 20–25 per cent to firm-specific experience; and over 50 per cent to general (transferable) experience.

Perhaps the best way to summarize the life-cycle relation between mobility and wages is to recognize that initial (first decade ?) job search has two major purposes: to gain experience, wages, and skills by moving across firms; and to find, sooner or later, a suitable job in which one can settle and grow for a long time. The life-cycle decline in mobility is, in part evidence of successful initial mobility, an interpretation which is corroborated by corresponding life cycle growth in wages.

In both older and younger age groups, stayers and successful searchers grow faster than unsuccessful searchers or 'noninvesting' movers. However, a comparison of movers and stayers puts successful searchers in the category of movers among the young, but in the category of stayers (they moved when younger) among the old. As a result, comparisons of stayers and movers show that young movers do as well as or better than stayers, but ultimate stayers show superior wage growth and higher wage levels in the later decades.

We note, in conclusion, that 'tenure and heterogeneity effects' are not restricted to job mobility. Whenever specific capital matters, comparable dualities between returns ('wages') and turnover may be expected. Some evidence on this generalization is available in analyses of location decisions (Da Vanzo, 1976), and of marital instability (Becker *et al.*, 1977).

In the second part of our paper we shall treat labor mobility and wage growth over the life-cycle as related stochastic processes. We first focus on the evolution of these processes for a given worker, interpreting our formulation within the context of existing theories of turnover and of wage growth and listing some of the implications of these theories. Next we take up the question of unmeasured heterogeneity in the population, and the problem of sample selection over time, known as the 'mover–stayer' problem. A simple result is proved (theorem 3 in section 10) which relates the behavior of a heterogeneous group to the behavior of the individual members of that group. In interpreting the result, we pay particular attention to the on-the-job-training hypothesis. Lastly, we describe a method to estimate various parametrizations of the separation and wage equations.

9. Evolution of stochastic processes
Definitions:

z = parameter indexing a particular worker
X = the worker's labor-market experience
t = the worker's job tenure
X_0 = market experience at which the worker started on his current job, so that, at each moment in time, $X_0 + t = X$

Let

$F(t|X_0, z) \equiv$ probability that for a worker of type z, job tenure does not exceed t on a job which started at X_0

Let $f(t|X_0, z) = \partial F/\partial t$ be the associated density, and let $\hat{s}(t, X_0, x)$ be the 'hazard function' of this distribution, defined by $\hat{s} = f/(1 - F)$. Then $\hat{s}$ is the conditional density of job separation at tenure t, given that a tenure level t has been attained. The definitions of $\hat{s}$ and f imply that F may be written as

$$F(t|X_0, z) = 1 - \exp\left[- \int_0^t \hat{s}(y, X_0, z)\, dy\right] \tag{5.3}$$

There may be a positive probability that a job episode never terminates, in which case

$$\lim_{t \to \infty} F(t|X_0, z) < 1, \text{ i.e., } \int_0^{\infty} \hat{s}(y, X_0, z) \, dy > \infty$$

It should be noted that F determines $\hat{s}$ uniquely and vice versa. Since $f \geq 0$, $\hat{s} \geq 0$ so that F is nondecreasing.

One purpose of this section is to draw some parallels between wage rates and separation probabilities. Let $\hat{w}(t, X_0, z)$ be the mathematical expectation of the wage that worker z, with experience $X_0 + t$, and tenure t, will receive. It may be noted that both $\hat{w}$ and $\hat{s}$ are mathematical expectations conditional upon t, X_0, and z.

Hereafter it is assumed that when a particular job episode terminates, it is immediately followed by a new job episode. That is, there are assumed to be no unemployment spells or spells of market nonparticipation. Given this assumption, consider now the special case in which $\partial \hat{s}/\partial X_0 = \partial F/\partial X_0 = 0$. Then each job episode is identically distributed. If, in addition, the job episodes are also assumed to be independently as well as identically distributed, then turnover becomes a pure renewal process (see Feller, 1966, ch. 11). In what follows, we study processes that are more general than the renewal process.

Let $a(X, z)$ be the probability density that worker z will experience a job separation at the point in time at which his market experience is equal to X. (For the special case where turnover is a renewal process, $a(X, z)$ is known as the renewal density.) Also let $h(t|X, z)$ be the probability density that a worker with market experience x will have current job tenure equal to t. Note that for this statement to be true, the worker must have experienced a job separation at exactly $X = t$ level of market experience, and no subsequent separations. Therefore,

$$h(t|X, z) = \begin{cases} 1 - F(X|0, z) & \text{if } t = X \\ a(X - t, z) \, [1 - F(t|X - t, z)] \\ \text{if } 0 \leq t < X \end{cases} \tag{5.4}$$

Then

$$a(X, z) = \hat{s}(X, 0, z) \, [1 - F(X|0, z)] + \int_0^X \hat{s}(t, X - t, z) \tag{5.5}$$
$$h(t|X, z) dt$$

$$= \hat{s}(X, 0, z) \, [1 - F(X|0, z)] + \int_0^X \hat{s}(t, X - t, z)$$
$$a(X - t, z)$$
$$\times [1 - F(t|X - t, z)] \, dt$$

Define $y(X, z)$ as the mathematical expectation of worker z's wage conditioned only on his market experience. Then

$$y(X, z) = \hat{w}(X, 0, z) [1 - F(X|0, z)] + \int_0^X \hat{w}(t, X - t, z) \tag{5.6}$$

$$\times a(X - t, z) [1 - F(t|X - t, z)]\, dt$$

Now define two new functions

$$s(t, X, z) = \hat{s}(t, X - t, z) \to \hat{s}_X = \hat{s}_{X_0}$$
$$\text{and } s_t = \hat{s}_t - \hat{s}_{X_0}$$

and

$$w(t, X, z) = \hat{w}(t, X - t, z) \to w_X = \hat{w}_{X_0}$$
$$\text{and } w_t = \hat{w}_t - \hat{w}_{X_0}$$

(where subscripts denote partial derivatives).
Making the substitution into (5.5) and (5.6):

$$a(X, z) = s(X, X, z) [1 - F(X|0, z)] + \int_0^X s(t, X, z) \tag{5.7}$$

$$\times a(X - t, z) [1 - F(t|X - t, z)]\, dt$$

and

$$y(X, z) = w(X, X, z) [1 - F(X|0, z)] + \int_0^X w(t, X, z) \tag{5.8}$$

$$\times a(X - t, z) [1 - F(t|X - t, z)]\, dt$$

There are several reasons for choosing this approach. First, the deterministic earnings function approach (see, for example, Mincer, 1974) is a special case of the above formulation. In the earnings function approach, turnover is not considered explicitly, so that job tenure is not included in the regressions. Such regression equations are here interpreted as expectations conditional on X and on the measured component of z, and the expressions that characterize such conditional expectations are provided in equations 5.8 and 5.11. A set of sufficient conditions under which the conditional expectation of the wage is a monotonically increasing function of experience is provided below.

Secondly, the job-matching theory of turnover as developed in Jovanovic (1978b) is fully consistent with the above formulation when the latter is restricted to $s_X = w_X = 0$ for all (X, t, z), so that the turnover process is predicted by the theory to be one of pure renewal. The key assumptions in generating such a result are a constant rate of discount and an infinite horizon, and an assumption about the job search process that makes the latter 'pure experience search', in the terminology of Nelson (1970). The model implies $w_t > 0$ for all t, and $s_t < 0$ for large enough t and perhaps for all t.

Two other search models that explicitly look at the implications for life-cycle mobility are those of Burdett (1973) and of Jovanovic (1978a). Both models involve the worker's moving up a fixed wage-offer distribution over his lifetime, with search of the 'pure search' kind (Nelson's terminology again). Both models imply that in the absence of on-the-job training, $s_X < 0$ and $w_X > 0$, while $s_t = w_t = 0$ for given X. When firm-specific human capital investment is introduced (Jovanovic, 1978a), the latter prediction changes to $s_t < 0$ and $w_t > 0$ for all workers except the very old, for whom $s_t > 0$ and $w_t < 0$ as they allow their human capital to depreciate toward the end of their lifetime.

General on-the-job training raises wages, implying $w_X > 0$ given a monotonic increase in general training over time. Since general training raises the worker's productivity in many firms, it is not expected to affect turnover, and therefore $s_X = 0$ is consistent with $w_X > 0$ and with the presence of general training. A somewhat different argument asserts that the presence of general training is the cause of turnover at younger ages, because it may be optimal for the training to be acquired in several different firms and such turnover is planned in advance. To the extent that such turnover is significant (and little evidence is available to support its significance), it may produce nonmonotonic effects on $s(t, X, z)$ for young workers as t and X increase.

Next, define

$$H(t, X, z) \equiv \int_0^t h(\tau|X, z) \, d\tau \geq 0 \qquad (5.9)$$

so that $H(0, X, z) = 0$ and $H(X, X, z) = F(X|0, z)$. Then, integrating by parts in (5.7) and (5.8), one obtains

$$a(X, z) = s(X, X, z) - \int_0^x s_t (t, X, z) H(t, X, z) \, dt \qquad (5.10)$$

and

$$y(X, z) = w(X, X, z) - \int_0^X w_t (t, X, z) H(t, X, z) dt \qquad (5.11)$$

Equations (5.10) and (5.11) should be compared for their identical structure.

The following results follow directly from equations (5.10) and (5.11), and are presented in theorem 1:

Theorem 1: Let $s_t < 0$ and $w_t > 0$ for all values of the arguments. Then
$$a(0, z) = s(0, 0, z) \text{ and } y(0, z) = w(0, 0, z)$$
$$a_X(0, z) = s_X (0, 0, z) + s_t (0, 0, z)$$
$$y_X(0, z) = w_X (0, 0, z) + w_t (0, 0, z)$$
$$a(X, z) > s(X, X, z)$$
$$y(X, z) < w(X, X, z) \text{ for any } X > 0$$

Proof: The assertions follow from the observation that

$$H(t, X, z) > 0 \text{ for any } t > 0 \text{ and from } H(0, 0, z) = 0$$

Next, consider the special case in which $s_x = 0$, as would be true if turnover was a pure renewal process. We then have the following theorem:

Theorem 2: Let $s(t, X, z)$ be independent of X. Then if $s_t < 0$ for all (X, t, z) then $a_X < 0$ for all (X, z).

Proof: Differentiating with respect to X in equation 10 and applying the assumption that $s_X = 0$ yields

$$a_X(X, z) = s_t(X, X, z) [1 - F(X|0, z)] - \int_0^X s_t(t, X, z) H_X(t, X, z) dt$$

and since, by assumption, $s_t < 0$, it is sufficient to prove that $H_X < 0$ for all (t, X, z). But since s does not depend on X, neither does F. Therefore, $H_X(t, X, z) = \int_0^t a_X(X - y, z) [1 - F(y|X - y, z)] dy$. Therefore, $H_X(t, X, z) < 0$ if $a_X(X - y, z) < 0$ for all $y \varepsilon (0, X)$. But then, $a_X(X, z) < 0$ for all X if there exists an $\varepsilon > 0$, no matter how small, such that $a_X(X, z) < 0$ for $X \varepsilon (0, \varepsilon)$. But such an ε must exist if $a_X(X, z)$ is continuous at zero, because by theorem 1, $a_X(0, z) = s_t(0, 0, z) + s_X(0, 0, z) < 0$. (The last inequality follows by the assumptions of the theorem.) This completes the proof of the theorem.

Intuitively, one expects that theorem 2 should extend to the case where $s_t < 0$ *and* $s_X < 0$, that is, to the case where the separation propensity declines with both tenure and market experience, and that the decline in the separation propensity considered as a function of market experience alone $[a(X, z)]$ should, if anything, be reinforced. While this conjecture may be true, an attempt at proving it along the lines of the proof of theorem 2 fails, because H_X cannot be signed.

Theorem 2 asserts that the renewal density declines monotonically if the interevent waiting time distribution possesses a monotonically decreasing hazard rate. Note that a parallel result for monotonically increasing hazard rate distribution does not hold. That is, $s_t > 0$ everywhere does not imply that $a_X > 0$ for all X, and an attempt at a proof along the lines of the proof of theorem 2 is quickly seen to fail (a counterexample is given in Brown, 1940).

It should be noted that $y(X, z)$ is the wage-experience profile for a homogeneous group of type z. By differentiating in equation (5.8), conditions may be derived under which the wage experience profile will be increasing and concave ($y_X > 0$), $y_{XX} < 0$) for each homogeneous group. These conditions involve restrictions on both $w(t, X, z)$ and $s(t, X, z)$. For example, one set of *sufficient* conditions for a monotonically increasing wage experience profile ($y_X > 0$) is: $s_X = 0$, $s_t < 0$, $w_t > 0$, $w_X > 0$ and $w_{tX} > 0$, as may be verified by direct differentiation in (5.8) (and by applying the result of theorem 2 which states that $s_t < 0$ and $s_X = 0$ jointly imply $a_X < 0$ everywhere). Assuming that $s_X = 0$ is theoretically consistent with assuming that $w_X > 0$, that is, the accumulation of purely general on-the-job training raises the worker's productivity in all firms by an equal amount, and it raises his wage (hence $w_X > 0$), but is not expected to have any effect on his separation propensity (hence $s_X = 0$). Sufficient conditions for concavity of the wage experience profile may also be derived but turn out to be much more complicated.

Let $T(X, z)$ be the mathematical expectation of current tenure. The latter is distributed according to (5.4), and, therefore,

$$T(X, z) = X[1 - F(X|0, z)] + \int_0^X th(t|X, z)dt \qquad (5.12)$$

$$= X - \int_0^X H(t, X, z)dt$$

The second equality follows after integration by parts. Since $H > 0$, $T(X, z)$ cannot exceed X. Differentiating with respect to X,

$$T_X(X, z) = 1 - F(X|0, z) - \int_0^X H_X(t, X, z)dt \qquad (5.13)$$

so that $T_X(0, z) = 1$. If turnover is a pure renewal process, with $s_t < 0$ everywhere, then, from theorem 2, $H_X > 0$, and $T_X > 0$ for all X. In other words, the average current job tenure will always be increasing for a cohort of workers as their market experience increases under these assumptions.

Let t_1, t_2, ... be the sequence of completed job durations. Then the distribution function for the length of the nth job episode is $F(t_n| \sum_{j=1}^{n-1} t_j, z)$. The t_i are therefore neither independent nor identically distributed random variables so long as the aging effect (s_X) is not zero. If there is no aging effect, then each job episode has the same distribution, and if, in addition, one assumes that the job episode durations are independently distributed, then turnover is a pure renewal process. Let $n(X, z)$ be the number of job changes (the number of completed episodes or the number of 'prior moves') on the experience interval $(0, X)$. Then

$$E\, n(X, z) = \int_0^X a(t, z)\, dt \qquad (5.14)$$

To see this, note that $a(X, z)\, \Delta X + 0\, [(\Delta X)^2]$ is the probability that exactly one job change will occur in the interval $(X, X + \Delta X)$. The expression in equation (5.14) is the sum of these probabilities over such disjoint intervals as Δt tends to zero. Dividing both sides of (5.14) through by X, taking the limit as X tends to infinity, and applying L'Hôpital's rule, one obtains

$$\lim_{X \to \infty} a(X, z) = \lim_{X \to \infty} \frac{En(X, z)}{X}$$

Of course, $(\partial/\partial X)\, [E\, n(X, z)] = a(X, z)$, and $(\partial^2/\partial X^2)\, [E\, n(X, z)] = a_x(X, z)$. Therefore, a monotonically decreasing experience profile of turnover implies concavity of the expected number of moves treated as a function of experience.

9.1 Example: A pure renewal process
Let F be the mixed exponential distribution:

$$F(t|X, z) = 1 - \frac{1}{2}[e^{-zt} + e^{-(z + b)t}]$$

so that no aging effects exist. Then

$$f(t|X, z) = \frac{1}{2}[ze^{-zt} + (z + b)e^{-(z + b)t}]$$

and

$$s(t, X, z) = z + \frac{b}{1 + e^{bt}}$$

$$s_t(t, X, z) = -\frac{b^2 e^{bt}}{(1 + e^{bt})^2}$$

The slope of the separation function is in this case independent of z. If $b = 0$, then $s_t = 0$, and so b is a parameter denoting the extent of duration dependence. Then let

$$\hat{T}(X, z) = \frac{1}{2}\left(\frac{1}{z} + \frac{1}{z + b}\right) < \frac{1}{z}$$

The renewal equation (5.5) has for this case explicitly been solved by Bartholomew (1972) to yield

$$a(X, z) = [\hat{T}(X, z)]^{-1} + (z + \frac{b}{2} - [(\hat{T}(X, z)]^{-1})e^{-(z + \frac{b}{2})X}$$

$$= \frac{2(z + b)z}{2z + b} - \frac{b^2}{2(2z + b)}e^{-(z + \frac{b}{2})X}$$

so that

$$a_x(X, z) = -\frac{b^2}{4}e^{-(z + \frac{b}{2})X}$$

If there is no duration dependence with tenure ($b = 0$), then separations also do not decline when considered as a function of age. Notice also that

$$a_{Xz}(X, z) = -X a_X(X, z) > 0$$

so that although the $s(t, X, z)$ curves are parallel in z, that is, ($s_{tz} = 0$), the

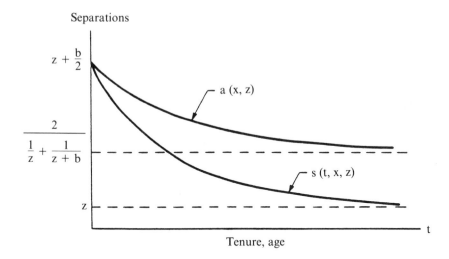

Separations

$z + \dfrac{b}{2}$

$a\,(x, z)$

2

$\dfrac{1}{z} + \dfrac{1}{z + b}$

$s\,(t, x, z)$

z

Tenure, age

t

Figure 5.1   Separations by age and by tenure

age curves are not – they diverge. The relationship between the tenure and age curves is depicted in Figure 5.1.

The divergence of age profiles therefore can be explained not only by divergences in levels of specific human capital (as argued in part 1) but also as a purely statistical phenomenon.

In this case, convexity of $s(t, X, z)$ implies convexity of $a(X, z)$ in X. As b (the duration-dependence parameter) tends to zero, both $a(z, z)$ and $s(t, X, z)$ tend to a constant, z.

10.   Group relationships

The individual-specific parameter z is by assumption unobservable. It is an 'incidental parameter'. The population distribution of z is assumed to be $p(z)$ with mean μ and variance σ. The nondegeneracy of this distribution gives rise to the dynamic version of the sample selection problem studied below.

Upon entering the labor market, a worker is assumed to be a random drawing from the distribution $p(z)$. On the other hand, a worker who is starting out on a job *other* than his first, at a market experience level $X > 0$, is *not* representative of the entire population in the sense that he cannot be considered a random drawing from the distribution $p(z)$.

Although $p(z)$ is interpreted to be an unmeasured personal characteristic, it is likely to be correlated with measured personal characteristics such as years of schooling, race, sex, and so on. The unmeasured variability in separation propensities decreases as the number of personal characteristics held constant increases, which is another way of saying that part of the variance of z is 'explained' by the variance of a set of personal characteristics. (Note that this is quite different from the statement that the variance of the conditional distribution is never greater than the variance of the marginal distribution. The latter statement is false.)

The objective now is to characterize the distribution of z conditional upon X and t. Let $p(z|X)$ be the distribution of z which applies to workers who are just *starting* a new job at experience level X. Applying Bayes's theorem,

$$p(z|X) = \begin{cases} \dfrac{a(X, z)\, p(z)}{\int a(X, z)\, p(z)dz} & X > 0 \\[2mm] p(z) & X = 0 \end{cases} \tag{5.15}$$

It follows that $p(z|X)$ is a continuous function of X except at $X = 0$. (The continuity of $p(z|X)$ at $X > 0$ follows if $a(X, z)$ is continuous.)

Now let $\hat{p}(z|X_0, t)$ be the probability density that the worker is of type z, given job tenure t and experience $X_0 + t$. At the time he joined his current firm, the worker was drawn from the population $p(z|X_0)$. Applying Bayes's theorem again,

$$\hat{p}(z|X_0, t) = \frac{[1 - F(t|X_0, z)]p(z|X_0)}{\int [1 - F(t|X_0, z)]\, p(z|X_0)dz} \tag{5.16}$$

Equation (5.16) follows because $1 - F(t|X_0, z)$ is just the probability that the worker of type z will attain tenure t in a job which he started at experience level X_0.

Writing $\hat{s}(t|X_0, z)$ instead of $\hat{s}(t, X_0, z)$ (thereby emphasizing the nature of the conditioning), let

$$\hat{s}(t, X_0) \equiv \int \hat{s}(t|X_0, z)\, \hat{p}(z|X_0, t)\, dz \tag{5.17}$$

be the probability that the worker will experience a separation at tenure t given X_0 and t. We then have

Theorem 3

$$\hat{s}_t(t, X_0) = \int \hat{s}_t(t|X_0, z)\, \hat{p}(z|X_0, t)dz - \sigma^2(\hat{s}|X_0, t) \tag{5.18}$$

and

$$\hat{w}_t(t, X_0) = \int \hat{w}_t(t|X_0, z)\hat{p}(z|X_0, t)dz$$
$$- \text{Cov}(\hat{s}, \hat{w}|X_0, t)$$

where $\hat{w}(X_0, t)$ is the mathematical expectation of the wage given X_0 and t, where $\sigma^2(\hat{s}|X_0, t)$ is the variance of $\hat{s}(t|X_0, z)$ in the population $\hat{p}(z|X_0, t)$, and where $\text{Cov}(\hat{s}, \hat{w}|X_0, t)$ is the covariance of $\hat{s}(t|X_0, z)$ and $\hat{w}(t|X_0, z)$ in the population $\hat{p}(z|X_0, t)$. Before proving this theorem, we elaborate on the meaning of its assertions. When t is increased by one unit while X_0 is held constant, tenure and experience both increase by one unit. Therefore, s_t is the sum of the tenure effect and of the pure age effect, and similarly for w_t. In words, the first assertion of the theorem may be expressed as: the slope of the average separation rate is equal to the average of the individual slopes, minus the variance of the separation rates in the *current* population $\hat{p}(z|X_0, t)$. This result is an extension of an earlier result of Barlow *et al.* (1963). Their result states that mixtures of decreasing hazard rate distributions also possess decreasing hazard rates.

Suppose that there are no true age or tenure effects on separations, so that $\hat{s}_t(t|X_0, z) = 0$ everywhere. Then, $\hat{s}_t(t, X_0) = -\sigma^2(\hat{s}|X_0, t)$, so that the group separation rate declines although the individual separation rates are constant. Furthermore, $\hat{s}(t, X_0)$ would in this special case be convex in t (which would be consistent with the evidence presented in Table 5.1), if $\sigma^2(\hat{s}|X_0, t)$ declines monotonically with t. For a wide class of distributions $p(z|X_0)$, one would expect such a monotonic decline because the selection out of the sample as t increases is such that 'movers' are (on average) selected out leaving behind only 'stayers', so that the sample of those left behind becomes increasingly more homogeneous. But σ^2 need not decline monotonically, as is demonstrated by the following example. Assume that at any X_0, $p(z|X_0)$ is such that z takes on only two values, say 1 and 0, and that the $z = 1$ workers have a higher separation propensity than do the $z = 0$ workers. Assume that the initial ($t = 0$) sample is such that nine-tenths of the workers are $z = 1$ types and that the remaining one-tenth are $z = 0$ types. Then the initial variance of z is $(1 - 0.9)0.9 = 0.09$. As tenure increases, the population proportions shift towards the stayers, and the variance of z increases steadily up to 0.25, at which point the population proportions are equal. Thereafter, the variance declines monotonically to zero.[17] Of course, a monotonic decline would occur even in this example if the initial proportions happened to be equal, or were weighted in favor of stayers.

According to the first part of equation (5.18), the change in the group separation rate is always an overstatement (in the negative direction) of the average of the individual changes. However, the same is not true of the group wage change, because the covariance term in the second part of equation (5.18) may be either positive or negative. The relevant question is whether a 'mover' (for whom $\hat{s}(t, X_0) - \hat{s}(t|X_0, z)$ is negative) would expect to receive higher or lower wages than a 'stayer' at a certain tenure level *given that it was optimal for both to remain in the firm up to that time*. A theory which predicts that a worker will separate from a job on which wages paid to him were low relative to his prior expectations implies nothing about this question.

The implications of human-capital theory for the sign and magnitude of $\text{Cov}(\hat{w}, \hat{s}|X_0, t)$ are ambiguous. In section 1 we emphasized the role of firm-specific human capital in generating a wedge between the worker's productivity in his current firm and his productivity elsewhere. Consider the polar case in which the ratio of general to firm-specific training is fixed and constant across workers, but in which workers differ in the total amount of training that they undertake. Suppose that z is an index inversely related to the worker's propensity to invest in on-the-job training. Under the assumptions, a higher propensity to invest also implies a higher investment in specific training, so that $\hat{s}_z(t|X_0, z) > 0$. Assume that z is not correlated with unmeasured ability components. Then, since investment in training involves forgone earnings early on in return for higher earnings later, this implies that $w_z(t|X_0, z) > 0$ for young workers (for whom X_0 and t are small), and $w_z(t|X_0, z) < 0$ for older workers. Therefore, $\text{Cov}(\hat{w}, \hat{s}|X_0, t)$ is *positive* for the young and *negative* for the old workers.

Suppose instead, however, that the total amount of training across individuals (with given X_0 and t and other observable characteristics) is constant while only the ratio of general to specific training varies positively with z. Now, high-z workers have higher separation propensities because their training is general in nature rather than firm specific. In view of the well-known argument (see Becker, 1975) that general training is financed by the workers, such workers earn lower wages initially, and higher wages later on, than do 'stayers' whose training is more firm specific in nature. (Again, this conclusion depends on the assumption that the preference for the type of training is not related to unmeasured ability differences.) The implication now is that $\text{Cov}(\hat{s}, \hat{w}|X_0, t)$ is *negative* for the young, and *positive* for the old workers.

Neither polar case is expected to obtain in practice. Both the total amount and the composition of the training may be expected to vary systematically with z. But which dominates? The wage function estimates reported in Table 5.6 strongly suggest that the dominant variation is in the total amount of training. This inference is made by comparing the second row with the fourth row in panel A, and the second row with the third in panel B. The variables PM and NIM are indexes of past mobility and are correlated with $\hat{s}(t|X_0, z)$. By definition, z is the unmeasured component of heterogeneity, and the inclusion of PM and NIM therefore has the effect of reducing the *absolute value* of $\text{Cov}(\hat{w}, \hat{s}|X_0, t)$. In both panels, there appears to be an effect of this reduction. The wage growth, measured as the sum of the coefficients on X and T, *increases* for the young men when NIM is included, and *decreases* for the older men when PM is included in the regression, and these changes are consistent with the first polar case, but not the second, as is clear from equation (5.18).

Proof: Substituting for $\hat{p}$ into (5.17),

$$\hat{s}(t, X_0) = \frac{\int f(t|X_0, z)\, p(z|X_0)dz}{\int [1 - F(t|X_0, z)]\, p(z|X_0)dz} \tag{5.19}$$

Differentiating with respect to t in equation (5.16).

$$\hat{p}_t(z|X_0, t) = \frac{-f(t|X_0, z)\, p(z|X_0)}{\int (1 - F)\, pdz} \tag{5.20}$$

$$+ \frac{[1 - F(t|X_0, z)]p(z|X_0) \int f(t|X_0, z)\, p(z|X_0)dz}{[\int (1 - F)\, pdz]^2}$$

$$= [- \hat{s}(t|X_0, z) + \hat{s}(t, X_0)]\, \hat{p}(z|X_0, t)$$

Multiplying both sides by $\hat{s}(t|X_0, z)$ and integrating both sides over z,

$$\int \hat{s}(t|X_0, z)\, \hat{p}_t(z|X_0, t) = \hat{s}(t, X_0)^2 - \int \hat{s}(t|X_0, z)^2\, \hat{p}dz \tag{5.21}$$
$$= [E(\hat{s})]^2 - E(\hat{s}^2) = - \sigma^2(\hat{s}|X_0, t)$$

and differentiating with respect to t in equation (5.17) and using equation (5.21), one obtains the first assertion of the theorem which has therefore been proved. Next,

$$\hat{w}(X_0, t) = \int \hat{w}(t|X_0, z)\, \hat{p}(z|X_0, t)dz$$

and differentiating with respect to t,

$$\hat{w}_t(X_0, t) = \int \hat{w}_t\, \hat{p}dz + \int \hat{w}\hat{p}_t\, dz$$
$$= \int \hat{w}_t\, \hat{p}dz + \int \hat{w}(t|X_0, z)\, [\hat{s}(t, X_0)$$
$$- \hat{s}(t|X_0, z)]\, \hat{p}(z|X_0, t)dz$$

where the second equality follows in view of equation (5.20), and this completes the proof of the theorem.

11. An estimation procedure[18]

The following estimation procedure exploits the property of $p(z|X)$ (defined in equation (5.15)) of having two different functional forms, implying, in turn, two different functional forms for $\hat{s}(t, X_0)$ in (5.17). We demonstrate below how identification of the parameters may be secured by subdividing the sample of all workers into two subsamples: one for which $X_0 = 0$ (workers on their first job ever), and the other for which $X_0 > 0$. In fact, in the following illustration for an *additive* fixed effect parametrization of $s(t, X, z)$, the parameters are overidentified, which suggests that identification may be secured for more complex functional forms which we hope to consider in future work. The following additive fixed effect formulation is perhaps inadequate in capturing the individual differences, but it is adequate as an illustration of the estimation method. Let

$$s(t, X, z) = z + S(t, X) \tag{5.22}$$

where, without loss of generality $S(0, 0) = 0$. One possible way to proceed is to take first differences in equation (5.22) and eliminate z, thereby also eliminating the selection bias. There are two problems with this approach. First, using differences in separation probabilities as the dependent variable leads to coefficients that are not significant. Secondly, there is then no possibility of estimating σ^2, the variance of z. We have therefore chosen a different procedure, which is based on deriving two separate relationships associated with equation (5.22).

Let $z(t, X)$ be the conditional expectation of z, and $s(t, X)$ the conditional expectation of the separation rate, given t and X. Then, taking conditional expectations in equation (5.22).

$$s(t, X) = z(t, X) + S(t, X) \tag{5.23}$$

where

$$z(t, X) = \int z\hat{p}(z|X - t, t)dz$$

Then since

$$F(t|X - t, z) = 1 - \exp\left[- zt - \int_0^t S(y, X - t + y)\, dy\right]$$

application of (5.16) and (5.15) leads to

$$z(t, X) = \frac{\int ze^{-zt} a(X - t, z)\, p(z)dz}{\int e^{-zt} a(X - t, z)\, p(z)dz} \text{ for } X > t \tag{5.24}$$

$$z(X, X) = \frac{\int ze^{-zX} p(z)dz}{\int e^{-zX} p(z)dz} \text{ for } X = t$$

(Workers with $X = t$ are on their first job.) Assume now that $p(z)$ is the normal distribution. Then a straightforward calculation yields

$$z(X, X) = \mu - \sigma^2 X$$

where μ and σ^2 are the mean and variance of z.

So that (for workers on their first job)

$$s(X, X) = \mu + S(X, X) - \sigma^2 X \qquad (5.25)$$

The discontinuity of the $\hat{p}$ distribution at $X = 0$ carries over to $z(t, X)$. It is seen from (5.24) that

$$z(0, 0) = \mu$$

while taking the limit in (5.24) and observing (5.7),

$$\lim_{X \to 0} z(0, X) = \mu + \frac{\sigma^2}{\mu}$$

To obtain a closed form approximation to $z(t, X)$ for $X > t$, a first-order Taylor's expansion is performed in equation (5.24) around the point ($t = 0, X = \varepsilon$) where $\varepsilon > 0$. Then

$$z(0, \varepsilon) = \frac{\int za(\varepsilon, z) p(z)dz}{\int a(\varepsilon, z) p(z)dz}$$

$$z_t(0, \varepsilon) = - \frac{[\int z^2 a(\varepsilon, z) p(z)dz + \int z\, a_x(\varepsilon, z) p(z)dz]}{\int a(\varepsilon, z) p(z)\, dz}$$

$$+ \frac{[\int z\, a(\varepsilon, z)p(z)dz + \int a_x(\varepsilon, z) p(z)dz]}{[\int a(\varepsilon, z) p(z)\, dz]^2} \int za(\varepsilon, z)p(z)dz$$

and

$$z_X(0, \varepsilon) = \frac{\int z\, a_x(\varepsilon, z) p(z)dz}{\int a(\varepsilon, z) p(z)dz} - \frac{\int a_x(\varepsilon, z) p(z)dz}{\int a(\varepsilon, z) p(z)dz} z(0, \varepsilon)$$

For *any* $X > t$, and any $\varepsilon > 0$ no matter how small,

$$z(t, X) = z(0, \varepsilon) + z_t(0, \varepsilon)t + z_X(0, \varepsilon)(X - \varepsilon) \tag{5.26}$$
$$+ \text{ higher order terms}$$

$$= \lim_{\varepsilon \to 0} z(0, \varepsilon) + [\lim_{\varepsilon \to 0} z_t(0, \varepsilon)] \, t$$

$$+ [\lim_{\varepsilon \to 0} z_X(0, \varepsilon)] \, X$$

$$+ \text{ higher order terms}$$

Evaluating the limits, and using theorem 1,

$$\lim_{\varepsilon \to 0} z(0, \varepsilon) = \frac{\int z \, a(0, z) \, p(z)dz}{\int a(0, z) \, p(z)ds}$$

$$= \frac{\int z \, s(0, 0, z) \, p(z)ds}{\int s(0, 0, z) \, p(z)dz}$$

$$= \frac{\int z^2 \, p(z)dz}{\int z \, p(z)dz} = \mu + \frac{\sigma^2}{\mu}$$

$$\lim_{\varepsilon \to 0} z_t(0, \varepsilon) =$$

$$- \frac{[\int z^2 s(0, 0, z) \, p(z)dz + \int z[s_X(0, 0, z) + s_t(0, 0, z)] \, p(z)dz]}{\int s(0, 0, z) \, p(z)dz}$$

$$+ \frac{\int z \, s(0, 0, z) \, p(z)dz + \int [s_X(0, 0, z) + s_t(0, 0, z)] \, p(z)dz}{[\int s(0, 0, z) \, p(z)dz]^2}$$

$$= - \mu^{-1}[\int z^3 \, pdz + \mu(\alpha + \gamma)] + \mu^{-2}(\int z^2 \, pdz + \alpha + \gamma)$$

where $\alpha \equiv S_X(0, 0)$ and $\gamma = S_t(0, 0)$.

If $p(z)$ is a symmetric distribution so that the third order moment about the mean is equal to zero, then one obtains $\int z^3 pdz = \mu^3 + 3\sigma^2\mu$, and therefore

$$\lim_{\varepsilon \to 0} z_t(0, \varepsilon) = (\mu^{-2} - 1)(\alpha + \gamma) + 1 - 3\sigma^2 - \mu^2 + \frac{\sigma^2}{\mu}$$

Also,

$$\lim_{\varepsilon \to 0} z_X(0, \varepsilon) = - \frac{\sigma^2}{\mu^2}(\alpha + \gamma)$$

Taking an expansion in (5.23),

$$s(t, X) = \alpha X + \gamma t + z(t, X) + \text{higher order terms}$$

But making the substitution into (5.26),

$$z(t, X) = \mu + \frac{\sigma^2}{\mu} + [(\mu^{-2} + 1)(\alpha - \gamma) + 1 - 3\sigma^2 - \mu^2 + \frac{\sigma^2}{\mu^2}]t$$

$$- \frac{\sigma^2}{\mu^2}(\alpha + \gamma) X + \text{higher order terms}$$

Therefore for $t < X$,

$$s(t, X) = \mu + \frac{\sigma^2}{\mu} + [(\mu^{-2} - 1)\alpha + \mu^{-2}\gamma + 1 - 3\sigma^2 - \mu^2 \quad (5.27)$$

$$+ \frac{\sigma^2}{\mu^2}]t + [\alpha - \frac{\sigma^2}{\mu^2}(\alpha + \gamma)]X$$

$$+ \text{higher order terms}$$

Also, expanding in (5.25)

$$s(X, X) = \mu + (\alpha + \gamma - \sigma^2)X + \text{higher order terms.} \quad (5.28)$$

Equations (5.27) and (5.28) are the two basic relationships estimated.

The separation propensity is of course unobservable. All that is observed is whether or not an individual has changed jobs within a particular period. Let $y = 1$ if the worker has changed jobs within the period $(X, X + \Delta X)$, and zero otherwise.

$$\text{Prob } (y = 1) = 1 - \exp\{ - \int_0^{\Delta X} s(t + y, X + y, z)dy\}$$

$$= s(t, X, z) \Delta X + 0 [(\Delta X)^2]$$

Similarly

$$\text{Prob } (y = 0) = 1 - s(t, X, z) \Delta X + 0 [(\Delta X)^2]$$

Therefore y_X has a mean equal to $s(t, X, z) \Delta X + 0 [(\Delta X)^2]$

Table 5.7   NLS young men's sample, 1967–73

	Separations		Quits		Permanent layoffs	
	$X = T$	$X > T$	$X = T$	$X > T$	$X = T$	$X > T$
Constant	0.78	0.64	0.5583	0.4439	0.103	0.1999
X	−0.1805	0.0137	−0.1112	0.0051	−0.0692	0.0086
	(23.22)	(1.13)	(14.55)	(0.4)	(12.51)	(0.844)
X^2	0.0098	−0.0012	0.0057	−0.0005	0.0042	−0.0006
	(15.38)	(1.27)	(9.02)	(0.524)	(9.09)	(0.862)
T		−0.1819		−0.0996		−0.0822
		(10.03)		(5.28)		(5.38)
T^2		0.0069		0.0032		0.0037
		(3.02)		(1.34)		(1.92)
XT		0.0037		0.0016		0.0021
		(1.65)		(0.696)		(0.924)
R^2	0.305	0.246	0.167	0.106		0.148
n	1,877	1,985	1,877	1,984	1,877	1,984

Ignoring the $0[(\Delta X)^2]$

$$y_X = [z + S(t, X)] \Delta X + u$$

where u is a disturbance with zero mean. In the data, ΔX was equal to two years. The regressions for the separation equations are reported in the first two columns of Table 5.7. (Separate regressions were also run for quits and for layoffs, and they are reported in the table, although they do not have an interpretation within the mathematical structure presented above.) The three linear coefficients and the two constant terms provide five restrictions on the four parameters so that the parameters are over-identified. However, the relative magnitude of the two constant terms is reversed from that implied by the theory, leading to an estimate of σ^2 which is negative, which may mean that the additive fixed effect formulation is inadequate. In future work, we intend to experiment with different functional forms for the separation and wage equations, focusing on the question of the best way to model the individual differences, and to organize the data so that the time interval ΔX is shortened: one year rather than two.

Acknowledgements
We are grateful to the National Science Foundation and the Sloan Foundation for support of this work. The research reported here is part of the

NBER's program in Labor Economics. Any opinions expressed are those of the authors and not those of the National Bureau of Economic Research.

Notes

1. The subject of women's labor mobility is reserved for separate study.
2. For analysis of geographic mobility see Bartel (1978) and Mincer (1978).
3. This is in contrast to the BLS data of Table 5.2 and may be peculiar to the NLS sample.
4. In his work, Jovanovic (1978b) has shown that job-matching processes produce downward-sloping tenure–separation functions and upward-sloping tenure–wage functions. Investments of employers and workers in their mutual association are a corollary. We use the language of specific capital to cover the combined phenomena.
5. We may note that even if returns to specific capital accumulation, and in particular W_s, did not decelerate with tenure, but grew in a linear fashion, the resulting growth of the reservation wage in job search would nevertheless lead to decelerating declines in the probability of quit, given a declining upper tail of the wage-offer distribution.
6. We must be careful, however, not to assert the converse: by itself, inertia does not bring about specific investments.
7. The deterministic treatment is for expository convenience only. See sections 9–11 for a more-formal and more-specialized analysis of the stochastic process.
8. Perhaps a simple way of illustrating the conclusion that dT/dX is larger with than without tenure dependence is to consider a case in which we go from none to some tenure dependence. Let the mean tenure in the group be T_{av} and the overall turnover rate s. Then, after a passage of a year, the $(1 - s)$ stayers have increased tenure by one year, while the s movers, without tenure dependence, have lost on average T_{av} years of tenure. The net change dT/dX is therefore $(1 - s) - sT$, which approaches zero since T approaches $[(1/s) - 1]$. Now, let s remain the same, but the process becomes tenure-dependent. In this case, the average tenure lost by movers is $T_{mav} < T_{av}$ since proportionately more of them are drawn from low-tenure classes. Consequently the net gain in tenure $dT/dX = (1 - s) - sT_m > (1 - s) - ST$.
9. Cf. theorem 3 in section 10. Such a decline in the variance need not be inconsistent with widening of differences in mobility rates.
10. For those men whose current tenure started before the initial year of reported prior mobility (1965 for the older men and 1966 for the young men in NLS, and 1968 for MID), no information on PM is available (12% of young men and 62% of the old men in NLS, and about 50% in MID). As a check on the results in Table 5.5 which implicitly assigns a value of PM $= 0$ to those whose tenure is too long, we used dummy variables on the complete samples, and we also replicated the regressions of Table 5.5 on the subsamples which contained information on prior mobility. The results were quite similar to those in Table 5.5 with one interesting feature: the tenure coefficients for the old men in NLS (with short tenure in the subsample) were as steep as for the young, and the inclusion of PM reduced the slope by a relatively small amount as it did for the young.
11. The longitudinal evidence is less familar. See Borjas and Mincer (1978) reporting Coleman–Rossi data, and Anderson *et al.* (1976) on the Continuous Work History Sample.
12. Dollar wage equations, not shown here, show similar patterns, but weaker predictive power.
13. This is true also in the sample with $T \leq 8$, in contrast to the short-tenure mobility equation (see note 11).
14. Supporting evidence is shown in (Bartel and Borjas (1981), as well as in previous research by Borjas. Borjas (1975) classified the older NLS men into movers and stayers. The latter were defined by the fact that their current job was the longest ever. Education

and experience were only slightly different in the two groups. The movers had lower wages (about 25%) and flatter experience profiles.

15.   See Freeman (1978), Borjas (1978), and others. The flatter union tenure slopes have been analyzed as effects of union policy. We suggest that they may also reflect lesser heterogeneity in the union compared with the nonunion sector.

16.   See Burdett (1973); Sorensen (1975). Jovanovic (1978a) is an adaptation of Burdett, which allows for on-the-job human-capital accumulation. It is doutful, however, that the assumption of a fixed wage-offer distribution can be maintained for workers whose skills are growing and changing over the life cycle.

17.   This example was supplied by R. Shakotko.

18.   Helpful comments by J. Heckman on an earlier version of this paper have led to considerable improvement of this section.

References

Anderson, R., Y. Balcer and D. Diamond (1976), 'A Model of Lifetime Earnings Patterns', in *Decoupling the Social Security Benefit Structure*: Hearings before the Subcommittee on Social Security, House of Representatives, 94th Congress, 2nd Session, on H.R. 14430, 1976, Washington, D.C.: US Government Printing Office.

Barlow, R. E., A. W. Marshall and F. Proschan (1963), 'Properties of Distributions with Monotone Hazard Rates', *Annals of Mathematical Statistics*, vol. 34, pp. 375–89.

Bartel, A. (1975), 'Job Mobility and Earnings Growth', NBER Working Paper no. 117.

Bartel, A. (1977), 'The Economics of Migration: an Empirical Analysis with Special Reference to the Role of Job Mobility', NBER Working Paper no. 198, August.

Bartel, A. and G. Borjas (1981), 'Wage Growth and Job Turnover', in S. Rosen (ed.), *Studies in Labor Markets*, Chicago: University of Chicago Press.

Bartholomew, D. (1972), *Stochastic Models for Social Processes*, New York: John Wiley.

Becker, G. S. (1975), *Human Capital*, 2nd edn, New York: Columbia University Press.

Becker, G. S., E. Landes and R. Michael (1977), 'An Economic Analysis of Marital Instability', *Journal of Political Economy*, December.

Blumen, I. M., M. Kogan and P. J. McCarthy (1955), *The Industrial Mobility of Labor as a Probability Process*, Ithaca, N.Y.: Cornell University Press.

Borjas, G. (1978a), 'Job mobility and Earnings Growth over the Life Cycle', NBER Working Paper no. 233, February.

Borjas, G. (1978b), 'Labor Turnover in the Union and the Public Sector', *Xerox*.

Borjas, G. and J. Mincer (1978), 'The Distribution of Earnings Profiles in Longitudinal Data', in Zvi Griliches (ed.) *Income Distribution and Economic Inequality*, John Wiley.

Brown, A. W. (1940), 'A Note on the Use of a Pearson Type III Function in Renewal Theory', *Annals of Mathematical Statistics*, pp. 448–53.

Burdett, K. (1973), 'On-the-Job Search', PhD thesis, Northwestern University.

Bureau of Labor Statistics (BLS) (1963), 'Job Mobility in 1961', Special Labor Force Report no. 35.

Bureau of Labor Statistics (BLS) (1975), 'Job Tenure of Workers, 1973', Special Labor Force Report no. 172.

Da Vanzo, J. (1976), 'Why Families Move', Rand Report, September.

Feller, E. (1966), *Introduction to Probability*, vol. 2, New York: John Wiley.

Freeman, R. (1978), 'Exit-Voice Tradeoff in the Labor Market', unpublished MS., Harvard University, April.

Greenwood, M. (1975), 'Research on Internal Migration in the U.S.', *Journal of Economic Literature*, June.

Heckman, J. (1977), 'Statistical Models for Discrete Panel Data', *Xerox*.

Heckman, J., and R. Willis (1977), 'A Beta Logistic Model for the Analysis of Sequential Labor Force Participation by Married Women', *Journal of Political Economy*, February.

Jovanovic, B. (1978a), 'Labor Turnover Where Jobs Are Pure Search Goods', unpublished MS., Columbia University, February.

Jovanovic, B. (1978b), 'Job-Matching and the Theory of Turnover', PhD thesis, University of Chicago.

Leighton, L. (1978), 'Unemployment over the Life-Cycle', PhD thesis, Columbia University.

Mincer, J. (1974), *Schooling, Experience and Earnings*, New York: Columbia University Press.

Mincer, J. (1978), 'Family Migration Decisions', *Journal of Political Economy*, October. (Chapter 7 of Volume 2.)

Mortensen, D. (1978), 'Specific Capital and Labor Turnover', *Bell Journal*, Fall.

Nelson, P. (1970), 'Information and Consumer Behavior', *Journal of Political Economy*.

Oi, W. (1961), 'Labor as a Quasi-Fixed Factor of Production', *Journal of Political Economy*, December.

Parnes, H. S. (1970), 'Labor Force Participation and Labor Mobility', in *A Review of Industrial Relations Research*, vol. 1.

Parsons, D. (1972), 'Specific Human Capital: Quits and Layoffs', *Journal of Political Economy*, November.

Parsons, D. (1978), 'Models of Labor Turnover', in *Research in Labor Economics*.

Rosen, S. (1966), 'Short-run employment variation on railroads', PhD thesis, University of Chicago.

Singer, B., and S. Spilerman (1976), 'Some Methodological Issues in the Analysis of Longitudinal Surveys', *Annals of Economic and Social Measurement*, NBER, Fall.

Sjastaad, L. (1962), 'Costs and Returns of Human Migration', *Journal of Political Economy*, part 2, October.

Sorensen, A. (1975), 'Growth in Occupational Achievement', in *Social Indicator Models*, New York: Russell Sage Foundation.

Stigler, G. J. (1961), 'Economics of Information', *Journal of Political Economy*, June.

Tuma, N. B. (1976), 'Rewards, Resources, and the Rate of Mobility', *American Sociological Review*, April.

6 Wage changes in job changes*

1. Introduction and overview

In this study we estimate short- and longer-run wage changes observed in the period of moving from one job to the next. Short-run wage changes are defined as the difference between the starting wage on the new job and the wage observed a year before on the old job. Longer-run changes are defined as the difference in wages between the two jobs at the same tenure levels, net of experience. In effect, this 'job gain' in wages measures the shift of the tenure–wage profile in the successive jobs. The wage changes of movers, as usually estimated, measure the difference between wage growth of movers and wage growth of all stayers during the observation period. Heterogeneity in wage profiles of workers creates a selectivity bias in using all stayers as the control group. We try to reduce the bias by using a more appropriate control group, namely, of those stayers whose mobility behavior, in addition to other observable characteristics, is similar to that of current period movers. Their wage growth on the job proxies for the wage growth forgone by movers.

Wage changes of movers were estimated in the period 1970–81, as well as in the more recent subperiod 1976–81, for white male workers, non-students, up to age 60. We distinguished subgroups of young (first decade of work experience) and of all other, more experienced workers. We also distinguished movers by type of separation – quit and layoff. Other characteristics, such as education, marital status, and union membership, were used as independent variables in the statistical regression equations.

Findings in both the shorter and longer run reveal similar facts: wage gains of movers are generally positive,[1] except for layoffs among the older workers. Wage gains in quits exceed wage gains in layoffs. Wage gains of older movers are smaller (or even negative) than wages of young movers. This is partly due to the greater frequency of layoffs (compared to quits) among older workers.

These systematic patterns are clearly observed, when the mobility wage gains are related to the group of next-period movers rather than to the less-appropriate control group of all stayers. Indeed, a large part of the gain is due to the lesser wage growth on the job of movers, compared to stayers. This is consistent with findings in our previous studies, according

*This chapter was first published in *Research in Labour Economics*, vol. 8 (1986), part A, pp. 171–97.

to which less-frequent movers receive more job training and grow more rapidly on the job.[2] This is one reason for the flatter lifetime trajectories of frequent movers. The other, according to our present findings is that movers – with the exception of young workers (especially quits) – despite average gains in moving, do not catch up with wage levels of stayers. This is true mainly of the more-experienced movers.

The adverse effect of layoffs compared to quits on mobility wage gains is not traceable to differential behavior on the prior job, in so far as it is reflected in wage levels and wage growth. Both are about the same prior to separation, and lower than among (the average) stayer. However, search behavior both on the job and off the job is apparently different. Unemployment encountered by most layoffs reduces wage gains, especially if it is prolonged. Fewer quits enter unemployment, which also tends to be shorter than in layoffs.

A search model which focuses on search efficiency, defined both as search effort and as personal or environmental (state-of-the-market) search productivity is capable of explaining differential mobility wage gains of layoffs relative to quits and by age, as well as by other characteristics such as education, marital status, national unemployment, and probably other criteria which we have not studied. The model suggests that differences in search efficiency create differences in duration of search (unemployment) and in acceptance wages, as well as a negative relation between the two. Differences in costs of search would, of course, create a positive correlation. In our findings, differences in search efficiency appear to dominate.

Although the decline in wage gains of older movers is largely due to the adverse effects of layoff unemployment (quit unemployment is not as deleterious), wage gains decline with age in quits as well. The work of Bartel and Borjas (1981) with National Longitudinal Survey (NLS) data indicates that quits which are exogenous (for family, health, and other reasons) result in wage losses, and so do, to a lesser extent, quits which represent trade-offs of wages for preferred other working conditions. We find one important example of the latter in our data: reduced wage gains are traded off for preferred changes in hours. The phenomenon is significant in the experienced labor force, but not so among the young. We may conclude that the reduction of wage gains in quits of older workers is due primarily to the greater prevalence of the exogenous and trade-off categories among them.[3]

2. Measuring wage changes in transitions

In estimating returns to interfirm job changes we should distinguish short-term wage changes obtained in the transition from longer-run changes

represented by a shift in the tenure profile of wages after the move relative
to that profile in the previous job. Job change decisions of workers are
motivated by both kinds of gains (or losses). Their relative importance
depends on the worker's discount rate. More generally, it is the present
value of the net gain that matters. Although present value effects of
mobility are not estimated in this study, some inferences about comparative magnitudes (as between younger and older workers) are discussed in
Section 4. It should also be noted that the wage gains we observe are net of
costs of forgone wages, but not of direct and other costs. While such costs
may be negligible in job change within the local labor market which is
preponderant (some 85 per cent in our data), they are surely important in
geographic mobility. Data limitations prevented us from properly distinguishing between local and geographic mobility in the present report.

(a)   Short-run wage gains

Most studies of longitudinal data contain estimates only of short-run
wage transitions,[4] but the quality of available findings is not secure. Wage
transitions observable in panel data cover an interval of at least one year[5]
between reports of the first wage on the new job and the last wage on the
old. Since wages change (usually grow) for stayers as well as for movers, a
correct estimate of the wage gain from moving is the difference between
the actual wage gains of movers over the interval and the unobserved but
expected wage gain of movers had they not moved over the same interval.
In the usual procedure, the coefficient of a job change dummy (S_t) in a
wage growth equation is used to estimate the wage transition. What it
really measures is the difference between the wage gain of movers and
wage gain of stayers both defined over this particular time interval (t).

Let us define the wage gains of movers over the interval t as $\Delta W_{m,t}$ and
the wage gain of stayers over this interval as $\Delta W_{s,t}$. Thus, the coefficient on
S_t is $\Delta W_{m,t} - \Delta W_{s,t}$. What is known as the 'selectivity problem' is that
wage growth of stayers ($\Delta W_{s,t}$) is not likely to be the same as the expected
wage growth of movers, call it $\Delta W_{ms,t}$, had they stayed. Put more strongly,
the coefficient on S_t tells us how much better (or worse) movers fare
compared to stayers, but this is an irrelevant and even faulty question. It is
prima facie faulty, because any answer would suggest that one or the other
group is acting irrationally: if $\Delta W_{s,t}$ is the opportunity cost of movers in
moving (we are ignoring other costs here), then $\Delta W_{m,t}$ must be the opportunity cost of stayers in staying. Hence if $\Delta W_{m,t} > \Delta W_{s,t}$, the stayers are
irrational; and conversely, if the inequality sign is reversed. It is irrelevant
because economic optimization means that movers are doing their best by
moving and stayers by staying. Strictly speaking this is true *ex ante*, as well
as, on average, *ex post*, so long as most people are not misled by incom-

plete information. We must replace the incorrect opportunity cost of movers $\Delta W_{s,t}$ by an estimate of the correct one, $\Delta W_{ms,t}$.

We should be careful to note, however, that the dichotomy of movers and stayers which bears on the selectivity problem was defined solely for the particular interval t. Some workers who moved in t might otherwise move very infrequently, whereas some of those who did not might otherwise move quite frequently. In a longer-term perspective, there is no dichotomy between movers and stayers; rather, there is a spectrum of workers ranging from those who move rarely to those who move very frequently. Since average job tenure in our sample is about seven years, movers observed in a one-year interval must have an above-average probability of moving, that is, of being repeat movers over their working lives. Indeed, their job tenure is on average closer to three years. As was shown in our previous study, workers who tend to invest more heavily in human capital formation on the job are likely to move less frequently and to have steeper wage growth while on the job.[6] Consequently, movers in period t should have systematically weaker on-the-job growth than do stayers in period t. The data on job training are consistent: while all workers had an average training period of 2.5 years, movers had training of about 1.3 years (in the 1976 and 1978 surveys). Hence the 'selectivity' bias: the correct opportunity cost of movers $\Delta W_{ms,t}$ is *smaller* than $\Delta W_{s,t}$. But it can be estimated on a subgroup of stayers in period t. Since the time period t is arbitrary, workers who have similar personal characteristics including mobility behavior should have similar wage growth on the job. If so, we can approximate the unobserved growth of movers had they not moved ($\Delta W_{ms,t}$) in period t by the observed wage growth of stayers in period t who are otherwise similar to our movers and who are observed to move in period $t + 1$; let us call it $\Delta W_{s,t}^{m,t+1}$. The only difference is that in period t the 'future' movers (those moving in $t + 1$) stay on the job.[7]

The wage growth equation now contains two change dummies, S_t, denoting separation in period t, and S_{t+1}, denoting separation in period $t + 1$, while the dependent variable is wage growth of all in period t. Here, S_t is 1 if a move takes place in period t, and 0 if no move occurs in that period nor in the next; $S_{t+1} = 1$ if a move occurs in period $t + 1$ but not in period t, and 0 if it does not occur in the second (or preceding) period. The coefficients on S_1 and S_2 are, respectively,

$$b_t = \Delta W_{m,t} - \Delta W_{s,t} = G(s) \tag{6.1}$$

and

$$b_{t+1} = \Delta W_{m,t+1} - \Delta W_{s,t}. \tag{6.2}$$

Hence the corrected estimate of the relevant wage gain is

$$b_t - b_{t+1} = \Delta W_{m,t} - \Delta W_{m,t+1} = G(m). \qquad (6.3)$$

The basic idea is that $\Delta W_{m,t+1}$, the wage growth of stayers observed in the period preceding their move (in $t + 1$), is a good approximation for the unobserved wage growth of movers in period t, had they stayed on the job ($\Delta W_{ms,t}$). This procedure may not eliminate the bias entirely, but we expect it to provide a much better control than $\Delta W_{s,t}$ in the naive procedure, which ignores the selectivity issue.

(b) Longer-run job gains in mobility

Longer-run changes in wages resulting from an interfirm change in employment are estimated as upward (or downward) parallel shifts in the tenure–wage profile in the new relative to the preceding job. The shift is basically an estimate of the difference between the starting wages on the new and the preceding job, net of wage levels resulting from accumulated experience. The same issue of selectivity arises here as it did in estimating short-run changes. Our procedure to deal with this problem is essentially the same. It permits us to compare wage gains of movers with wage gains of all stayers, as well as with wage gains of comparable stayers during the year of tenure which was forgone by the movers.

Both wage level and wage change equations are used in the estimation of job gains. Wage level equations are used separately for prior and subsequent surveys bracketing the move.[8] Both equations contain the same separation dummies. In time t the coefficient on the separation dummy indicates the cross-section wage difference between otherwise similar movers and stayers prior to the move, while in time $t + 1$ it measures this differential after the move. Separation dummies one year forward are added in each equation to provide for the control group of future movers. While the prospective equation (at t) indicates the wage level selectivity of movers, the difference between coefficients on the same separation in retrospective at $t + 1$ and the prospective equation measures the gain from moving relative to all stayers.

The gain relative to comparable (next-period) movers is obtained by subtracting the difference in coefficients on the future move from the difference in the coefficients of the current move: the prospective equation (P) containing levels at time t has (in addition to other variables) dummies on S_t, the move in the subsequent period, and on S_{t+1}, the move in the following period. The dummy on S_t denotes the differential between wages (at t) of next-period movers before they moved and stayers (at t),

$$b_t^P = W_{m,t}^t - W_{s,t}^t.$$

The dummy on S_{t+1} denotes the differential between wages at (t) of those who will move two periods ahead, and of stayers,

$$b_{t+1}^P = (W_{m,t+1}^t - W_{s,t}^t).$$

In the retrospective equation (R) containing levels at $t + 1$ the dummy on S_t denotes the differential between wages (at $t + 1$) between those who moved in the preceding period and those who stayed,

$$b_t^R = (W_{m,t}^{t+1} - W_{s,t}^{t+1}).$$

Again, the dummy on S_{t+1}, the move in the subsequent period, denotes the differential between wages (at $t + 1$) of such movers and of stayers,

$$b_{t+1}^R = (W_{m,t+1}^{t+1} - W_{s,t}^{t+1}).$$

The wage gain of movers relative to stayers is therefore measured by the difference between the dummies on S_t in the following equations:

$$G(s) = b_t^R - b_t^P = (W_{m,t}^{t+1} - W_{s,t}^{t+1}) - (W_{m,t}^t - W_{s,t}^t) = \Delta W_{m,t} - \Delta W_{s,t}. \tag{6.1a}$$

The difference between the wage growth of next period movers and of stayers is measured by the difference between the dummies on S_{t+1} in the following two equations:

$$G(ms) = b_{t+1}^R - b_{t+1}^P = (W_{m,t+1}^{t+1} - W_{s,t}^{t+1}) - (W_{m,t+1}^t - W_{s,t}^t)$$
$$= \Delta W_{m,t+1} + 1 - \Delta W_{s,t}. \tag{6.2a}$$

Hence the corrected estimate of wage gains of movers is

$$G(m) = G(s) - G(ms) = (\Delta W_{m,t} - \Delta W_{s,t}) - (\Delta W_{m,t+1} - \Delta W_{s,t})$$
$$= \Delta W_{m,t} - \Delta W_{m,t+1}. \tag{6.3a}$$

As Equation (6.3a) suggests, instead of taking differences between coefficients in two-level equations, we may use a wage change equation which is derived from the two-level equations. This alternative procedure is, in principle, equivalent to the first. However, estimates in the two procedures may differ in so far as wage change equations require panels in neighbouring years, which reduces the sample size somewhat, and in so far as the error structure is altered. Although the estimate of short-term gains in equation (6.3) is algebraically the same as the estimate of longer-run 'job gains' in equation (6.3a), the estimates are derived in a different manner: the short-term estimates are derived from a wage change equation in which all variables (other than the separation dummies) are levels prior to moving. In the job-gain estimates, these variables are in form of first difference over the relevant periods. Note that in differencing the independent variables of the level equations, the experience variable becomes $\Delta X = 1$ for all, and its coefficient enters the intercept, but ΔX^2 differs with the level of experience. The tenure variable ΔT equals 1 for job stayers but becomes negative, $-T$, for movers, where T is length of job tenure on the preceding job. Similarly, ΔT^2 is positive for stayers but is negative and equals $-T^2$ for movers. The use of ΔT is the key to estimating 'job' gains. When tenure *levels* before separation were held fixed in the equations, the mobility dummies indicated the more immediate wage change in moving from one job to another. To estimate 'job gains', ΔT is 'held constant'.[9] The present specification estimates the wage change from the prior job to the current one at comparable tenure levels, in effect at starting wages, assuming the same shapes (but not level) of the tenure curve for both jobs. This is corrected for selectivity by the dummies on future movers.

3.   Empirical findings

Tables 6.1a, 6.2a and 6.3 show real wage gains[10] from job changes. Table 6.1a shows the short-run gains of movers over the year the move took place; Table 6.1a shows the longer-run gain we call 'job gain' obtained from a wage change specification; and Table 6.3 measures the same using pairs of wage levels equations 'prospective' and 'retrospective' bracketing the move. In our PSID (Panel Study on Income Dynamics) data, the period 1976–81 contains a comprehensive wage and salary coverage for straight-time real wages on the main job. The earlier period (1970–5) data are restricted to wage earners (hourly rated).[11] Tables 6.1a, 6.2a, and 6.3, which extend the period back to 1970, utilize a dummy for the 1976–81 period to distinguish the subperiods both by coverage and possible historical differences.[12]

Tables 6.1 to 6.3 utilize coefficients of dummy variables for separations in one and two adjacent periods, after inclusion in wage regressions of a number of relevant independent variables. In effect, we are asking how much do movers gain relative to comparable workers who did not move over the period, and how much relative to a more similar subgroup of stayers, namely, those who move in the subsequent period.

In Table 6.1a short-run ('transition') wage gains were estimated in pooled wage growth equations. Year-to-year wage growth measured as

Table 6.1a   Short-run wage gains in job change annual, 1970–81[a,b]

	Separations			
	(1) $G(s)$	(2) S_t	(3) S_{t+1}	(4) $G(m)$
All	−0.005	0.0034	−0.035	0.039
$n = 7246$	(0.6)	(0.4)	(3.9)	
Young[c]	0.024	0.031	−0.033	0.064
$n = 2689$	(1.8)	(2.3)	(2.7)	
Older[d]	−0.032	−0.022	−0.043	0.021
n = 4571	(2.4)	(1.5)	(3.1)	

	Quits			
	$G(s)$	Q_t	Q_{t+1}	$G(m)$
All	0.010	0.019	−0.034	0.053
$n = 7246$	(0.9)	(1.7)	(3.1)	
Young[c]	−0.006	0.024	−0.050	0.074
$n = 2689$	(0.4)	(1.4)	(3.1)	
Older[d]	0.020	0.027	−0.019	0.046
$n = 4571$	(1.3)	(1.7)	(1.3)	

	Layoffs			
	$G(s)$	L_t	L_{t+1}	$G(m)$
All	−0.036	−0.026	−0.044	0.018
$n = 7246$	(2.4)	(1.6)	(3.0)	
Young[c]	0.009	0.008	−0.049	0.057
$n = 2689$	(0.4)	(0.8)	(2.6)	
Older[d]	−0.071	−0.059	−0.041	−0.018
$n = 4571$	(3.2)	(2.6)	(1.8)	

Notes
[a]Conventional t statistics in parentheses.
[b]*Columns*: (1) gains relative to stayers (S_{t+1} not in the equation); (2) coefficient on separation in t; (3) coefficient on separation in $t + 1$; (4) gains relative to movers (column (2) − column (3)).
[c]Young = experience ≤ 10 years.
[d]Older = experience > 10 years.

$\Delta\ln(W)$ is the dependent variable. We shall look at net dollar gains in some of the subsequent tables (4, 6, and 8) when we try to rank present

Table 6.1b   Other variables in short-run wage change regressions[a]

Variables[b]	All 1976–81	All 1970–81	Young 1976–81	Young 1970–81	Old 1976–81	Old 1970–81
C	0.097	0.097	0.130	0.104	0.079	0.096
	(4.4)	(5.8)	(2.6)	(2.7)	(2.1)	(3.6)
Ed	−0.0008	−0.0002	0.00002	0.0016	−0.0008	−0.0005
	(0.6)	(0.2)	(0.01)	(0.8)	(0.5)	(0.5)
X	−0.0037	−0.0035	0.0021	−0.0020	−0.0032	−0.0029
	(2.6)	(3.4)	(0.1)	(0.2)	(1.2)	(1.5)
X^2	0.00004	0.00005	−0.0009	−0.0004	0.000026	0.00003
	(1.2)	(2.0)	(0.7)	(0.5)	(0.5)	(0.8)
CS	0.005	0.005	0.011	0.009	0.0025	0.004
	(0.6)	(0.9)	(0.7)	(0.8)	(0.2)	(0.5)
$Dsab$	−0.008	−0.00008	−0.020	−0.012	−0.005	0.003
	(5.6)	(0.1)	(0.7)	(0.6)	(0.4)	(0.3)
ΔU	−0.024	−0.014	−0.029	−0.016	−0.021	−0.012
	(5.2)	(4.7)	(3.4)	(2.9)	(3.9)	(3.6)
Mar	0.0008	0.0002	0.008	0.011	0.0007	−0.004
	(0.1)	(0.02)	(0.5)	(0.8)	(0.04)	(0.4)
SMA	0.006	0.006	0.0026	0.005	0.006	0.005
	(0.8)	(1.0)	(0.2)	(0.5)	(0.7)	(0.8)
Ten	−0.006	−0.0050	−0.036	−0.032	−0.003	−0.0026
	(4.0)	(4.4)	(3.9)	(4.2)	(1.8)	(2.4)
Ten^2	0.0002	0.00015	0.003	0.0027	0.0001	0.00008
	(3.8)	(4.0)	(2.6)	(2.7)	(2.0)	(2.3)
$D(76–81)$[c]		−0.017		n.s.		−0.024
		(3.2)				(4.1)

Notes
[a]Conventional t statistics in parentheses.
[b]Variables: C = intercept; Ed = education; X = experience; CS = city size; $Dsab$ = health impairment; ΔU = annual change in the unemployment rate; Mar = married; SMA = Standard Metropolitan Area = 1; Ten = tenure in firm.
[c]D(76–81), 1 if in 1976–1981
n.s. = not significant

values of gains from moving in different age groups. The independent variables, other than the separation dummies, are shown in Table 6.1b.

   Table 6.1a shows coefficients on dummies for separation (S), quits (Q), and layoffs (L) for periods t alone (column (1)), and of pairs of dummies in

Table 6.2a   Job gains in mobility[a,b] *(Δln wage), 1970–81*

	Separations			
	(1) $G(s)$	(2) S_t	(3) S_{t+1}	(4) $G(m)$
All	0.032	0.040	−0.032	0.072
	(3.0)	(3.3)	(3.5)	
Young	0.089	0.099	−0.044	0.143
	(4.2)	(4.4)	(3.1)	
Older	0.035	0.048	−0.030	0.078
	(2.4)	(2.8)	(2.4)	
	Quits			
	$G(s)$	Q_t	Q_{t+1}	$G(m)$
All	0.044	0.056	−0.030	0.086
	(3.6)	(4.0)	(2.8)	
Young	0.113	0.130	−0.052	0.182
	(5.0)	(5.4)	(3.2)	
Older	0.028	0.038	−0.016	0.054
	(1.6)	(1.9)	(1.0)	
	Layoffs			
	$G(s)$	L_t	L_{t+1}	$G(m)$
All	0.007	0.008	−0.041	0.049
	(0.5)	(0.5)	(2.7)	
Young	0.059	0.057	−0.039	0.096
	(2.4)	(2.1)	(1.7)	
Older	0.012	0.029	−0.004	0.033
	(0.6)	(1.2)	(2.4)	

Notes
[a] Conventional t statistics in parentheses.
[b] Columns: (1) gains relative to stayers; (2) coefficient on separation in t; (3) coefficient on separation in $t+1$; (4) gains relative to movers (column (2) – column (3)).

(t) and ($t+1$) in columns (2) and (3), respectively. Column (1) measures the gain of movers relative to all stayers $G(s)$, while column (4) = column (2) − column (3), measures the gain $G(m)$ relative to movers in period $t+1$ who stayed on the job in period t. Here, $G(s)$ is the coefficient of S_t,

Table 6.2b   Variables in job gains (Δ) regressions[a]

Variables[b]	All		Young		Old	
	1976–81 (1)	1970–81 (2)	1976–81 (3)	1970–81 (4)	1976–81 (5)	1970–81 (6)
C	0.64 (2.7)	0.63 (3.8)	n.s.	n.s.	0.066 (22.0)	0.067 (3.4)
ΔX^2	−0.001 (5.0)	−0.0008 (6.2)	n.s.	−0.0033 (2.4)	−0.001 (3.7)	−0.0007 (4.0)
ΔU	−0.018 (3.3)	−0.014 (4.5)	−0.018 (1.7)	−0.015 (2.5)	−0.016 (2.6)	−0.012 (3.5)
ΔTen	0.017 (2.1)	0.011 (3.8)	0.072 (4.9)	0.061 (5.7)	n.s.	0.004 (1.4)
ΔTen^2	−0.0004 (2.4)	−0.0004 (3.1)	−0.005 (3.0)	−0.004 (3.6)	n.s.	n.s.
D(76–81)		−0.018 (3.2.)		n.s.		−0.025 (4.0)

Notes
[a]n.s. = not significant.
[b]*Variables:* see Table 6.1b.

when S_{t+1} is excluded, while $G(m)$ is the difference between the coefficients of S_t, when S_{t+1} is excluded, while $G(m)$ is the difference between the coefficients of S_t and S_{t+1}, shown in columns (2) and (3).

   The separation dummies are added to a list of other, standardizing variables measured in the survey prior to the move. The variables include education (*Ed*), experience (*X*), and tenure (*Ten*) in linear and quadratic terms; marital and health status (*Mar*) and (*Disab*); and location variables (city size, whether in a Standard Metropolitan Area (SMA) or other geographic area). Also, the percent-point change in the national unemployment rate (ΔU) of adult males (ages 35–54)[13] over the interval *t*, and an interaction of the separation with union membership in any of the periods *t* and (*t* + 1). Statistically significant effects were observed on several of the standardizing variables, shown in Table 6.1b: wage growth of all workers (mainly stayers in any given year) diminishes with experience and with tenure in the firm, both in a decelerating manner – features similar to those in cross-section wage profiles. Changes in the adult male unemployment rate are significant, indicating a procyclical fluctuation in

Table 6.3 Job gains in mobility: prospective (P) and retrospective (R) cross sections,[a] 1970–81

Eq.	All S	All Q	All L	Eq.	Young S	Young Q	Young L	Eq.	Older S	Older Q	Older L
P_t	−0.131	−0.13	−0.128	Q_t	−0.125	−0.131	−0.122	P_t	−0.122	−0.119	−0.112
	(10.5)	(8.8)	(6.6)		(8.1)	(7.1)	(5.0)		(6.2)	(4.9)	(3.6)
P_{t+1}	−0.085	−0.0982	−0.087	Q_{t+1}	−0.062	−0.050	−0.075	P_{t+1}	−0.100	−0.111	−0.088
	(6.7)	(5.4)	(3.9)		(3.9)	(2.6)	(2.9)		(5.0)	(4.3)	(2.9)
R_t	−0.109	−0.082	−0.148	R_t	−0.067	−0.033	−0.096	R_t	−0.083	−0.057	−0.135
	(8.6)	(5.5)	(7.7)		(3.5)	(1.6)	(3.7)		(3.9)	(2.3)	(4.2)
R_{t+1}	−0.121	−0.118	−0.126	R_{t+1}	−0.125	−0.117	−0.133	R_{t+1}	−0.109	−0.111	−0.105
	(10.1)	(8.1)	(6.7)		(8.3)	(6.6)	(5.6)		(5.7)	(4.6)	(3.6)
$G(s)$	0.022	0.047	−0.020	$G(s)$	0.060	0.098	0.026	$G(s)$	0.039	0.062	−0.023
$G(m)$	0.058	0.085	0.019	$G(m)$	0.123	0.167	0.083	$G(m)$	0.048	0.062	−0.006

Notes
[a] S = separation; Q = quits; L = layoffs.
Other independent variables listed in Table 6.1b.

real wages of homogeneous labor. The response of real wage changes to unemployment changes is stronger in the more recent period (1976–81) than in the longer period back to 1970.

Table 6.1a shows wage gains between jobs calculated from coefficients of mobility dummies. The effects of separations, quits, and layoffs are shown for all workers in the sample, young workers (defined by at most one decade of work experience), and the older, more experienced workers (defined by $x > 10$).

Findings in both the shorter and longer period show the following similar patterns:

(a)   Starting with short-run gains in Table 6.1a, wage growth between jobs does not exceed on-the-job wage growth for the average separation (column (1)). It is even less than the wage growth of stayers, if the separation is due to layoff among the more experienced workers. However, the gain in wages between jobs relative to comparable movers who stayed on in period t, shown in column (4), is positive – again, with the exception of layoffs among the more experienced workers. This positive gain is, therefore, largely due to the fact that movers have weaker wage growth on the job than stayers.

(b)   Gains of quitters are positive and exceed gains from layoffs which are small or negative, especially for the more experienced workers. This despite the fact, evident in column (3), that the flatter on-the-job growth of movers, which represents the opportunity cost of moving, is about the same whether the following separation is a quit or a layoff. The adverse effect of layoffs on wage growth between jobs has been noted before, albeit in terms similar to our column (1) than to the more appropriate column (4). This finding appears natural to some and puzzling to others.[14]

(c)   Gains from separations, as shown in Table 6.1a, column (4), decline with age (experience), both in quits and in layoffs. Once again, the facts are familiar, although based on diverse methodologies. Numerically, the gains from separations range from − 1.8 per cent in layoffs of older workers to 7.4 per cent in quits of young workers in the longer period.

Before we proceed to interpretations of the findings, we turn to estimates of longer-run effects of mobility shown in Tables 6.2a and 6.3, since they are qualitatively similar to those in Table 6.1a. The layout of Table 6.2 is the same as that in Table 6.1a. The coefficients on separation dummies come from wage change regressions in which the dependent and independent variables are the same as in those underlying Table 6.1a, except that levels of experience and of tenure are now replaced by annual changes in them.

The job gains (tenure–wage profile shifts) estimated in Table 6.2a are numerically larger than the 'transition' gains shown in Table 6.1a. This is pronounced for the younger movers, suggesting perhaps that, beyond the immediate gain, young movers gain also in wage growth on the new job. Otherwise the pattern of profile shifts by type of separation and by age is similar to that found for short-run gains in Table 6.1a.

Table 6.2b shows the significant coefficients of the standardizing variables: thus the coefficient of ΔX^2 is negative. This is consistent with a negative sign on X in Table 6.1b, since $\Delta X^2 = 2X + 1$. The sign of ΔTen^2 is similarly negative, but positive for ΔTen, suggesting a negative effect of longer tenure on subsequent gain from moving. Increases in unemployment reduce wage growth as before, though the effects are smaller than in the shorter run. Interactions of union membership with separations are generally positive, probably reflecting moves from nonunionized to unionized firms.

Table 6.3 shows the job gain (profile shift) estimates obtained by using prospective (P) and retrospective (R) wage functions in successive cross sections.[15] Here G_s, the gain relative to all stayers, is the difference between separation coefficients ($R_t - P_t$), in row (3) minus row (1); G_{ms} is the gain of future movers relative to current stayers, $R_{t+1} - P_{t+1}$, that is, row (4) minus row (2); and G_m is the gain of movers relative to comparable (next period) movers, $(R_t - P_t) - (R_{t+1} - P_{t+1})$, that is, rows $[(3) - (1)] - [(4) - (2)]$.[16]

It is reassuring to find that the numerical estimates of the relative gains G_m in Table 6.3 are quite close to those in Table 6.2a. The conclusions are therefore the same as in Table 6.2a. There is, however, additional information in Table 6.3, namely, observations on wage *levels* of movers and stayers before and after the move. Thus the fact that all coefficients in rows (1) through (4) are negative means that movers have lower wages than stayers both *in the old and in the new job*, although the discrepancy is reduced by moving. Also, prior to moving, the wage disadvantage (relative to stayers) is about the same for quits and for layoffs (row (1) in Table 6.3). In conjunction with the findings in Tables 6.1 and 6.2 to the effect that wage growth on the job is about the same for quits and layoffs, it would seem on the whole that there is no significant difference in on-the-job wage experience of quits and layoffs prior to separation.

By moving, young quits make up the bulk of the deficit, whereas older quits only cut it in half. Young layoffs remove less than half of the deficit, whereas older layoffs worsen it if they change it at all. Apparently, it is behaviour during the transition rather than on the job that distinguishes quits from layoffs. Since mobility does not compensate for the slower wage growth on the job of frequent movers, their wage trajectories are flatter, and even flatter for those movers whose separations are dominated by layoffs. However, in the long run more frequent movers are not distinguishable by quits or layoffs. No significant correlation between frequency of moving and relative frequencies of quits to layoffs was found among movers in the PSID.

Interaction effects

Mobility wage gains differ by type of separation and by age, according to Tables 6.1 to 6.3. Do mobility wage effects differ also by other characteristics, such as education, experience, tenure, and so on? To detect these interactions, we restrict our observations to episodes of moves. In Table 6.4, in the upper panel we show relative wage gains as before; in the lower panel we show dollar wage gains. In both panels we look at wage changes during the move (in period t) and before the move (at $t - 1$). The latter are substitutes for the wage changes of stayers who will move in $t + 1$.

We find that both the relative and dollar gains differ by education, tenure, by health, by location (in SMA), and less significantly by experience and by marital status. These results are qualitatively similar in the per cent and dollar measures, and are stronger when lagged wage effects (coefficients in period $t - 1$) are subtracted from current effects (in t) which refer to current movers without reference to any comparison group.

Gains from job mobility increase with education, mainly because gains from quits do. In relative terms the effect of education is negative only in layoffs of young workers. Note also, in column ($t - 1$), that more educated workers tend to quit jobs which are relatively inferior (in terms of wage growth); also, they gain more by moving, the more inferior the previous job was. Gains decline with tenure in a decelerating fashion. They are reduced in ill health, and they are smaller in SMAs. They are larger (certainly in dollar terms) for married than for single men. Experience effects are negative and near significance when health variables are left out.

Recessions (increases in national unemployment) have a stronger negative effect on wage growth of movers (-3.7 per cent in Table 6.4 as compared to -2.5 per cent in Table 6.1b) than on wage growth of stayers. Thus, the cyclical variability of real wages is greatest for movers and declines with experience (and/or tenure) among stayers (Table 6.1b). Lesser cyclical fluctuations in wages may be expected of workers who have accumulated more firm-specific capital than others, or, more generally, carry greater fixed labor costs to employers. The comparative findings on

Table 6.4   Effects of mobility on wage gains by characteristics of movers.[a]
1976–81

Variables	Relative wage change			
	Separations		Quits[b]	
	At t^c	At $t - 1^d$	At t^c	At $t - 1^d$
Ed	0.068	−0.048	0.0767	−0.088
	(1.9)	(2.1)	(2.0)	(3.2)
Ed²	−0.0024	0.002	−0.0028	0.0036
	(1.7)	(2.1)	(1.8)	(3.1)
Ten	−0.028	−0.011	−0.037	n.s.
	(2.2)	(1.8)	(3.4)	
Ten²	0.0017	0.0005	0.002	n.s.
	(2.7)	(1.8)	(3.4)	
ΔU	−0.037	n.s.	−0.027	n.s.
	(1.8)		(1.6)	

Variables	Dollar wage change			
	Separations		Quits[b]	
	At t^c	At $t - 1^d$	At t^c	At $t - 1^d$
Ed	0.85	−0.66	1.002	−1.071
	(4.5)	(4.5)	(4.1)	(4.9)
Ed²	−0.032	0.026	−0.037	0.041
	(4.1)	(4.3)	(3.7)	(4.6)
Ten	−0.095	−0.063	−0.127	n.s.
	(1.8)	(1.6)	(1.8)	
Ten²	0.006	0.002	0.008	n.s.
	(2.1)	(1.4)	(2.2)	
ΔU	−0.15	n.s.	−0.13	n.s.
	(2.4)		(0.9)	

Notes
[a]Of the additional variables (listed in Table 6.1b), Disability was negative, Marital Status positive, both nearly significant. Experience variables had the same signs as Tenure (at t) but were not significant when Tenure was included. (For separations, $n = 763$). For quits, $n = 352$.)
[b]Layoff variables had the same signs as separations but were less significant.
[c]At t, wage growth in move.
[d]At $t - 1$, wage growth a year before move.

movers and stayers, young and old, and early vs. later tenure are consistent with this hypothesis.

Table 6.5   Effects of layoffs and of unemployment on wage gains: sample of job changes, 1970–81

	Separation[a]			Quits		Layoffs	
	(1)	(2)	(3)	(4)	(5)	(6)	(7)
Sample	L	U	D	U	D	U	D
All	−0.046	−0.070	−0.011	−0.050	−0.008	−0.064	−0.014
(n = 1082)	(2.1)	(3.2)	(3.1)	(1.6)	(1.3)	(1.8)	(3.0)
Young	−0.044	−0.060	−0.008	−0.038	−0.014	−0.036	−0.007
(n = 675)	(1.5)	(2.1)	(1.7)	(1.1)	(1.2)	(0.6)	(1.1)
Older	−0.041	−0.085	−0.016	−0.064	0.007	−0.119	−0.025
(n = 407)	(1.3)	(2.7)	(3.2)	(1.3)	(0.6)	(2.3)	(4.3)

Notes
Columns: (1) coefficient of dummy for Layoff = 1, for Quit = 0; (2) coefficient on dummy for Unemployment in Transition = 1, for no Unemployment = 0; (3) coefficient on duration of unemployment measured in two-week intervals, linear terms only, in addition to dummy as in column (2).

4.   Wage changes and unemployment in job transitions

Why do gains from quits exceed gains from layoffs?

As was noted in Tables 6.1 to 6.3, gains from quits exceed gains from layoffs in all groups and periods, both in the transition and in the job sequence. The differential is rather stable. Gains from quits exceed gains (or losses) from layoffs by about 4 percentage points. A dummy for layoffs (= 1) and quits (= 0), included in the wage change equations for moves only, indicates the difference; it is shown in column (1) of Table 6.5.

Explanations of the disadvantage of layoffs in the transition are put forward by several analysts. Cline (1980) argues that quitters move from inferior jobs when better jobs become available, while involuntary separations (layoffs) affect workers in both inferior and superior jobs. The implication is that the pre-separation wage levels are, on average, higher for layoffs, whereas post-separation wages are about the same. Our findings in the prospective and retrospective regressions of Table 6.3 show exactly the opposite: pre-separation wages of both quits and layoffs are about the same, both significantly lower than wages of stayers, whereas post-separation wages, although not equal to wages of stayers, are lower for layoffs than for quits. Rosen argues against the asymmetry between layoffs and quits in his preface to an NBER volume (1981, p. 4): who initiates the turnover decision should be irrelevant, 'since job separations should occur if and only if productivity on the current job is less than productivity on an alternate job'. Rosen adds the speculation that perhaps layoffs are more heavily selected from unstable sectors, and hence a greater average loss (or lesser gain) may be expected for layoffs than for quits. This assumes higher (compensatory) wages in unstable sectors and (some) moves from unstable to stable sectors; while our prospective regressions are consistent with the symmetry argument, they reject the unstable sector hypothesis.

A hypothesis that may explain the larger gains of quitters relies on job-search behavior: most quitters change jobs directly without intervening unemployment, whereas most layoffs are unemployed between jobs. The implied on-the-job search of quitters carries a reservation wage which exceeds the wages on the old job (abstracting from nonwage components of the real wage package), while the reservation wage of the laid-off unemployed searchers is lower.[17] The starting wage on the new job may be, but need not be, higher than on the old job. In our data, two-thirds of quits changed jobs without unemployment, while about the same proportion of layoffs became unemployed. If reservation wages are indeed lower for unemployed than for employed searchers, we should find that the reduction in wage gains due to unemployment is greater than that due to layoff. This is shown in Table 6.5 (cf. column (2) with column (1)).

The disadvantage of searching while unemployed is less significant for quits than for layoffs (cf. column (4) with column (6)), especially among the more experienced workers. Quit into unemployment is deliberate – it is likely to be prompted by high costs of searching while on the job. It therefore indicates the intent to search more intensively. Moreover, the intensity of search by unemployed quitters is likely to be strengthened by lack of unemployment compensation for which layoffs are eligible. Indeed, average duration[18] of layoff unemployment is almost twice as long as of quit unemployment (as shown in Table 6.7; see section 4(b), below).

If intensity of search of unemployed quitters is greater than that of those on layoff, it should also follow that *for the same length of search* quitters should be more successful in locating a better (higher wage) job. This is confirmed in our regression (Table 6.5) in which a duration variable is added to the unemployment dummy: The coefficient on duration is not significant for quits but is negative and significant for layoffs. That is, each additional month of unemployment reduces the acceptance wage of unemployed layoffs by an additional 2.8 per cent. Apparently, longer duration reflects lesser or decreasing efficiency of search[19] of those laid off but not of those who quit.

(b)   Why do gains from moving decline with age?
According to Table 6.1, short-run gains from separations of experienced workers ($X > 10$) are much smaller (about a third), than gains of young

Table 6.6   Average relative and dollar wage gains of subgroups, by age and separation

Wage gains	Separations		Quits		Layoffs	
	%	$	%	$	%	$
1970–81						
Young	4.7	0.129	5.3	0.154	1.6	0.090
Older	3.5	0.104	4.2	0.121	0.9	0.030
1976–81						
Young	3.7	0.134	4.5	0.160	2.6	0.091
Older	2.7	0.096	3.0	0.103	0.9	0.038

workers. The reduction is somewhat less in quits (about a half), but goes from positive to negative in layoffs. The use of percent gains may, of course, be misleading. It is possible for the *net* dollar gain (the difference between the dollar gains of movers and the dollar gains of the control group) to increase when the percent gain declines. Table 6.6 shows that the *gross* dollar gain from moving of young workers was larger than the corresponding gain of older workers. This implies that the net dollar gain declines as well, given the decline in the percent measures[20](G_m).

As Tables 6.2 and 6.3 indicate, the decline in G_m with age is even greater in our job gain estimates, which are conceptually closer to present values.

One reason for the decline in the wage gain of the older job changers is that a greater proportion of them experience layoff. The ratio of layoffs to separations is close to 70 per cent among the older workers, compared to about 50 per cent for the younger ones. And, as was shown in Table 6.5, the effects of unemployment are especially severe for laid-off older workers, and more so in prolonged unemployment, which is more typical of laid-off workers. It follows that the differential effects of unemployment, especially in layoffs, explain the wage gain differences between quits and layoffs as well as the decline of gains for older job changers.

An explanation of all these patterns, already alluded to, may be found in differential efficiency of search by type of separation, age, education, or other characteristics of workers or labor markets. Greater efficiency in search may be a matter of personal efficiency, or greater intensity of search, or of a more favorable environment. We define it as the probability (p) of finding a vacancy (whether or not the job is ultimately acceptable) per unit of time. Of course, p is a function of resources invested in search and of the environment, but it will suffice for our purposes to treat it as a parameter.[21]

In the terminology of search models, we argue that, on average, older workers who separate from jobs have a smaller probability of finding a job per unit of search time, not because they are holding out for a higher acceptance wage within the relevant wage offer distribution (though it is true of some), but because the probability of getting any offer, that is, the probability of finding a vacancy, is smaller. On this assumption we can show that older workers who separate will search longer when unemployed, and quit less frequently, while their acceptance wage will be relatively lower, so the wage gain will be smaller for older job movers than for younger ones.

In the initially standard search model, the individual samples from his/her wage offer distribution $f(w)$ receiving one offer per unit of time. The worker decides on an optimal wage floor which equates the gain from an additional unit of search to the cost of it. The resulting rule is

$$(1) \quad P_a(\bar{W}_a - W_a) = c,$$

where W_a is the lowest acceptable wage; P_a is the probability of getting an acceptable wage offer, that is, of $W > W_a$; $\bar{W}_a$ is the mean of all acceptable wage offers; and c is the (marginal) cost of search which includes opportunity and other costs. Income offsets z which are contingent on a continued search, such as unemployment compensation, enter costs with a negative sign. Expected duration of search D is inverse to P_a. In this model, search is longer the higher the acceptance wage, which is higher the lower the cost of search.

However, the probability of accepting a wage offer must be redefined given that the probability of finding any offer in a unit period can be less than 1. A lower frequency of vacancies may be a result of depressed business conditions in general, or depressed markets for a particular type of labor, or a function of lesser efficiency or intensity of search. The optimum condition becomes

$$(2) \quad p \cdot P_a(\bar{W}_a - W_a) = c.$$

Here p is the probability of finding a job offer; P_a, the probability of finding an acceptable job conditional on finding a vacancy; and $p \cdot P_a$, the probability of finding an acceptable job. Note that D is now the inverse of the product $p \cdot P_a$. As before, changes in c produce a positive relation between W_a and D. However, changes in p over the business cycle, or differences in p across people, are likely to produce a negative correlation between W_a and D.

A reduction in p leads to a downward revision of W_a, hence to an increase in P_a. The question is whether $p \cdot P_a$ will rise or fall when p declines. No perfectly general answer can be given to this question, but a most plausible answer is that $p \cdot P_a$ will fall, hence the duration of search will lengthen even though W_a is revised downward in consequence of a fall in p. It is easy to see that the difference $(\bar{W}_a - W_a)$ increases as W_a is lowered in a uniform or triangular wage offer distribution.[22] When W_a is reduced, $\bar{W}_a$ is reduced by a smaller amount, so that $p \cdot P_a$ must fall if c is fixed or reduced.

The conclusion that a lower p is very likely to produce longer search and lower acceptance wages holds both for unemployed and for employed searchers. An increased duration of search on the job, of course, means a reduction in the frequency of quit.

In sum, workers facing fewer vacancies in their search may be expected to have a longer duration of search and a smaller wage gain when unemployed, and to inhibit their job change (quitting) when employed.[23] These conclusions are consistent with worker behavior during the business cycle: duration of unemployment increases and quits decline while layoffs increase, partly because employment demand has declined and partly to substitute for a decline in attrition (quits).

Applying the same model to the life cycle, we may argue that either p or c declines at older ages. A decline in c is not plausible except very early when labor market entrants become eligible for unemployment compensation. A decline in c would lead to increases in W_a and in wage gains, but the opposite is implied by a fall in p and is observed. The implications that older men have a lesser tendency to quit, a reduced Q/L ratio, and a lower W_a when changing jobs are confirmed in our data.

The longer duration of unemployment of older workers is a well-known feature of national statistics. In our data this fact is observed in Table 6.7, in which duration of unemployment of unemployed job changes is regressed on a number of variables. In rows 1 and 3, where the variables are restricted to education and experience, duration initially decreases (over the first half of a dozen years of experience), then increases with experience. When tenure and other variables are added in rows 3 and 5, it is lengthening of tenure that appears to be responsible for the increased duration of uemployment by age. Apparently, unemployed older movers with longer tenure face greater hardships in job search – a fact consistent with the smaller wage gains of longer-tenured movers, as observed in Table 6.4. It is also consistent with losses of firm- and industry-specific capital due to structural changes affecting older, longer-tenured workers

Table 6.7   Duration of unemployment between jobs: unemployed movers, 1970–81

Variables	Coefficients	
Ed	−0.56	−0.54
	(2.0)	(2.0)
Ed^2	−0.018	0.017
	(1.6)	(1.5)
X	−0.032	0.028
	(0.9)	(0.6)
X^2	0.003	0.0014
	(2.2)	(1.0)
U		1.40
		(8.1)
Disab		0.72
		(1.8)
Mar		−0.72
		(2.1)
Ten		−0.45
		(4.5)
Ten^2		0.020
		(3.8)
Layoff		1.71
		(6.3)

in manufacturing industries especially. Sectoral information as well as that on plant closings is required to probe these matters more deeply.

Looking at the other variables, Table 6.7 also shows that duration of unemployment diminishes with education. The hypothesis that the efficiency parameter (*p*) increases with education is therefore consistent with both implications of the search model: greater wage gain (Table 6.4) and shorter duration of unemployment. Similarly, duration increases with the level of the national unemployment rate (Table 6.7) and wage gains decline (as we saw in Table 6.4). Here, *p* reflects the decline of vacancies in recessions. Effects of health disabilities and of marital status similarly fit the search model: longer duration of unemployment and smaller wage gain of the disabled; and the converse for married compared to single men. Finally, if unemployment results from layoff, its duration is 70 per cent longer than if it results from quit and, as shown before, the wage gain is far smaller.

Table 6.8   Wage changes by type of quit in NLS data

	Personal			Push			Pull		
	%	$	P^a	%	$	P^a	%	$	P^a
Young[b]	12.8	−0.365	0.15	0.6	0.054	0.42	6.9	0.30	0.43
Old[c]	−19.5	−0.46	0.27	−2.8	−0.097	0.48	7.1	0.60	0.25

Notes
[a] P = proportion of quits in each category.
[b] At most 30 years old.
[c] At least 45 years old, not retired.
Source: Bartel and Borjas (1981, p. 68, Table 2.1).

(c)   Why do wage gains from quits decline with age?
Although the smaller gains from mobility can be in large measure attributed to unemployed search, wage gains decline also in quits where unemployment plays a minor and not necessarily deleterious role. In their study of NLS data, Bartel and Borjas (1981) were able to classify quits into three categories: (a) for personal or family nonmarket reasons, such as change in health, in family status, and so on; (b) for reasons of dissatisfaction with working conditions, which they call 'push'; and (c) 'job-related' wage-maximizing reasons, which they call 'pull'. Their findings are shown in Table 7.8. Quits in the first two categories led to smaller wage gains or to losses, and the incidence of them was greater among older workers (age over 45 in the NLS) than among the younger ones: 75 per cent vs. 57 per cent. Although the gains estimated by Bartel and Borjas are calculated relative to all stayers, therefore probably understated, the differential patterns of gains by age are consistent with our estimates.

The distinctions *within* quit categories are not available in our data. However, the role of changes in nonwage conditions can be explored in one rather important case, which fits category (b) of Bartel and Borjas, namely, when the job change contains a significant change in hours per week. The different wage-hours schedules offered in different jobs, firms or industries are due to various technologically and administratively conditioned systems of coordination of the production process, as well as to the presence of fixed labor costs which differ among firms. Consequently, desired changes in hours are more likely to be accomplished in job transitions than within the firm.[24] Where the change is in the direction opposite to the desired one, workers must be compensated by an increase in the wage. When the change in hours is in the desired direction, workers are willing to trade off some of the acceptance wage for the preferred change

Table 6.9   *Interaction effects of separation and changes in hours on wage*
gains, 1970–81

	Wage and salary earners		
	All	Young	Older
Short-run gains	−0.012	n.s.	−0.04
	(1.0)		(2.1)
Job gains	−0.016	n.s.	−0.042
	(1.1)		(2.1)
$\Delta H > 5^{a}$	n.s.	n.s.	−0.057
			(2.3)
$\Delta H < 5^{a}$	−0.024	−0.029	−0.028
	(1.5)	(1.1)	(1.7)

	Wage earners only		
	All	Young	Older
Short-run gains	−0.022	n.s.	−0.058
	(1.5)		(2.9)
Job gains	−0.026	n.s.	−0.061
	(1.7)		(2.9)
$\Delta H > 5^{a}$	−0.026	n.s.	−0.076
	(1.4)		(2.9)
$\Delta H < 5^{a}$	−0.026	n.s.	−0.047
	(1.5)		(1.8)

Notes
[a]In job gain equations
n.s. = not significant

in hours. Note that the negative effect of wages applies whether or not the desired change is negative or positive, and that the trade-off applies to search and match mobility rather than to moves in response to widespread shifts in demand. In the latter case, wages would rise with increases in hours and decline with decreases. Thus, if most of job changing associated with significant changes in hours is not in response to demand fluctuations and is in the direction of preferred hours, we should expect to see a negative effect of absolute (positive and negative) changes in hours schedules on the wage gain.

In Table 6.9 we find that coefficients on the interaction of separations[25] and change of hours in wage gains are negative, suggesting that trade-offs dominate in moves with sizable changes in hours (> 5 hours per week, in absolute value).

We find also that changes in hours do not significantly affect wages of young workers. Apparently job-matching and experimentation apply to work schedules and other working conditions during the early years of work experience.[26] Since reports on hours worked are conceptually less reliable for salaried than for hourly rated workers, we show separately effects of changes in hours in the sample of wage earners. The results are equally significant, despite the smaller sample size. More importantly, the effects are observed not merely on starting wages; the effects on the longer-run ('job') wage gains are at least as clear and significant.

In demand fluctuations, hours decline in downturns and so do real hourly wages, but the opposite is true in upswings. To test whether we were not confounding effect of utility trade-offs with demand fluctuations, we also distinguish increases from decreases in hours. If a negative sign on the latter dominates, we may have misinterpreted our findings as a utility trade-off. We find, however, that each of the changes carries a negative coefficient, not significant for the young, but significant for workers with more than 10 years of experience. The trade-off is a 3–6 per cent reduction in wage for more than 5 hours change in work schedule for wage and salary earners. It is between 5 and 8 per cent for wage earners alone.

The illustration of effects of changes in hours on wage gains fits category (2) of the Bartel and Borjas classification of quits shown in Table 6.8. The preponderance of 'personal' and 'push' types of quits among older workers explains the anomaly that gains from quits decline with age in both relative and dollar terms. It is an apparent anomaly, because a declining payoff period would require increases in gains to induce workers to move. Note that this requirement is indeed fulfilled in the 'pull' category of quits. Here returns to strictly wage motivated quits are twice as high in dollar terms for the old movers than for the young ones. The percent gain is about the same. If the gains are assumed to be permanent, the present value of older quits is probably not smaller than that of the younger movers.[27]

Acknowledgements

I am grateful to the National Science Foundation and to the US Department of Labor for support of this work.

Notes

1.   Of course, the dispersion is not small. Hence significant numbers of movers incur losses.
2.   Mincer and Jovanovic (1981) provide the human capital explanation and limited empirical evidence. Much stronger evidence is shown in Mincer (1984).

3. According to Table 6.8, about half of quits of young workers are mainly wage maximizing ('pull'). This is true of only one-quarter of older quits.
4. The exceptions are Borjas and Rosen (1980); Cline (1980); Mincer (1983); and Polachek and Horvath (1977). These studies differ both in methodology and in population coverage.
5. One exception is the DIME–SIME data set, in which intervals are as short as one month (Mortensen and Neumann, 1984).
6. Mincer (1984).
7. Although one might use the wage growth of movers in the year before they moved, $W_{m,t}^{s,t-1}$, instead of $W_{s,t}^{m,t+1}$, there are several disadvantages due to differences in (calendar) period, nonlinearity in tenure–wage profiles, and significant loss of observations, given short tenure of movers.
8. This approach was used also in Mincer (1983) in the study of union effects on wages.
9. Among the other independent variables listed in Table 6.1b.
10. Wages and salaries on the current, main job, were divided by scheduled hours and deflated by the Consumer Price Index (CPI).
11. Hourly rated wages were truncated at $9 before 1978, causing some (small) biases.
12. In fact, most of the estimates in the shorter period are similar to those in the longer period.
13. This index of unemployment is not affected by compositional changes in the labor force, and it is less likely to reflect supply responses to the business cycle, as do some of the other demographic components of the aggregate unemployment rate.
14. Bartel and Borjas (1981) term the differential effect of quits and layoffs 'not surprising', while Rosen in his introduction to the 1981 volume calls it 'a puzzle.'
15. These equations exhibit the usual coefficients found in cross-section wage functions.
16. See the following paragraphs for derivation.
17. Recall unemployment is excluded from our data, by definition.
18. Our measures of duration of unemployment in Tables 6.5 and 6.7 are weeks unemployed during the year when job change took place. This may represent more than one spell and may create some inaccuracy.
19. Although job changers do not, by definition, return to their previous jobs, some of the unemployed may have expected recall. These expectations may wane as duration lengthens, resulting in a drop in the reservation wage.
20. Let the gross dollar gain of movers be g and of the control group (movers who stay) g_{ms}. The net dollar gain is therefore $g_m = g - g_{ms}$. But $g_m = g/(1 + G_m)$, so

$$g_m = g[1 - 1/(1 + G_m)] = g \times G_m/(1 + G_m).$$

It follows that the net dollar gain g_m declines with age if g does, even if G_m is the same. For g_m to remain the same or to increase, g must rise at least as fast as G_m declines. The decline in G_m is therefore not merely a matter of arithmetic. it does indicate a decline in the gross dollar gain. Indeed, the relative measures (G_m) shown in Tables 6.1 to 6.3 would have to increase with age to keep the net dollar gains from falling.
21. This parameter is called the 'arrival rate' (of offers) in the mathematical search literature. In the version that follows, the model was described in Leighton and Mincer (1982).
22. Barron (1975), Feinberg (1977), and Nickell (1979) analyze wider classes of wage offer distributions, with similar results. These distributions belong to a more general class of log-concave probability distributions, including uniform, triangular, normal, and exponential among others. Proofs that such wage offer distributions generate a negative correlation between our p and D are given by Flinn and Heckman (1983) and by Burdett and Ondrich (1985).
23. We need not assume that p is exogenous. It may decline as a result of the search process (e.g., see Salop, 1973). The distinction is immaterial for our purposes.
24. See Altonji and Paxson (1985).

25. Altonji and Paxson (1985) have similar findings for quits of workers who previously expressed the desire to change hours.
26. Also, moves toward *higher wages* in preference to other components of the job dominate the mobility of young compared to older workers according to Table 6.8, taken from Bartel and Borjas (1981).
27. Let i be the discount rate; g_o and g_y, the dollar gains of old and young movers, respectively; and R, the remaining payoff period in years ($R = 10$ for the older movers in the NLS, while $R = 40$ for the young, which is almost infinity for discounting purposes). For the present values of older quits to be no less than for the younger, the following inequality must hold:

$$\frac{1}{i[1 - 1/(1+i)^R]g_o} \geq \left(\frac{1}{i}\right) g_y$$

$$[1 - 1/(1+i)^{10}]1/2;$$

hence

$$[1/(1+i)]^{10} \leq 1/2,$$

so

$$(1+i)^{10} \geq 2.$$

The inequality holds for $i \geq 7$ per cent, a quite realistic condition.

References

Altonji, J. and C. Paxson (1985), 'Labor Supply, Hours Constraints, and Job Mobility', US Department of Labor (DOL) Report, ch. 3.

Barron, J. M. (1975), 'Search in the Labor Market and the Duration of Unemployment', *American Economic Review*, December.

Bartel, A. and G. Borjas (1981), 'Wage Growth and Job Turnover', in S. Rosen (ed.), *Studies in Labor Markets*, Chicago: University of Chicago Press.

Borjas, G. and S. Rosen (1980), 'Income Prospects and Job Mobility of Younger Men', in R. G. Ehrenberg (ed.), *Research in Labor Economics*, vol. 3, Greenwich, Conn.: JAI Press, pp. 159–81.

Burdett, K. and J. Ondrich (1985), 'How Changes in Labor Demand Affect Unemployed Workers', *Journal of Labor Economics*, vol. 3, January.

Cline, H. (1980), 'The Effect of a Job on the Wage', University of Rochester, December, *mimeo*.

Feinberg, R. M. (1977), 'Search in the Labor Market and the Duration of Unemployment', *American Economic Review*, December.

Flinn, C. J. and J. Heckman (1983), 'Are Unemployment and Out of the Labor Force Behaviorally Distinct Labor Force States?', *Journal of Labor Economics*, vol. 1, January.

Leighton, L. and J. Mincer (1982), 'Labor Turnover and Youth Unemployment', in R. B. Freeman and D. A. Wise (eds), *The Youth Labor Market Problem*, Chicago: University of Chicago Press.

Mincer, J. and B. Jovanovic (1981), 'Labor Mobility and Wages', in S. Rosen (ed.), *Studies in Labor Markets*, Chicago: University of Chicago Press. (Chapter 5 of this volume.)

Mincer, J. (1983), 'Union Effects: Wages, Turnovers, and Job Training', in R. G. Ehrenberg (ed.), *Research in Labor Economics*, Supplement 2: *New Approaches to Labor Unions* (ed. Joseph Reid), Greenwich, Conn.: JAI Press, pp. 217–52. (Chapter 11 of Volume 2.)

Mincer, J. (1984), 'Labor Mobility, Wage Growth, and Job Training', in U.S. Department of Labor (DOL) Report.

Mortensen, D. and G. Neumann (1984), 'Interfirm Mobility and Earnings', *Econometrica*, September.

Nickell, S. (1979), 'Estimating the Probability of Leaving Unemployment', *Econometrica*, September.

Polachek, S. and F. Horvath (1977), 'A Life Cycle Approach to Migration', in R. G. Ehrenberg (ed.), *Research in Labor Economics*, vol. 1, Greenwich, Conn.: JAI Press.

Rosen, S. (ed.) (1981), Preface to *Studies in Labor Markets*, Chicago: University of Chicago Press.

Salop, S. S. (1973), 'Systematic Job Search and Unemployment', *Review of Economic Studies*, pp. 191–201.

7 Education and unemployment*

1. Components of unemployment and differentials by education

Accounting schemes and gross differentials

Educated workers enjoy at least three basic advantages over less-educated workers in the labor market: higher wages, greater upward mobility in income and occupation,[1] and greater employment stability. An immense literature is available on the wage structure by education; much less research is devoted to mobility and unemployment aspects of education. This study explores the relation between education of workers and their unemployment experience. That this relation is negative is well known from nearly ubiquitous observation.[2] But the reasons for it have not been subjected to thorough scrutiny.

The approach we take is to analyze several aspects of labor market behavior which combine to affect the unemployment rate of a group of workers. The analysis is facilitated by a decomposition of the unemployment rate into factors which correspond to somewhat distinct behavioral aspects. The same rate can obtain if more workers experience unemployment for a shorter time or fewer for a longer time. The probability of leaving employment, which we call unemployment incidence, is separable from, though not unrelated to, the probability of leaving unemployment, that is, to its duration.

The decomposition of the unemployment rate (u) is best seen if we define it as the fraction of time lost by all members of the labor force within a unit period, say a year: let L be the number of workers in the labor force, $Wk(l)$ the number of weeks in the labor force, N_u the number of workers who experienced unemployment, and $Wk(u)$ their weeks of unemployment. Thus, the average weekly unemployment rate is:

$$u = \frac{\sum_i Wk(u_i)}{\sum_i Wk(l_j)} = \frac{N_u}{L} \cdot \frac{\overline{Wk(u)}}{\overline{Wk(l)}} = P(u) \cdot \frac{D_u}{52 - D_o} = P(u)\frac{d_u}{1 - d_o} \quad (7.1)$$

Here, incidence, or the probability of unemployment, is $P(u) = \frac{N(u)}{L}$, while D_u is the average duration of unemployment for those who exper-

*This chapter is the previously unpublished National Bureau of Economic Research (NBER) Working Paper no. 3838, 1989; revised 1991.

ienced it, and D_o is the average number of weeks out of the labor force of all workers; d_u and d_o represent fractions of time spent in unemployment and out of the labor force, by the unemployed and by all workers respectively. Equation 7.1 shows that the unemployment rate of a group of workers is the *product* of their probability of experiencing unemployment $P(u)$ during the time they are in the labor force, and of the fraction of labor force time spent in unemployment of those who experience unemployment $(\frac{d_u}{1 - d_o})$.

Going behind the incidence factor, we note that:

$$P(u) = P(s) \cdot P(u/s) \qquad (7.2)$$

which is to say that the probability of being unemployed in the period depends on the probability of having separated from the previous job $P(s)$, and on the probability of encountering unemployment while separated. If restricted to job changes in the labor market,[3] equation 7.2 points to the significance of labor mobility or turnover, and to on-the-job search as (partly distinct) behavioral factors affecting incidence. Off-the-job search behavior is, presumably, the basic content of the duration of employment.

Combining equations 7.1 and 7.2, the composition of the unemployment rate is:[4]

$$u = P(S) \cdot P(u/s) \cdot d_u \cdot \frac{1}{1 - d_o} \qquad (7.3)$$

Table 7.1 illustrates the fact that each of the components of unemployment gets smaller as the level of education in the group increases.[5]

It is worth noting that the behavioral data shown in Table 7.1 are rather closely duplicated by subjective expectations of workers. Two surveys conducted by the National Opinion Research Center in 1977 and 1978 asked a nationwide sample of employed workers whether they expect to lose their jobs in the next 12 months, and whether they could easily find another comparable job if they were separated from their current firm.[6] Interpreting the responses to the first question as expectations about $P(u)$, and the second as expectations about $P(u/s)$,[7] compare column 1 of Table 7.1a with row 2 in Table 7.1, and column 2 of Table 7.1a with row 4 in Table 7.1.

Returning to Table 7.1, unemployment of the least educated (< 12 years) groups of male workers is typically over three times higher than that of the most educated (16+) groups. This ratio (R) shown in the last column of Table 7.1 can be decomposed following our equations, into

Table 7.1   Education and unemployment components: some gross
              (unadjusted) facts

Ed	< 12	12	13–15	16 +	< 12 / 16 +	Key to variables
u^a	7.0	4.1	3.3	1.9	3.7	unemployment rate
$P(u)$	9.5	6.4	4.7	3.5	2.7	probability (incidence) of unemployment
$P(s)$	17.9	13.4	12.8	10.5	1.7	probability of separation
$P(u/s)$	53.2	48.6	37.8	33.2	1.6	probability of unemployment of job separators
Du	13.8	12.1	11.6	11.0	1.26	duration of unemployment of job separators (in weeks)
LFP^b	92.1	97.0	96.4	98.2	0.94	labor force rate

Notes
[a]BLS data, white men, age 25–54, in 1979
[b]BLS data, same, age 35–44, in 1979
All other rows: PSID, white men, years 1976–81, 11–25 years of work experience.

Table 7.1a   Worker expectations about job loss and difficulty in job finding
               if separated

Education	Percent expecting to lose job	Percent expecting difficulty in finding another
Grade school	9.0	51.2
High school	8.8	43.1
Some college	9.0	31.6
College degree	2.7	37.8
Graduate work	1.3	27.7

Source: Monthly Labor Review, April 1980, p. 53.

products of component ratios, all of which are shown in the last column of
Table 7.1.

Thus,

$$R(u) = RP(s) \cdot RP(u/s) \cdot R(d_u) \cdot R\frac{(1)}{1-d_o} =$$
$$= 1.7 \times 1.6 \times 1.26 \times 1.06 = 3.5 \qquad (7.4)$$
$$= 2.7 \times 1.3$$

Here incidence of unemployment is 170 per cent greater, but duration is
only 30 per cent greater in the least-educated compared to the most-
educated group. Clearly, duration of unemployment is a relatively minor
aspect of the educational unemployment differentials, a finding familiar
from previous research.[8]

However, if the distinction is not between the probability of losing
employment and that of leaving unemployment, but between labor
mobility across firms and both on-the-job and off-the-job search behavior,
we find that:

$$R(u) = RP(s) \times \text{Remainder} = 1.7 \times 2.0, \text{ where the remainder} =$$
$$\ldots RP(u/s) \; R(du) \; R(\frac{1}{1-do}) \qquad (7.5)$$

While incidence is far more important than duration, job-search behavior (on and off the job) is as important as job turnover in affecting the
educational unemployment differentials.

Net unemployment differentials by education
Table 7.1 illustrated the patterns of educational unemployment differentials from various data sources. These differentials are gross, not standardized for other worker characteristics. We proceed to a description of the
net or partial effects of education, in the presence of such characteristics.
In this effort, we restrict the sample to adult white males, non-students,
age 18–60. We consider unemployment of job-changers only, so that recall
unemployment and that of labor force entrants and exits is excluded.
These exclusions are, in part, necessitated by the imperfections of our
data. Although we may lose close to a half of the usually observed
unemployment by these exclusions, the patterns of unemployment by
education are quite similar[9] whether or not we make the exclusions.
However, the behavioral analysis pertains most directly to the group we
study.

The PSID (Panel Study of Income Dynamics) sample we use contains observations on about 1200 males in years 1976–83, with some differences in temporal coverage, depending on availability of survey questions. The effective size of the samples varies also due to missing or faulty observations.

Table 7.2 shows the relation between education and the incidence of unemployment $P(u)$, and its components $P(s)$ and $P(u/s)$, net of other measured worker characteristics. In the linear specification of Table 7.2 (col. 2), each additional year of schooling reduces the probability of unemployment by 1.3 per cent points at given levels of working age ('experience').[10] The effect is smaller (0.8 per cent) when other variables, especially training in the firm, are included. Looking across the row of coefficients on education, we see that both separation probabilities $P(s)$ and conditional unemployment (i.e., unemployment of movers) $P(u/s)$ are reduced by education.

The reduction in turnover and the lesser exposure to unemployment of those who turn over bring about the reduction in unemployment incidence of the better-educated in just about equal measure. From the definition of $P(u)$ in equation 7.2, we have

$$\frac{\partial P(u)}{\partial Ed} = \frac{\partial P(s)}{\partial Ed} \cdot P(u/s) + \frac{\partial P(u/s)}{\partial Ed} P(s) =$$

$$= -.014 \times .47 - .036 \times .18 =$$

$$= \qquad -.007 \qquad -.006$$

(7.6)

The effects of education on the incidence of unemployment are reduced somewhat when additional variables are added in column 3 of Table 7.2. The (net) effect of education on the duration of unemployment, after standardization for other factors and characteristics, is shown in the first column of Table 7.6. An additional year of education (at $Ed = 12$) reduced duration of unemployment by nearly one week.

This effect amounts to about one-fourth of the decline in the unemployment rate due to an additional year of schooling. Since, in our sample, $u = P(u)\,d(u)$, the derivative is:

$$\frac{\partial u}{\partial Ed} = \frac{\partial P(u)}{\partial Ed} \cdot d(u) + \frac{\partial d(u)}{\partial Ed} \cdot P(u)$$

(7.7)

Given that $d(u)$ was, on average,[11] close to 0.24, and the mean (at $Ed = 12$) of $P(u) = 0.06$,

$$\frac{\partial u}{\partial Ed} = -1.32 \times .24 - 2.4 \times .06 =$$

$$= \qquad (-.32 \qquad -.12)$$

Table 7.2 Factors in the incidence of unemployment* (white men, PSID, 1976–81)

Variables	P(u)			P(s)		P(u/s)		Means
Intercept (c)	0.41 (21.6)	0.36 (15.2)	0.35 (13.7)	0.55 (19.5)	0.61 (15.4)	0.93 (120)	0.81 (6.8)	P(u) = 0.082 P(s) = 0.18 P(u/s) = 0.47
Education (Ed)	−0.018 (14.6)	−0.0132 (11.1)	−0.008 (9.8)	−0.014 (7.7)	−0.008 (7.8)	−0.036 (6.4)	−0.018 (5.8)	12.7
Experience (x)	−0.012 (10.7)	−0.0076 (7.0)	n.s.	−0.018 (9.7)	n.s.	n.s.	n.s.	17.2
x^2	0.0002 (6.6)	0.00012 (4.2)	n.s.	0.00026 (5.7)	n.s.	n.s.	n.s.	
Tenure (Ten)			−0.021 (15.7)		−0.038 (20.2)		−0.036 (3.9)	9.1
Ten^2			0.00056 (11.8)		0.0012 (15.0)		0.0011 (2.6)	
Married (Mar)			−0.038 (4.0)		−0.055 (4.0)		−0.061 (1.6)	0.88
Union member (Union)			−0.024 (3.4)		−0.076 (7.3)		0.083 (2.2)	0.35
Nat'l. unempl. Rate[a] (NUR)			0.007 (1.6)		n.s.		0.054 (2.0)	0.032
Training (RQT)			−0.0026 (1.8)		−0.0031 (2.1)		−0.010 (2.5)	2.2

Notes
*Recall unemployment excluded except for the first left column.
[a] of white men, age 35–44
n.s. = not significant
t = t-ratio

As in the unadjusted data (equation 7.4 above), the importance of education in reducing unemployment is nearly three times as great via reduction of turnover than via reduction of duration.

2.   Term by term analysis

Reasons for Lower Turnover P(s) *at Higher Education Levels*
In employing human-capital analysis it is important to distinguish the more comprehensive concept of investments in human capital from investments in school education. According to early calculations, (returns on) investments in school education – in dollar volumes – represent no more than a half of (returns on) total human-capital investments. Investments in job learning and training, in information, and labor mobility represent the other half of the total volumes.[12]

While higher wage trajectories of the more-educated workers reflect returns on investments in schooling, patterns of wage growth and of turnover of workers are, in principle, related to training and learning in the labor market, not in school. Therefore, the relations that are observed – steeper wage growth and greater attachment to the firm for the more educated worker – are causally indirect. It is because job training tends to be (a) positively related to schooling, and (b) negatively related to turnover, that we observe a negative relation between education and turnover.

Consequently, we break our questions into three parts: (a) is job training positively related to education, and why? (b) is turnover negatively related to job training, and why? and (c) does education affect labor mobility apart from its correlation with training?

(a)   Is job training positively related to education, and why?   Direct information on volumes of job training is provided in the PSID surveys of 1976 and 1978. The measure we use (*RQT*) is given by respondents' answers to a question: 'On a job like yours, how long would it take the average new person to become fully trained and qualified?' The question followed several other questions about training *prior* to the current job, and it 'was intended to measure the volume of the training investment attached to the current job'.[13]

That volumes of job training are positively related to school education of workers (when other characteristics are taken into account) is shown in Table 7.3 (column 1). In the PSID surveys conducted annually by the Institute for Social Research, University of Michigan, volumes of training were measured by the length of time in training and learning on the

Table 7.3 *Training and wages in current job (PSID, 1976 and 1978 pooled for* ROT, *1976–81 for ln* W)

Variables*	RQT	ln W
c	−0.50	0.26
	(6.6)	(7.2)
Ed	0.245	0.071
	(10.8)	(42.2)
x	0.107	0.024
	(5.1)	(13.9)
x²	−0.0013	−0.0004
	(2.5)	(10.2)
Ten	0.04	0.021
	(1.8)	(12.1)
Ten²	n.s.	−0.0004
		(6.5)
Mar	0.46	0.067
	(2.8)	(5.3)
Union	−0.55	0.13
	(4.8)	(14.0)
Ed × PG		0.073
		(4.5)
RQT × PG		0.078
		(1.9)
RQT		0.043
		(14.4)
Ed × RQT		n.s.
NUR		−0.039
		(4.8)

Notes
*PG = total factor productivity growth in industry 1970–79. Its level was also included in the wage regression.
NUR = national unemployment rate
ln w = logarithm of wages
Source: Conrad and Jorgenson (1985)

current job required for reaching a proficient ('fully qualified') level of productivity in the job.

Although this measure is far from accurate and ignores intensity (hours per period) of training,[14] results shown in Table 7.3 (column 1) are supported in other data sets utilized by other investigators. In the most comprehensive study, Lillard and Tan (1986) analyzed the distribution of training across workers in larger and, in some respects, more detailed Current Population Survey (CPS) and National Longitudinal Survey (NLS) samples. The training measure in both data sets is its incidence in the year before the survey. The location of training (whether in or outside of firms) is also indicated. (Our PSID data aim at in-firm training.) Their findings regarding the incidence of training by education – with similar standardizing variables – provides strong support for the inferences based on Table 7.3 here.

But why do more-educated workers engage in more on-the-job training? The general answer is that persons who have greater learning ability and better opportunities to finance the costs of human capital investments do invest more in all forms of human capital, including schooling and job training. Although this answer is sufficient, some analysts claim in addition that school education is a complementary factor to job training in producing human capital. In other words, education enhances the productivity of job training at work. It is clear, however, that schooling can also be a substitute for job training: thus, the decline in apprenticeships has been attributed to growth in educational levels over the long-run.

One direct test of complementarity fails in Table 7.3 (column 2): the coefficient of the interaction of education and training in the wage equation is not significant. However, the same test applied to upward occupational mobility (or wage growth in the long run) was positive (Sicherman, 1987). The wage equation in Table 7.3 also reveals another reason for a link between education and training: both are more profitable where productivity growth (*PG*) is more rapid.

(b)   Is turnover negatively related to education, and why? We saw in Table 7.2 that job training (measured by RQT) has a negative effect on separation rates, that is to say, it reduces the probability of leaving the firm in which training was received.[15] The reason is that training which enhances skill and productivity in the firm is not fully transferable to otherwise comparable jobs in other firms. Since training processes at work tend to be integrated with production processes, idiosyncrasies in the latter create some degree of firm specificity in training. Consequently, workers who acquire large volumes of training on the job are less likely to move from one firm to another. Similarly, employers are less likely to lay off such workers (permanently) if they share in the costs and returns to training. Indirect evidence of such cost-sharing appears in the negative effects of training on quits and layoffs, in separate regressions.[16] We may

conclude that the observed negative relation between education and turnover is, in part, attributable to the positive correlation between education and on-the-job training.

(c)   Does education affect labor mobility, apart from (net of) its correlation with training?   The answer is provided in Table 7.2, where the effect of education on turnover is reduced, but remains negative after training is introduced ('held constant') in the $P(s)$ regression, suggesting that factors other than training may be important as well.

One possibility is that firms with high fixed labor costs – such as costs of screening, hiring, and fringes which do not depend on hours of work – will aim to cut these costs by reducing turnover. This may be done by selecting more productive, capable, and stable workers, substituting adjustments in hours for adjustments in employment, and postponing rewards to workers in the form of steeper wage growth and/or of pensions. In substituting quality for quantity of employment, such firms tend to hire a larger proportion of better-educated workers. Information on the amount of fixed labor costs is scarce.[17] However, many firms that are large and more capital-intensive (the two tend to be correlated) are likely to have higher fixed costs of employment and therefore tend to engage in the above described policies in order to reduce turnover. Of course, another reason for lesser turnover in large firms is that their size permits job changes and, especially, upward mobility within the firm, thus limiting inter-firm mobility. There is abundant evidence that larger firms employ larger proportions of better-educated workers, and that turnover is lower in such firms.[18]

It may also be true that more-educated persons are more efficient in job matching, that is in finding suitable employment with less job-shopping – resulting therefore in lesser turnover. If matching gains are equated with wage gains in moving from one firm to another, the proposition is testable and we do find that wage gains (in percent terms) are greater for more educated workers (see Table 7.6) who move, especially by quitting.[19]

The greater mobility gain of educated workers, in part results from their longer-distance geographic migration, in which costs and therefore returns are higher. Indeed, geographic mobility is an exception to the proposition that more-educated workers engage in less job mobility. While less mobility of more-educated workers holds within local markets, and local mobility dominates the overall picture,[20] geographic mobility increases with education. Indeed inter-regional migration is twice as frequent among workers with 16 or more years of schooling than for those with 12 or less. Of course, having migrated, educated workers stay much longer on the job and in the new locality than do others (Da Vanzo, 1983).

The apparent contradiction between effects of education on local and on geographic job mobility can be reconciled on the following grounds: although educated workers change jobs less frequently, when they do, they are more likely to migrate geographically. It should be noted that most job changers have accumulated very little of specific capital,[21] that this is especially true of young workers, and that migration is especially selective of young workers. At the same time, job-search by the more-educated is likely to be more efficient where information is less complete (such as in long distance opportunities) because they accumulate more information and process information more efficiently. Indeed, educational selectivity is greater the longer the distance (e.g., in interstate vs. inter-county migration), and return migration is much less frequent among more-educated than less-educated migrants (Da Vanzo, 1983).

The purpose of this section was to explore the negative relation between education and labor turnover, because the latter is an important component of unemployment incidence. The following factors appear to give rise to this relation: job training which is partially specific to the firm; high turnover costs which induce firms to substitute schooled and trained workers for others; more intensive screening by firms; and more efficient job-search of more-educated workers.

Tied to these factors are sources of demand for educated workers in the labor market: firms in which training is important; firms in which turnover costs are high; large firms; and firms in geographically diversified industries. At the sectoral (industry) level we can add two additional sources: sectors with more rapid productivity growth; and sectors in which product demand, hence employment demand, is stable.

That demand for educated workers is greater in industries with more rapidly growing productivity is evident in Table 7.3 (column 2): the return to education (and to training) is greater in sectors with more rapid productivity growth.[22]

Industries in which employment fluctuations are mild are also likely to demand more-educated labor. This is because training is less risky in stable industries, as capital losses due to infrequent layoffs are smaller. Since more training is received by the more-educated workers, more of the latter are hired and sort themselves to such industries. The evidence is shown in Table 7.4, where sectoral instability is measured by unemployment incidence of high school graduates, showing that the proportion of workers with over 12 or with 16+ years of schooling as well as frequency of training are inversely related to instability.[23]

Table 7.4 *Unemployment incidence and the proportion of educated labor by industry, PSID 1976–81 (i = 25, $n_i \geq 30$)*

	P(Ed>12)		P(Ed≥16)		RQT
C	0.56	0.27	0.34	0.06	2.38
	(8.4)	(1.3)	(5.3)	(0.3)	(3.4)
$P(U_{12})$	−0.76	−0.56	−0.56	−0.37	−2.47
	(2.5)	(1.9)	(2.0)	(1.5)	(2.8)
x		0.024		0.022	n.s.
		(2.0)		(2.0)	
UnM		−0.31		−0.31	−0.26
		(1.9)		(1.9)	(1.6)
R^2		0.37		0.32	0.24

Notes
i = industry, n_i = sample size in industry i
C = intercept
$P(U_{12})$ = incidence of unemployment of high school graduates in industry
x = average years of experience in industry
UnM = unionization rate in industry
n.s. = not significant

Reasons for lower unemployment of job changers P(u/s) at higher educational levels

As we saw in Table 7.2, more-educated job changers are less likely to experience unemployment in the transition to a new job. The probability of becoming unemployed upon separation $P(u/s)$ depends, in part, on whether the separation was a quit or a layoff, since close to 70 per cent of layoffs but only 25–30 per cent of quits become unemployed. Indeed, more-educated job changers are somewhat less likely to separate by layoff than by quit (column 3 in Table 7.5). But this is a minor part of the reason for the lesser probability of unemployment of educated job changers. The major part is played by the lesser probability of unemployment of educated job changers both in quits and in layoffs.

This conclusion is based on the sizes of the coefficients of the education variables in Table 7.5. Given that, by definition:

$$P(u/s) = P(u/L)\frac{L}{S} + P(u/Q)(1 - \frac{L}{S}),$$ (7.8)

where P represents conditional probabilities of unemployment, given separation (s), layoffs (L), and quits (Q), respectively.

The effect of education is

Table 7.5   Unemployment in quits and layoffs

Variables	P(U/Q) (1)	P(U/L) (2)	L/S (3)
Ed	0.049	0.076	0.038
	(1.3)	(1.8)	(2.1)
Ed^2	−0.003	−0.004	−0.002
	(2.2)	(2.5)	(2.5)
x	−0.006	−0.006	0.009
	(1.0)	(1.0)	(2.6)
x^2	0.0001	0.0001	−0.0001
	(0.7)	(1.1)	(1.4)
Slope at $Ed = 12$	−0.023	−0.020	−0.010

Notes
$P(U/Q)$ = probability of unemployment in quits
$P(U/L)$ = probability of unemployment in layoffs
L/S = ratio of layoffs to all separations

$$\frac{dP(u/s)}{dEd} = \frac{dP(u/L)}{dEd} \cdot \frac{L}{S} + \frac{dP(u/Q)}{dEd}(1 - \frac{L}{S}) + \quad (7.9)$$

$$[P(u/L) - P(u/Q)] \cdot \frac{d(\frac{L}{S})}{dEd}$$

At the means of education ($Ed = 12$) and of L/S (0.4), the numerical value of the last term is no more than one-sixth of the total effect.

We know by now that more-educated workers are less likely than others to quit or to be laid off. But why are they less exposed to unemployment when they do quit or are laid off? The general answer to this question lies in job-search behavior of workers and hiring efforts of firms.

It is important to realize that job-search of workers takes place both on the job (while employed) and off-the-job (while unemployed). (Indeed, over half of all job changes occur without unemployment, involving search or accepting offers while employed.) The proportion is even greater among the more-educated, who are more likely to search on the job rather than off-the-job. A basic reason from the worker's point of view is that the cost of off-the-job search (while unemployed) relative to the cost of on-the-job search is greater for the more-educated. Larger forgone earnings and smaller unemployment compensation offsets make search off-the-job more costly, while greater efficiency in accumulating information and greater flexibility in time at work lower the cost of on-the-job search.

Consequently, while over 40 per cent of less-educated (*Ed* < 12) quitters quit into unemployment in order to search, only 20 per cent of the more-educated (16 +) do so.

The greater stock of information and greater efficiency in search can also account for the lesser risk of unemployment of more-educated workers who are laid off, provided layoff notices permit some time for search on the job, and especially if the more-educated workers are more likely to receive advance notices of layoff. Indeed, a recent study by Ehrenberg and Jakubson (1987) indicates that (a) workers who receive advance notices of layoff or of plant shutdown are less likely to experience unemployment; and (b) advance notices are more likely to be received in plants where proportions of skilled blue-collar workers and of college-educated workers are larger. The study also shows that, given advance notice, the laid-off more-educated white-collar workers are less likely to become unemployed.

On the hiring side, one would expect a greater intensity of search for more-educated workers by firms, since costs of unfilled vacancies for skilled jobs, in terms of forgone production, are clearly higher. Hence more-educated workers are likely to receive offers from other firms while they are employed elsewhere. In other words, the costs of search shift in part to employers as education of workers rises.[24]

Direct evidence on the informational efficiency in job-search of educated workers is not available. Indirect evidence of migration behavior was cited before. Greater wage gains in job-changing will be shown in the next section, together with other evidence on efficiency which applies both to on-the-job and off-the-job search.

Job search and the duration of unemployment
The hypotheses concerning search efficiency of workers and greater search effort of employers in hiring educated workers apply to workers' search on as well as off-the-job. These hypotheses provide explanation for the educational patterns of unemployment durations and of wage gains in moving, both observable in our data.

To understand the findings about effects of education on unemployment of job-changers, its duration, and on wage gains in moving, we view them as implications of a theoretical model of job search. It can be described, in a simplified manner, as follows: workers sample from sets of alternative wages available in potential jobs (the set is called the 'wage offer distribution') finding at least one vacancy per unit of time with probability p. The worker's strategy in accepting a job offer is to decide on a minimum acceptable wage ('wage floor') which equates the gain from an

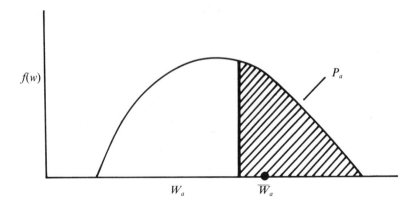

W_a = acceptance wage
$P_a = P(W > W_a)$ = area to the right of W_a
$\overline{W}_a$ = mean wage in the truncated area

Figure 7.1   Wage offer distribution

additional period of search to the cost of it. Formally, the decision rule
(see Appendix 7.1) is:[25]

$$\frac{k}{i} p \cdot P_a(\overline{W}_a - W_a) = C, \text{ where } k = [1 - (\frac{1}{1+i})^t] \qquad (7.10)$$

Costs (*c*) are on the right side of equation (7.10); gains on the left.

Since gains accrue over a long period following accession to a new
job, their capital value appears on the left hand side of equation (7.10),
when divided by the discount rate *i*. The term $\frac{1}{i}$ is multiplied by
$k = [1 - (\frac{1}{1+i})^t]$, a correction for the finite payoff period *t*. The shorter
the period the smaller the gain ($k < 1$ and declines as *t* declines).

These concepts are easily visualized in Figure 7.1. The probability of
finding a vacancy is *p*, so the probability of finding an acceptable job is
(pP_a).

The cost of search includes opportunity costs of time (C_o), direct costs
of search (travel, communications, and of other forms of acquiring information) (C_d). Income offsets (*z*) which are contingent on continuing
search, such as unemployment compensation, enter costs with a negative
sign: thus $c = c_o + c_d - z$. The discount factor *k* depends on time preference, on the terms of credit available to the workers, and on the expected

Factor	Up (↑) Down (↓)	*du*	W_a
c	↑	↓	↓
i	↓	↑	↑
t	↑	↑	↑
p	↓	↓	↑

Figure 7.2   Changes

duration of the next job (*t*). Duration of unemployment (D_u) when identified with duration of search is the inverse of the (unconditional) probability of finding an acceptable job:

$$D_u = \frac{1}{p \cdot P_a} \qquad (7.11)$$

Decision rule (equation (7.10)) contains several factors differing by education, which determine both the duration of search unemployment and the minimal acceptable wage in the new job.

The model produces several important implications:

(a)   The lower the cost of search (*c*), the more time the worker can afford to spend searching and choosing among alternatives, and the higher the wage demanded.

(b)   The lower the discount rate (*i*) and the longer the expected stay on the new job, the greater future gains loom relative to current costs. The result is longer duration of search and better terms (here W_a) on the new job resulting from the more thorough search.

(c)   The higher the probability of finding a vacancy (*p*), the more likely is a worker to find an acceptable job during a given period. Hence the duration of search is likely to be shorter, and the new wage likely to be obtained is higher.[26]

Schematically, the effects of these factors on duration of search and on reservation wages are indicated in Figure 7.2. Variations (across people) in costs of search (per unit of calendar time), in ease of financing (*i*), and in the expected payoff period (*t*) induce the same direction of effect on duration as on the acceptance wage. Only variations in (*p*), the efficiency of search, produce opposite signs.

In the first column of the diagram we assume variations that distinguish

Table 7.6   Duration of unemployment between jobs, and wage gains of unemployed movers, 1976–81, PSID

Variables	Duration coefficients		Wage gain ($\Delta \ln W$) coefficients
	(1)	(2)	(3)
Ed	−0.56	−0.54	0.068
	(2.0)	(2.0)	(1.9)
Ed²	−0.018	−0.017	−0.002
	(1.6)	(1.5)	(1.7)
x	−0.032	0.028	−0.010
	(0.9)	(0.6)	(1.0)
x²	0.003	0.0014	0.0002
	(2.2)	(1.0)	(0.8)
u		1.40	
		(8.1)	
u			−0.037
			(1.8)
Disabled		0.72	−0.049
		(1.8)	(1.6)
Mar		−0.72	0.044
		(2.1)	(1.8)
Ten		−0.45	−0.028
Ten²		0.020	0.0007
		(3.8)	(2.7)

Notes
Ed = years of schooling
u = unemployment rate

more- from less-educated workers. Cost (c) of search (given its efficiency) is assumed to be higher per unit of calendar time, the discount rate (i) lower, expected stay in the new firm (t) longer, and probability of finding a vacancy (p) per unit of calendar time greater.

The analysis may be described as follows: cost of search, c (on the right side of our decision rule, equation (7.10), is likely to be higher for educated workers because of their greater forgone earnings and lesser offset by unemployment compensation. Of the left side variables, the discount rate i, reflecting the ease of financing search as well as time preference, is likely to be lower – as this is a factor, in addition to ability, which induced greater investment in education in the first place. Empirical evidence from

Table 7.7   *Ratio of reservation wage and new job wage to last wage of movers, and average duration of the unemployment spell, 1980–2*

	Education	< 12	12–15	16+
$\dfrac{W_R}{W_O}$	Unempl. Q	0.88	1.05	1.23
		(12)	(22)	(6)
	Unempl. L	0.82	0.78	1.04
		(51)	(69)	(14)
	Unempl. M	0.83	0.85	1.07
		(63)	(91)	(20)
$\dfrac{W_N}{W_O}$	Unempl. Q	1.08	1.06	1.17
		(37)	(78)	(17)
	Unempl. L	0.97	0.98	1.12
		(34)	(96)	(17)
	Unempl. M	1.01	1.02	1.14
		(71)	(174)	(34)
$\dfrac{W_N}{W_O}$	Empl. M	1.14	1.17	1.21
		(63)	(163)	(81)
Duration of spell	Unempl. Q	11.3	11.0	7.5
		(41)	(113)	(25)
	Unempl. L	17.4	14.0	12.8
		(59)	(174)	(28)
	Unempl. M	14.9	13.2	10.9
		(116)	(333)	(60)

Notes
Sample sizes in parentheses.
W_R = reservation wage Q = quits
W_O = last wage on prior job L = layoffs
W_n = new starting wage M = all movers

Table 7.7, utilized in Appendix 7.2, confirms this hypothesis. Because of lower i and greater ability, educated workers also benefit more from all other forms of human capital, including information and training. Therefore, their search is more informed and they expect to continue training and learning on the next job. Hence they expect to stay longer in the new job than the less-educated job-changers do. The greater accumulation of information in turn raises p, the efficiency of search. The lower i and higher k and p raise the value of the gain from search.

We have already alluded to several factors affecting efficiency. As just indicated, efficiency is not exogenous. It is affected by incentives of workers and firms to acquire information about alternative jobs and employees, and to search more intensively. Formally, we can express p (the probability of finding vacancies per unit (of calendar time) as a function:

$$p = p(\tau,x;e_i,e_m) \qquad (7.12)$$

Here τ is the intensity of search (hours per week spent in search), x is other expenditures, such as advertising, transportation, etc. Educated workers have an incentive to spend more resources (τ and x) in order to shorten the period of unemployment, which is more costly in terms of forgone earnings to them compared to other workers. Evidence on greater job-search intensity of more-educated workers is available in Barron and Mellow (1979) and in Zuckerman (1982), based on a Bureau of Labor Statistics (BLS) survey of unemployed workers (1976) and (1973). The greater investment in (accumulation of) job market information appears in a larger e_i, personal efficiency variable, and the greater intensity of search by employers for more-educated workers appears in the market efficiency variable e_m. Indirect evidence on e_i and e_m was cited before.[27] In support of a larger e_m, there is also evidence that more-educated workers are less vulnerable in cyclical declines, partly because they are employed in more stable sectors (Table 7.4), and that greater demand for educated workers is generated by economic growth, as seen in the positive coefficient on $Ed \times PG$ in Table 7.3, and in other recent studies.[28]

Comparing more-educated to less-educated workers, using decision rule (equation (7.10)), we see that the right side (c) is raised, but so is the left side, because of higher p and $\dfrac{k}{i}$. The empirical findings suggests that the product $p\dfrac{k}{i}$ increases (with education) more than the opportunity cost c.[29]

The adjustment to achieve optimum results in search when gains exceed costs is to equate the two sides of equation (7.10) by raising the acceptance wage W_a. This reduces the conditional probability P_a, but the unconditional probability of finding an acceptable job ($p.P_a$) may remain higher after the adjustment.[30] Duration of search, therefore, may decline, since

$$d_u = \frac{1}{p \cdot P_a}.$$

The opposite scenario, where costs c increase more than gains in equation (7.10) would produce the opposite effects; reservation wages would be reduced and duration of search increased for more- compared to less-educated workers. This scenario is decisively rejected by the empirical findings in Tables 7.6 and 7.7.

Note that for empirical purposes (Tables 7.6 and 7.7), we are equating duration of unemployment with duration of search, and that both reservation wages and wages on the new job are deflated (divided) by the wage on the old job (W_o). Since $\overline{W}_a > W_a$, it must be true that $\frac{\overline{W}_a}{W_o} > \frac{W_a}{W_o}$, i.e., percent gains in wages are larger the higher the reservation wages. Deflation by W_o is necessary in order to standardize (keep fixed) the level of the wage offer distribution, which differs by education.

Reservation wages of workers unemployed during the survey were reported in 1980–2.

Table 7.7 shows that $\frac{W_a}{W_o}$ moves up with education of job-changers in quits and in layoffs with and without unemployment.[31] Wage gains ($\frac{W}{W_o}$) move correspondingly.

The behavior of variables in the decision rule equation (7.10) is similar for on-the-job searchers, and perhaps less ambiguous than in the case of unemployed searchers. p and $\frac{k}{i}$ are greater for the more-educated workers whether or not they are employed. They also have lower costs of on-the-job search, if they are more flexible in their use of work time, while the unemployed may have somewhat less efficiency than the employed – as evidenced by their winding up in unemployment. Wage gains are indeed larger for employed than for unemployed searchers (Table 7.7). We conclude that $P(u/s)$, discussed in the previous section, is smaller among more-educated workers not only because they find it more economical to search on- rather than off-the-job, but also because their search is more efficient. The fact, shown earlier, that education reduces conditional unemployment $P(u/s)$ to a greater extent than it reduces the duration of unemployment is also consistent with this analysis.

3. Summary and concluding remarks

A major benefit of education in the labor market is the lower risk of unemployment at higher levels of education. In order to understand this relation, we analyze several aspects of unemployment which combine to produce the usually reported unemployment rates. We find that the reduction of the incidence of unemployment, that is, of the probability of experiencing unemployment in a calendar period, is far more important than the reduced duration of unemployment in creating the educational differentials in unemployment rates. While this finding is not new, further analyses of components and factors in the incidence and duration of unemployment yield insights into the relevant behavior of workers and firms in the labor market.

The behavioral phenomena of basic importance are: training processes in firms, and search of workers and firms for one another. These phenomena are not quite unrelated, although they are analytically separable. We find that the lesser unemployment incidence of the more-educated workers is, in about equal measure, due to their greater attachment to the firms employing them, and to the lesser risk of entering unemployment when separated from the firm. This lesser risk applies to both quits and layoffs and is, only in small part, due to the somewhat greater likelihood of quit than of layoff among the more-educated job-changers.

The lesser frequency of job turnover of more educated workers, which creates fewer episodes of unemployment, is in large part attributable to a greater likelihood of their engaging in on-the-job training. Because such training contains elements of firm-specificity, its costs tend to be shared by workers and firms, and turnover, both in quits and in layoffs, is reduced. It should be understood that job training and learning is a comprehensive concept, not restricted to formal training programs or apprenticeships in firms.

Factors other than job training also play a role in the greater firm attachment of educated workers. Firms which bear relatively high fixed labor costs – in terms of hiring, screening, fringes – tend to substitute both physical and human capital for less-skilled labor. Large firms, which tend to have higher fixed labor costs, recruit larger proportions of educated workers, whose turnover is lower. Training costs are, of course, also a part of fixed costs and, indeed, there is evidence that screening costs tend to correlate with training costs.[32]

In explaining the lesser conditional unemployment of educated workers and the somewhat lesser duration of their unemployment, we focus on search behavior. Moving from one firm to another without unemployment implies search on the job. The lesser risk of unemployment in job-changing suggests greater efficiency of on-the-job search. We provide largely indirect evidence that (a) costs of on-the-job search relative to costs of searching while unemployed are lower for more educated workers; (b) that these workers are also more efficient in acquiring and processing job search information; and (c) that firms and workers search more intensively to fill more-skilled vacancies.

All three reasons explain the more successful on-the-job search of the more-educated workers. The second and third apply to off-the-job search as well. However, efficiency of search is not the only factor affecting duration of search unemployment. Three other factors – opportunity costs, the rate at which the future is discounted, and the expected length of the payoff period, that is of duration of stay on the next job – have conflicting implications for the duration of search. Information on wage gains in moving is useful in disentangling these contradictory forces. We conclude that the somewhat shorter duration of unemployment coupled with larger wage gains from search is due to the dominating effect of greater efficiency and intensity of search in the market for educated labor.

The interrelation between human capital investment behavior and search behavior can be seen in the following mutual links: since educated workers tend to invest more in training, they expect to continue doing so when they move to the next firm. Consequently they expect to stay at a firm longer than other workers. According to the economic model they will, therefore, search more thoroughly (though, as we have seen, not necessarily longer), and obtain greater wage gains in moving, as we observed.

At the same time, the more informed the search, the more likely is a successful job match, hence the longer are workers likely to stay on the next job.[33] Thus search efficiency, which is characteristic of educated workers, may be an additional factor in their lesser turnover.

Having restricted our sample basically to workers who are in almost continuous employment – white men, non-students, age 18–60, we could ignore non-participation including entries into and exits from the labor force as components of unemployment. The bottom row of Table 7.1 showed that, for our sample, the differences by education are negligible, except for the least-educated (*Ed* < 12) high-school dropouts. The entry probabilities are likely to be higher for the more educated because they have fewer difficulties in finding jobs – as was shown in our search analysis. Lesser probability of leaving the labor force is suggested by the likelihood of greater training on the job: to the extent that the training is specific, losses of human capital deter workers from leaving the employing firm whether it is to go to another or to leave the labor force. But even when the training is transferable to other firms, as most of it tends to be, leaving employment for a longer time can erode the acquired human capital. Consequently more-educated workers are less likely to drop out and stay out. In analyzing labor force groups in which continuity of employment is far from permanent, non-participation and labor force turnover must be singled out in addition to job turnover as an important factor in analyzing unemployment differentials.

Appendix 7.1: Derivation of Equation (7.10)
The decision rule in (sequential) optimal search is:

$$c = \int_{w_a}^{\infty} (w - w_a) f(w) dw$$

where c = search cost, w_a = reservation wage, $f(w)$ = wage offer distribution. This may be rewritten as follows:

$$c = \int_{w_a}^{\infty} w f(w) dw - w_a \int_{w_a}^{\infty} f(w) dw = \int_{w_a}^{\infty} f(w) dw \cdot [\bar{w}_a - w_a] = P_a[\bar{w}_a - w_a]$$

where

$$\bar{w}_a = E(w > w_a) = \frac{\int_{w_a}^{\infty} w f(w) dw}{\int_{s_a}^{\infty} f(w) dw}, \text{ and } P_a = \int_{w_a}^{\infty} f(w) dw$$

This is correct, if at least one wage offer (vacancy) appears in a unit period. More generally the probability of a vacancy encountered is p. Also, the gain from search will accrue at least over the period of the next job (t), hence the complete equation, taking account of discounting (i), is:

$$c = \frac{k}{i} p \, P_a(\bar{w}_a - w_a), \text{ where } k = 1 - \frac{1}{(1+i)^t}$$

Duration (D_u) is the inverse of pP_a. In most plausible distributions ($\bar{w}_a - w_a$) moves in the same direction as P_a (Flinn and Heckman, 1983). Hence the effects of any of the variables on w_a, P_a, and D_u are easily shown.

Appendix 7.2: Evidence (from Table 7.7) that discount rate i is lower at higher levels of education

Optimal search:[34]
$$\frac{k}{i} p P_a(\bar{w} - w_a) = c$$

Let $\bar{w}_a = w_n$ and $c = \alpha w_n = \alpha \bar{w}_a$

Assume α same for all levels of education (e.g., employment agency fees proportional to the wage in new job).

So
$$\frac{k}{i} p P_a(1 - \frac{w_a}{w_n}) = \alpha$$

Therefore ratio R of educ < 12 to educ ≥ 16:

$$R(\frac{k}{i})R(p \cdot P_a)R(1 - \frac{w_a}{w_n}) = 1$$

Since $D_u = \dfrac{1}{pP_a}$, substitute numbers from Table 7.7 to get

$$\frac{k_1}{k_2} \frac{i_2}{i_1} = \frac{1{,}065}{2{,}255} \simeq \frac{1}{2}$$

hence

$$i_2 \simeq \frac{1}{2} i \cdot \frac{k_1}{k_2}$$

Discount rate of educated $(16+)$ is at most half the size of that of the least-educated.[35]

(*Note*: $k = 1 - \dfrac{1}{(1+i)^t}$ and if $t_2 = 2t_1$, (average tenure) while $i_2 = 1/2\, i_1$, k_2 $\simeq k_1$, since $\dfrac{1}{(1+i)^t} = \dfrac{1}{(1+1/2i)}2t$, when i is small enough.)

Acknowledgements
I am grateful to Tom Melito for research assistance, to David Bloom and other members of the Columbia Labor Seminar, and to members of the National Center for Education and Employment Seminar for helpful comments.

Notes
1. On occupation, see Sicherman (1987).
2. Some exceptions have been reported in less-developed countries (e.g., India in the 1950s and '60s) (Blaug *et al.*, 1969).
3. Separation can be generalized to include labor-force entrants and exits. In the current report it is restricted to job changes.
4. The last term $\dfrac{1}{1-d_0}$, is ignored in the empirical analyses of workers who are (almost) continuously in the labor force.
5. The statement refers to each row in Table 7.1. Comparisons of *levels* within columns are distorted by differences in sources and definitions of data. *Ratios* in the last column are comparable.
6. *Monthly Labor Review*, April 1980.
7. Perhaps the relative difficulty of finding another job (col. 2 of Table 7.1a) is more properly compared with $P(u/s) \times D_u$. Either way, the results are similar.
8. See Ashenfelter and Ham (1979).
9. Some preliminary evidence suggests that inclusions would actually steepen the relations observed here. See first column in Table 7.2.

10. The reduction accelerates at medium and higher levels of education, when a non-linear formulation is used.
11. Assuming an average of 50 weeks per year in the labor force.
12. This is net of investments in health which represent investments in 'maintenance and repairs' of human capital (Mincer, 1974).
13. A check on whether the RQT measures in the PSID refer to the length of current training in the firm or to total (cumulated) on-the-job training needed for the particular job was performed by Sicherman (1987). A comparison by detailed occupation in PSID responses with DOT (Dictionary of Occupational Titles) estimates supports the assertion that RQT is not a cumulative measure antedating the current firm for most occupations, except for a minority of highly skilled professional occupations where RQT is overstated. When added to probably sizable errors of measurement this discrepancy creates an additional downward bias on estimates of effects of RQT in statistical regressions.
14. Supplementary information on intensity is available in a 1980 study of PSID time budgets by Duncan and Stafford (1980). It contains data on the proportion of workers who were engaged in job training during the survey week and the hours spent in training by those engaged in it. Both components and their product increase with education (except for the highest level (16+)). Our measure (RQT) is, therefore, not misleading in terms of direction of effect of schooling on training.
15. For additional evidence see Mincer (1987).
16. Ibid.
17. See, however, Oi (1962), and Mincer and Higuchi (1988).
18. For a summary of a growing literature, see Idson (1986).
19. See also Table 4 in Mincer (1986).
20. Geographic mobility amounts to about 25% of total job mobility in Census data. It was less than 20% in the PSID.
21. Most job movers had short tenures in the firm they left.
22. Similar and related findings were obtained by Lillard and Tan (1986) and in Japanese data (Mincer and Higuchi, 1988). Reasons were analyzed by Da Vanzo (1983) and in Bartel and Lichtenberg (1987).
23. Instability here is an industry characteristic, not a consequence of more training received by more educated workers.
24. Another reason for this shift (proposed by Stigler, 1962) is that the ratio of workers to potential employers declines at higher education levels.
25. See Appendix 7.1 for derivation. For an extensive survey of job search models see Mortensen (1987).
26. On average, the new wage equals $\overline{W}_a$, which exceeds W_a.
27. Direct evidence on the number of contacts with potential employers during the previous month shows that it was larger for the more educated unemployed searchers in the sample of Table 7.7. Similar evidence is reported by Yoon (1981) for earlier periods. This evidence reflects greater efficiency or greater intensity of search. Holzer (1988) reports greater diversity of search methods by more-educated young unemployed workers in the NLS. Generally, he finds this variable reduces the duration of unemployment as well.
28. See Bartel and Lichtenberg (1987); Lillard and Tan (1986); Mincer and Higuchi (1988).
29. Appendix 7.2 uses data of Table 7.7 to test the proposition.
30. For proofs see Flinn and Heckman (1983). The theorem they prove is that the (negative) elasticity of P_a with respect to p is less than unity. This guarantees a reduction in duration of search when its efficiency (p) increases. Note that when a higher (rather than p) distinguishes more- from less-educated workers, duration of search increases. Our empirical findings indicate that p dominates the educational differentials.
31. There are very few layoffs among employed movers, hence only total separations are shown for them in Table 7.7.
32. See Barron *et al.* (1986); also, Mincer and Higuchi (1988).
33. Some evidence is available in Mincer (1987).

34. Here i is the discount rate, $k = 1 - \dfrac{1}{(1+i)^t}$, where t is the payoff period.

    p = arrival rate of vacancies

    P_a = Prob $(w > w_a)$, w_a − reservation wage, $\bar{w}_a$ − expectation of wage in new job, c − cost of search.

35. Ratio is smaller when the lesser offset by unemployment compensation is taken into account.

References

Ashenfelter, O. and J. Ham (1979), 'Education, Unemployment and Earnings', *Journal of Political Economy*, part 2, October.

Barron, J., D. Black and M. Loewenstein (1986), 'Job Matching and On the Job Training', Working Paper E-97-86, University of Kentucky, September.

Barron, J. and W. Mellow (1979), 'Search Effort in the Labor Market', *Journal of Human Resources*, Summer.

Bartel, A. and F. Lichtenberg (1987), 'The Comparative Advantage of Educated Workers in Implementing New Technologies', *Review of Economics and Statistics*, vol. 69.

Blaug, M., P. R. G. Layard and M. Woodhall (1969), *The Causes of Graduate Unemployment in India*, London, Penguin.

Borsch-Supan, A. (1987), 'The Role of Education in Geographic Mobility', *NBER Working Paper no. 2329*, July.

Conrad, K. and D. W. Jorgenson (1985), 'Sectoral Productivity Gaps between the United States, Japan and Germany, 1960–1979', in *Probleme und Perspektiven der Weltwirtschaftlichen Entwicklung*, Berlin: Duncker & Humboldt.

Da Vanzo, J. (1983), 'Repeat Migration in the U.S.', *Review of Economics and Statistics*, November.

Duncan, G. and F. Stafford (1980), 'The Use of Time and Technology by Households in the United States', *Research in Labor Economics*, vol. 3.

Ehrenberg, R. and G. Jakubson (1987), 'Advance Notice Provisions: Do They Matter?', Cornell University, draft, July.

Flinn, C. and J. Heckman (1983), 'Are Unemployment and Out of the Labor Force Behaviorally Distinct Labor Force States?', *Journal of Labor Economics*, January.

Holzer, H. (1988), 'Search Methods Used by Unemployed Youth', *Journal of Labor Economics*, January.

Idson, T. (1986), *Establishment Size Differentials*, PhD thesis, Columbia University, May.

Lillard, L. and H. W. Tan (1986), *Private Sector Training*. Rand Publication for Department of Labour, March.

Mincer, J. (1974), *Schooling, Experience and Earnings*, New York: Columbia University Press.

Mincer, J. (1986), 'Wage Changes in Job Changes', *Research in Labor Economics*, vol. 8A. (Chapter 6 of this volume.)

Mincer, J. (1987), 'Job Training, Wage Growth, and Labor Turnover', Columbia University, draft. (Chapter 8 of this volume.)

Mincer, J. and Y. Higuchi (1988), 'Wage Structures and Labor Turnover in the U.S. and in Japan', *Journal of the Japanese and International Economy*, June. (Chapter 11 of this volume.)

Mortensen, D. (1987), 'Job Search and Labor Market Analysis', *Handbook of Labor Economics*, vol. II, Amsterdam: North Holland.

Oi, W. (1962), 'Labor as a Quasi-Fixed Factor of Production', *Journal of Political Economy*, December.

Sicherman, N. (1987), *Human Capital and Occupational Mobility*, PhD Thesis, Columbia University, May.

Stigler, J. (1962), 'Information in the Labor Market', *Journal of Political Economy*, Supplement, October.

Yoon, B. J. (1981), 'Unemployment Duration with Variable Search Intensity', *Review of Economics and Statistics*, November.

Zuckerman, S. (1982), *Job Search with Varying Search Effort*, PhD. Thesis, Columbia University, May.

8   Job training, wage growth, and labor turnover*

1.   Introduction: Background

Until recently, the absence of empirical measures of job training has made much of the human capital analysis of wage structures largely indirect. Levels of school education are important in analyzing *levels* of lifetime earnings, but not shapes of wage profiles. These are affected by time patterns of post-school (working life) human capital investments (Becker, 1962; Ben-Porath, 1967). Training or learning on the job is understood to be of major substantive importance among such investments. The idea that job investments contain elements of firm-specificity introduced by Becker (1964) and Oi (1962) produces a link between human capital investments and interfirm labor mobility,[1] or labor turnover. These ideas were elaborated and applied by Kuratani (1973) and Hashimoto (1980). Completing the syllogism, Mincer and Jovanovic (1981) proposed an inverse relation between slopes of tenure–wage profiles and labor turnover. This hypothesis has proven useful in analyzing interoccupational, interindustry, and intercountry differences in turnover.[2]

The emphasis on human capital in producing an indirect relation between wage growth and labor mobility does not preclude the possible validity of direct effects of upward-sloping wage profiles on turnover. Such effects are envisaged in work-incentive models (Lazear, 1981) and in selectivity models (Salop, 1976). Individual growth in productivity, due to skill training or otherwise, plays no role in these models. No empirical evidence has emerged to discriminate between them and the specific-capital hypothesis. One major reason is the lack of measures of productivity.

Another interpretation of the relation between wage growth and turnover which both limits the upward slope in wages to an initial 'probation' period in the firm and relates the length of stay in the firm to the magnitude of the initial boost in wages is the 'matching' hypothesis of Jovanovic (1979). As is true of the other theories, matching and specific-capital hypotheses are, in principle, not mutually exclusive. Indeed, there are reasons to believe that training is more likely to be undertaken the more successful the match, since worker–firm complementarity should raise

*This chapter is a previously unpublished National Bureau of Economic Research (NBER) Working Paper, revised 1988.

both current productivity and returns to training. For this reason, training and trainability are themselves likely to be important matching (and screening) criteria. If this reasoning is correct, matching and specific capital models may be difficult to distinguish, even when information on training is available.

The purpose of this study is to take advantage of the availability of information on the incidence and timing of training in conjunction with information on wage profiles and mobility behavior of workers in the Panel Study of Income Dynamics (PSID) micro-data. Short- (within the firms) and longer-run effects of training on mobility and on wages are estimated in PSID data which cover intervals as long as two decades.[3] Aside from PSID data, job training information is also available in other data sets, such as the National Longitudinal Panels (NLS), and in a 1983 Current Population Survey (CPS). Fragmentary evidence on the positive effect of training on wages appears in these and other data sets. Systematic studies of wage structures in relation to training begin with Duncan and Hoffman (1978) and Brown (1983, 1989) who used PSID data, Parsons (1986) who used NLS Young Men's Panels, Lillard and Tan (1986) who used the CPS and NLS data in a comprehensive and detailed analysis, and Bishop (1984) who used Equal Opportunity Pilot Project (EOPP) data.

The present study extends these efforts in two directions: (a) it analyzes effects of training on mobility, that is on length of tenure in the firm in which training was received and on the frequency of job change over longer periods of time, and (b) it looks at effects of training on changes in wages over time, distinguishing in-firm and across-firm wage effects. Although the main reliance is on the PSID data, findings or data from other studies are used or cited where relevant.

The study confirms empirically the validity of human-capital factors in producing the wage–turnover relation. The question about reality and importance of other hypotheses is not thereby resolved, but some implications regarding alternative interpretations are considered in the empirical context.

Although job training information lets some light into the black box, it cannot fully illuminate it. This is so not only because the data are imperfect, but also because a direct measurable distinction between general (transferable) and specific human-capital investments is not available. A working assumption which obviates this problem is that, at the firm level, training, even if largely transferable to other firms, perforce contains some elements of firm specificity. Since the greatest opportunities for training are likely to exist in firms in which training processes are closely related to and integrated with their production processes, we may infer a positive relation between total volumes of training and amounts of both general and specific training received in firms. Hence the hypothesis that the larger the volume of training in the firm, the steeper the growth of wages of trainees in the firm and over experience, and the stronger their attachment to the firm. Since the experience–wage profile includes gains (or losses) in wages in moving between firms, a needed qualification is that these mobility gains of the more-frequent movers do not compensate for their lesser wage-growth within firms. This qualification is verified in the present study. What may appear as a paradox, that mobility is undertaken for wage gain, yet wages of frequent movers grow less in the long run, is thus resolved.

Empirical work reported here is based on PSID data, and is restricted to white male heads of households, up to age 60, excluding students and self-employed. Section 2 presents information on cumulative patterns of individual interfirm mobility, on annual separations rates, and on the distribution of job training across workers reported in the 1976, 1978 and 1985 PSID surveys. Job training is shown in section 3 to be positively related to the length of tenure and negatively to current and longer-run mobility behavior. Section 4 provides evidence on the positive effects of training on wage growth in the firm, and Section 5 over longer periods. Section 6 contains findings on mobility wage gains. Section 7 contains concluding remarks.

2.   Mobility profiles, separation rates, and job training

Experience profiles of interfirm mobility

Information on the number of interfirm moves (N) was accumulated over time (working age, X) for each worker in the sample. It was available for all moves since 1958.[4] In the pooled (1968–83) sample, profiles of mobility show a typically concave shape – decelerating growth of N with experience, as in Figure 8.1 – with individual interfirm moves ranging from near zero to 16 over a maximum range of 25 years of work experience (X). Converted into a 'mobility rate' (N/X), it has an average of one move in five years.[5]

The separation rate (s) which measures the incidence of turnover during a year is the usual measure of labor mobility. The cumulative measure (N) is a time integral of (s): the concavity of the experience profile $N(X)$ is implied by a decline of (s) over experience.[6] Coefficients on X and X^2 in Table 8.1 confirm the decelerating growth of N, and decline of S over experience.

Reasons for the decline of the experience–turnover profile $s(X)$ can be briefly described.[7] By definition, changes in separation probabilities over the working life can be decomposed into a sum of two factors:

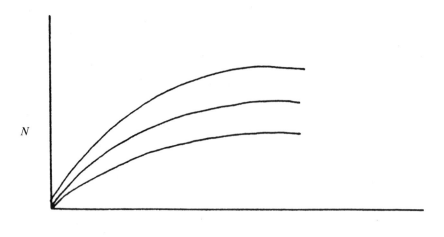

Figure 8.1   Typical experience–mobility profiles

$$\frac{ds}{dX} = \frac{\partial s}{\partial T} \times \frac{dT}{dX} + \frac{\partial s}{\partial X}$$

The decline of $s(X)$ with X reflects a decline in the probability of moving as tenure in the firm lengthens and as workers age, holding tenure levels constant.[8] Note that a negative aging effect implies a positive growth of tenure (T) with experience (X).

$$\left(\frac{\partial s}{\partial T} < 0\right); \text{ and } \left(\frac{\partial s}{\partial X} < 0\right) \rightarrow \left(\frac{\partial T}{\partial X} > 0\right), \text{ hence } \left(\frac{ds}{dX} < 0\right)$$

The decline of turnover with tenure reflects costs of separation which result from the accumulation of firm-specific capital. Such accumulations raise productivity and wages in the firm more than elsewhere, so mobility declines as the wage increases, resulting in longer tenure.

Other variables
Judging by the regression coefficients on the other independent variables in Table 8.1, individual profiles of mobility are lowered by education, marital status, and union membership, and by national unemployment.[9] Most of these findings are familiar as are some of the reasons for them. Thus, the lesser mobility of union workers has been explained by the wage, fringe, and other union benefits (Freeman, 1980; Mellow, 1983; and Mincer, 1983). Lesser mobility of married men is, in part, attributable to

Table 8.1 Mobility profiles (N), mobility rates (N/X), and separations rate(s) by worker characteristics, pooled 1958–83, and 1958–87

Variables	N (1958–83) (A)	(B)	N/X	S	N (1958–87)
C	7.63		1.20	0.43	4.95
	(14.5)		(19.2)	(13.2)	(7.0)
Ed	−0.64		−0.039	0.0144	−0.31
	(7.9)		(4.1)	(2.9)	(6.6)
Ed²	0.022		0.0014	−0.0012	
	(6.5)		(3.6)	(5.6)	
X	0.225	0.40	−0.035	−0.017	0.37
	(15.9)	(4.2)	(20.3)	(18.8)	(8.4)
X²	−0.0018	−0.01	0.0006	0.0003	−0.007
	(5.1)	(3.6)	(14.6)	(11.2)	(4.9)
X³		0.0001			
		(3.2)			
Mar	−0.71		−0.108	−0.077	−0.48
	(5.6)		(7.2)	(9.0)	(2.0)
UM	−0.30		−0.038	−0.067	−0.88
	(3.4)		(3.7)	(9.4)	(3.6)
NU	−0.08		−0.007	−0.009	−0.06
	(2.0)		(1.1)	(1.2)	(1.7)

Notes
C = intercept; ED = years of schooling; X = labor-force experience; Mar = married; UM = union member; NU = national unemployment rate of men age 35–54, *t*-values in parentheses.

greater opportunity costs inherent in the presence of family ties, especially in geographic mobility (Mincer, 1978). Married men, however, change jobs less frequently than single men even within local labor markets. The unemployment effect is due to a lower probability of job finding which apparently inhibits quits. The increase in layoffs is smaller than the reduction in quits, mainly because layoffs terminating by recall are not included in separations.

Reasons for lesser mobility of the more educated workers have not been investigated in the past. A positive association between education and job training is theoretically predictable, however, and has been inferred from differential slopes of experience-profiles of wages (Mincer, 1974) and is shown more directly in Table 8.2. If training is in part specific, the effect of education follows.[10] A similar association of training and marital status

244 Studies in human capital

(Table 8.2) is likely to be a factor, in addition to family ties, in the lesser mobility of married men.

Job training: measures and incidence

Direct information on volumes of job training is provided in the PSID surveys of 1976 and 1978. The measure we use (RQT) is given by respondents' answers to a question: 'On a job like yours, how long would it take the average new person to become fully trained and qualified?' The question followed several other questions about training prior to the current job, and it was intended to measure the period of time during which training was received in the current job.[11] The period was measured in months, but not in actual hours of training during those months.

Table 8.2 (col. 1 in panel A) shows a regression of the duration of training (RQT) in the 1976 and 1978 jobs on experience, education, marital status, union coverage, and other variables in the 1976 and 1978 pooled cross sections. A similar regression of training (RQT) reported in 1985 is shown in col. 1 in panel B. It appears that training, as measured, increases with working age (experience) and with education, is lengthier among married than single men, and is longer in nonunion than in union jobs. The coefficients on experience X and X^2 are positive and negative, respectively. This indicates that training per job increases with experience in a decelerating fashion.

The increase of training (RQT) with experience may seem puzzling: according to human-capital theory, investments in human capital, especially if measured in time units, as RQT is, should decline over the life-cycle, for good theoretical reasons, and if such investments are to imply a concave growth of wages over the life cycle. There is no inconsistency, however, if we realize that RQT is an investment volume per job, not per year. A rough adjustment to convert RQT into a rate per year is to divide it by the length of completed tenure on the job on which the training was received. When this is done, the regression of RQT/Ten shows a negative coefficient on X and a much smaller positive coefficient on X^2 (col. 2 of Table 8.2). This means that the rate of training per year declines with experience, at a diminishing rate.[12]

The decline of training with experience is also apparent in col. 3 of both panels in which the dependent variables are the incidence of training in 1976 and in 1985, respectively. Given the length of training (RQT) and the assumption that it started with the start of the current position, we assign a value 1 if the worker received training during the year, 0 if not. The sample for col. 3 is almost twice as large as that of col. 2, as it includes all those in the 1976 job whether or not they left it prior to 1983 or 1987. The truncated sample of col. 2 contains workers with shorter completed

Table 8.2 Factors associated with job training (1976 and 1978 cross-sections, pooled, and 1985)

A

Variables	RQT (1976–8)	RQT/Ten (1976)	Incidence of training in 1976 job
Intercept	−1.52	0.49	0.16
	(3.4)	(2.9)	(7.0)
Ed	0.24	0.065	0.014
	(6.8)	(2.5)	(10.1)
X	0.107	−0.016	−0.012
	(3.6)	(6.4)	(8.0)
X^2	−0.0013	0.005	0.0002
	(1.6)	(6.0)	(5.4)
Mar	0.46	0.058	0.011
	(1.8)	(1.5)	(1.8)
Union	−0.56	−0.056	−0.023
	(2.9)	(1.8)	(2.7)
R^2	0.19	0.11	0.15
N	1,216	564	

B

Variables	RQT, 1985	Indicence, 1985
Intercept	−2.42	0.34
	(8.5)	(7.1)
Ed	0.25	0.013
	(14.2)	(2.0)
X	0.114	−0.006
	(7.6)	(2.2)
X^2	−0.0014	0.0001
	(4.3)	(1.4)
Mar	0.014	−0.067
	(2.7)	(3.7)
Union	−0.25	−0.052
	(2.7)	(3.3)
R^2	0.17	0.13
N	1,509	

tenure, and significantly, with shorter average training (mean $RQT = 1.8$) than the complete sample (mean $RQT = 2.4$). It is also worth noting that the respective coefficients on X and X^2 imply that training duration reaches a minimum at $X = 16$ while minimal incidence is reached at $X = 30$.

The net positive coefficients of education in the RQT regression of Table 8.2 correspond to the negative coefficient of this variable in the mobility regressions in Table 8.1. The interpretation is that job training with its firm-specific elements, being positively related to schooling, reduces mobility at progressively higher levels of schooling. The same inference is applicable to marital status. Lesser mobility of union workers, however, is not a consequence of their job training, as they engage in *less* training than non-union workers. Here the effects of wage-premiums and of other rents received by union workers appear to play the major role in inhibiting mobility.[13]

There are several shortcomings in the measures of 'years of required training on the current job' (RQT) in the PSID: the total period of training 'for the average new worker on this job' is a blunt measure of the individual training periods. Moreover, the intensity of training, that is, the actual amount of time devoted to training during the year or week, is not indicated. Supplementary information on intensity is available in a 1980 study of PSID time budgets by Duncan and Stafford. It contains data on the proportion of workers who were engaged in job training during the survey week and the average weekly hours spent in training by those engaged in it. Appendix Table A8.1 provides a check on the decline in training over experience (here age), and the increase in training with education, both of which were indicated in our regression in Table 8.2. Both percent engaged and their hours decline with age, and increase with education (up to college). Note, however, that the data are not standardized for other characteristics. Consequently, the gross effects may be exaggerated, as younger people are on average more educated.

We tried to check our inferences based on the rather imperfect measures of training in the PSID with results in other studies based on other sources of data. Lillard and Tan (1986) analyzed the distribution of training across workers in larger and in some respects more-detailed CPS and NLS samples. The training measure there is its incidence during the year between surveys, and it is distinguishable by its locus. Since firm-specificity is more likely to be found in company training than in outside sources such as business or vocational courses, and because it is the larger part of job training, we show their regressions of company training in three data sets in Appendix Table A8.2.

Despite minor differences in some of the variables, the estimated regression coefficients on education, experience, and marital status in Table A8.2 are similar to those based on PSID data.

Table 8.3   *Effects of training on attachment to the 1976 job*

Variables	Length of tenure completed before 1987 (1)	Probability of staying in the 1976 firm beyond 1987 (2)
Intercept	9.2	0.25
	(4.8)	(2.9)
RQT	1.10	0.024
	(7.2)	(3.5)
P_rX	0.065	0.004
	(1.5)	(2.1)
Mar	1.96	0.13
	(2.5)	(3.3)
Union	2.85	0.14
	(4.4)	(5.2)
Ed	0.40	0.02
	(3.3)	(0.7)
N	−0.26	−0.012
	(1.7)	(1.7)
R^2	0.10	0.05
n	819	1,528

Notes
P_rX = years of experience prior to the 1967 job
N = number of firms in which employed before the 1976 job
t values in parentheses

3.   Effects of job training on turnover

Attachment to the 1976 firm

Effects of training in the 1976 job on the probability of leaving the firm in which training was received are observed in Table 8.3. In col. 1 the dependent variable is the completed length of the 1976 job, which is observable in over a half of the PSID sample who changed jobs before 1987. The effects of *RQT* reported in 1976 on the length of completed tenure were positive and significant, despite the truncation which selects shorter tenured workers into the sample. The information is extended beyond the truncation in col. 2. Here the dependent variable indicates the probability of staying in the 1976 firm beyond 1987. Again, the effect of training (*RQT*) is positive and significant.

More frequent mobility prior to the 1976 job predicts shorter tenure in it. That the effect of training remains positive and significant, conditional on prior mobility, suggests that training affects mobility behavior, whether or not the converse is also true.

Education has a positive effect on firm attachment, net of training. More efficient and intensive job search may well be the cause (Mincer, 1988). Marriage and union variables are also positive, as expected.

For younger workers ($X \leq 12$), the regression results (not shown here) are similar, except for much smaller effects of training, and of prior experience. These age differences in effects of training are clearly not due to differential intensity of training. The latter *declines* with age, as was shown in Table A8.1. More likely, the age differences reflect lesser specificities of training and of work experience among younger workers. Finding a successful match on productivity and training requires repeated employment trials (job shopping) which takes time, so the probability that the current match will not be a lifetime job is very high at young stages. Consequently, the payoff period to specific training is substantially shorter than the payoff period to general (transferable) training. Hence, the bulk of general training investments is incurred as early as possible, while specific investments may actually grow over the first decade or so. At any rate, the specific content of training can be expected to grow over time in the individual lifetime allocation of human capital investments. The coefficients of the experience variables behave as the training variables do: they are larger in size and significance for older workers. The reasons are presumably similar, especially as the training variables are unlikely to capture all the learning processes on the job.

Longer-run effects of training on turnover
While training obtained in the firm reduces the worker's probability of leaving it, it need not follow that it also reduces his turnover in subsequent or previous employments. Workers who received training in their 1976 jobs may have received little or no training in prior or later jobs. It appears, however, that workers who received substantial training in the 1976 job were likely to receive training in subsequent jobs.

Persistence of training is predicted by a lifetime optimization hypothesis on human-capital investment behavior. Workers with better abilities and opportunities tend to invest more in their human capital both at school and in a successive series of jobs. This is one reason for the observed positive correlation between schooling and job training in Table 8.2. The serial correlation of training in successive jobs was tested by regressing *RQT* reported in the 1978 jobs of those who left their 1976 job (about one-fourth of the workers) between 1976 and 1978, with reported training in their 1976 jobs. The result of the regression is shown in the first column of

Table 8.4 Persistence of training and long-run mobility effects

(A) Persistence of training across jobs

Independent variables	Dependent variables		
	RQT_{78}	RQT_{85}	RQT_{85}
RQT_{76}	0.42		0.43
	(8.5)		(9.4)
RQT_{78}		0.36	
		(7.6)	
Ed	0.16	0.19	0.22
	(4.0)	(4.8)	(5.4)

Other variables as in Table 8.3.

(B) Effects of training[a] on long term mobility rate[b]

	Mobility rate		Quit rate	Layoff rate
RQT	−0.072	−0.048	−0.038	−0.033
	(4.0)	(2.6)	(1.7)	(1.9)
Ed		−0.012		
		(8.6)		

Notes
[a]Average of reported training in 1976, 1978, and 1985
[b]Number of moves (N/X) per year of experience since 1958
Other variables as in Table 8.3.

Table 8.4, panel A. Regressions of training reported in 1985 on that reported in 1978 and in 1976 (cols 2 and 3) show undiminished positive correlations, as well as the positive effects of education on subsequent training in the sequence of firms in which the workers were employed. The correlation is clearly positive, and it is probably biased downward: the information comes only from workers who have recently joined the new firm, and positions with training need not start immediately at entry into the new firm.

The persistence of training over time can also be inferred from the NLS data on the incidence of training provided by Lillard and Tan (1986). Appendix Table A8.3 shows the reported incidence of training over intervals of varying lengths, and incidence predicted on the assumption of serial independence (Bernouilli trials). It is clear from Table A8.3 that the lengthening of intervals increases incidence much less than would be predicted by random trials. The same individuals tend to receive repeated (or continuing) training over longer periods. A similar test is used in the lower panel of Table A8.3 which covers successive annual periods. More than twice the proportions predicted on the basis of randomness receive lengthy repeated (3–8 years) training.

The persistence of training implies persistence of mobility behavior. This is confirmed in panel B of Table 8.4, where the dependent variable is the mobility rate (number of jobs per year) over the longest observed interval and the independent variables are training (RQT averaged over 1976, 1978, and 1985), as well as education (Ed), experience (X), marital status, and union membership. All have negative effects, including education which may, in part, be a proxy for training intensity not reported in the PSID. It is also noteworthy that the negative effects of training on separations is symmetric in quits and layoffs, an indication that investments in job training are shared by employers and workers.

4. Job training and wage growth in the firm

That greater volumes of job training imply steeper wage profiles on the job and over longer experience is a theorem in human-capital analysis. The availability of the training measures in the PSID makes it possible to observe more directly individual wage differences and growth in relation to the observed volumes of their training.

A positive relation between measured volumes of training and slopes of wage profiles was observed by Duncan and Hoffman (1978); Gronau (1982); Brown (1983 and 1989); and Parsons (1986). A more-comprehensive empirical exploration of the relation between training and the wage structure is available in the study by Lillard and Tan (1986). The study utilizes CPS cross sections and NLS panels. It contains measures both of incidence and of hours of training. The effects of training on wages are strong in cross-section wage functions. In the NLS panel of young men the effects are strongest for company (in-house) training.[14]

Brown's study had shown that, when the tenure profile of wages is decomposed into three segments (see Figure 8.2), wages grow slowly before the training period (*Pre*) and rapidly during training (*RQT*). The level off after training (*Post*). The pre-training period may actually contain some training, but this was not reported in the data. It is clear that the usually observed concavity of the tenure–wage profile is due to the completion of *RQT*.

We have replicated the regressions with tenure decomposed into the three segments in the 1976 and 1978 cross sections. The regression coefficients in Table 8.5a show that wage growth during the training period is

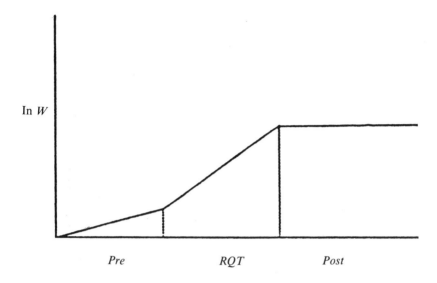

Figure 8.2   Tenure profile of wages

most rapid (4–5 per cent per year), it is only 1–2 per cent in the prior period, and about 1 per cent thereafter. Wage growth is somewhat steeper when previous (before the current job) rather than total experience is held constant.

In order to detect effects of RQT on wage growth rather than on wage differentials in the cross-section, we observe changes in wages of the 1976 workers over time. This is done in Table 8.5b. The dependent variable is the year-to-year growth in (real) wages of workers in the 1976 job whether or not their tenure was completed. *RQT* and *Learning* are (1,0) dummies. The coefficient in the left-hand column measures the effects of reported training compared to no or unreported training each year between 1968 and 1982. This *RQT* coefficient shows that a year of training increased wage growth by 4.4 per cent. When restricted to the 1975–76 period (col. 2) the effect was 6.7 per cent. The *Learning* variable (col. 3) showed a similar effect, 6.4 per cent. None of the other independent variables were significant, including a very small negative and decelerating effect of prior experience, measured at the start of tenure in the 1976 job. Perhaps surprisingly, the training coefficients are no smaller than those shown in the cross section.[15]

The effect of training on wage growth is greater at younger ages (9.5 per

Table 8.5a   The tenure–wage profile components (1976 and 1978 cross-sections)

Segments	1976		1978	
	b	t	b	t
Pre-pos	0.012	7.9	0.021	11.5
D (TICP)	0.042	5.5	0.054	9.1
$(1 - D) RQT$	0.054	7.6	0.047	8.4
$(1 - D)$ Post	0.008	1.8	0.012	6.8
R^2	0.28		0.34	

Note
$D = 1$, when in training; TICP = tenure in current position. Other RHS variables as in the other regressions. Experience was measured at the start of tenure.

Table 8.5b   Effects of training on year-to-year wage growth

Variable	RQT_{76} pooled sample	RQT incidence in 1976	Learning in 1976
b	0.044	0.067	0.064
t	(3.9)	(4.6)	(4.3)

Notes
Dummy $= 1$, when training or learning during the year.
The learning variable is a positive ($=1$) answer to the question asked in 1976: 'Are you learning on the job, so you can be promoted or get a better job?'

cent for $X < 12$, 3.6 per cent for $X > 12$), reflecting greater intensity of training among young workers, a fact shown in Table A8.1 in terms of age differences in weekly hours of job training. In this respect Table 8.5 is a first in documenting empirically the importance of job training or learning in producing the upward-sloping and concave experience–wage profiles.

5. Training, turnover, and wage growth in the long run

We now turn our attention to effects of job training on wage growth trajectories which transcend one firm. A positive effect is expected on the human capital hypothesis, given largely transferable skills and some persistence in training. Using the longest interval, from 1968 to 1987 in Table 8.6, we find a positive effect of training averaged over years 1976, 1978, and 1985.

Table 8.6   Training and long-run wage growth (1968–87)

| | In 1968 Sample | | Entered after 1968 | |
	All	Young	All	Young
RQT	0.008	0.011	0.009	0.012
	(3.2)	(2.8)	(2.7)	(2.9)
N/X	−0.004	−0.003	0.003	−0.003
	(2.4)	(0.2)	(0.3)	(0.2)
Ed	0.001	0.0015	0.0015	0.0018
	(2.0)	(1.6)	(1.8)	(1.7)
X	−0.008	−0.002	−0.001	−0.002
	(6.3)	(3.2)	(3.4)	(2.6)
Δ*Ten*	−0.0002	−0.0008	−0.0008	−0.0005
	(2.5)	(1.7)	(2.1)	(2.0)

Notes
RQT = average training in 1976, 1978, and 1985
N/X = separation per year of experience
X = experience in 1972.   Young = $x \leq 12$
Δ*Ten* = Tenure in 1987 minus tenure in initial year in panel
Other variables as in preceding Tables.

The effect of (average) training on long-run wage growth is positive. The effect is larger among young workers. The wage trajectory is also flattened by mobility, as might be expected if training contains firm-specific components. Mobility is not significant for young workers whose training is less likely to be firm-specific. Education has a small positive effect on wage growth, even net of RQT. But, as already mentioned, the net education effect may still reflect training intensity or other unreported training with which education is positively correlated. The same proxy effect may be showing through the mobility variable, net of reported RQT. As expected, wages grow less rapidly at more-advanced working ages (X). We should note that tenure effects which would bias estimates of long-run wage growth are eliminated by the inclusion of tenure levels at the beginning and end of the interval.

The negative coefficient of the mobility variable in Table 8.6 implies that per-year growth of wages *within firms* is smaller when tenure in the firm is, on average, shorter. This finding has recently become controversial in the econometric literature,[16] but it is not likely to be an artifact in our approach, especially after account is taken of an important qualification. A qualification is required because the wage change analyzed in Table 8.6 includes gains due to interfirm moves: total wage change over an interval is the sum of intrafirm growth and of interfirm (mobility) wage changes (*m*). For the conclusion to be correct, the sum of mobility gains (defined as wage change between starting wage on the new job and last wage on the previous job) should not be greater for the less-frequent movers. More precisely, the elasticity of *m* (mobility wage gain) with respect to *N* (frequency of moving) should be either positive or, if negative, less than unity (in absolute value).

A regression of *m* on *N*, with the other independent variables as before, showed a small positive coefficient with *t*-values close to zero. Thus the wage gain per move was about the same for frequent and infrequent movers, so the differences in intrafirm wage growth between 'stayers' and 'movers' were actually greater than the differences in total growth calculated from the coefficients of *N* (number of moves per year) in Table 8.6.

A numerical example illustrates these results. At the observed mean, individual wage growth was 3.1 per cent per year. Wage gain per move (*m*) was 2.2 per cent, and the average number of moves 4.0 (probably an underestimate). Thus wage growth over the 20-year period was 62 per cent of which close to 9 per cent were mobility gains. Growth within jobs was therefore 53 per cent. According to the coefficient on *N* in Table 8.6, doubling of moves would reduce growth over the 20 years by $20 \times 0.004 = 8$ per cent while doubling mobility gains to 18 per cent. Hence wages of workers who move twice as frequently as the average would grow 54 per cent (compared to the 62 per cent average) over the period, while their growth within jobs would be 36 per cent (compared to the 53 per cent average).

On average, mobility gains accounted for about 15 per cent of total growth over the period. Clearly, the bulk of the rise in the life-cycle wage trajectory cannot be ascribed to mobility. Indeed, the opposite is true: long-term growth of wages (total and intrafirm) is flatter for the more-frequent movers, even though they gain from repeated mobility.

These findings show that a 'pure search theory' of a rising (and decelerating) wage profile is inadequate, although it does contribute, in part, to the explanation of lengthening tenure and declining mobility wage gains over the working life.[17]

6.   Mobility wage gains and training

The findings concerning the relation between mobility wage gains (*m*) and frequencies of job change (*N*) warrant further discussion as they shed additional light on labor market processes that we are exploring. Theoretically, we expect a negative relation between *m* and *N*, that is a positive relation between the wage gain in moving to a new firm and the length of stay in the new firm, as a result of a successful job search and match.

Now, if the job change does not involve job training on the next job, the observed m equals m^*, the true search gain. However, if training is involved, m differs from m^*. Indeed, $m = m^* - k$ where k is the worker training cost (measured in percent reduction of the new starting wage). Given m^*, the more training, the larger k and the smaller m. In that case the relation between m and N could become positive.

More generally,

$$\text{Cov}(m,N) = \text{Cov}(m^* - k,N) = \text{Cov}(m^*,N) - \text{Cov}(k,N)$$

If training is not involved, only the first term matters and the sign of Cov (m,N) is negative as a result of pure search or match gains m^*. If prospective training is involved, the second term matters, and is positive since Cov $(k,N) < 0$ and the sign of Cov (m,N) is positive if search or match behavior is unimportant.

We found a positive, but practically zero effect of N on m when $m = \ln W_0 - \ln W_{-1}$. Here W_0 is the wage in the survey after the job started and W_{-1} in the survey of the preceding year. This implies either that the two factors are at play and offset each other, or that neither matters.

This evidence would be consistent with a partial role of matching in affecting the duration of tenure, provided initial wages are reduced in consequence of training. The initial reduction in wages due to costs of training is usually assumed, but it has not been previously observed. Workers' heterogeneity is the problem in cross-sections. If more able individuals are selected or select themselves to training, their starting capacity wages on the new job as well as previous wages are higher, compared to those of other workers. The transition wage differential we use to describe matching gains eliminates this personal component, and makes possible a more direct test which is to observe whether workers moving to a job with training accept a reduction in their transition wage gain.

Let K be the measure of the prospective volume of training

$$\text{Cov}(m,K) = \text{Cov}(m^*,K) - \text{Cov}(k,K)$$

Since k reflects the volume of training K, $\text{Cov}(k,K) > 0$, the sign of $\text{Cov}(m,K) < 0$ if the correlation between the pure matching or search gain and training is small.

We regressed wage growth (e) over the training period (T) on m (alongside other independent variables) and found it to be negative. The partial regression coefficient on m was -0.075 ($t = 2.4$). Since $m =$

$\ln W_0 - \ln W_{-1}$, and $e = \ln W_T - \ln W_0$ we shifted e to $\ln W_{T+1} - \ln W_1$, in order to avoid a spurious negative correlation due to errors in W_0. This is a strong result, both because e is (in part deliberately) underestimated and because $\mathrm{Cov}(m^*,e)$ is likely to be positive, if more successful search (larger m^*) is followed by training.

7. Conclusions

Using short- and long-run wage changes in PSID panels which cover intervals as long as twenty years and information on intrafirm job training, we were able to estimate negative effects of job training on turnover and positive effects on wage growth in the firm and over longer periods. The turnover effects are consistent with the view that (a) intrafirm job training contains elements of firm-specificity, whose amount is positively related to the volume of total training, and (b) training investments of workers are to some extent persistent across firms.

Assumption (b) is standard in human-capital theory in which individual abilities and opportunities tend to be long lasting: it is supported by empirical evidence of a positive serial correlation in training and in turnover. The training variable does not distinguish general from specific components, but the positive correlation between them produces both job duration effects and the effects of wage growth within firms (during the training period), and in the longer-run experience profiles.

Although wage growth may be largely a result of general (transferable) training, its negative relation with turnover indicates existence of firm-specific components in training. A possible qualification to this inference is that workers with an exogenously low propensity to move may tend to acquire more training rather than conversely. If so, training would not reduce turnover which is low to begin with. Our findings tend to reject this implication but they do not rule out a two-way causality.

At the most basic level, we confirm empirically the human-capital hypotheses that training increases wage growth over the period of training, and that job training or learning is a major factor in producing the typically increasing and decelerating long-run individual wage trajectory.

The more training is observed, the steeper are the experience and the tenure profiles of wages. The inferred positive correlation between general and specific components of training explains also the apparent paradox that while, on average, mobility wage gains are positive, frequent movers earn less in the long run than stayers do because their wage growth within firms is smaller. They tend to be less-engaged in training, and so their moves are more frequent because they are less costly.[18]

Observed wage changes in transitions reinforce these conclusions, since the contribution (sum) of mobility gains to total wage growth of more-frequent movers is substantially greater than the corresponding (sum of) mobility gains of less-frequent movers.

To distinguish between matching and training effects we used information on the wage gains in moving and related them to frequencies of moving and to growth of wages over the training period. The analyses yielded the following conclusions: (a) matching alone does not explain job duration nor wage growth within and across firms. If it plays a role, it is a factor in addition to training; (b) effects of training on turnover and wage growth are significant whether or not training is related to matching; (c) mobility gains are reduced by worker investments in training, again regardless of the presence or absence of a relation between training and matching.

In some of the literature the alleged absence of a net tenure effect on wages is ascribed to a predominant (exclusive?) firm share in specific training costs. Our data cast doubt on this possibility in view of an apparently symmetric effect of training on quits and on layoffs.

It is not clear what light, if any, our finding sheds on the work-incentive hypothesis popularized by Lazear (1979, 1981). The work-incentive hypothesis does not represent a contradiction of the human capital hypothesis in principle, but no attempt was made here to assess its contribution to our findings.[19]

Finally, the usual word of caution is especially relevant in this kind of study: our information on training, tenure, and wage changes is beset by a host of errors. The findings are tentative, albeit suggestive. Other data sets should be used to replicate the analyses, although they are likely to contain perhaps different but equally troubling errors. In the longer run, more accurate data in relevant detail, especially as regards training concepts and activities should provide more definite answers to the questions we have investigated in the present study.

Acknowledgements

This publication is based on work sponsored by the US Department of Education, by the Spencer Foundation, and the National Science Foundation.

I thank Tom Melito and Lalith Munasinghe for excellent research assistance, Jim Brown and Aloysius Siow for useful discussions, and other members of the Columbia University Labor Workshop for helpful comments.

Notes

1. Of course, the specificity is not restricted to firms and to inter-firm mobility. Occupation, region, and industry specificities affect corresponding types of mobility.
2. See Sicherman (1987) and Mincer and Higuchi (1988).
3. The initial version of the present study covered annual data 1968–83. They are now extended to 1987.
4. This includes retrospective information provided in the 1968 survey back to 1958.

5. The frequency of moving is underestimated in this data set, since at most one job change can be ascertained between two annual surveys.
6. The quadratic form of $s(X)$ in Table 8.1 implies a cubic form of $N(X)$, and this is verified in col. (B) of Table 8.1. The cubic form has only minor effects on the coefficients of the other variables.
7. A more thorough explanation of factors underlying the decline and convexity of $s(X)$ can be found in Mincer and Jovanovic (1981).
8. In cross sections, an observed negative relation between turnover and tenure may come from heterogeneity, without *any* tenure dependence. If so, for the individuals over time, any observed changes over the working life would be due to aging effects only. However, experience–turnover profiles decline much more steeply than the declines due to aging (that is, declines in separation rate with experience, *at the same levels of tenure*). This is evidence of the reality of the asserted 'tenure-dependence' despite the heterogeneity bias. See Mincer and Jovanovic (1981).
9. The unemployment rate of adult males ages 35–54 was used in order to abstract from changes in the demographic composition of the labor force.
10. Negative effects of education on turnover are reduced when training effects are accounted for, but not eliminated (Mincer, 1988).
11. A check on whether the RQT measures in the PSID refer to the duration of current training in the firm or to total (cumulated) on-the-job training needed for the particular job was performed by Sicherman (1987). A comparison by detailed occupation in PSID responses with DOT (Dictionary of Occupational Titles) estimates supports the assertion that RQT is not a cumulative measure antedating the current firm for most occupations, except for a minority of highly skilled professional occupations where RQT is overstated. When added to probably sizable errors of measurement this discrepancy creates an additional downward bias on estimates of effects of RQT in statistical regressions.
12. Both RQT and RQT/Ten level off at about two decades of work experience. The quadratic smoothing function forces peaks and troughs at about that time. The regression of RQT divided by completed tenure in the 1976 job is restricted to a subsample of workers (about half of the total) who left their 1976 jobs by 1983.
13. For evidence and analysis see Mincer (1983).
14. Lillard and Tan (1986), Table A7. There the effect of an additional year of training is a 15% increase in wages. The effect of training (higher wage level after training) decays over a period of 13 years, due to depreciation of human capital or to job change which erodes firm-specific capital.
15. The estimated effects of training on wage growth over the training period are larger in Brown's study of the same PSID data (1989). Brown restricted the sample to those workers whose training was certain to have started at entry to the firm, and who reported that prior training was not required in entering the firm.
16. See articles by Altonji and Shakotko (1985); Abraham and Farber (1987); and Marshall and Zarkin (1987).
17. The theory assumes no human capital accumulation and a fixed wage offer distribution facing the individual worker. Progressive upward moves in the distribution, which has a central tendency, result in a declining probability of an incremental wage gain in the next move. See Burdett (1973).
18. For evidence, see Mincer (1986).
19. Findings in Mincer (1990) that about three quarters of the observed wage growth over working ages is attributable to job training and to mobility leaves some scope for additional hypotheses concerning slopes of wage profiles.

References

Abraham, K. and H. Faber (1987), 'Job Duration, Seniority, and Earnings', *American Economic Review*, June.

Akerloff, G. and R. S. Main (1980), 'Unemployment and Unemployment Experience', *American Economic Review*, December.

Altonji, J. and R. Shakotko (1985), 'Do Wages Rise with Job Seniority?', Working Paper no. 87, Princeton University, April.

Barron, J., D. Black and M. Lowenstein (1986), 'Job Matching and On-the-Job Training', Working Paper E98\7-86, University of Kentucky, September.

Becker, G. S. (1962), 'Investment in Human Capital: A Theoretical Analysis', *Journal of Political Economy*, Supplement, October.

Becker, G. S. (1975), *Human Capital*, 2nd edn, Chicago: University of Chicago Press.

Ben-Porath, Y. (1967), 'The Production of Human Capital and the Life-Cycle of Earnings', *Journal of Political Economy*, August.

Bishop, J. (1984), 'Hiring and Training Workers', National Commission for Research in Vocational Education, Ohio State, June.

Brown, J. (1983), 'Are Those Paid More Really No more Productive?', Working Paper, SUNY-Stony Brook.

Brown, J. (1989), 'Why Do Wages Increase with Tenure?', *American Economic Review*, December.

Burdett, K. (1973), 'On the Job Search', PhD thesis, Northwestern University.

Duncan, G. and S. Hoffman (1978), 'Training and Earnings', in *Five Thousand American Families*, ed. G. Duncan and J. Morgan, Institute of Social Research, University of Michigan.

Duncan, G. and F. Stafford (1980), 'The Use of Time and Technology by Households in the United States', *Research in Labor Economics*, vol. 3.

Freeman, R. (1980), 'The Exit-Voice Tradeoff in the Labor Market', *Quarterly Journal of Economics*, June.

Garen, J. (1986), 'Wages and Tenure: Some Approaches', Working Paper, University of Kentucky, September.

Garen, J. (1988), 'Empirical Studies of the Job Matching Hypothesis', *Research in Labor Economics*.

Gronau, R. (1982), 'Sex Related Wage Differentials', *National Bureau of Economic Research* Working Paper no. 1002, October.

Hashimoto, M. and B. Yu (1980), 'Specific Capital, Employment Contracts and Wage Rigidity', *Bell Journal of Economics*, Autumn.

Jovanovic, B. (1979a), 'Job Matching and the Theory of Turnover', *Journal of Political Economy*, October.

Jovanovic, B. (1979b), 'Firm Specific Capital and Turnover', *Journal of Political Economy*, December.

Kuratani, M. (1973), 'A Theory of Training, Earnings and Employment', PhD thesis, Columbia University.

Lazear, E. (1979), 'Why Is There Mandatory Retirement?', *Journal of Political Economy*, December.

Lazear, E. (1981), 'Agency, Earnings Profiles, Productivity, and Hours Restrictions', *American Economic Review*, September.

Lillard, G. and H. Tan (1986), *Private Sector Training*, Rand Corporation, R-3331, March.

Marshall, R. and G. Zarkin (1987), 'The Effect of Job Tenure on Wage Offers', *Journal of Labor Economics*, July.

Mellow, W. (1983), 'Employer Size, Unionism and Wages', in *Research in Labor Economics*, ed. J. Reid, Part 2, New York: JAI Press.

Mincer, J. (1974), 'Schooling, Experience and Earnings', New York: Columbia University Press.

Mincer, J. (1978), 'Family Migration Decisions', *Journal of Political Economy*, October.

Mincer, J. (1983), 'Union Effects: Wages, Turnover and Job Training', in *Research in Labor Economics*, ed. J. Reid, New York: JAI Press. (Chapter 11 of Volume 2.)

Mincer, J. (1986), 'Wage Changes in Job Changes', in *Research in Labor Economics*, ed. J. Reid, New York, JAI Press, vol. 8, part A. (Chapter 6 of this volume.)

Mincer, J. (1988), 'Education and Unemployment', National Center for Education and Employment Working Paper. (Chapter 7 of this volume.)

Mincer, J. (1990), 'Job Training; Costs, Returns, and Wage Profiles', Columbia University, November. (Chapter 9 of this volume.)

Mincer, J. and Y. Higuchi (1988), 'Wage Structures and Labor Turnover in the U.S. and in Japan', *Journal of Japanese and International Economics*, June. (Chapter 11 of this volume.)

Mincer, J. and B. Jovanovic (1981), 'Labor Mobility and Wages', *Studies in Labor Markets*, ed. S. Rosen, Chicago: University of Chicago Press. (Chapter 5 of this volume.)

Oi, W. (1962), 'Labor as a Quasi-Fixed Factor of Production', *Journal of Political Economy*, December.

Parsons, D. (1986), 'Job Training in the Post-Schooling Period', draft, Ohio State University.

Salop, J. and S. Salop (1976), 'Self-Selection and Turnover in the Labor Market', *Quarterly Journal of Economics*, November.

Sicherman, N. (1987), 'Human Capital and Occupational Mobility', PhD thesis, Columbia University.

Topel, R. (1987), *Wages Grow with Tenure*, draft, University of Chicago.

Appendix

Table A8.1   Job training in survey week (1976 PSID survey)

Age	% engaged	Their hours	Average* hours	Education	% engaged	Their hours	Average* hours
< 25	76	12.7	9.7	0–8	39	3.1	1.2
25–34	72	9.3	6.7	9–11	56	8.2	4.6
35–44	58	8.1	4.7	12	59	9.6	5.6
45–54	48	2.5	1.2	13–15	71	9.7	6.9
55–64	29	3.9	1.1	16+	58	7.2	4.2

*The third column is the product of the first two columns, yielding average hours in training of all workers.
Source: Duncan and Stafford (1980).

Table A8.2   Incidence of company training

Variables*	CPS men (1983)	NLS young men (1973–80)	NLS mature men (1967–71)
Education: < 12	− 0.48	− 0.44	− 0.33
	(7.1)	(6.2)	(4.8)
13–15	0.23	0.30	0.19
	(5.9)	(6.8)	(2.4)
16	0.48	0.45	0.11
	(11.0)	(8.8)	(0.9)
17 +	0.31	0.26	− 0.08
	(7.0)	(4.9)	(0.7)
Non-white	− 0.25	− 0.17	− 0.22
	(4.8)	(3.9)	(3.1)
Union	− 0.09	− 0.06	− 0.59
	(1.8)	(1.2)	(3.4)
X	− 0.008	0.009	− 0.016
	(4.0)	(2.2)	(3.2)
Tenure	0.034		0.004
	(11.2)		(2.0)
Mar	0.39		
	(5.2)		
NU		− 0.02	0.014
		(0.1)	(2.8)

*Variables: see Table 8.1.
Source: Lillard and Tan (1986).

Table A8.3

(A) Incidence of training in intervals of varying length in the NLS

Length of interval (years)	Observed %	Predicted[1] %	Observed %	Predicted %
1	24.3			
2	29.7	42	10.2	
4				
5				19
6			17.2	
				27

[1]Predicted figures are rounded.

(B) Cumulated annual incidence of training in the NLS (young men cohorts)

Number of periods in which training was received	0	1	2	3–8
Observed %	37.2	25.0	14.2	23.6
Predicted %	35.0	38.0	17.0	10.0

9 Job training: costs, returns, and wage profiles*

1. Introduction: background

The emergence of job training as an observable – albeit still a fragmentary one – has the potential of filling some important gaps in the empirical analyses of human capital investments and of related wage structures. It enables us to pursue questions which were not amenable to research in the past. Thus, while a vast literature, accumulated over several decades, contains a wealth of findings on volumes and on profitability rates of educational investments, corresponding estimates of job training investment could not be constructed. Instead, growth of earnings over working age, known as the 'experience wage profiles', was assumed to reflect returns on workers' investments in the labor market, especially in job training. Indeed, a first (and last) indirect estimate of on-the-job training costs by schooling level and in the aggregate was obtained using this interpretation nearly three decades ago (Mincer, 1962).

Job training was used as a latent variable not only in analyzing shapes of wage profiles but also in the study of labor mobility, or turnover. In particular, turnover and slopes of wage profiles were linked in a hypothesis according to which training affects both: on the assumption that some degree of firm-specificity usually attaches to on-the-job training, we may conjecture that, on average, the more training a worker receives, the more it tends to be specific to the firm. Consequently, with more training the worker's wage profile is steeper and turnover slower. This 'duality hypothesis' was proposed in a paper coauthored with Jovanovic in 1981. In the absence of empirical data on job training or learning, the duality hypothesis provides insights into labor market behavior, as was shown in that paper as well as in a more recent study (with Higuchi, 1988). The latter compares wage structures and labor turnover in Japan with those in the US. The negative relation between slopes of wage profiles and labor turnover is shown to hold across industrial sectors within each country. Much larger investments in job training in Japan were adduced to generate both the steeper Japanese wage profiles and the much stronger attachment to the firm in Japan.

*This chapter is a paper presented at the *Conference on Job Training*, 1988, Madison, Wisconsin; a revised version was published in *Market Failure in Job Training?* ed. J. H. H. Ritzen and D. Stern, Springer Verlag, 1991.

As usual, the absence of direct information leads to a proliferation of theories. Thus, the lack of direct evidence on job training stimulated the development of alternative theories that attempt to explain upward slopes of wage profiles as devices to economize on costs of supervision (Becker and Stigler, 1974; Lazear, 1979), or turnover (Salop and Salop, 1976), or as consequences of job-sorting or job-matching of new hires (Jovanovic, 1979).

The recent growth of information on job training in several data sets has led to empirical studies of the effects of training on wage growth.[1] In my own work, information available in the University of Michigan's Panel Study of Income Dynamics (PSID) was brought to bear on the duality hypothesis. Job training magnitudes were explored as a factor in wage growth and in labor mobility in a National Bureau of Economic Research (NBER) Working Paper (Mincer, 1988): using information on timing and duration of job training among PSID men, I found negative effects of training on turnover and positive effects on wage growth in the firm and over longer periods transcending tenure in one firm. The positive correlation between general and specific training which explains these results also explains the apparent paradox that, despite wage gains in moving, frequent-movers' wages grow less in the long run than those of less-frequent movers.

Another effect of job training which has been observed is the reduction in the incidence of unemployment among workers who receive training. This is a corollary of the reduced turnover, as close to half of firm separations involve unemployment. Finally, there are two important observations bearing on the determinants of job training: (a) workers with more years of schooling are more likely to engage in job training,[2] and (b) more training is provided in industries in which technological progress is faster.[3]

The potential significance of these initial research accomplishments is of a high order: (a) they indicate that human capital analyses of labor-market behavior based on proxies for post-school training hold up when direct measures of such training are used; (b) the documented link between training, schooling, and technological change directs attention to the sources of demand for human capital and to its role in economic growth.

As we reach better, empirically based insights into the effects and determinants of job training, it is necessary to return to a task that I attempted in an indirect fashion in 1962: to estimate the extent and profitability of private sector job training, this time based on direct, albeit imperfect information. Although precise estimates cannot be hoped for, given the quality of current data and the conceptual complexities, orders or ranges of magnitude are feasible, and should yield insights into important issues.

This is the primary purpose of the present study. At a time when concern is raised about the quality of the American workforce and statements about under-investment in human capital abound in public rhetoric, an attempt at comprehensive estimates of volumes of investment and of their profitability is a prerequisite for public discussion. Another objective of this paper is to compare the directly estimated magnitudes of training investments with indirect estimates obtained from wage profiles, as was done in the 1962 study. Such comparisons can help in gauging how much of the growth (slope) in the wage profile is attributable to observable training processes. If the magnitude is significant, a link between the direct and indirect estimates can be used to infer changes in training investments over time.

2. Data sources and related literature

Direct information on the incidence, timing, and duration of job training is available in several data sets. The information represents responses, mainly from household surveys, to questions about formal or informal job training or learning in the firm or outside the firm during the preceding year. The questions are phrased differently in the various surveys, both in detail and in degree of subjectivity. Nevertheless, the elicited information makes possible qualitative and quantitative estimates from which a degree of consensus may emerge.

The available data on job training suffer from poverty amidst plenty. Table 9.1 indicates both the proliferation and the shortcomings of the data. Although concentrating on one consistent source of data would provide single-valued results, I attempt in addition to draw on results based on various data sets to gauge a degree of robustness, if any.

The PSID, an annual survey of about 5000 households, provides usable information on job training for about 1200 male heads of households in 1976, 1978, and 1985. The information covers the length of time of training required during the current job, as well as its learning contents in 1976.[4] Information on intensity (hours per week) of training is available in a supplementary time study of PSID workers by Duncan and Stafford (1980). The PSID data have been analyzed by Duncan and Hoffman (1978), Brown (1988), Gronau (1982), and Mincer (1988a).

The National Longitudinal Samples (NLS) surveys covering several thousand households conducted at Ohio State University contain annual or biannual information on job training for two cohorts of young men (aged 14–24 in 1968, and 14–21 in 1979), and for mature men (aged 45–59 in 1968). The new (1979) cohort of young men contains information on

Table 9.1   Information on job training*

Data set	Coverage	Incidence	Duration of spells	Duration in hours
CPS	1983 survey All workers Cross-section	During current job	Not available	Not available
PSID	Question on current job asked in 1976, 1978, 1985 All males	Dates estimated within current job	In months	In a separate 1976 survey
NLS previous young cohort	A number of periods Young males	Variable survey periods	Not available	Not available
NLS new young cohort	A number of periods Young males	Over 3 years	In weeks	Not available
EOPP	Young male new hires at low wages 1980–82	Within 3 months after hire	Within 3 months	Available, incompletely

*Available and utilized in the references. More information and broader coverage may exist in the data sets.

the duration of a spell of training. In-house training reported in the 1968 cohorts has been studied by Lillard and Tan (1986). The new young cohort has been analyzed by Parsons (1986) and Lynch (1988).

The Current Population Survey of the US Census, the largest periodic sample of US households, contains the incidence of training in its March 1983 survey. The data have been analyzed by Lillard and Tan (1986).

Finally, the 1982 EOPP (Equal Opportunity Pilot Project) is the only survey of employers (about 2000 in 31 areas). It provides information on hours of training of new hires during the first three months on the job. These data have been described and analyzed by Lillard and Tan (1986), and Barron, Black, and Lowenstein (1989) and reanalyzed by Holzer (1989).

In my work with the PSID (1988a), I compared year-by-year wage growth of workers in the 1976 firm in periods with training with workers and periods without training. The effect of a year with training on wage growth in the 1976 job was 4.4 per cent, using the 1968–82 annual PSID surveys. No other variables had much of an effect on wage growth, except for a small negative effect of prior experience.

The effect of training on wage growth was greater (9.5 per cent) at younger ages (working age 12 years or less) than at older ages (3.6 per cent). The difference reflects greater intensity of training among young workers, as is shown in the Duncan and Stafford (1980) time study (see Table 3).

The findings that wage growth decelerates with age because training does, and that no other variable appears to affect individual wage growth, indicate the importance of job training or learning in producing the typical upward-sloping and decelerating wage profiles over working lives.

The same conclusion is reached in a study by H. Rosen (1982). Using the 1976 PSID data, Rosen divided the sample into two groups: workers who received training during the year and those who did not. (Cross-sectional) wage profiles were steep and concave in the first group, and very flat in the second. This suggests, once again, the importance of job training or learning in creating the typical shapes of wage profiles.

As with the PSID, all the studies based on other data sets found positive and significant effects of training on wages and on wage growth.

Barron, Black and Lowenstein (1989) use the EOPP survey of over 2000 employers located in 31 areas across the country. They measure training in hours spent in training by new hires and by their supervisors and co-workers during the first three months of employment in the firm. The mean training hours were 151 in the three months. They report that in a two-year period, training raised wages by 15 per cent, or 7.5 per cent per year. It will be recalled that a year of training in the PSID raised wages of young workers, whose average age was about the same as the new hires in the EOPP, by 9.5 per cent, and by 3.6 per cent for workers who, on average, were 15 years older, and who had correspondingly smaller intensity (hours per week) of training. This is also consistent with the 9 per cent effect per year found by Brown (1988) for new hires who had no previous training.

Holzer's (1989) reanalysis of the EOPP data yields a smaller wage growth effect of 4.7 per cent. Lynch (1988) uses the new young cohort of the NLS. Here information is available on all training spells of recent male entrants into the labor force during the three-year period 1980 to 1983. She finds that wages of young workers with job training during the year rose by 11 per cent, while an additional year of tenure without training increased wages by 4 per cent; the net effect is therefore 7 per cent.

Lillard and Tan (1986) also find significant effects of training on wages

Table 9.2   Rates of return on investments in job training

Data set	w	k	r^1	corrected r			Average tenure
	(1)	(2)	(3)	(4)	(5)	(6)	(7)
PSID[a], all males	4.4	0.15	29.3	23.5	25.0	6.5	8
EOPP[b], young new hires	4.7	0.20	23.5	8.7	8.5	0	3
NLS$_1$[c], new young cohort	7.0	0.22	31.8	16.0	16.2	5.2	3
NLS$_2$[d], previous young cohort	10.8	0.25	43.2	26.0	31.0	22.8	4

Notes
[a]Based on Mincer (1988a); k from Duncan and Stafford (1980).
[b]Based on Holzer (1988).
[c]Based on Lynch (1989).
[d]Based on Lillard and Tan (1986); k from Duncan and Stafford.
Col. (3): $r^1 = w/k$.
Col. (4): $r = r^1 (1 - d) - d$; here $d = 0.4$ in the PSID, 0.12 in the other data sets.
Col. (5): $r = r^1 [1 - (1/1 + r)^T]$; T as shown in col. (7).
Col. (6): $r = r^1 (1 - d) [1 - (1 - d/1 + r)^t] - d$; here d as in col. (4).

in the CPS and in the 1963–80 young cohort of the NLS. In the CPS (their Table 4.1), company training raises wages by 11.8 per cent; in the NLS (their Table 4.5), job training raises wages of young workers by 10.8 per cent initially, but the effect declines subsequently.

In sum, estimated effects of an additional year with training appear to range from 4.4 per cent in the PSID for all new hires to 9 per cent for young workers in the PSID, 7 per cent for the new young cohort in the NLS, and 11 per cent for the previous young cohort in the NLS. The 12 per cent 'effect' for CPS men is a cross-sectional finding that trainees have higher wages than non-trainees, but it takes no account of the pretraining wage. It is not included in the profitability analysis in Table 9.2.

3.   Profitability of job training investments

Table 9.2 presents the rates of return on investments in job training. *Prima facie*, these estimates of effects of a year with training on wage growth (column 1) are comparable to effects of an additional year of schooling at the average level of schooling. Yet, viewed as measures of profitability or as rates of return on the cost of job training (column 3), these numbers appear to be much too large.

The reason is that job training is not a full-time (full-year) activity. If it

takes 25 per cent of worktime during an average week of a year with
training, the rates of return on worker opportunity costs are four times
higher than the estimated rates of wage growth.

Let $k = h/H$, the fraction of work time devoted to job training. Here h
is hours of training during the period (week, month, or year) and H
average hours of work during the period. Let w_0 be the pre-training and w_1
the post-training wage. Then the (uncorrected) rate of return on training is
$r^1 = (w_1 - w_0) \times H/w_0 \times h$. Here the numerator is the annual dollar
increase in earnings, the return on the investment, while the denominator
is the opportunity cost of training. Let $\overset{\circ}{w} = w_1 - w_0/w_0$ be the percent
increase in wages due to training; then the (uncorrected) rate of return is
$r^1 = \overset{\circ}{w}/k$. The first three columns of Table 9.2 show estimates of $\overset{\circ}{w}$, k, and
r^1 based on the PSID, the EOPP, and the two young cohorts of the NLS.

The r^1 rates appear to be implausibly high. However, they need to be
corrected downward, if skills acquired in training depreciate, and if the
payoff period is short. If training is portable, the latter factor may be
ignored, as the median age of trainees is about 30, so that, without
depreciation, the payoff period may exceed 30 years. Depreciation, however, can be substantial, as suggested by Lillard and Tan (1986). For the
previous NLS young cohort, they estimate an initial wage gain of 10.8 per
cent due to training and a subsequent decline of 1 per cent per year during
years since training. This translates[5] into a 12 per cent exponential rate of
decline due to depreciation in returns per year. My attempts to estimate a
depreciation rate in the PSID using the Lillard and Tan procedure yielded
a depreciation rate close to 4 per cent. This smaller figure in the PSID may
be due to the broader coverage of all males, compared to younger males in
NLS: if training has substantial elements of specificity, mobility would
create wage depreciation. Since mobility of young workers exceeds substantially the mobility of older workers, a smaller depreciation rate in the
PSID may be reasonable.

The estimate of corrected rates of return (r) is obtained as follows: given
annual depreciation rates (d), and the payoff period T, equate costs or
forgone earnings while training (kw_0) to the present value of the stream of
gains (Δw) the first year following training,

$$\Delta w \frac{1 - d}{1 + r} \text{ the next year,}$$

$\Delta w (\frac{1 - d}{1 + r})^2$ the year after, and so on:

$$kw_0 = \Delta w \left[\frac{1 - d}{1 + r} + (\frac{1 - d}{1 + r})^2 + \ldots (\frac{1 - d}{1 + r})^T\right] = \Delta w \frac{1 - d}{r + d}, \text{ when } T = \infty$$

more generally

$$\frac{kw_0}{\Delta w} = \frac{k}{\dot{w}} = \frac{1 = d}{r + d}[1 - (\frac{1 - d}{1 + r})^T]$$

It follows that corrected $r = r^1 (1 - d) [1 - (\frac{1 - d}{1 + r})^T] - d$ (9.1)

Since the estimates of d were obtained by ignoring labor mobility, they could be an artifact created by negative effects of mobility on gains from (partly) firm specific (nontransferable) training. The polar alternative of complete specificity makes the payoff period T equal to the length of tenure in the firm in which training was received, and $d = 0$, if there is no obsolescence within the period T. (The observed average values of T are shown in col. (7)). In this case, $r = r^1[1 - (1/1 + r)^T]$ according to equation (9.1); r was solved by iteration, and the results are shown in col. (5). These numbers are rather surprisingly close to those in col. (4). Thus, the estimates do not depend much on whether the observed depreciation is true and training is largely transferable, or it is an artifact due to substantial specificity.

To calculate the profitability rate of employer's investments in training we need to know their returns and costs. In principle, the way to assess returns is to compare increases in productivity resulting from training with increases in wages. The excess is the return on costs borne by the firm. Two recent studies using very different data and approaches suggest that the productivity increase is over twice that of the wage increase caused by training. This is found by Barron *et al.* (1989) in the EOPP data, where a productivity scale is used to gauge the increase. Blakemore and Hoffman (1988) use production and turnover data by industry to estimate effects of tenure on wages and on output per unit of time. They find a doubling of productivity compared to wages, implying that returns to employers are similar to returns to workers. If employer costs are also about the same as those of workers, the uncorrected r^1 (in col. 3 of Table 9.2) would be the same for employers as for workers. And if depreciation is negligible, the employer rate of return would be again the same as that of workers as listed in col. (5) in which observed tenure is the assumed payoff period. Note that this is always true for the employer who gains only as long as trainees stay in the firm – whether or not training is transferable. However, if depreciation is positive *during* workers' stay in the training firm, employers' rates are lower than those indicated in cols (5) or (4). Assuming a 4 per cent depreciation rate for the PSID and 12 per cent for the young group results in a lower limit for employer profitability rates, shown in col. (6).

The assumption that employer costs are just about equal to worker costs is more speculative than the proposition of roughly equal returns (r^1). It can be defended, if we consider time costs of workers ($\sum kw_0$) to be absorbed by workers, while time costs of supervisors, trainers, and of co-workers are absorbed by employers. Except for the time when trainees learn by watching others at work, the time spent on training is the same for trainers and trainees. If so, the EOPP data (Table 1 in Barron *et al.*, 1989) suggest that trainers spend two-thirds of the 150 hours of training reported to be spent by trainees during the three months of new hires. Since wages of trainers, supervisors and co-workers are higher than wages of trainees, employer costs are likely to be about as high as employee time costs in the groups covered by the EOPP. Whether this ratio of employer to employee time inputs can be generalized is unknown. Neither is there any evidence that employees absorb precisely the costs of time they spent and employers the rest.[6] In the absence of information on the actual division of costs between employers and workers, we can still consider the profitability of training if we know total costs and total returns. The fragmentary evidence described above suggests a (more than?) doubling of costs ascribed to workers and returns observed for workers. Consequently, the profitability rates in cols. (4), (5), and (6) remain conceptually valid, as measures of profitability of training, regardless of who bears the cost.

What does the range of estimates in Table 9.2 tell us about adequacy of training? As soft as it may be, this is the evidence that could be marshalled. Are the rates too high, suggesting under-investment? Column (5) in which depreciation is negligible suggests quite ample profitability, even if trainees stay in the firm no longer than non-trainees! In other words, average worker mobility would deter neither them nor employers from investment in training. However, depreciation is probably not zero, and we need to keep in mind that: (a) the rates in Table 9.2 are average, not marginal. Bishop (1989) suggests that marginal rates in the EOPP are about half the size of average rates; (b) rates of return to schooling of about 10 per cent are not considered exorbitant, and they do not include consumption returns, which are negligible in training.

Consequently, there is no definite evidence of under-investment, though it clearly cannot be ruled out, given the wide range of estimates.

4. Estimating volumes of annual job training investments

I proceed to estimate economy-wide annual volumes (flows) of investments in job training, measured in worker opportunity costs. To estimate these costs, we need to know the number of workers engaged in training in the survey period ($n = p \times N$, where N is the total workforce and p the

Table 9.3   Time use in training (survey week, 1976, PSID, all workers)

Group	Hourly wage rate	Whether any	On-the-job training mean weekly hour		Sample size
Age			Jointly with production	Separate from production	
	(1)	(2)	(3)	(4)	(5)
< 25	3.68	0.76	9.5	3.2	50
25–34	5.55	0.72	7.5	1.8	139
35–44	6.19	0.58	6.4	1.7	80
45–54	6.69	0.48	2.1	1.3	56
55–64	6.26	0.29	2.6	0.4	42
Education (years)					
0–8	4.08	0.39	2.8	0.3	26
9–11	4.47	0.56	6.9	1.3	36
12	4.79	0.59	8.2	1.4	147
13–15	5.44	0.71	6.5	3.2	80
16+	8.33	0.58	5.7	1.5	85

Source: Duncan and Stafford (1980), Table 3, Col. (3): Hours of training joint with production.

proportion of workers engaged in some training or learning on the job), the time (h = hours) they spend in training during the period, and their hourly pre-training wage (w_0). The total worker opportunity costs of training are then the product $C_w = w_0 h\, p\, N$. Information on such statistics for a sample of the whole US labor force is available only in a PSID survey of Time Use at Work during a week in 1976 (Duncan and Stafford, 1980), a part of which is shown here in Table 9.3. Information on hours spent in training by new hires during the first three months is available in the EOPP survey and in weeks in the new NLS young cohort. Both cover subgroups of new labor-force entrants rather than the whole labor force. The CPS is a large national survey with information on the incidence but not on the hours of training.

Table 9.4 applies the data from the 1976 Time Use Survey to calculate weekly worker opportunity costs of training on the job, by age groups. The first three columns on wages (w), hours (h), and incidence (p) of

Table 9.4   Worker opportunity costs of job training, 1976

Age	Hourly wage ($) ($w_0$)	Hours of training per week (h)	Percent with training (p)	Number of employees (millions)	Costs ($mil) per week ($w_0 h p N$)
	(1)	(2)	(3)	(4)	(5)
< 25	3.7	6.4	76	20.0	360
25–34	5.6	4.3	72	22.5	390
35–44	6.2	3.8	58	16.5	225
45–54	6.7	2.2	48	16.1	114
55–64	6.3	1.1	29	10.9	22
				Total cost	$1111

Sources: Cols (1), (2), and (3) from Duncan and Stafford (1980); and Table 9.3 above.
Training hours in col. (3) calculated as sum of separate hours in training and one-third of hours spent jointly in training and production.
Col. (4) from Employment and Earnings, BLS, 1976.
Col. (5) is the product of cols (1)–(4).

training are taken from Duncan and Stafford (1980), here shown in Table 9.3. Column (4) contains BLS national employment figures (by age) for 1976. Column (5) shows total costs per week; it is a product of columns (1)–(4).

Statistics on time spent in training by trainees shown in Table 9.3 overstate the time cost of training: to the extent that training is joint with production and the marginal product is positive. It is the loss of production during training that represents pure training costs. Thus, if production during training is half of that achieved without training, half the work time with training should be counted as training time. The Time Use Survey lists separately the hours trainees spent in training with and without production (columns (3) and (4) in Table 9.3).

Weekly hours spent in training by trainees were obtained as a weighted sum of these two components: only one-third of time spent jointly with production was considered as a loss of production, hence as pure training. This is probably a conservative estimate, judging from the work of Bishop (1989). The sum adds up to roughly four hours a week per trainee.[7] The average wage in the age group is an approximate estimate of a pre-training or non-training wage of trainees.[8] The estimates are made separately by age groups, as all components vary systematically with age, then summed to obtain a total of $1.11 billion per week, or $57.7 billion per year in 1976.

Expressing this figure as a fraction of the total wage bill (total compensation), which was $1.04 trillion in 1976, yields a 5.6 per cent figure. If the fraction of work time spent in training did not change over time,[9] so that the same ratio held in 1987, it would amount to $148 billion in 1987 dollars.

Worker time costs represent a part of total investment in job training. Time costs of trainers and other resource costs are the other part. If estimates based on the division of time reported in the EOPP can be generalized, total costs would be (over?) double of worker time costs. Total cost would, therefore, amount to $115 billion in 1976 and to $296 billion in 1987.

One check on these orders of magnitude is available from a survey of companies (with 100 or more employees) published in *Training Magazine* (1988). The survey reported expenditures on formal training programs of about $40 billion in 1987. Based on a Columbia University survey of a national sample of firms, Bartel (1989) reports a larger figure of $55 billion in 1987. These estimates clearly leave out the apparently much larger expenditures on informal training processes. Thus our conservative estimate based on the 1976 Time Use Study suggests that trainees spent an average of four hours per week or close to 200 hours in training per year. This is over six times the number of hours (32) reported for formal training by *Training Magazine*. If the hourly costs of training were the same for formal and informal training, a global estimate based on formal training costs alone would be $240 billion or $330 billion, depending on which survey is used. Our figure of $296 billion for 1987, estimated in an entirely different manner, is very much within the range of such estimates.

5.   Comparing direct with indirect estimates of training

Extrapolating our estimate of 1976 worker training costs back to 1958 in the same manner as we did in the 1987 extrapolation, that is, assuming that the time spent in training (per worker) did not change, yields a figure of $14.4 billion for 1958. This 'direct' estimate for the whole workforce compares closely with the indirect estimate of $13.5 billion obtained from wage profiles for the 1958 male labor force (Mincer, 1962, Table 2). Adding another 10–15 per cent for costs of women's training would have raised the 1958 indirect estimate for the whole work force to about $16 billion.

Still the $16 billion indirect estimate needs to be revised downward because it should exclude gains from job changes, which, according to calculations in PSID data, accounts for about 15 per cent of growth in the wage profile of males (Mincer, 1988a). On the other hand, the reduced figure ($13.5 billion) is an underestimate, since it estimates net investments

in job training, while the 'direct' costs measure the larger gross investments. At the same time, the 1958 estimate of direct costs is probably
overstated because it assumes that time costs of training amount to the
same fraction of the wage bill in 1958 as in 1976. But the fraction must
have been lower in 1958, if time spent in training did not change *within*
education groups, since time spent in training increases with schooling, as
the PSID data indicate (Mincer, 1988 and Table 9.3 above). Workers with
less than high school spent a little over one-half the hours in training that
more educated workers did. The size of the two groups in the labor force
was about equal in 1958, but the group with less than 12 years shrank to
25 per cent of the labor force by 1976. Hence, average hours of training
would have increased by over 15 per cent if hours within each educational
level remained fixed. If so, the 'direct' estimate of $14 billion in 1958
should be corrected downward to $12.2 billion. Even the reduced estimate
suggests that over 75 per cent of the growth observed in the wage profiles
can be attributed to job training, if the biases in the indirect estimates
roughly cancel.

However, a positive relation between education and training does not
mean that they are related in fixed proportions. To the extent that an
(exogenous) expansion of education leads to a substitution of school
education for job training, education may grow faster than job training.
Indeed, (direct) educational expenditures grew from 4.8 per cent to 7.1 per
cent of GNP between 1958 and 1976. If substitution was present, job
training grew more slowly than education, suggesting that hours of training declined within school groups. In the aggregate, therefore, time spent
in training may not have grown over the period, in which case the initial
extrapolation may be valid.

The comparison of direct and indirect estimates is less problematic if
carried out for the same year. This requires a calculation of job training
costs based on the 1976 wage profile. The use of a parametric wage
function (Mincer, 1974) makes such calculation much less laborious than
was necessary when the 1958 data were analyzed (Mincer, 1962). The
human-capital earnings functions contain, among other variables, years
of work (experience), variable X, which enters in a nonlinear fashion. Its
coefficients are interpretable as post-school human-capital investment
parameters. On the assumption that time spent in investment declines
linearly as working age increases, the expression is:

$$lnw = Z + rk_0X - (rk_0/2T)X^2 + ln[1 - k_0 + \frac{k}{T}X]$$

Here Z is a set of other independent variables, while k_0 is the fraction of

Table 9.5   Calculation of 1976 worker OJT investments derived from wage function

Age	Mean age	k	Nw	Nwk		
< 25	22	0.23	74	17.0		
25–34	30	0.15	126	18.9		
35–44	40	0.05	102	5.1		
45 +		0	182	0	Ratio	Dollars
		Total	484	41.0	8.5%	88.4 billion

Sources: k estimated from Rosen (1982); N and w from Table 9.4.

earnings devoted to human capital investments in the early working age, T the period in the working life at which investments cease, and r the rate of return on the net investments.

In a recent paper, Rosen (1982) estimated these parameters from the 1976 PSID for the male sample. He found $k_0 = 0.32$, $T = 26$, and $r = 12$ per cent. Assuming that investments of a typical woman worker (in terms of k, or time) are half as large, k_0 for all workers is a weighted average of the male and female investment ratio, the weight being total earnings ($N \times w$) of each. Since the female work force was two-thirds the size of the male workforce, and earnings per woman worker 60 per cent of male earnings, the weights are 1 to 0.4, yielding a k_0 of 0.27. Since $T = 26$, k falls approximately 0.01, or 1 per cent per year. Thus investments cease at about age 44. Average k in each age group is shown in Table 9.5. The ratio of training investments to wage per hour is $\sum Nwk / \sum Nw = 41/484 = 8.5$ per cent. This is higher than the direct estimate of 5.6 per cent. Translating the 8.5 per cent ratio to dollar figures by applying it to total compensation of workers in 1976 (it was $1040 billion) yields a figure of $88.4 billion for the cost of worker training based on wage profiles. This figure is reduced to $75 billion if 15 per cent of the estimate based on wage profiles is attributable to job mobility rather than training. Direct estimates of annual worker investments in training (5.6 per cent of the wage) amounted to $57.7 billion in 1976. The comparison with the $75 billion figure estimated by the wage function suggests that three-quarters (75 per cent) of the growth in the wage profile can be attributed to worker investment in training in 1976. This conclusion is supported by another piece of indirect evidence contributed by Rosen (1982). The PSID sample was divided into two parts: workers who received some training in 1976 and those who did not. Wage functions of the form indicated above were estimated for each group. The estimated k_0 for the group without training was less than one-

Table 9.6   Wage profiles with and without training

Group	B_1	B_2
With some training in 1978	0.0226 (10.2)	-0.00027 (5.6)
No training in 1978	0.00686 (1.7)	-0.000082 (0.8)

Note
t-ratios in parentheses.

third the size of the k_0 for the group with training. Indeed, the experience wage profile was very flat in the no-training group.

Since new information on training was provided in the 1978 PSID survey, I replicated the procedure for that year. The linear (B_1) and quadratic (B_2) coefficients on experience (x and x^2) are shown in Table 9.6. The growth of wages over a year is $(B_1 - 2B_2X)$. It is over three times as fast for any given working age in the group with training as compared to the group without training.

It is noteworthy that three entirely different methods of estimating volumes of job training yield comparatively similar figures, as shown in Table 9.5. It is also interesting to note that by 1976 directly estimated job training costs (see columns marked (b)) amounted to about half of schooling costs (direct and opportunity costs). In the 1962 study the ratio for 1958 appeared to be higher (first row of Table 9.7). If a decline in the ratio actually occurred, the substitution of schooling for training may have been dominant. Apparently, increased public expenditures on schools (including especially the growth of two-year colleges) moved relative prices against training.

The comparison of direct and indirect estimates of job training investments summarized in Tables 9.5 and 9.7 for 1976 (where no extrapolation is involved) suggests that OJT investments account for more than two-thirds of the observed growth in the (cross-sectional) wage profiles. This is consistent with a preponderant human capital interpretation of the wage profile. As suggested in the introduction, an empirically substantial link between wage profiles and training volumes can be used to infer changes in training investments over time. Such changes cannot be observed directly, as training data are reported only sporadically and fragmentarily. Whether and in what way job training was a factor in the pronounced changes in the wage structures over the past two decades in the US is a question left for future research.

Table 9.7   Estimates of job training (OJT) and of its ratio to total compensation (TC)

	OJT ($billions)			OJT/TC			School/TC
Workers[a]	(a)	(b)	(c)	(a)	(b)	(c)	
1958	16.0	14.4		6.2%	5.6%		8.3%
1976	88.4	57.7		8.5	5.6		11.7
	(75.0)			(7.2)			
1987		148.0			5.6		11.3
Total[b]							
1987		296.0	240.0	11.2%	9.0%		22.6%
1987			330.0		12.4		

Notes
[a]Upper panel: worker investments in OJT, school direct expenditures.
[b]Lower panel: worker and employer investments in OJT, school direct and opportunity costs.
Col. (a) OJT estimates derived from wage profiles. 1976 estimate (in parenthesis) is adjusted for wage growth attributable to job mobility.
Col. (b) OJT estimates based on time spent in training in 1976.
Col. (c) Two OJT estimates based on costs of formal training in 1987, multiplied by ratio of time in all training to time in formal training.
Col. (d) Direct costs of education, from OERI, *Digest of Education Statistics*, 1989. Opportunity costs assumed equal to direct costs.

Summary and conclusions

With information on time costs of training and gains in wages attributable to training, rates of return for training can be computed. A downward adjustment is required, however, as the acquired skills erode due to obsolescence, or, to the extent that the skills are firm specific, to job mobility. The range of estimates of *worker* returns to training based on several data sets seems to exceed the magnitude of rates of return usually observed for schooling investments. Given the data on workers' firm tenure, it appears also that training remains profitable to firms, even in the face of average worker mobility.

The rates of return here calculated may be large enough to suggest underinvestment in training relative to that in schooling. However, such conclusions must be qualified in several respects: (a) marginal rates of return to training are lower than the reported average rates; (b) schooling investments receive heavy public subsidies, which may lead to over-investment; and (c) returns to schooling contain leisure during school years and lifetime consumption benefits (skills) not included in the calculation. For both these reasons observed rates of return are lower on schooling than on job training. Another relevant comparison concerns the trade-off between training and labor mobility: optimal allocation of human resources in the labor market requires equal marginal rates of return in both activities. The image of the US labor market as one in which mobility is rampant and job training modest (in comparison with Japan and Western Europe) does not necessarily imply that the marginal rates are far out of line: many American workers may search more intensively for better opportunities afforded by job changing than by attachment to a firm. The picture is suggestive, but better data and deeper studies are needed.

This is not to say that training activities could not or should not be increased. If quality of educational background affects the efficiency of training, the much-clamored improvements in education would increase the profitability and the utilization of training.

A further objective of this paper was to estimate total annual costs of job training in the economy. Three entirely different methods were used to estimate these volumes for 1958, 1976, and 1987. (a) The 'direct' method used information on time spent in training and on wages. For 1976, investments so calculated amounted to 11.2 per cent of total employee compensation, and about half of the costs of school education.[10] (b) In the 'indirect' method, training costs were estimated from wage profiles, using a wage function fitted to 1976 PSID data. The indirect estimate provides an upper limit, since other factors, job mobility among them, also affect the slope of the wage profile. Indeed, the direct estimate for 1976 is about 75 per cent of the indirect estimate once gains due to labor mobility are netted out of the wage growth in the profile. (c) A third method uses information on costs of formal training programs and on average time spent in them and inflates the figures to a total training level. Rather remarkably, the three estimates are not far apart. Of course, the estimate based on wage profiles represents an upper limit.

An important corollary purpose of this work was to evaluate the usefulness of data on job training. Potentially, such data could provide important insights into the wage structure and into a wide range of labor-market behavior. Procedures for determining volumes and profitability rates of job training were illustrated here, and these should be instructive. The analysis was performed on the available data which are still incomplete and fragmentary. The conclusions reached are therefore not definitive, even if highly suggestive. Harder estimates will require proper accounting of time and other resources absorbed by training, of its distribution across workers and over time, and corresponding histories of wages and of labor mobility.

Acknowledgements
This report is based on work sponsored by the National Science Foundation, grant SES-8921357, and in part by the Office of Educational Research and Improvement, US Department of Education.

I am grateful to Lalith Munasinghe for research assistance, and to David Stern for editorial comments.

Notes
1. See section 2 below.
2. All studies described in section 2 found this positive relation. See also the data in the Time Use Study shown in Table 9.3.
3. See Lillard and Tan (1986) and Mincer (1988a).
4. One question asked was: 'On a job like yours, how long would it take the average new person to become fully trained and qualified?' This question followed another about training prior to the current job, therefore intending to measure training attached to the current job. Another usable question was whether the current job provides 'learning which could help in promotion or getting a better job'.
5. Half of the gain vanishes in 5.4 years according to the linear estimate. A depreciation rate (d) of 12 per cent produces a half-life of 5.4 years; d is solved from $(1 - d)^t = 0.5$, where $t = 5.4$.
6. Doubts are sometimes expressed concerning absorption of any costs by trainees on the job in the form of initially lower wages. Three kinds of indirect evidence, however, favor the hypothesis that trainees' wages are initially lower than wages they could receive if they did not train, even if they are not lower than wages of non-trainees: (a) matching and screening selects more promising (productive) workers for training (Barron *et al.*, 1989); (b) training affects negatively both quits and layoffs (Mincer, 1988a); and (c) initial wage gains in job changing are (non-spuriously) negatively correlated with wage growth during training in the new firm (Mincer, 1988a).
7. This is an average for all workers, including women. For men alone, average hours are closer to 6. The profitability estimates in Table 9.2 were calculated for men for whom wage gains were estimated in the PSID.
8. Even if all their opportunity costs were financed by trainees, training costs would be underestimated by no more than 6%, according to the Time Use data. They would be overestimated somewhat if starting wages of trainees and non-trainees are the same.
9. A preliminary estimate of the average time spent in training in the 1985 PSID sample is quite close to that in 1976.
10. These include total, private and public, expenditures and opportunity costs of students.

References
Barron, J., D. Black and M. Lowenstein (1989), 'Job Matching and On-the-Job Training', *Journal of Labor Economics*, January.
Bartel, A. (1989) 'Formal Employee Training Programs', paper presented at Symposium on Job Training, Madison, Wisconsin, May.
Becker, G. S. (1975), *Human Capital*, 2nd edn, Chicago: University of Chicago Press.
Becker, G. and J. Stigler (1974), 'Law Enforcement, Malfeasance, and Compensation of Enforcers', *Journal of Legal Studies*.
Bishop, J. (1989), 'On the Job Training of New Hires', paper presented at Symposium on Job Training, Madison, Wisconsin, May.
Blakemore, A. and D. Hoffman (1988), 'Seniority Rules and Productivity', Discussion Paper, Arizona State University.
Brown, J. (1989), 'Why Do Wages Increase with Tenure?', draft, SUNY-Stony Brook; published in *American Economic Review*, December.
Duncan, G. and S. Hoffman (1978), 'Training and Earnings' in *Five Thousand American Families*, vol. 6, Institute for Social Research, University of Michigan.

Duncan, G. and F. Stafford (1980), 'The Use of Time and Technology by Households in the United States', *Research in Labor Economics*, vol. 3.

Gordon, J. (1988), 'Who is Being Trained to do What?', *Training Magazine*, October.

Gronau, R. (1982), 'Sex-related Wage differentials', NBER Working Paper no. 1002.

Holzer, H. (1989), 'The Determinants of Employee Productivity and Earnings', NBER Working Paper no. 2782.

Jovanovic, B. (1979), 'Job Matching and the Theory of Turnover', *Journal of Political Economy*, October.

Lazear, E. (1979), 'Why is There Mandatory Retirement?', *Journal of Political Economy*, September.

Lillard, G. and H. Tan (1986), *Private Sector Training*, Rand Corporation, R-3331, March.

Lynch, L. (1988), 'Private Sector Training and its impact', draft, Massachusetts Institute of Technology, October.

Mincer, J. (1962), 'On the Job Training: Costs, Returns, and Implications', *Journal of Political Economy*, Part II, October. (Chapter 4 of this volume.)

Mincer, J. (1974), *Schooling, Experience and Earnings*, New York: Columbia University Press.

Mincer, J. (1988a), 'Job Training, Wage Growth, and Labor Turnover', NBER Working Paper no. 2680. (Chapter 8 of this volume.)

Mincer, J. (1988b), 'Education and Unemployment', NCEE Working Paper. (Chapter 7 of this volume.)

Mincer, J. (1988c), 'Labor Market Effects of Human Capital', NCEE and NAVE conference paper.

Mincer, J. and B. Jovanovic (1981), 'Labor Mobility and Wages', in *Studies in Labor Markets*, ed. S. Rosen, Chicago: University of Chicago Press. (Chapter 5 of this volume.)

Mincer, J. and Y. Higuchi (1988), 'Wage Structures and Labor Turnover in the US and in Japan', *Journal of Japanese and International Economics*, June. (Chapter 11 of this volume.)

Parsons, D. (1986), 'Job Training in the Post-Schooling Period', Discussion Paper, Ohio State University.

Rosen, H. (1982), 'Taxation and On-the-Job Training Decisions', *Review of Economics and Statistics*, August.

Salop, J. and S. Salop (1976), 'Self-selection and Turnover in the Labor Market', *Quarterly Journal of Economics*, November.

Sicherman, N. (1987), 'Human Capital and Occupational Mobility', PhD thesis, Columbia University.

Topel, R. (1987), *Wages Grow with Tenure*, draft, University of Chicago.

PART III

TECHNOLOGY AND THE DEMAND FOR HUMAN CAPITAL

10 Human capital and economic growth*

1. Introduction

As an economic concept human capital is at least two centuries old, but its incorporation into the mainstream of economic analysis and research is a new and lively development of the past two decades. The need for this development became apparent in the 1950s, when the application of empirical economic research to the concerns about economic growth and about income distribution revealed major defects not only in our under-standing of each but also in our way of thinking about these matters. Two types of findings were especially significant: (a) the observed growth of conventionally measured inputs of labor and capital was far smaller than the growth of output in the US and other countries for which long time series were available; and (b) data on personal income distribution, which began to appear with greater frequency and detail, showed that the vari-ance of labor incomes, rather than the 'functional' differences between returns to labor and to capital, represented the major component of personal income inequality.

The development of human-capital theory was a response to these twin challenges. This response did not require a revolution in economic theory or a resort to extra-economic explanations which economists sometimes invoke when answers to pressing questions escape their competence. It merely involved the abolition of two simplifying, but, as it turned out, unduly inhibiting assumptions: (a) the restriction of the concept of capital to physical capital, even after a more general definition was provided by Fisher (1930); and (b) the assumption of homogeneous labor, which underlies both the concept of functional income distribution and the measurement of labor input in man-hours.

Fisher's definition of capital as any asset that gives rise to an income stream requires the inclusion of human capital, even if it cannot be bought and sold (it is, of course, rented), and even though investments in such capital often involve non-market activities. But non-market activities are not necessarily extra-economic. To the extent that they involve costs and returns, whether explicit or implicit, they are amenable to economic analy-sis, even if measurement problems are difficult. The contribution of human capital theory to economics does not lie in a reformulation of

*This chapter was first published in *Economics of Education Review*, vol. 3 (1984), pp. 195–205.

economic theory, but in pushing back the boundaries of economics beyond the sphere of market transactions. The payoff is now apparent in both of the problematic contexts: (a) at the macro-economic level the social stock of human capital and its growth are central to the process of economic growth; and (b) at the micro-economic level differences in individual human capital stocks and in their growth can explain much of the observed variation in the wage structure and in the personal distribution of income.

The applications of the human-capital concept to economic growth and to labor economics were initially pioneered independently.[1] The concepts are the same, and are applied basically to the same problem: individual economic growth at the micro-level and growth of the economy at the macro-level.

2. Human capital and personal economic growth

Individuals differ in both inherited and acquired abilities, but only the latter clearly differ among countries and time-periods. Human capital analysis deals with acquired capacities which are developed through formal and informal education at school and at home, and through training, experience and mobility in the labor market. The central idea of human-capital theory is that, whether deliberate or not, these activities involve costs and benefits and can, therefore, be analyzed as economic decisions, private or public. The costs involve direct expenses and earnings or consumption forgone by students, trainees and workers engaged in labor mobility. Since production and consumption benefits from these activities accrue mainly in the future, and are for the most part quite durable, the costly acquisition of human capacities is an act of investment. Deterioration of health and erosion or obsolescence of skills represent the depreciation of human capital which is offset, though not indefinitely, by maintenance activities such as the production of health and retraining.

The general categories of human-capital investments can be described in a life-cycle chronology: resources in child care and child development represent pre-school investments. These overlap and are followed by investments in formal school education. Investments in labor-market mobility, job choice, job training and work effort occur during the working life, while investments in health and other maintenance activities continue throughout life.

School education

Initially, investment in school education has been the subject of almost exclusive attention by human-capital analysts. While economists since Adam Smith have recognized the importance of education as a type of private or social investment, only recently have economists undertaken rigorous conceptual and statistical examination of the evidence on costs, returns and rates of return to education.

The costs of education borne by the student or his parent consist not merely of tuition and other school expenditures, but also of forgone earnings – the loss of what the student could have earned if he had spent the school years in gainful employment instead. Beyond early schooling, forgone earnings are the largest component (over a half) of schooling costs.

As in the analysis of physical capital, the difference between the discounted future returns and costs represents the profit or loss on the investment. Gains do or ought to induce further schooling, and losses discourage it. Another way to represent this decision-making process is to calculate that rate of interest which makes the profit equal to zero, that is, it makes the investment just about worthwhile. This rate is called the internal rate of return on the investment; further schooling is encouraged if the internal rate of return on schooling exceeds the rate on alternative investments. The advantage of this approach is that while individual discount rates are not observable, internal rates of return can be calculated given estimates of costs and of earnings streams. Comparisons of rates of return to education with rates of return on other (say, in business capital) investments can indicate the desirability of existing allocations or of changes in them, since equality of rates in all types of investments is required for a social optimum.

It is understood, of course, that relevant concepts of costs and benefits are real, that is, not restricted to pecuniary terms. Education itself may be attractive and it may enhance future enjoyment of life, apart from the monetary gain.

Employers pay higher wages to the more-educated workers because their skill and productivity are seen and experienced as greater than that of less-educated workers. In the absence of strong barriers to supply, the wage differential translates into a rate of return comparable to those on alternative human or other investments. Increases in demand favoring more-educated workers raise the rate of return on schooling, inducing growth of enrollments until the increased return has been reduced back to an equilibrium level. Autonomous increases in supply, given no changes in demand, reduce the rate of return to education and thus become self-limiting. The estimated rates of return to schooling in the US have remained relatively stable in the past several decades despite the continuous growth of educational attainment, suggesting that the trend is mainly a response to the continuous growth of demand for educated labor.

If financial and social barriers to education are stronger than in other fields of investment, the rate of return on education exceeds that on physical capital. Reduction of these barriers brought about by widespread growth of family incomes and by public policy has also been a factor in the long-term growth of education. As an example, the growth of education in the US between 1890 and 1950 was accompanied by a decline in the rate of return to education to levels which no longer exceed the return to business investment.[2]

A recent survey of estimates made in 32 countries (Psacharopoulos, 1973) shows that rates on physical and especially on human-capital investments are higher in developing countries (LDCs) than in the industrialized ones (DCs).[3] This is perhaps not surprising as it reflects the greater scarcity of capital in LDCs. More interesting is the finding that rates of return to human capital exceed the rates on business capital in LDCs while, if anything, the opposite appears to be true in the DCs. Evidently, the scarcity of human capital is significantly greater than the scarcity of physical capital in the LDCs.[4]

The calculations that are available do not include non-pecuniary or 'consumption components' of costs or returns. To the extent that these are positive and important in the benefits of schooling (an assumption dear to the hearts of educators), the rates are underestimated, though the pattern of their historical changes need not be affected.

An important distinction is made between private and social rates. Thus, in calculating private rates, costs and returns to students and their families are computed from after-tax data, and schooling costs do not include public financing of schools. In contrast, the calculation of social cost is based on before-tax earnings, and school costs are total costs of the relevant school systems (including opportunity costs of students) regardless of the source of financing. The real difficulty in calculating social rates of return is the problem of measuring externalities. To the extent that the gain to society exceeds the sum of gains to students, social returns are underestimated. An assumption of public policy which is difficult to verify and to quantify is that such externalities are substantial and positive.

It is often suggested that these externalities include, among others, informed and responsible citizenship, communication skills, lawful behavior and standards of health. The existence of such externalities is invoked to justify public efforts to stimulate educational investments. Such efforts can take the form of a publicly owned school system and/or of direct subsidies to students. The extent of required support is always debatable as the magnitude of externalities is unknown.

There are also other reasons for public intervention. This is the concern with the distribution rather than with the total volume of educational investments. Helping children of the poor to acquire a minimal degree of earning power is an objective for which schooling is also viewed as an instrument. Since poverty is often viewed as a relative concept, the amount of minimal universal government-supported education has been progressively lengthening as average education (and income) have increased. It is not always clear, however, to what extent these policies are efficient in alleviating poverty. There is some evidence that public spending on primary education tends to be redistributive toward the poor, but that above that in LDCs, and above secondary education in DCs, the opposite may be true since children of the poor are less likely to acquire higher education.[5]

Post-school human-capital investments[6]

There is no reason to believe that human capital investments cease with the termination of schooling. The educated have higher earnings, but the earnings are not fixed. They grow over the working life, albeit at a decelerating pace. This growth is additional to and largely independent of economy-wide trends in earnings. These patterns of growth also differ among persons whose education is similar.

The economic interpretation of lifetime earnings growth is as follows: wages of a worker are proportionate to the size of his human-capital stock. Thus wage differentials among workers are due primarily to differences in the sizes of human-capital stocks, not in the 'rental price' employers pay per unit of the stock. The individual's human-capital stock grows over the life-cycle by means of investment, which is initially in schooling, later in job choice, job training, work effort and job mobility, and in health. At any stage the level of earnings depends on the size and utilization of the human capital which accumulated up to this point, and its growth depends on the rate of net additions to the stock, that is, on the net investment rate. The deceleration in the rate of growth which is observed in individual earnings reflects the rate of decline of investments as the worker ages. Investments diminish over time because (a) benefits decline as the payoff period (remaining work life) shortens; and (b) the opportunity costs of time, which is an input in the learning process, are likely to rise over the working life.[7] While gross investment proceeds at a slackening rate throughout working life, net investments (gross minus depreciation) vanish or turn negative earlier. This happens when depreciation (including obsolescence) begins to outstrip maintenance, a progression which eventually brings about retirement.

An alternative interpretation of the earnings profile is that it is an intrinsic age phenomenon; initial productivity growth corresponds to inherent biological and psychological maturation, while later stability and decline are due to first stable then declining physical and intellectual vigor. In the perspective of human capital, this view is incomplete since it explains the earnings profile solely by a life-cycle pattern of the depreciation rate, seen as negative in early years, zero in middle life and positive in later years. There is evidence, however, which indicates that this inherent age–depreciation factor affects earnings only to a minor degree, except at teenage and in the near or post-retirement years; in data where age and length of work experience are statistically separable, levels and shapes of earnings curves are mainly a function of experience rather than of age. Moreover, earnings profiles differ by occupation, sex and other characteristics in systematic ways that cannot be attributed to aging.[8]

One may also interpret the shape of the earnings profile as a 'learning curve' or a reflection of growth of skills with age and experience known as 'learning by doing'. This view is not at all inconsistent with the human-capital investment interpretation as long as opportunities for learning are not costless. Since more learning, hence a more steeply rising wage, is available in some jobs compared to others, qualified workers would gravitate to such jobs if learning were thought to be costless. In consequence, entry wage levels in such jobs would be reduced relative to entry wages elsewhere for workers of the same quality, thereby creating opportunity investment costs in moving to such jobs. Thus it is not merely training on the job (formal or informal) but also the processes of occupational choice that give rise to investments beyond schooling. Similarly, geographic mobility and other labor turnover in search of higher real earnings represent investments in human capital.

It follows that barriers to occupational choice and to job mobility reduce the opportunities for investment in human capital. The elimination of such barriers increases individual economic growth and the overall efficiency of allocation of resources in the economy, hence total product.

Empirical economic research indicates that the relation between schooling and post-school investment is positive: more-educated people invest more in the labor market. One interpretation is that ability and opportunity factors which induce individuals to have more schooling affect their post-school behavior similarly, even though the correlation is far from strict: abilities and opportunities change over the life-cycle, and there is a fair amount of substitution between the two forms of skill accumulation. Another interpretation is that schooling improves the efficiency with which people can absorb learning on the job, thereby leading to greater job investments. This hypothesis is consistent, in a dynamic context, with evidence on the so-called 'worker allocative effect' propounded by Schultz (1975a) and Welch (1970). Their proposition that education promotes the adjustment to technological change has been documented, mainly in studies of agricultural production activities. The more limited macroeconomic evidence of a positive relation between rates of return to schooling and rates of economic growth is also suggestive.

Pre-school investments and women's education

Inherited abilities, or what is called the 'original' endowment, is an important part of the human capital stock, yet the line between heredity and environment is by no means clear. Much of the physical and intellectual deficiency shown by infants born in poor conditions can be avoided by improved nutrition of mothers and sanitary environments for childbirth. Similarly, subsequent child care represents an investment in better adult health and so in greater productivity of the adult worker.

Especially in low-income countries, the effects of a healthier child-rearing on adult productivity are double: not only is a healthier adult more productive but he also lives longer.[9] Consequently, the incentives to invest in lengthier schooling and training increase, since with the lengthened payoff period the profitability of such investments increases. Thus it is inappropriate to view reductions in mortality with alarm as a cause of the 'population explosion'. The mitigating effects on population growth and improvements in work quality eventually predominate, since the costs of investing in child quality, including health and education, represent a powerful force toward reduction of family size, given the families' limited resources. Indeed, research has shown (Belmont and Marolla, 1973) that, even at the same level of family income, children in smaller families tend to be healthier, more able and better educated.

Much of the accumulation of a person's human capital takes place in the home, particularly during the pre-school stage of the life-cycle. It appears that education of parents is a significant influence in this process, even after controlling for family income and numbers of siblings. This suggests that, aside from expenditures on schooling and health, child care is also an important qualitative input into the production of human capital. The time inputs are usually those of the mothers who take the major child-care responsibilities and reduce their market activities to engage in them. The consequent reduction in their earnings may be viewed as a partial measure of opportunity costs of these investments. So viewed, the opportunity cost of child care is greater for more-educated women. The observed positive effects on children's health, ability, education and future earning power may thus be viewed as an indirect return on the investment in maternal education.

An important consequence of the larger opportunity cost per unit of time spent in child care by more-educated mothers is the reduction of total time so spent. This is accomplished largely by a reduction in the number of children. The strong inverse relation between fertility and education of mothers has been documented repeatedly. Thus the growth of women's education and of their wages induces declines in fertility coupled with increased investments in the resultant smaller number of children per family.

Since, in most countries, even educated women spend less time in the labor market than men, the direct earnings benefits of education are smaller for women. From this point of view, it might seem that the provision of equal amounts of education to both sexes is wasteful. However, if better-educated mothers produce greater human capital in children and a better quality of family life, apart from contributing to family money income, educational equality need not be questioned. Indeed, it is rarely questioned as a matter of public policy.

It appears, however, that private schooling decisions are still very much influenced by the expected participation in the labor market, and therefore by the directly expected payoff in earnings. In the US sex differentials in enrollment now appear only at the postgraduate university level. In Latin America and in other LDCs there remains a pronounced differential above primary school enrollment.[10]

3.   Human capital and national economic growth
Human capital as a factor of production
The micro-economic analysis of investment in human capital is the underpinning of our understanding of the contribution of human capital to the aggregate level of income and to its rate of growth. The micro-economic view is most directly applicable to the analysis of labor heterogeneity and of the resulting wage structure. Given sufficient labor mobility, wages tend to be similar for the same human capital stock in various employments, regardless of differences in size and quality of other factors of production in such employments. Equilibrium wage differentials within the economy may therefore be viewed as solely reflecting differences in individual magnitudes of human capital stocks. Although international mobility of labor is not negligible and it mitigates somewhat the disparities in wages of the same human capital in different countries, it is costly and largely restricted. Therefore national wage levels differ because of differences in volumes of human capital as well as of other forms of capital. For the understanding of macroeconomic differences in levels and in growth of income, it is best to start with the view of human capital as a factor of production alongside physical capital in an aggregate production function.

The traditional trinity of factors of production contains land viewed as fixed, 'original and indestructible', labor, measured in numbers and hours, and capital, restricted to tangible plant and equipment. It is now well-recognized that this conception is false. The notion of a quantity of land as a fixed factor of production had already been discarded prior to the realization that the measurement of labor in man-hours is entirely inadequate. As Schultz (1980) has emphasized, differences in amount and 'original quality' of arable land (in terms of land population ratios) do not at all help in accounting for differences in income levels among countries. Experience and research have shown that it is not the quantity and the original endowment of land so much as the improvement or modernization of agriculture that matters. Inferior raw lands and even deserts have been transformed into superior productive resources while total acreage has declined. Investment in modernization of agriculture is a capital investment, and the capital nature of land is now fully recognized.

The capital nature of the sources of labor services is now also receiving its proper recognition. The inadequacy of the traditional view of labor in the field of growth accounting is well known. But the biases went beyond description to affect policy: the misunderstanding of the nature of expenditures on health, education, labor mobility and information as consumption which reduces saving leads to investments in steel mills rather than in people.

Land, by itself, is no longer a limiting or critical factor. But the quality and behavior of people is increasingly recognized as such. Indeed, it appears that indexes of human capital, such as average levels of education, are more strongly correlated with average income levels across countries than measures of physical capital per unit of labor (Krueger, 1968; Psacharopoulos, 1973). Although suggestive, this finding is not conclusive since the demand for education as a consumer good is income-elastic. In this sense, education is an effect rather than a cause of income. The role of education as a cause, however, is evident from the micro-economic findings that the relation between education of persons and their own future income is strong and largely unaffected by parental income, even though parents' income does affect the amount of education their children receive.[11]

Some critics question the inference that education increases productivity from the observation that it increases wages, and still others assert that schools do not affect skills but serve merely as a filter to sort differences in ability which exist independently of schooling. If so the micro-economic relation between education and income would not carry over to the economy as a whole. This argument is contradicted by research: studies of empirical production functions have shown that not only differences in wage rates but differences in productivity are related to differences in education and training of the labor force across states and regions and over time.[12]

This is not to say that the screening or sorting function of education is unimportant or unproductive. Indeed, the search for talent by the school and by the student are activities no less productive than the search for any other scarce natural resource. Human capital is augmented both by learning and by selection. The interaction of the two is efficient: the more-able student learns more at the same cost.

The view of human capital as a factor of production coordinate with physical capital implies that its contribution to growth is greater the larger the volume of physical capital. This relation is symmetric: the contribution of physical capital is larger the higher the average level of human capital. In this light, the success of the Marshall Plan in Europe and the failure of foreign aid to LDCs are perhaps not surprising. To quote Johnson (1975, p. 283):

> Europe had available the industrial and commercial organization, and the skilled people required for modern industry; what it lacked was precisely physical capital which was largely destroyed or obsolete. The problem of LDCs was different: they lacked virtually everything necessary for a higher standard of economic productivity, and the injection of only one element (physical capital) was found to be both wasteful and disappointing.[13]

For the more-recent period the problem of absorption of massive amounts of physical capital in the human-capital-poor OPEC countries is another example of the significance of complementarity between the two forms of capital. But, while physical plant and equipment can be acquired or built quite rapidly, the development of a significant and broadly based level of human capital of a nation is a lengthy process which involves profound social and cultural changes.[14]

The framework of an aggregate production function makes it clear that the growth of human capital is both a condition and a consequence of economic growth. The growth of human capital raises the marginal product of physical capital which induces further accumulation of physical capital, thus raising total output both directly and indirectly. Conversely and symmetrically, the growth of physical capital raises the marginal product of human capital. This produces an increased demand for human capital relative to unskilled labor, if human capital is more complementary with physical capital than is unskilled labor.[15] The resulting increase in the skill–wage differential exceeds the increase in (opportunity) costs, so the acquisition of human capital by students and workers becomes more profitable. As already indicated, the continuous long-term growth of human capital in the US and elsewhere is consistent with this interpretation of supply responses to growing demand.

The differential shifts in demand for skilled and unskilled labor implied by the complementarity hypothesis also tend to produce the well-known skill differentials in unemployment rates, observable in most countries which experience economic growth. The greater cyclical stability of employment of skilled labor is also consistent with the hypothesis that skilled labor is complementary with fixed plant and equipment. Recent research also suggests that employment of skilled labor is relatively insensitive to the business cycle, because human capital acquired on the job contains elements of firm specificity which make separations unprofitable to both workers and firms.[16]

Growth of human capital is also spurred on the supply side by growth of family incomes. Since human capital cannot serve as collateral, markets for its financing are scarce. Consequently, it is growth of income that enables increasing numbers of people to self-finance their human capital investments. In poor countries these financial restrictions create monopolistic advantages for the children of the wealthy, and high rates of return on human capital. Both are reduced by the spread of education made possible by growing incomes. However, human capital growth due to growth of family incomes is eventually self-limiting when rates of return become sufficiently depressed in consequence of 'over-education'. Public subsidies are also self-limiting in the same sense, and they may become unprofitable from a social point of view (when the social rate of return on human capital drops below the corresponding rate on physical capital) before they inhibit private incentives. It follows that for a sustained growth of human capital we must look to increasing market demands for skills and technology.

Human capital and technology
Although the effects of human-capital growth and some of its causes can be described in the framework of an aggregate production function in which technology is fixed, few will argue against the view that growth of technology is the ultimate force which propels all factors of production by increasing their productivity. A fixed technology may be maintained for analytical convenience by viewing all technical change as embodied in human and physical capital (Griliches and Jorgenson, 1967). Whether or not such a device is purely semantic, I think it is helpful to distinguish between the stock of human capital as a standard factor of production and the stock of knowledge as the source of technology. Human capital activities involve not merely the transmission and embodiment of available knowledge in people but also the production of new knowledge, which is the source of innovation and of technical change. Without new

knowledge it is doubtful that larger quantities of existing physical capital and more-widespread education and health would create a continuous growth in productivity on a global scale. In a fundamental sense, modern economic growth is a result of the scientific revolution, that is, of the growth of systematized scientific knowledge.

The geographic origin and spread of the industrial revolution since the eighteenth century supports this view and the pivotal role of human capital in generating and facilitating it. The industrial revolution started with the scientific revolution in the north-west of Europe and spread most rapidly to those areas where educational development has made the transfer of technology most feasible.

It is clear now that the process of growth and diffusion is worldwide. Human capital as embodiment of skills is a convenient conceptualization of its role as coordinate factor of production in its contribution to national economic growth. Human capital as a source of new knowledge shifts production functions upward and generates worldwide economic growth.

Even though 'knowledge knows no bounds', its utilization requires local adaptation which is more costly the more dissimilar ('distant') the economies and societies to which it is transmitted. Moreover, as technical progress continues, the slower the diffusion the wider the technological gap between the initiators and the 'latecomers'. Consequently, the capacity to absorb and adapt new technology requires an increasingly specialized and sophisticated labor force backed by a broadly educated population. For reasons that certainly make sense in the technology-exporting countries, the imported modern technology is capital- and skill-intensive. Thus problems of 'labor absorption' are added to the difficulties of absorbing modern technology.

Yet the disadvantages of factor bias are transcended by the advantages of being able to skip several generations of technology in a short time. It is true that the most modern technology is most readily available. But somewhat older vintages which are more labor-intensive may be used to some extent if complementary or ancillary industries are not obsolete. Even if the initial effects on the creation of highly productive employment are relatively small, the simultaneous adaptation of human capital by job training and some job redesign can help to widen the process. Initially, the pressure of modernization is most acutely felt at the highest education levels: specialized scientists, technicians and researchers are needed to adopt, master and modify the new technologies. But only widespread educational growth, especially at basic levels of literacy and numeracy, can lead from islands of modernity to a complete transformation of the economy.[17]

4. Human capital and population

According to Malthus, economic growth can only be sporadic: it is self-defeating, since it produces population growth, which in turn swallows all the gains. This theory has long been contradicted by empirical evidence. The notion that this hypothesis may be applicable to LDCs, which was entertained by some, is also being discredited by events. Economic growth has not been eliminated by rapid population growth in these countries.

Moreover, the patterns of population change associated with the 'demographic transition' in the West are now being visibly repeated in the rest of the world.[18] Indeed, the congruence of spatial and temporal patterns of economic growth and demographic change suggest an important interrelation between the two. Human capital is a link which enters both the causes and effects of economic-demographic changes.

Human capital, or population quality, was left out of Malthusian theory. The theory actually omits any economic motivation. It presents a strictly biological view of mortality as a mechanism which adjusts numbers of people to available resources. The contrary facts of economic growth and of the demographic transition have led to a reformulation of population theory in terms of parental decisions about numbers and 'quality' of children.[19] In primitive, pre-modern regimes of very high mortality, especially in an agricultural setting, unlimited fertility may be viewed as a rational response, which is also (or therefore?) culturally sanctioned. Declines in mortality, brought about by public health measures or by higher levels of living, create the need for family-size decisions, given the family's limited resources. Implicitly such decisions must consider both material and 'psychic' costs and returns from children. Intentions about human capital formation in children, or child 'quality', play a part in the decision. Given the family budget, resources spent on 'quality' compete with the number of children the family might otherwise want. This trade-off becomes pronounced in the context of economic growth, which raises the payoff to human capital formation.

In the West mortality reductions had little impact on fertility initially, but after a long lag they were followed by fertility declines. Surviving average family size grew initially but eventually declined to the present-day low levels. Roughly speaking, family size begins to decline when fertility rates drop more sharply than mortality rates. Although even exogenous declines in mortality tend to induce declines in fertility, it appears that for birth rates to fall more than death rates, the additional stimuli of economic growth and widespread education are necessary.

This generalization is supported both by the history of DCs and by current experience in LDCs. An intercountry analysis of changes during the 1965–75 decade in Latin America[20] showed that declines in birth rates were positively related to declines in death rates, but the declines in births were steeper than the declines in deaths only in countries whose economic growth rates were above average during the decade and whose educational enrollments of the population aged 5–14 were significantly above average at the outset. The regression analysis showed that at a rate of 2 per cent growth of per capita income the enrollment rate must be at least 80 per cent to generate a reduction in family size. With a growth rate of 3 per cent the minimum enrollment rate was 60 per cent.

But what is there in the process of economic and educational growth that makes incipient incentives toward reductions in family size widespread, effective and progressive? In a way, the emergence of strong economic growth implies that some of the cultural inhibitions to rationalism have already weakened. More directly, economic theory contains three implications of economic growth which point to deliberate reductions in family size: (a) urbanization; (b) the rising cost of time; and (c) educational growth.

(a) Since demands for agricultural products are relatively income and price inelastic, the growth of productivity reduces the demand for farm labor, which in turn flocks to cities in search of employment and higher wages. With children less productive and more costly to raise in the city than on the farm, incentives of migrants to limit family size are strong.

(b) The growth of wages in the labor market attracts people from non-market activities (households and subsistence sectors) to the labor market. To the extent that child-rearing is a time-intensive activity, increases in market wages represent a rising forgone cost of time spent in child care rather than in gainful work. Therefore incentives of women to limit family size and to enter (or stay in) the labor market appear and grow. This is especially true of educated women, since opportunity costs increase with education. A strong negative correlation between education of mothers and family size has been widely documented.[21]

(c) With growing incomes and industrial demands for literate, disciplined and skilled labor, both private and public demands for education increase. At the family level the demands for prolonged education of children represent an additional incentive to substitute 'quality' for the quantity of children, as the reduction in numbers of children increases the available family resources per child. The inducement to invest in quality and in greater future earning capacity of the children is strengthened by increased life expectancy as it constitutes a lengthened 'pay-off period' on the investments. In turn, when the educated children become parents they tend to have more-favorable attitudes and more information about birth control behavior and greater demands for education and health of their children.

In sum, we should expect growing urbanization, education, female labor-force participation and declining family size to follow economic growth. Such trends are, indeed, widely observed under conditions of sustained economic growth, although intensities and time lags in these processes can and do differ from one setting to the next. For example, growing market wages may induce women into the labor market without reducing their fertility if the extended family and cheap domestic service can help in child-rearing and if the nature of the work, such as farming or cottage industry, is not incompatible with the immediate presence of children. Also, for a time, growth of wages may reduce fertility without increasing the labor force: this happens when women employed in the occupations just described, including domestic service, move to better paid factory work. All the same, the extended family institution and the occupations compatible with uninterrupted mother's child-care eventually decline as incomes and education continue to grow, and all the predicted effects become apparent, as they do in the industrially developed countries.

The significance of these demographic events for the quality of labor is two-fold:

(a) High birth rates imply an age distribution of the population heavily weighted toward youth. For example, close to one-half of the Mexican and Brazilian population is less than 15 years of age. This represents a heavy burden on the economy, since the consumption and educational needs of the young population are paramount and their economic contribution small. Continuation of declines in birth rates changes the age distribution toward a more-productive labor supply.

(b) Beyond improving the quality of the labor force via changes in age distribution, reductions in the size of large families apparently also affect educational progress, as was already alluded. Families with fewer children can more readily afford educational expenditures. If the frequency of large families is greater among the poor, the induced demographic changes have important positive effects on the future distribution of income and on social mobility.

5. Conclusion

In this brief exposition it was not possible to do more than sketch the theory and allude to some of the empirical research which documents the vital and manifold role of human-capital formation in personal, national and global economic development. I think it is fair to conclude that even if substantial levels of human capital may not be a prerequisite for an acceleration of economic growth at a certain time and place, the concurrent growth and diffusion of human capital appear to be necessary to ensure sustained economic development.

The endogeneity of demographic developments to the processes of scientific, economic and educational progress means that the population explosions of the past two centuries should not be viewed as causes of poverty. On the contrary, they are part and parcel of the transition, completed in the West and current in most LDCs, from low to high levels of income, to be enjoyed by a vastly increased world population.

Notes
1. For an exposition of these origins see McNulty (1980, pp. 192–200). The works cited are: Schultz (1961), Becker (1964) and Mincer (1958).
2. Findings in Becker (1964).
3. Psacharopoulos (1973, Table 5.3, p. 86) shows that in a sample of countries whose per capita income was under $1000 in the early 1960s, the average rate of return on education was 19.9% and on physical capital 15.1%. In countries with higher income, the educational rate of return was 8.3% while the rate on physical capital was 10.5%. An estimate for Mexico at about that time was 21.9% for education and 14.0% for business capital. These estimates appear in Carnoy (1967).
4. Indeed, in a recent study Harberger (1978) shows that around 1970 rates of return (social or private) on physical capital no longer differed between advanced and less-developed countries. One may speculate that the growth of international investments has led to this result. Does this mean that physical capital is no longer scarce in developing countries? Not at all, its quantity is still limited by the scarcity of human capital: an increase in the latter will raise the rate of return on the former, increasing the demand for it until marginal returns on both forms of capital have equalized.
5. See Hansen and Weisbrod (1969), and World Bank (1980, pp. 49–50). The Hansen–Weisbrod findings are disputed by a number of authors; see, for example, Pechman (1979), Cohn (1979) and Blaug (1982).
6. This section draws on Mincer (1979).
7. The notion that human-capital productivity in earning activities increases relative to its productivity in learning activities over the life cycle is consistent with Ben-Porath's findings (1970).
8. Carnoy (1967); Psacharopoulos (1973).
9. For an empirical study of India, see Ram and Schultz (1979).
10. See World Bank (1980, p. 47).
11. For a survey of US findings, see Mincer (1979). Similar findings are shown by Carnoy (1967) for Latin America. However, his data contain father's occupation, rather than parental income.
12. For references, see Mincer (1979), World Bank (1980, p. 38) and Elias (1978).
13. Japan should be added to the European example in this quotation.
14. See Stone (1976) and Caldwell (1980).
15. Some evidence is provided in Griliches (1969). Complementarity of human capital with technology would produce the same results. This is stressed in Schultz (1975a) and Welch (1970). Evidence from time series is provided in Parvin (1963).
16. See Becker (1964) and Mincer and Jovanovic (1981).
17. See Anderson and Bowman in Stone (1976) and Caldwell (1980).

18. See Figure 5.3 in World Bank (1980, p. 64).
19. See the compendium edited by Schultz (1975b), World Bank (1980), Caldwell (1980) and Easterlin (1976).
20. Mincer (1975).
21. See Schultz (1975b), Easterlin (1976) and Caldwell (1980).

References

Becker, G. S. (1964), *Human Capital*, New York: Columbia University Press.

Belmont, L. and F. A. Marolla (1983), 'Birth Order, Family Size, and Intelligence', *Science*.

Ben-Porath, Y. (1970), 'Production of Human Capital over Time', in *Education, Income, and Human Capital*, ed. W. L. Hansen, New York: Columbia University Press, pp. 129–147.

Blaug, M. (1982), 'The Distributional Effects of Higher Education Subsidies', *Economics of Education Review*, vol. 2, pp. 209–31.

Caldwell, J. C. (1980), 'Mass Education as a Determinant of Fertility Decline', *Population Development Review*, pp. 225–56.

Carnoy, M. (1967), 'Rates of Return to Schooling in Latin America', *Journal of Human Research*, vol. 2, pp. 359–74.

Cohn, E. (1979), *The Economics of Education*, 2nd edn, Cambridge, Mass.: Ballinger.

Easterlin, R. (ed.) (1976), *Population and Economic Change in Developing Countries*, Chicago: University of Chicago Press.

Elias, V. J. (1978), 'Sources of Economic Growth in Latin American Countries', *Review of Economics Statistics*, pp. 362–70.

Fisher, I. (1930), *The Theory of Interest*, New York: Macmillan.

Griliches, Z. (1969), 'Capital–skill complementarity', *Review of Economics Statistics*.

Griliches, Z. and D. W. Jorgenson (1967), 'The Explanation of Productivity Change', *Review of Economics Studies*, pp. 249–83.

Hansen, W. L. and B. A. Weisbrod (1969), *Benefits, Costs, and Finance of Public Higher Education*, Chicago: Markham.

Harberger, A. (1978), 'Perspectives on Capital and Technology in Less-developed Countries', Xeroxed copy.

Johnson, H. (1975), *On Economics and Society*, Chicago: University of Chicago Press.

Krueger, A. O. (1968), 'Factor Endowments and Per Capita Income Differences', *Economics Journal*, pp. 641–59.

McNulty, P. J. (1980), *The Origins and Development of Labor Economics*, Cambridge: MIT Press.

Mincer, J. (1958), 'Investments in Human Capital and Personal Income Distribution', *Journal of Political Economy*, pp 1–32. (Chapter 1 of this volume.)

Mincer, J. (1975), 'Populaçao e Forca de Trabalho', *Revista Brasileira Da Economia*, pp. 25–39.

Mincer, J. (1979), 'Human Capital and Earnings', *Economic Dimensions of Education*, Report of the National Academy of Education. (Chapter 3 of this volume.)

Mincer, J. and B. Jovanovic (1981), 'Labor Mobility and Wages', in *Studies in Labor Markets*, ed. S. Rosen, Chicago: University of Chicago Press, pp. 21–64. (Chapter 5 of this volume.)

Parvin, M. (1963), 'Technological Adaptation and Income Growth', PhD thesis, Columbia University.

Pechman, J. A. (1970), 'The Distributional Effects of Public Higher Education in California', *Journal of Human Research*, vol. 5, pp. 361–70.

Psacharopoulos, G. (1973), *Returns to Education*, Amsterdam: Elsevier.

Ram, R. and T. W. Schultz (1979), 'Life Span, Health, Savings, and Productivity', *Economic Development and Cultural Change*, pp. 399–42.

Schultz, T. W. (1961), 'Investment in Human Capital', *American Economic Review*, vol. 51, pp. 1–17.

Schultz, T. W. (1975a), 'The Value of the Ability to Deal with Disequilibria', *Journal of Economic Literature*, pp. 827–46.

Schultz, T. W. (Ed.) (1975b), *Economics of the Family*, Chicago: University of Chicago Press.

Schultz, T. W. (1980), 'The Economics of Being Poor', Nobel Lecture, *Journal of Political Economy*, pp. 639–51.

Stone, L. (ed.) (1976), *Schooling and Society*, Baltimore: Johns Hopkins University Press.

Welch, F. (1970), 'Education in Production', *Journal of Political Economy*, vol. 78, pp. 35–59.

World Bank (1980), *World Economic Report*, Washington, D.C.: World Bank.

11 Wage structures and labor turnover in the United States and Japan*

1. Introduction

The relation between labor mobility, or turnover, and the structure of wages, especially by age, seniority, and skill level, is a subject of research in the United States and a topic of lively interest in the analyses of Japanese labor markets. In particular, theories of human-capital investment in worker skills and in hiring and screening have been used to explain tenure and experience–wage profiles and to link them to turnover patterns across workers. This linkage, which we shall refer to as the duality hypothesis,[1] has been invoked by several researchers[2] to explain the very low Japanese turnover rate, often portrayed as a product of the 'lifetime employment system'. Although hard estimates are not readily available, it is well-known that the labor policies of Japanese firms involve a strong emphasis on recruitment for jobs, and on training and retraining of workers. The greater volume and greater firm-specificity of such human capital investments in Japan than those in the United States is claimed to be the central, proximate reason for the large differences in the degree of attachment to the firm in the two countries.

Our research is guided by the same hypothesis: put briefly, larger investments in workers on the job result in steeper tenure–wage profiles and, given a degree of specificity in each unit of human capital, turnover is smaller the steeper the profile. This is a testable proposition in contexts other than United States–Japan comparison, and we report on such tests by industry sectors within the two countries.

Of course, observed dualities of this sort need not arise from specific human capital alone. Wage–tenure profiles may be steepened, independently of skill formation, to deter shirking,[3] or to deter worker-quitting in order to amortize fixed costs of employment, such as recruitment and training costs. If training costs are important and recruitment efforts are related to training needs,[4] the fixed costs and specific capital hypotheses overlap, and may be treated as one.

To the extent that the reputation of Japanese workers for loyalty and discipline can be ascribed to their cultural background in upbringing and in historical tradition, steeper wage profiles in Japan are not likely to

*This chapter was written with Y. Higuchi and was first published in *Journal of the Japanese and International Economics*, vol. 2 (1988), pp. 97–133.

reflect greater needs to deter shirking. Moreover, contrary to the monitoring model[5] in which steep profiles substitute for greater supervision, there is a great deal of supervision in Japan, though it is largely a matter of guidance and training. As Koike (1984) describes it, a young recruit who joins a work group, following a period of (orientation) training, 'is usually backed up by the sub-foreman for a period of several months. Even after that he is instructed and attended by a senior worker who occupies the next position in the rotation sequence.' Indeed, Koike remarks, 'the foreman in Japanese labor markets is much more involved than his Western counterpart in a worker's career.'

It may, of course, be argued that the cultural traits of Japanese workers which obviate the need to deter shirking are sufficient to explain low turnover behavior or the so-called 'lifetime employment system'. Although it may well be a facilitating condition, cultural background has long historical roots, but very low turnover in the labor market appears to be a modern-day phenomenon in Japan. While the evidence is incomplete, there are indications that major declines in turnover accompanied the onset of rapid economic growth in Japan in the early 1950s.[6] Figure 11.1 shows that in manufacturing the turnover rate is significantly lower in the recent decades than in the interwar period.

We think that the timing is not coincidental. We also think that the nature of training processes and of labor policies in Japanese firms, which makes the specific human capital hypothesis particularly useful, derives in part from the context of rapid economic growth. There is evidence in US data that rapid productivity growth promotes training and retraining, by increasing its profitability.[7] The special emphasis on training for job flexibility and rotation in Japanese firms[8] strongly suggests a policy geared to the progressive introduction and absorption of technological improvements. To the extent that the adaptations vary across firms, greater specificities are generated in human capital investments on the job.

This study is an attempt to deepen our understanding of the Japanese labor market by comparing it with the US labor market. We take the differences in on-the-job skill formation of workers as the central source of differences in wage profiles and in turnover behavior, while placing the skill formation and related labor policies in the context of economic growth and technological change.

In section 2 we use microdata for both countries, not previously employed for this purpose, to contrast the two national labor markets, as well as to test the relation between wage growth and turnover at the sectoral (industry) level within the countries.[9] In section 3 we trace inter-country differences in labor policies to differences in rates of economic growth or technical change. We utilize information on productivity

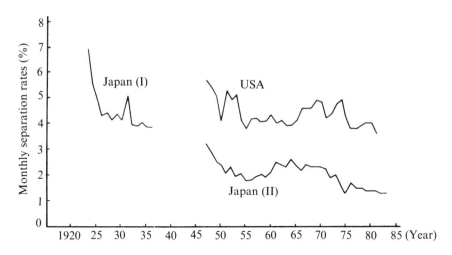

Notes
Japan (I): The average monthly separation rates of workers in the plants with 50 workers or more (the figure in 1923 is the average from May through December). Japan (II): The average monthly separation rates of regular workers in establishments with 30 workers or more (manufacturing). United States: The average monthly separation rates of workers in all establishments (manufacturing).
Sources: Japan (I): *Statistics on Labor Movement History in Japan*, vol. 10, Chūō Kōron Sya; Japan (II): *Monthly Labor Survey*. Japanese Ministry of Labor; United States: *Monthly Labor Review*. Bureau of Labor Statistics.

Figure 11.1   Historical changes in monthly separation rates in the manufacturing industry (Japan and the United States)

growth by industrial sectors to assess effects on training and on shapes of wage profiles. We also explore corollary evidence on the effects of rapid economic growth on depreciation (obsolescence) of human capital and on mandatory retirement. In section 4 we compare the wage–turnover relation in a sample of Japanese firms employing American workers in the United States with the relation in comparable American firms, and in the general Japanese and US labor markets. This comparison reveals the effects of differential labor policies, net of differences in cultural backgrounds of workers which are often emphasized in discussions of Japanese labor markets. Section 5 contains a summary and concluding remarks.

2.   The human capital duality hypothesis and the microevidence

That greater volumes of job training imply steeper wage profiles on the job and over longer work experience, is a theorem in human-capital analysis. A similar theorem predicts a negative effect of job training on turnover, on the plausible assumption that larger volumes of training also contain more firm-specific training, even if the latter is not a fixed part of the former.

The theory of specific human capital (Becker, 1962; Oi, 1962; Kuratani, 1973; and Hashimoto, 1981) postulates that some of the increased productivity resulting from training in the firm is applicable only in the firm in which training was received. As a hedge against capital losses, the costs of such training are shared between workers and firms, thereby deterring each party to this 'implicit contract' from quits and layoffs, respectively.

Until recently, the absence of empirical measures of job training has made much of the human capital analysis of wage structures (Mincer, 1974) and of its effects on mobility (Mincer and Jovanovic, 1981) largely indirect. What was testable was the relation between wage growth and labor mobility, both of which are, according to the theory, affected by job training.

More recently, useful measures of job training have become available in US microdata sets, such as the Current Population Survey (1983), recent panels of the National Longitudinal Samples, and the Panel Studies of Income Dynamics (PSID). Direct evidence on the effects of training on wage growth has appeared in the research literature. Brown (1983), Parsons (1986), Tan (1987),[10] and Mincer (1984a) all show evidence of the wage-growth effect in the cross-section and over time.[11] In particular, Brown and Mincer (separately) showed that when the *tenure* profile of wages was decomposed into three segments in the PSID data, wages grew slowly before the training period, rapidly during the training period, and levelled off after it. Training periods were defined as months and years during which training occurred. An additional year with training raised wage growth in the firm by 4–5 per cent over the year, in cross-sections and over time.

The effects of training on mobility are explored in Mincer (1984a) using the PSID data panel of working men: an additional year with training reduces the separation rate of workers by about 1 percentage point while it lengthens the completed duration of tenure in the firm in which training is received by less than a year at younger ages and by more than a year at older ages. The lesser effect during the early stage of working life is due to a prevalence of 'job-shopping': specific training is postponed until a reasonably favorable job match is achieved. These effects hold for workers with the same education, experience, marital status, union status, and health. The same study shows that more-educated and married men tend to receive more training, which also helps to explain why turnover is lower for more-educated and married workers.

We proceed to estimate wage functions in US and Japanese national sample microdata, in order to derive experience and tenure–wage profiles for otherwise similar workers in the two countries and in a set of industrial sectors in each country. Mobility behavior is then estimated on the same data using the same independent variables for standardization. Tests of the duality hypothesis – that turnover is inversely related to tenure–wage growth – are then performed at the sectoral levels. It should be noted that while previous research invoked this relation as a plausible explanation of the intercountry differences, the hypothesis was never tested empirically. Our sectoral analysis provides both a test of the duality hypothesis as well as estimates of parameters with which to gauge the magnitude of inter-country differences that can be ascribed to the hypothesis.

(a)   Wage functions in Japanese and US microdata

Our data are drawn from the 1979 Japanese Employment Structure Survey (ESS) and the US Panel Study of Income Dynamics for the period 1976–81.[12] The Japanese sample consists of male employees from 15 years of age through 55. The sample surveyed in the 1979 ESS contains about 330,000 households. A sample of 21,140 male employees (about 10 per cent of the total) was selected at random. Because ESS does not provide direct information about the hourly wage rate, we substitute the ratio

$$\frac{\text{annual earning from main job}}{\text{annual working hours in main job}}$$

for it.[13] The US (PSID) sample consists of over 7000 observations on white males, heads of household (ages 18–60),[14] who were employed during each survey. The real wage rate in the main job was deflated by the 1979-based CPI. Marital status (M), union membership (U), and the dummy of job changes (C) are entered as independent variables in addition to education, experience, and tenure.[15] In the US equation, year dummies are added to eliminate aggregate wage changes over time. Due to lack of exact infor-mation about years of schooling in ESS, nine years is selected if the person is a junior high school graduate, 12 years if a senior high school graduate, and 16 years if a college graduate or beyond. Total work experience is calculated for both countries as the employee's age minus his years of school completed minus six (the elementary school entrance age).

The estimated wage function is of the form

$$\ln w = \alpha_0 + \alpha_1 E + \alpha_2 E^2 + \alpha_3 X + \alpha_4 X^2 + \alpha_5 T + \alpha_6 T^2 + \alpha_7 Z \quad (11.1)$$

Here, the human capital variables are E years of schooling, X years of work experience, and T years of tenure in the firm. As these are expressed in time units, wages are expressed in logarithms, and the coefficients measure rates of increase in wages with E, X, and T, respectively.

Table A11.1 shows means and standard deviations of variables for Japan and the United States. Average current tenure in the employing firm is 3.5 years longer in Japan, and the average annual separation rate is over three times greater in the United States. Other differences are small. Wage functions are shown in Table A11.2 for all workers, younger workers (up to age 30), and older workers (over 30) for the United States and Japan.

The coefficients in Table A11.2 show the usual signs in all groups, except for differing signs of the quadratic on education in the United States (positive) and Japan (negative).[16] As described in equations (A), where tenure is not included, wages grow with experience over twice as rapidly in Japan as in the United States. When tenure is added, the experience coefficients are reduced in both countries, but more drastically in Japan. This indicates that the growth of wages with experience is in large part due to growth of wages with tenure, especially in Japan. The inference is that larger volumes of human capital, mainly within a firm, are accumulated in Japan.

Other important differences emerge in the complete equations (C), when age groups are compared: growth of wages with tenure is similar in both countries in the younger age group; the big difference – and steeper slope in Japan – is evident in the older (> 30) age group. Put another way, there is little, if any, decline in wage growth in the firms as age advances in Japan, compared to a large decline in the United States. The human-capital interpretation is that on-the-job training processes are much more continuous and more evenly distributed over working age in Japan.

In summary, Table 11.1 shows the partial derivatives of (log) wages with respect to education, experience, and tenure based on wage equations in Table A11.2. These were calculated at common (average) levels of the independent variables, and show the much steeper tenure–wage trajectories in Japan compared to those in the United States in the national microdata samples.

If tenure is viewed as 'internal' experience as distinguished from prior experience in other firms, the tenure–wage growth shown in Table 11.1 can be reinterpreted as the difference between wage growth due to internal and to prior external experience. Using a linear approximation (at the means as in Table 11.1), equation (11.1) can be written:

$$\ln W = \beta_0 + \beta_1 E + \beta_2 X + \beta_3 T. \qquad (11.1a)$$

Since $X = X_p + T$, where X_p is prior or external experience, the equation is

$$\ln W = \beta_0 + \beta_1 E + \beta_2 X_p + (\beta_2 + \beta_3)T. \qquad (11.1b)$$

Table 11.1   Growth of wages with education, experience, and tenure

	Equation type:	Japan (C)	US (C)	US (D)
All age group				
Schooling	12 years	17.05%	6.45	6.94
Experience	17 years	0.65	0.95	0.63
Tenure	9 years	4.19	1.22	1.01
Young age group				
Schooling	12 years	15.63%	5.78	6.27
Experience	6 years	2.25	1.94	1.91
Tenure	3 years	3.72	3.18	1.01
Old age group				
Schooling	12 years	17.70%	6.48	6.94
Experience	23 years	0.66	0.50	0.32
Tenure	12 years	4.07	1.13	0.91

Hence β_3 shown in Table 11.1 as the coefficient of tenure can also be interpreted as $(\beta_2 + \beta_3) - \beta_2$, the difference between returns on investments in the firm and returns on investments in prior employments. It is clear that this difference is far greater or that prior experience is relatively far less important in Japan.

Note on the interpretation of the coefficients in the wage functions.   The human capital interpretation of the coefficients in the wage functions requires a little more elaboration: in principle (Mincer, 1974), the coefficients of experience and tenure reflect (multiplicatively) rates of return to the respective investments, volumes of them (measured as ratios to labor costs, or time equivalents of training costs), and the rate of decline of such investments over time. It is sufficient, for our purpose in this note, to look at the linear coefficients: thus, the linear coefficient of experience X in (A) of Table 11.2 equals $r_x K_{0x}$, where r_x is the rate of return to post-school investments, including general and specific job investments, indexed by the initial investment ratio K_{0x}, assumed to decline linearly over experience. Similarly, the coefficient of tenure (T) in Table A11.2 equals $r_t K_{0T}$ with a corresponding interpretation for specific investments in the firm, given that X is in the equation.

Table 11.2   Adjusted and unadjusted mean turnover rates (%)

| | US | | Japan | | |
	Adj.	Unadj.	Adj.	Unadj.	At X
All	13.9	16.6	3.3	4.9	17
Young	28.4	28.1	8.1	8.6	6
Older	10.1	10.0	2.5	3.5	23

Note
Education is 12 years for all three groups.
Source: Table A11.3, col. (A).

Since the rate of return to schooling (r_s) measured as $\partial \ln W / \partial E$ is over twice as high in Japan as it is in the United States (in Table 11.1), and the same is true of coefficients of X (col. A of Table A11.2) and of T, it may be true that volumes of job training (measured by K_{0x} for total training, and by K_{0T} for specific training) are similar in both countries, but that the rate of return on it is over twice as high in Japan.[17]

Even in this case the implication for turnover of the over-twice steeper tenure–wage profile in Japan would still be the same, since returns (to workers and employers) from a unit of investment would be increasing more rapidly in Japan, providing a greater deterrent to turnover. Judging, however, by fragmentary evidence on the comparative prevalence[18] and on ratios of job training (and recruitment) costs to labor costs in Japanese and American firms (see section 4), an emphasis on differences in both magnitudes and efficiency of job training is probably correct.

(b)   Turnover functions
We proceed to estimate turnover functions in Table 11.3, corresponding to the wage functions in Table A11.2.

Table A11.3 utilizes US data in the PSID for the period 1976–81, as in the wage equation. But, because the data on firm tenure in the previous job are not available in the 1979 ESS, the Japanese sample is drawn from the 1982 ESS. The samples are male employees of the same age group as in the wage equation including part-time and temporary workers in both countries. In this paper we define labor mobility by whether the worker changes firms during the past year. We exclude exits from and entries into the labor market. Consequently, job separation is synonymous with job change in our data.

Table A11.3 shows regressions of turnover rates for each country and for age groups. The dependent variable in each equation is denoted as unity if the employee changed firms during the past year, and zero if the employee stayed within the same firm.[19] Independent variables, such as experience, tenure, and industry, are defined on the information in the previous year of the survey period.

The main purpose in estimating turnover functions is to compare turnover rates in the United States and Japan for similar workers by adjusting for worker characteristics specified in the turnover equations. For this purpose we use the coefficients in col. (A) of Table A11.3, to standardize separation rates by education, experience, and marital status at common (average) levels of these variables. The tenure variable is not included in the standardization, as its length already reflects (inversely) turnover probabilities. The results are shown in summary Table 11.2. It appears that the over-threefold higher US turnover rate shown in the unadjusted data (Table 11.1) is true for similar workers as well.

Another purpose of the turnover regressions A11.3 is to observe intercountry differences or similarities in the effects of education, experience, and tenure on turnover. Thus a positive relation between schooling and job training, which is partly specific, should lead to a negative relation between education and turnover. Of particular interest is the relation between tenure in the firm and turnover: the more specific training he accumulates in the firm, the longer the worker is likely to stay with the firm. The larger the volume of training and the more it is bunched in early tenure the bigger the decline in the separation as tenure lengthens. Moreover, the less intensive the screening of workers before hiring, the more important is job matching after hire, hence the bigger the separation rate in early tenure. Consequently, the decline in separations with tenure is steeper, the less prior screening, the larger the volume of training, and the shorter the period of training in the firm, given the volume.

Also, a decline in turnover(s) should be observed as age (experience, X) advances since

$$\frac{dS}{dX} = \frac{\partial S}{\partial T}\frac{dT}{dX} + \frac{\partial S}{\partial X} < 0 \tag{11.2}$$

because $\partial S/\partial T < 0$, as already suggested, while $dT/dX > 0$ (it would be zero, only if $\partial S/\partial T$ and $\partial S/\partial X = 0$), and $\partial S/\partial X$, the effect of 'pure aging' (given tenure), is also likely to be negative, as costs of moving increase with age, apart from specific capital reasons. If 'pure aging' is unimportant, as seems to be the case, the main reason for a negative age effect $dS/dX < 0$, is the negative tenure effect, $\partial S/\partial T < 0$.

The negative effect of schooling on separations is observable in both countries in Table A11.3. This is due to a positive correlation between schooling and training, a relation consistent with the theory of investment in human capital over the life cycle[20] or with complementarity between the two. The relation is a bit weaker in the United States, but it gets stronger at higher levels of schooling. The experience effect, where tenure is not included, is expected to be negative. This is induced by the pattern of tenure coefficients as seen in equations (B), according to the decomposition of dS/dX, shown above. The larger negative coefficients on X (without tenure) are due to the larger coefficients on T (given X).

It is surprising, at first glance, to find that the decline of separations with tenure is slower in Japan than in the United States. However, the more-intensive recruitment and prehiring screening effort in Japan (see section 4) means that separations are reduced in the immediate post-hiring period, and the spreading out of training activities over longer periods of tenure implies that the decline of initially low separations with tenure is rather slow. Indirect evidence on the spreading out of training (and retraining) activities in Japan was noted in the wage profiles of Table A11.2: tenure–wage profiles continued to grow for senior workers in Japan, while their slopes decline much more in the United States, hence the difference in the steepness of wage growth between the countries was much more pronounced among older workers.

It may be argued that the observed negative relation between turnover and tenure ($\partial S/\partial T < 0$) is an artifact of heterogeneity in turnover propensities among workers.[21] The greater the heterogeneity, the steeper the observed decline ($\partial S/\partial T < 0$) even if the true effect is $\partial S/\partial T = 0$ for a given individual. If this were the case, the decline of turnover with experience (dS/dX) would be due only to 'aging effects' ($\partial S/\partial X$). Hence the experience effect would be the same whether or not tenure is held constant. This is not the case in our data or in previous studies. To the extent that some degree of heterogeneity bias exists it could also be argued that the greater homogeneity (in tastes or moving propensities) among Japanese may be responsible for their flatter tenure profile of separations. But, if so, the same bias would also apply to the tenure–wage profile, making it *flatter* for Japan. Apparently, the heterogeneity differences are of little consequence in the intercountry comparison, as the Japanese wage profile is so much *steeper*, not flatter.

(c)   Sectoral evidence on wage-growth–turnover dualities

While the steeper tenure–wage profile and lower turnover in Japan than those in the United States are consistent with the human-capital-induced duality, one such comparison does not by itself represent compelling evidence. It is plausible that industrial sectors within the countries also differ in skill-acquisition processes of their workers, given differences in production functions. If so, dualities can be tested across sectors in both countries.

We proceed to do this by (a) including industry dummy variables (shown in Table A11.4), interacted with tenure (IND_iT_i) as well as (IND_i) dummies without interaction in the wage equations. The respective coefficients on these variables measure differential industry tenure–wage slopes (α_1) and industry levels (α_2). The α's are shown in Table A11.5. The next step (b) is to include these α's as variables in the separation equations. The coefficients on α measure the effects of industry tenure–wage slopes on industry turnover in each country. These results are shown in Table 11.3 for the United States and Japan. The coefficients on α_2 are negative, as would be expected if differential industry wage levels reflect unionization or other barriers to mobility. Our main interest is in the coefficients on α_1, which provide a test of the duality hypothesis, and they are negative. All US coefficients are statistically significant. The tenure–wage slope effect is larger in the over-30 age group, and is stronger in the non-union sector than in the total sample. The coefficients for Japanese industries are also negative in the whole sample, but stronger for the younger (≤ 30) group, and positive but not significant for the older group. We suggest in section 3(b) that the lack of effect of tenure–wage slopes on turnover in the older group in Japan is affected by the proximity of mandatory retirement.

Using the effects observed in Table 11.3, and the (standardized) magnitudes of tenure–wage growth and turnover shown in Tables 11.1 and 11.2, respectively, we can estimate the extent to which differences in tenure–wage slopes account for the differences in turnover rates between the United States and Japan. Since wage slopes are more likely to reflect training in non-union rather than union firms we prefer to use the US coefficient in the last column of the US panel. Multiplying it (-2.03) by the intercountry difference in tenure–wage growth shown in Table 11.1 (3.18 per cent) we get a predicted difference in turnover of 6.4 per cent. Since the observed difference is 10.6 per cent (Table 11.2), about 61 per cent of the intercountry gap is explained by the differences in tenure–wage slopes, which we ascribe to more-intensive and continuous training in Japanese firms.

The same calculation using the coefficient on α_1, in the first column of Table 11.3 which includes unionized firms (over 30 per cent of the sample is unionized) yields a predicted estimate which would account for 45 per cent of the gap. The higher estimate is more appropriate for reasons indicated and because of the different nature of unionism in Japan.

Table 11.3 Effects of industry tenure–wage slopes on separation rates[a]

United States

Variable	All (18–60)		Young (18–30)		Older (31–55)		All non-union
α_1	−0.0226	−0.0150	−0.0048	−0.0104	−0.0292	−0.0289	−0.0203
	(2.9)	(1.9)	(0.9)	(1.8)	(3.8)	(3.7)	(2.3)
α_2	—	−0.0023	—	−0.0022	—	−0.0013	−0.0020
		(4.6)		(2.3)		(2.8)	(2.8)

Japan

Variable	All (15–55)		Young (15–30)		Old (31–55)	
α_1	−0.3156	−0.1183	−0.2029	−0.1209	0.2490	0.1644
	(1.8)	(0.7)	(3.2)	(1.9)	(1.2)	(0.8)
α_2	—	−0.0105	—	0.0288	—	−0.0202
		(2.5)		(2.8)		(3.1)

[a]See Table A11.4.

314

3.   Economic growth, human capital, and wages

Why do labor policies of Japanese firms emphasize human-capital invest-ments which result in low turnover rates, or conversely, what explains the greater efforts of Japanese firms to strengthen worker attachment?

Although Japan was already an industrial power with a relatively educated labor force early in this century, the industrial relations system which produces low turnover became especially prominent in the post-World War II era. The successful effort to rebuild industrial plants, to catch up with Western technology, and to continue improvements yielded a very rapid rate of economic growth, initially capitalizing on the boom created by the Korean War in the early 1950s. The evolution of labor policies in the firms may be viewed as a response to actual and anticipated rapid technological change. Introduction of new technologies requires complementary, growing, and changing worker skills on the job, as well as a strong basic educational system which promotes continued learning skills. Technology is not quite a public good,[22] and its use is uncertain at any point. The result is considerable variation among firms in the techno-logies they create and adapt, particularly in industries where technology is advancing rapidly. Hence the emphasis on skill upgrading and remolding on the job, with strong elements of specificity.

Whether or not firm specificities are inherent in technological change, in its face firms must make choices: should the present workers be retrained and reassigned to new or modified tasks or should new workers be hired and trained while the old employees are laid off? If the training which is called for is general, that is, fully transferable, the firm is indifferent between hiring a new trainee and retraining and reassigning an old worker. It may prefer hiring new workers if new technology is already embodied in skills outside the firm or if newer vintages of education are helpful.[23] But, to the extent that training conditioned by the new techno-logy is specific, the firm will offer retraining, especially if it builds on the previously acquired specific capital which becomes only partly obsolete.

Training for flexibility, retraining, and job rotation represent the char-acteristic adjustment in Japan. It is of particular importance in facilitating long-term attachments in the face of changing technology: the resulting perception of job security eliminates worker-resistance to technological change and encourages innovative contributions on their part.[24]

If these arguments are correct, the steeper wage growth in the firm and the resulting lower turnover in Japan compared to that in the United States can be attributed, at least in part, to the differential rates of productivity growth in the two countries in the postwar decades.[25] To test this proposition we analyze several links between rates of productivity growth and behavior in the labor market.

Recent research in the United States (Lillard and Tan, 1986) reveals that job training is increased in industries which experience more rapid long-term productivity growth. It also shows that in-house training is encouraged while outside vocational training as well as prior on-the-job training in other firms is de-emphasized in such industries.[26] If these findings apply to differences across countries which differ in rates of economic (productivity) growth, the steeper tenure–wage profiles in Japan and lower turnover would follow as a consequence.

(a)   Sectoral evidence on effects of productivity growth
Using indexes of total factor productivity growth constructed by Conrad and Jorgenson (1985) for a set of (roughly 2-digit) US and Japanese industries, we are able to test the predicted effects by industry sector in each country.[27] Table 11.5 shows these indexes for both countries. As we have more information in US data, we can analyze them more comprehensively, in both substance and form. Thus, we first inquire into evidence of greater demand for education and training in sectors with greater productivity growth underlying the greater use of human capital in such industries. Panel A of Table 11.4 shows the effect of long-term productivity growth on the incidence of training, by education level. It is positive without the interaction, as well, according to Lillard and Tan (1986). Panel B shows the positive effects of productivity growth – both long and short term – on the profitability of (returns to) education and training. This we see in the positive coefficients of interactions of productivity-growth indexes with educational attainment ($PG \times E$) and with training ($PG \times RQT$) when they were alternately included in the 1976–81 PSID wage equations. These results suggest that the demand for education and for training increases as productivity grows, a fact of great importance for the understanding of the long-term growth of human capital in growing economies, and of its very rapid growth in recent Japanese history. Indeed, the fact that the relatively high rate of return to education was maintained in Japan despite the very rapid growth of educated labor supplies is consistent with the technologically based rapid increases in demand for educated labor.

We now proceed to test the effects of differential sectoral productivity growth on tenure–wage slopes in each country.

In Table 11.5 we interact productivity growth indices with tenure in the wage equation to ascertain whether tenure–wage slopes are steeper in industries where total productivity growth is faster.

The coefficients of the interaction variables, using long- and short-term productivity growth separately, are both positive and significant in Japan. In the US panel, each separate effect is also positive, but not significant for

Table 11.4 *Effects of productivity growth in US industries on (A) the incidence of training by education level and (B) returns to education and training*

Education	<12	12	13–15	16	17+
		(A)			
Coefficient of $PG \times E$[a]	1.92	0.41	2.88	3.56	5.32
		(B)			
		1960–79			1970–79
$PG \times E$		0.082			
		(8.0)			
$PG \times E$					0.061
					(4.0)
$PG \times RQT$		0.164			
		(10.1)			
$PG \times RQT$					0.100
					(4.0)

Note
The wage equation includes the PG variables in addition to their interactions with education and training shown here. The first column used longer-term productivity growth (PG) measured by the 1960–79 increases in the indexes, the second – shorter-term – over the 1970–79 period. RQT is the measure of (years or months) of training received in the current job, reported in 1976 and 1978 in the PSID. t values in parentheses. PG = productivity growth over the periods; RQT = training on the job, in years.
[a]All coefficients significant at the 1% level.
Sources: (A) Lillard and Tan (1986); (B) PSID males, 1976–81.

the short-run (1970–9) productivity growth interaction. When both variables are included together we get the impression of a distributed lag effect which is shorter in Japan. The lack of significance of the productivity growth variable in the 1970s in the United States may be due to its very low level during that period. Although productivity growth rates were also lower in Japan in the 1970s than before, they were still quite sizable. It is plausible that effects of low industry levels and hence of differentials in productivity growth are less clearly detectable, or that these effects take hold in a nonlinear fashion, a proposition we have not tested.

If the steepness of the tenure–wage slopes is increased by productivity growth, an effect of productivity growth on turnover should also be visible. This is verified in Table 11.6 by including the productivity indexes in the turnover equation.

Table 11.5 Coefficients of interaction of productivity growth in industry with tenure in wage functions

United States

	All (18–60)			Young (18–30)			Older (31–60)		
PG (60–79)	0.0139 (4.3)	—		0.040 (2.7)	—		0.015 (3.8)	—	
PG (70–79)	0.006 (1.5)	0.008 (1.1)	0.010 (1.2)	−0.003 (0.2)	0.093 (3.0)	−0.083 (2.0)	0.001 (0.2)	0.005 (1.1)	0.023 (2.6)

Japan

	All (15–55)			Young (15–30)			Older (31–55)		
PG (60–79)	0.009 (6.7)	—		0.016 (2.5)	—		0.009 (6.3)	—	
PG (70–79)	0.013 (7.5)	−0.010 (2.0)	0.024 (3.9)	0.027 (3.2)	−0.052 (2.2)	0.088 (3.1)	0.012 (6.9)	−0.008 (1.4)	0.021 (3.3)

Note
See Table A11.5.

Table 11.6 Effects of sectoral productivity growth on separation rates

United States

	All (18–60)		Young (18–30)		Older (31–60)	
PG (60–79)	−0.111	−0.248	−0.146	−0.372	−0.080	−0.130
	(4.2)	(4.3)	(2.9)	(3.6)	(2.6)	(2.2)
PG (70–79)	−0.081	0.197	−0.010	0.358	−0.075	0.083
	(2.2)	(2.4)	(1.4)	(2.5)	(1.7)	(1.0)

Japan

	All (15–55)		Young (15–30)		Older (31–55)	
PG (60–79)	−0.002	0.028	−0.021	0.038	0.006	0.021
	(0.5)	(1.3)	(1.8)	(0.7)	(1.2)	(1.0)
PG (70–79)	−0.007	−0.064	−0.047	−0.124	0.009	−0.034
	(0.8)	(1.6)	(2.0)	(1.1)	(1.0)	(0.8)

Note
See Table A11.5.

Table 11.7   Observed and predicted tenure–wage slope

	United States	Japan	Difference
Mean value of $(PG \times Ten)$	0.625	2.500	0.1875
Observed tenure–wage slope	0.011	0.042	0.031
Predicted (a)	0.011	0.037	0.026
(b)		0.028	0.017

When the long- and short-run indexes are used alternatively, they are negative, as expected, in the US data (Table 11.6). When both indexes are included, the short-run effects are positive, so that the negative effects reflect a long lag. The Japanese data show negative effects as well, but here again, the short-run effects dominate in Japan, reflecting a shorter lag.

As in Table 11.3 where the effects of tenure–wage slopes on separations of older workers were not clear in Japan, neither are they clear as effects of productivity growth on separations of older workers in Table 11.6. As suggested in the discussion of findings in Table 11.3, the greater-than-expected turnover rate is likely to be due to the earlier retirement in sectors with steeper wage profiles and/or faster productivity growth. These facts and reasons for them are described in the next section.

Returning to Table 11.5 we can ask the question posed at the outset of this section: to what extent does the more rapid economic growth in Japan account for the steeper wage profiles there?

According to the US data (Table 11.5) the effect of adding a unit of long-term growth, measured by the interaction variables $(PG \times \text{tenure})$, is to add 1.4 per cent to the tenure–wage slope. The mean value of $(PG \times \text{tenure})$ in the United States was 0.625. Since Japanese productivity growth was four times as rapid over the period, the corresponding mean value for Japan was 2.500. The predicted difference in tenure–wage growth was therefore (a) $(2.500 - 0.625) \times 1.4 = 2.62$ per cent, using the US table, or (b) 1.69 per cent using the Japanese table. (It would be 2.33 per cent if short-run PG which dominates in Japan were used.) As the summary Table 11.7 indicates, the differences in productivity growth account for 55–84 per cent of the differences in tenure–wage slopes in the two economies.

(b)   Obsolescence, lifetime distribution of training, and early retirement
One effect of rapid changes in technology is an increased depreciation of physical and human capital, due to obsolescence. In effect, the payoff period of investments in human capital is shortened. Hence less is invested

at any given time, but investments (training) are repeated over the work-ing life.[28] Since the investments do not decline much over the working life, wage profiles do not decelerate much. To the extent that training is specific, and it is plausible that such specificity is accentuated by firms' adaptations to technology, the lack of deceleration is pronounced in tenure–wage profiles. We saw evidence of this lack of deceleration in Japanese data, contrasted with significant declines in tenure–wage slopes at older ages in the United States. We also saw, in part (a) of this section, that effects of productivity growth on steepness of wage profiles were no smaller for older than for younger workers in Japan, but much smaller in the United States. Apparently, the overall much weaker productivity growth rate in the United States did not involve obsolescence, or potential obsolescence, as much as in Japan.

Despite the greater potential obsolescence, total volumes of training are increased in conditions of rapid productivity growth as was indicated in part (a), presumably because of the greater profitability (indicated by positive coefficients $PG \times RQT$ in Table 11.4) of the up-to-date training. We should note, of course, that obsolescence of human capital does not necessarily imply obsolescence of workers. By gradual adjustments in continuous training, with emphasis on flexibility and job rotation, poten-tial obsolescence is overcome without changing much of the work force in the firm. If the new cycle of training builds on the partially obsolete previous cycle, and both contain elements of firm specificity, skill adjust-ments are accomplished at lesser cost using the existing work force rather than new hires.

However, workers who interrupt their work experience for a long period are much more handicapped when returning to work in a regime of rapid technical change than in one where changes are milder. One way to gauge the difference in rates of potential obsolescence of worker skills in Japan compared to the United States is to observe the rate of decline in wage rates of persons who drop out of the labor force for a prolonged period. Such estimates are available for the United States (Mincer and Polachek, 1974, 1978), Sweden (Gustafsson, 1977), and Japan (Higuchi, 1987a) for married women who withdraw from the labor force (usually for child-bearing and child-rearing purposes). While such interruptions are now much less frequent in the United States, they were still pronounced in the late 1960s period covered by Mincer and Polachek in the United States and by Gustafsson in Sweden.

The estimates of depreciation 'through nonuse' are provided by the coefficient in the wage function of the form

$$\ln w = \alpha_0 + \alpha_1 E + \alpha_2 X + \alpha_3 T + \delta D$$

Table 11.8   Depreciation rates in wage functions of married women (%)

	Age	Educ: 9–11	12–15	16+	Period
Japan	35–39	−3.99	−4.44	−5.35	Late 1970s
	30–34	−1.35	−3.59	−3.05	
United States (a)	30–44	−0.20	−1.30	−2.30	Late 1960s
(b)	30–44	−1.16	−1.40	−4.30	
Sweden (c)		−0.16	−2.75	−1.57	Early 1970s

Note
(a): all married workers; (b): married women with children; (c): women with interrupted careers.

Here X measures *actual* work experience in the labor market, T the most recent job tenure, and D the length of interruptions of work activity, all in years. The 'depreciation' coefficient on D is in part due to 'forgetting' or erosion of skills used in the market prior to interruption. But, even without 'forgetting', skills become obsolete if they are rapidly modified in the market place when technology changes rapidly. This obsolescence effect ought to have been greater in Japan than in the United States. Indeed, estimates of the depreciation coefficient (δ) in married women's wage functions shown in Table 11.8 are clearly larger in Japanese data than in US or Swedish data.

Note also that the estimated depreciation rates tend to increase with level of education. This would be expected if retraining on the job is complementary with education and with technical change – a hypothesis consistent with our findings in Table 11.4.

The estimates are not quite comparable in terms of procedures, time periods, and data sources. Nevertheless, they represent a strong suggestion that obsolescence is an important additional component to 'forgetting' in Japan, augmenting the depreciation of skills which are not used over several years (the lengths of interruption periods are similar in the country comparisons).

Another implication of rapid technological change which necessitates continuing training and retraining of workers is an adverse effect on continuing employment of older workers. This could happen if it is more difficult, that is, more costly, to retrain older workers, while at the same time, the low turnover rates throughout prime ages result in a disproportionate number of such workers in sectors with rapid technological change. Early mandatory retirement from the job – though not from the

Table 11.9   *Productivity growth (X_1), wage slopes (X_2), and early*
retirement[a] (Y_1, Y_2) in Japan in nine industrial sectors.

	Y_1	Y_2
X_1	17.7	-1.39
	(1.5)	(2.5)
X_2	590.17	-26.17
	(4.6)	(2.4)

Notes
Y_1 = the incidence (in % of firms) with mandatory retirement. Y_2 = the average age of uniform mandatory retirement.
[a]*Source: 1980 Survey on Employment Management*, Japanese Ministry of Labor

labor force and not necessarily from the firm – is a solution apparently practised in Japan.

A weak test of this hypothesis is performed in Table 11.9. Here we relate the incidence (in percentage of firms) with mandatory retirement (Y_1) and, alternatively, the average age of uniform mandatory retirement (Y_2), given in nine industrial sectors (we had to aggregate from the larger numbers used before), to long-term productivity growth by sector (X_1) and to tenure–wage slopes for the 31–55 age groups by sector (X_2). The Xs are used alternatively; they cannot be used jointly, since they are strongly correlated on this highly aggregative level, as we would expect.

A similar test was not performed for the United States, where mandatory retirement is much less common and information is not readily available. A suggestive study by Hutchens (1986) indicates that mandatory retirement is more likely in firms in which turnover of older workers (especially the new hire rate) is low. Although the author interprets the result in the light of Lazear's (1979) hypothesis, it is clearly consistent with our hypothesis as well. Further work on this matter will be undertaken.

As the results show, sectors with more rapid productivity growth (X_1) tend to have mandatory retirement rules and an earlier retirement age. The same is true of sectors with steeper tenure–wage profiles in the 31–55 age group (X_2). Of course, these are very much the same sectors.

Since the average retirement age is close to 55 in the rapidly growing sectors, a significant proportion of workers below 55 are induced (by severance pay and other benefits) to change their jobs earlier. This is the likely reason for the previously observed apparent anomaly, namely that turnover rates appeared not to be smaller for older Japanese workers in sectors with faster productivity growth (Table 11.6) and with steeper wage slopes (Table 11.3).

4. Another control: a look at Japanese plants operating in the United States

In this section we summarize our findings on recruitment, job training, wage structures, and turnover in a sample of Japanese plants operating in the United States (JPUS). Details of the survey and of the data are more comprehensively described in Higuchi (1987b).

A popular view of Japanese industrial relations stresses discipline and company loyalty as a cultural characteristic of Japanese workers which is reflected in low turnover. The steep tenure–wage profile is ascribed to company policies of increasing wages with seniority as a reward for loyalty and for disciplined effort. Our comparison of Japanese and US labor markets yields findings that are consistent with the economic analysis of human-capital investments on the job, especially under conditions of differential rates of technical change, without attention to cultural conditioning. Nevertheless, the cultural background of workers is not irrelevant. The system of economic incentives that we described may be more effectively implemented, when favorable attitudes are engendered by the culture. In the language of Hashimoto and Raisian (1985) 'transaction costs' of the 'implicit contract' based on human-capital formation in the firm are lower in Japan.

The question that arises is: Would similarly intensive labor practices applied to a work force that is not Japanese, but American, yield results similar to those observed in Japan? If the answer is affirmative, it would prove that cultural factors are neither necessary nor sufficient, though they may well be facilitating. Such a test is available in data on recruitment, job training, wage structures, and turnover in a sample of Japanese plants operating in the United States which were surveyed by Higuchi (1987b). An additional benefit of this survey is direct information on costs of training and recruitment in JPUS and in comparable American plants – a key latent variable in our analysis. We examine (a) whether there are differences in modes of recruitment and job training between the JPUS and American plants, and (b) if so, how these differences influenced individual wage growth and job separation rates.

The survey covered 83 JPUS plants employing 17678 workers. Summary statistics are shown in Table A11.6. In interviews we found that most of the JPUS plants apply, with some modifications, similar technology and production systems to those in their parent plants. Both Japanese and American managers in these plants stress the importance of job training. Orientation and job training are used not merely to enhance a given skill but also to acquire job flexibility for rotation purposes and to maintain good conditions of machinery without relying on outside experts. Recruitment and hiring efforts are intensive.

Table 11.10   Industrial distribution of JPUS workers

Industry	Percentage of workers	Rate of productivity growth (1960–79) United States	Japan
Textiles	6.9	33	27
Chemicals	10.1	13	45
Fabricated metals	9.8	11[a]	48
Electrical machinery	36.5	46[a]	89[a]
Transportation equipment	22.7	13	21
Other	14.0	—	—

[a]Separate category in Conrad and Jorgenson (1985). All other rates from Table A11.5.

Table 11.11   Training and recruitment costs in JPUS and American plants

	JPUS	American
Proportion of workers who received training last year (%)	24.35	13.48
Cost of training per worker ($)	134.2	52.9
Cost of training per new hire ($)	1000.0	215.0
Recruitment cost per new hire ($)	759	411

The findings we now describe are based on difference and regression statistics shown in Higuchi (1987b). All the test statistics are significant at the 5 per cent level.

It should be noted first that the industrial distribution of workers in JPUS plants (Table 11.10) shows them to be concentrated in a few industries, most of which experienced relatively (to country average) high rates of productivity growth in Japan and in the United States. For this reason alone, the emphasis on Japanese labor practices in JPUS plants is not misplaced, according to our previous findings.

According to Table 11.11, the proportion of workers who received training in the past year (1985) was about twice as high in JPUS than in comparable American plants. This proportion was also about twice as high as the new hire rate in the JPUS plants, but the proportion receiving training in the American plants was less than the new hire rate. This means that JPUS plants provide not only training for new employees but also continuing training and retraining for the existing work force. Training costs per worker were over two times higher in the JPUS plants, and over four times higher for new employees. Given the strong emphasis on training and its specificity it is not surprising that JPUS firms make strong efforts to recruit more-adaptable and stable workers. Indeed, the recruitment costs are twice as high in the JPUS as in American firms. And the positive correlation between training and recruitment costs is clearly observable in Japanese industries as well.[29]

These findings, it should be noted, refer to production workers, not managers. As such they are not small: $1759 of recruitment and training costs per year of a new employee in JPUS, compared to $626 in American firms. Still, these are underestimates: opportunity costs of job training (forgone productivity) escape the accounting. Similarly, recruitment costs do not include compensation for recruiters' and interviewers' time.

Wage rates are similar in JPUS and American plants, although average tenure is less in JPUS plants, which are newer (the oldest plant dates back to 1963). Total labor costs per American worker are about $2500 (or 10 per cent) higher in JPUS. Over $1000 of the difference is due to higher training and recruitment costs and another $1000 to higher fringe benefits (unspecified); the rest is accounted for by (rather small) period bonus payments.

Table 11.12 shows the rates of growth of wages with schooling, experience, and tenure for JPUS, comparable American industries, and for the United States and Japan in the aggregate. The estimates are based on wage functions of the form we used before.[30] Tenure–wage growth in JPUS is over twice as steep (3.3 per cent) as in comparable American firms (1.4 per cent), but lower than in Japan (4.2 per cent). Prior experience has little or no effect on wages (for workers over 30, who were hired from other firms) in JPUS, in contrast to American firms. While prior experience is de-emphasized in JPUS, selectivity at upper education levels is apparent among white-collar workers and managers. This shows up in the schooling coefficient of the wage equation which is far higher for workers over 30 years of age in JPUS plants than those in American firms: since prior work experience is less valuable in the JPUS plants whose technology and labor utilization differ from those in US plants, quality and education may have been used as substitutes in hiring older workers for higher level positions.

Table 11.13 presents a comparison of turnover rates. As expected, all the rates are lower in Japanese plants, despite the fact that they are more recent and have a much larger proportion of younger workers. One seeming exception is the layoff rate which is not much lower in JPUS than in the American plants. But the statistic is unduly affected by one large

Table 11.12 Percentage growth in wage rate attributable to schooling, work experience, and job tenure in the JPUS plants, American firms, and Japanese firms (%)

	JPUS (with bonus)	JPUS (without)	United States (all industries)	United States (non-union workers in textile, chemicals, metal, machinery, and equipment)	Japan (all industries)	At (years)
All ages						
Schooling	18.92	18.78	6.62	8.76	16.79	(12.33)
Experience	0.57	0.64	0.98	0.82	1.46	(17.41)
Tenure	3.33	3.23	1.54	1.49	4.75	(9.60)
Under 30 years old						
Schooling	9.74	9.06	6.05	8.53	14.39	(12.65)
Experience	2.23	2.16	1.79	0.49	3.76	(6.58)
Tenure	5.25	5.00	3.69	4.02	6.36	(3.77)
Over 30 years old						
Schooling	22.41	22.60	6.55	8.76	17.16	(12.17)
Experience	-0.19	-0.04	0.53	0.57	0.66	(23.11)
Tenure	2.47	2.43	1.31	1.30	4.28	(12.55)

Note: The percentage growth in wage rate attributable to schooling calculated by the equation $\partial \log W/\partial E = b + 2CE$ is the simple average of mean years of schooling in the United States and Japan, which are shown in parentheses (the common value is given to the above five categories). The percentage growth in wage rate attributable to experience and tenure is similarly calculated. None of these calculations takes account of marital status which was not available in the JPUS data.

327

Table 11.13   Turnover rates in JPUS and American plants

| | JPUS | | American | |
	Annual	Monthly	Annual	Monthly
Separate rates	19.5	1.7	28.2	3.5
Quit rates	9.3	0.8	17.9	2.3
Layoff rates	7.3	0.7	8.6	0.9
Layoff rates[a]	1.6	0.1		
Percentage of plants with layoff	16.1		55.0	

[a]Excluding one JPUS plant which accounted for 40 per cent of all layoffs.

Table 11.14   Tenure–wage growth and turnover in three environments

	Japan	JPUS	United States
Tenure–wage growth	4.7[a]	3.3[a]	1.5[a]
Separation rate (monthly)	0.9[b]	1.7[c]	3.5[c]

Sources: [a]Table 11.12; [b]1985 *Monthly Labor Survey*; [c]Table 11.13.

electrical machinery plant which laid off 40 per cent of its workers. Without this exception, the layoff rate is, like the quitting rate, about half as large in JPUS than in US plants. Quite remarkably, as in the comparison of tenure–wage slopes, the JPUS turnover rate is about two-thirds of the distance from the higher national US rate to the lower national Japanese rate, as shown in Table 11.14.

We may conclude that the relation between the wage structure (the tenure–wage profile) and turnover is similar in all three cases, but that the (transplanted) hiring and training practices of Japanese firms account for about two-thirds of the differential between the US and Japanese wage and turnover behavior.

5.   Summary and Conclusions

The starting point of this study is the proposition that intensive formation of human capital on the job is the basic proximate reason for the strong degree of worker attachment to the firm in Japan. The greater emphasis on training and retraining, much of it specific to the firm, also results in steeper wage trajectories, due to growth of skills in the firm.

Several previous studies viewed the differences between Japanese and US labor markets in the light of the same hypothesis. We explore this insight more thoroughly by a detailed use of microdata for the two countries: we measure wage profiles and turnover in age groups and we *test* the inverse relation between the two on industry sectors within each of the countries. Numerical estimates of this relation permit us to conclude that about two-thirds of the differential in turnover between the two countries is explicable by the differences in the steepness of the profiles.

As we indicated, the relation between wage slopes and turnover is indirect – attributable to the effects of human capital formation on each. This is in contrast to theories of seniority wage incentive schemes which encourage worker effort, thereby permitting reductions in monitoring costs. In such theories, the effects of wage profiles – which rise *more* rapidly than productivity – on turnover is direct. In our opinion, this interpretation of differences in wage profiles between the United States and Japan is inappropriate, *prima facie*, in view of the traditional reputation of Japanese workers for discipline and loyalty to the firm. Moreover, there is evidence that supervision plays a larger role in the careers of Japanese workers – but the purpose is to guide worker development and not to monitor shirking behavior. Neither do we agree with the view that cultural attitudes are the major reason for the intercountry differences, especially because the system we observe has been changing over time. We do not deny that cultural factors may play a facilitating role.

The question remains why the emphasis on human capital formation on the job is so much greater in Japan than in the United States. Our answer is that such emphasis is conditioned by rapid economic growth. More specifically, Japanese labor policies in the firm represent adjustments of worker skills and activities to the very rapid technological changes of the past decades.

Several indications lead us to this hypothesis: (a) the timing of strong reductions in turnover during the 1950s, when economic growth accelerated in the postwar period; (ii) the lack of deceleration in the wage profile of mature workers relative to younger workers in Japan – suggesting continuous training and retraining processes characteristic of rapid technological change; (c) actual obsolescence of skills reflected in larger declines (than in the United States) in wages of workers who interrupt labor force participation for several year periods; (d) earlier retirement age in sectors with more rapid productivity growth in Japan. Research on US data suggests that the more rapid the productivity growth in an industry, the greater the demand for education and training in it.

Using productivity growth indexes for industries in the United States and in Japan we test the hypothesis that rapid technical change, which induces greater and continuous training, is responsible for steeper profiles, hence indirectly for lesser turnover. The hypothesis is confirmed on the sectoral level in both countries. We conclude that differences in productivity growth between the United States and Japan account for 70–80 per cent of the differences in the steepness of wage profiles, hence indirectly for the differences in turnover.

Finally, we try to standardize for the cultural background of workers, by observing a sample of Japanese plants in the United States which employ American workers and use Japanese labor policies in recruitment and training. We find that the steeper tenure–wage slopes and lower turnover place this sample closer to Japan than to the United States – about two-thirds of the distance.

The question whether these transplanted policies are profitable and may serve as a model for American industry to emulate is not easily answered, certainly not within the scope of this study. In answering such questions one should keep in mind that the JPUS ventures are highly selective not only with respect to choice of sector (Table 11.10), but also in regard to tax advantages and other incentives provided by local governments to induce their location, non-unionized and carefully recruited employees, and industrial activities in which their parent firms excel.

Acknowledgements

This research was supported by the National Science Foundation and the Spencer Foundation. Seminal ideas of M. Kuratani and of H. W. Tan stimulated our research. We are grateful to Hitoshi Hayami, Tom Melito, and Gus Baker for their excellent research assistance. Helpful comments were received from Linda Edwards, John Garen, Daniel Hamermesh, Masanori Hashimoto, Koji Taira, and members of the Columbia University Seminar on the Japanese Economy and of the Econometric Society meeting in Tokyo.

Notes

1. Explicated by Mincer and Jovanovic (1981).
2. References: Kuratani (1973); Shimada (1981); Tachibanaki (1984); Hashimoto (1981); Hashimoto and Raisian (1985).
3. See Becker and Stigler (1975) and Lazear (1981).
4. Some evidence is cited in note 29.
5. References in note 3.
6. In his survey of the steel industry, Koike (1984) found that tenure lengthened over that decade. A similar finding is shown by Saxonhouse (1976) for cotton textiles. In a most recent paper Saxonhouse (1987) writes: 'The large amount of intra-firm training which has come to be so characteristic of post-war Japan . . . is found only rarely in early twentieth century in Japan' (p. 14).
7. See Lillard and Tan (1986) and section 3, below.
8. According to Koike's survey (1984) there was a large number of rotations within Japanese plants. By contrast he finds that rotation in US firms is infrequent. Mary Brinton (1987) emphasizes rotation as an important component of training in Japanese firms.
9. The negative relation between wage growth and turnover is the 'duality hypothesis' proposed by Mincer and Jovanovic (1981). In it, tenure–wage trajectories are related to

probabilities of leaving the firm. In the present study we more precisely relate *slopes* of tenure–wage profiles to levels of turnover.

10. Parsons uses NLS data, Tan the CPS.
11. Similar findings are shown by Lillard and Tan (1986) in CPS and NLS data.
12. Most studies of Japanese wage structures use the Wage Structure Basic Survey (Shimada, 1981; Hashimoto and Raisian, 1985). The reasons for employing the ESS in this paper are as follows: (a) While the WSBS is an establishment survey, the ESS is a household survey which is comparable to the PSID (Mellow and Sider (1986) suggest that there are discrepancies between the estimated results of wage equations in establishment data and household data). (b) We were required to employ microdata which contain information on wage, job separation, and other related variables at the same time, and the ESS is the only nationwide data source available in Japan which satisfies these conditions. (c) While the WSBS conducts a survey of wages in June only for the employees in firms with more than 10 workers who worked for more than 18 days a month and more than 5 hours a day, the ESS covers annual earnings and working hours of all workers.
13. The 1979 ESS contains a question about the annual working days. In addition, the survey asked workers with more than 200 working days a year and workers with less than 200 working days who worked regularly during the survey period about their weekly working hours. But seasonal workers and day-workers did not provide information on their weekly working hours. So, these workers are excluded from our wage data because information about both the annual working days and the weekly working hours is necessary for calculating the annual working hours. (These workers are included in the sample for the separation equations.) The seasonal employees and the day workers account for just 3.6% of the total employees in non-agricultural industries. The annual working days and the weekly working hours were answered on a multiple-choice form. The annual working hours was calculated as the median of the selected answers to both questions.
14. Working age upper limits of 55 in Japan and 60 in the United States are used, as they precede retirement.
15. Our data did not include firm-size variables, often emphasized in analyses of Japanese labor markets. Larger firm-size provides greater scope for training and intrafirm mobility (rotation and promotion) which substitutes for interfirm turnover. Human capital differences which characterize firm size differentials are captured by our independent variables, so the firm size variable is to some extent redundant in our microanalyses. At any rate, other studies (e.g., Hashimoto and Raisian, 1985) have shown that the intercountry differences hold in all firm sizes. Moreover, the distribution of firms by size is not very different in the United States and Japan.
16. Greater homogeneity in abilities and/or larger inequality in opportunities in Japan could lead to such differences (see Becker, 1975, ch. 3). More surprising is the very high coefficient ('rate of return') on education in Japan. Although a higher rate may be expected in Japan – given the greater intensity of education, at least in terms of annual school days – our estimate may be problematic in view of the smaller coefficients shown in other studies (Kuratani, 1973; Shimada, 1981). The education coefficient on Japanese annual earnings (not shown here) is closer to the coefficient in US earnings, suggesting that annual hours of the more-educated Japanese workers are understated relative to hours of less-educated workers. Life-cycle patterns, however, do not seem to be affected.
17. See, however, note 16, which suggests that the differences (at least in schooling) are probably in investments rather than in rates of return.
18. Cf. Koike (1984) and Brinton (1987).
19. For a more rigorous formulation, see Mincer and Jovanovic (1981). OLS procedures were used instead of the more expensive probit. Experiments with US data showed little difference in the results of the two procedures. Note also that the wage variable does not enter directly into our turnover equations. Indirectly, expected wages are captured by the human capital variables in A11.3. Our tests of duality in Table 11.3 do utilize

industry wage levels (α_2) and wage slopes (α_1) in addition to the variables listed in A11.3.

20. The positive relation between schooling and job training is observed in Lillard and Tan (1986) and Mincer (1984a). Human capital theory (Becker, 1975) suggests that individuals with greater ability and/or opportunity tend to invest more in schooling and in job training.
21. See Mincer and Jovanovic (1981).
22. The notion of 'proprietary' technological knowledge is stressed by Nelson (1981). In an unpublished paper, Hong Tran (1987) translates this notion into firm technology-specific worker skills.
23. This appears to be an initial phase for technological adaptations in American industries (Bartel and Lichtenberg, 1987). According to Saxonhouse (1976), the unavailability of skills embodying new technology on the outside of the firm, led to major firm specific efforts to mold worker skills in Japan in the 1950s.
24. This resistance, or fear that workers 'will work themselves out of a job', is a common theme in the industrial-relations literature. As Koike (1984) puts it, the job-rotation training system in Japan produces a 'deeper' career pattern of company specific skills which underlies worker attitudes toward technological change and their commitment to the company.
25. We do not deny that the more successful worker adjustment to technology, the greater the gain in productivity. This feedback effect is stated in the preceding paragraph. Still, we view technical change as the largely exogenous factor and labor practices as endogenous, instead of the converse, which is sometimes expressed or implied in the literature. Incidentally, we do not intend the terms technological change, productivity growth, and economic growth to be synonymous. But each underpins the next in the expressed order.
26. Lillard and Tan (1986). Tables 3.4 and 3.5.
27. We combined some of the indexes in order to apply them to the smaller number (aggregated) of industries in our data sources (PSID in the United States). We used total factor productivity indexes as a reflection of technological change. We did not use labor productivity indexes which reflect, in addition, factor intensities. We did not theorize about the latter in our context, and we did not have all the required data in any case.
28. See Becker (1975), pp. 73–4.
29. The R^2 is 0.43 in 26 industries, excluding public utilities and textiles. Data are from the 1983 *Survey on Welfare Facilities Systems for Employees* and 1983 *Survey on Employment Trend*.
30. Tables in Higuchi (1987b).

References

Bartel, A. and F. Lichtenberg (1987), 'The Comparative Advantage of Educated Workers in Implementing New Technology', *Review of Economic Statistics*, Feb.
Becker, G. (1962), 'Investment in Human Capital: Theoretical Analysis', *Journal of Political Economy*, October.
Becker, G. (1975), *Human Capital*, 2nd edn, Chicago: University of Chicago Press.
Becker, G. S. and G. Stigler (1974), 'Law enforcement, malfeasance, and compensation of enforcers' *Journal of Legal Studies*, vol. 3, January.
Brinton, M. C. (1987), 'Women Workers and Human Resource Development in Japanese Firms', paper presented at the 1987 Association of Asian Studies Meeting. Boston.
Brown, J. (1983), 'Are Those Paid More Really No More Productive?', Princeton Working Paper no. 169.
Conrad, K. and D. W. Jorgenson (1985), 'Sectoral Productivity Gaps between the United States, Japan and Germany, 1960–1979' in *Probleme und Perspektiven der Weltwirtschaftlichen Entwicklung*, Berlin: Duncker and Humboldt.

Gustafsson, S. (1977), 'Depreciation Rates of Human Capital Due to Nonuse', Stockholm University, *mimeo*.

Hashimoto, M. (1981), 'Firm-specific Human Capital as a Shared Investment', *American Economic Review*, vol. 71.

Hashimoto, M. and J. Raisian (1985), 'Employment, Tenure, and Earnings Profiles in Japan'. *American Economic Review*, vol. 75.

Higuchi, Y. (1987a), 'Labor Force Withdrawal, Re-entry and Wage by Educational Attainment of Japanese Women', Columbia University Center on Japanese Economy and Business, Discussion Paper no. 7. Paper presented at the 1987 Association of Asian Studies Meeting, Boston.

Higuchi, Y. (1987b), 'A Comparative Study of Japanese Plants Operating in the U.S. and American Plants: Recruitment, Job Training, Wage Structure and Job Separation', Columbia University Center on Japanese Economy and Business, Discussion Paper no. 8.

Hutchens, R. (1986), 'Delayed Payment Contracts and a Firm's Propensity to Hire Older Workers', *Journal of Labour Economics*, vol. 4, no. 4.

Koike, K. (1984), 'Skill Formation System in the U.S. and Japan: A Comparative Study', in *The Economic Analysis of the Japanese Firm*, ed. M. Aoki, Amsterdam: North-Holland.

Kuratani, M. (1973), 'A Theory of Training, Earnings, and Employment: An Application to Japan', PhD thesis, Columbia University.

Lazear, E. P. (1979), 'Why is There Mandatory Retirement?', Journal of Political Economy, vol. 87.

Lazear, E. P. (1981), 'Agency, Earnings Profiles, Productivity, and Hours Restrictions', *American Economic Review*, vol. 71.

Lillard, L. A. and H. W. Tan (1986), *Private Sector Training: Who Gets It and What Are Its Effects?*, Rand Corp.

Mincer, J. (1974), *Schooling, Experience and Earnings*, New York: Columbia University Press.

Mincer, J. (1983), 'Union Effects: Wages, Turnover and Job Training', in *Research in Labor Economics*, Suppl. 2, ed. R. Ehrenberg, New York: JAI Press. (Chapter 11 of Volume 2.)

Mincer, J. (1984a), *Labor Mobility, Wages, and Job Training*, US Department of Labor.

Mincer, J. (1984b), 'Human Capital and Economic Growth', *Economics of Education Review*, vol. 3, no. 3. (Chapter 10 of this volume.)

Mincer, J. and B. Jovanovic (1981), 'Labor Mobility and Wages', in *Studies in Labor Markets*, ed. S. Rosen, Chicago: University of Chicago Press. (Chapter 5 of this volume.)

Mincer, J. and S. Polachek (1974), 'Earnings of Women', *Journal of Political Economy*, vol. 82, no. 2.

Mincer, J. and S. Polachek (1978), 'Women's Earnings reexamined', *Journal of Human Research*, vol. 13, no. 1.

Nelson, R. (1981), 'Research on Productivity Growth and Differences', *Journal of Economic Literature*, September.

Oi, W. (1962), 'Labor as a fixed factor', *Journal of Political Economy*, December.

Parsons, D. (1986), 'Wage Determination in the Post-Schooling Period', Ohio State, Center for Human Resources.

Saxonhouse, G. R. (1976), 'Country Girls and Communication Among Competitions in the Japanese Cotton-spinning Industry', in *Japanese Industrialization and its Social Consequences*, ed. H. Patrick, Berkeley: University of California Press.

Saxonhouse, G. R. (1987), 'Mechanism for Technology Transfer in Japanese Textile Industry', draft, University of Michigan.

Shimada, H. (1981), 'Earnings Structure and Human Investment: A Comparison between the United States and Japan', Keio Economic Observatory.

Tachibanaki, T. (1984), 'Labor Mobility and Job Tenure', in *The Economic Analysis of Japanese Firm*, ed. M. Aoki, Amsterdam: North Holland.

Tan, H. W. (1987), ed., 'Technical Change and its Consequences for Training and Earnings', paper presented at the Labor Workshop, Columbia University.

Appendix

Table A11.1   Means and standard deviations[a] of variables

	United States (18–60)	Japan (15–55)	United States (18–30)	Japan (15–30)	United States (31–60)	Japan (31–55)
Log wage rate[b]	1.470	9.030	1.308	8.696	1.564	9.191
	(0.42)	(1.58)	(0.37)	(1.51)	(0.42)	(1.59)
Schooling	12.73	11.94	12.83	12.48	12.67	11.67
(*E*) (years)	(2.70)	(2.49)	(2.10)	(2.32)	(3.00)	(2.52)
Total work						
experience (*X*)	16.30	18.53	6.24	6.93	22.10	24.12
(years)	(10.93)	(10.63)	(2.66)	(3.99)	(9.60)	(7.98)
Tenure at the						
current firm	7.85	11.35	2.82	4.72	10.75	14.35
(*T*) (years)	(8.31)	(8.94)	(2.52)	(3.61)	(9.07)	(8.99)
Separation (*S*)	0.166	0.049	0.281	0.086	0.100	0.035
	(0.377)	(0.22)	(0.45)	(0.28)	(0.30)	(0.18)
Married (*M*)	0.874	0.757	0.814	0.382	0.910	0.938
	(0.33)	(0.43)				

Note

The Japanese samples consist of male employees. The US sample consists of white male employees who are household heads.

Sources: Japanese Employment Status Survey, 1979; US Panel Study of Income Dynamics, 1976–81.

[a]Figures in parentheses are standard deviations.

[b]The Japanese wage rate is shown at 0.1 yen/hour. The US wage rate is deflated by the 1979-based CPI (in dollars/hour).

Table A11.2   Regressions of male wage equations in Japan and the United States

$$(\log W = a_0 + a_1E + a_2E^2 + a_3X + a_4X^2 + a_5T + a_6T^2 + a_7C + a_8M)$$

| | Japan (1979) | | | United States (1976–81) | | | |
Equation type:	(A)	(B)	(C)	(A)	(B)	(C)	(D)
Age group:	15–55	15–55	15–55	18–60	18–60	18–60	18–60
Constant	3.511**	4.414**	4.588**	0.5185**	0.5752**	0.5706**	1.0587**
E	0.5668**	0.4491**	0.4489**	0.0198**	0.0144	0.0141	0.0070
	(12.66)	(10.15)	(10.17)	(2.13)	(1.59)	(1.56)	(0.79)
E^2	−0.0149**	−0.0114**	−0.0116**	0.0019*	0.0021**	0.0021**	0.0026**
	(−8.43)	(−6.51)	(−6.81)	(5.26)	(5.72)	(5.74)	(7.16)
X	0.0843**	0.0390**	0.0167**	0.0347**	0.0237**	0.0231**	0.0233**
	(22.37)	(8.87)	(3.35)	(22.87)	(14.33)	(13.95)	(14.30)
X^2	−0.0013**	−0.0007**	−0.003**	−0.006**	−0.0004**	−0.0004**	−0.0005**
	(−13.71)	(−6.85)	(−2.93)	(−14.87)	(−10.96)	(−10.72)	
T		0.00629**	0.0491		0.0231	0.0158**	0.0137**
		(14.80)	(10.23)		(14.16)	(8.46)	(7.40)
T^2		−0.0008**	−0.0004**		−0.0004**	−0.0002**	−0.0002**
		(−5.89)	(−2.77)		(−7.24)	(−3.32)	(−2.69)
C			−0.1070**			−0.0964**	−0.0923**
			(−1.78)			(−7.60)	(−7.38)
M			0.2639**			0.0725**	0.0664**
			(8.22)			(6.07)	(5.65)
U							0.1308**
							(15.13)
R^2	0.098	0.129	0.134	0.268	0.305	0.313	0.333

335

Table A11.2 Regressions of male wage equations in Japan and the United States continued

$$(\log W = a_0 + a_1E + a_2E^2 + a_3X + a_4X^2 + a_5T + a_6T^2 + a_7C + a_8M)$$

	Japan (1979)			United States (1976–81)			
Equation type:	(A)	(B)	(C)	(A)	(B)	(C)	(D)
Age group:	15–30	15–30	15–30	18–30	18–30	18–30	18–30
Constant	3.9588**	4.4086**	4.744**	0.3914**	0.5048**	0.4963**	1.0806**
	(7.54)	(8.34)	(8.95)	(2.14)	(2.85)	(2.79)	(6.73)
E	0.5121**	0.4456**	0.4395**	0.0224	0.0099	0.0122	−0.0093
	(6.20)	(5.37)	(5.30)	(0.81)	(0.37)	(0.46)	(−0.38)
E^2	−0.0138**	−0.0117**	−0.0118**	0.0017*	0.0020**	0.0019**	0.0030**
	(−4.34)	(−3.67)	(−3.72)	(1.62)	(1.97)	(1.87)	(3.32)
X	0.1138**	0.0587**	0.0333*	0.0790**	0.442**	0.422**	0.0383**
	(7.21)	(3.31)	(1.77)	(7.51)	(4.11)	(3.90)	(4.31)
X^2	−0.0035**	−0.0016	−0.0009	−0.0036**	−0.0020**	−0.0019**	−0.0016**
	(−3.14)	(−1.28)	(−0.74)	(−4.48)	(−2.44)	(−2.35)	(−2.50)
T		0.0982**	0.0422*		0.0769**	0.0637**	0.0498**
		(5.84)	(1.71)		(9.62)	(5.81)	(5.41)
T^2		−0.0046**	−0.0009		−0.0052**	−0.0041**	−0.0030**
		(−3.45)	(−0.57)		(−5.69)	(−3.69)	(−3.36)
C			−0.1243			−0.0340*	−0.0366*
			(−1.26)			(−1.64)	(−1.95)
M			0.2054*			0.0456**	0.0506**
			(4.86)			(2.83)	(3.41)
U							0.1794**
							(14.17)
R^2	0.055	0.064	0.070	0.173	0.228	0.225	0.293

Table A11.2 Regressions of male wage equations in Japan and the United States concluded

Age group:	31–55	31–55	31–55	31–60	31–60	31–60	31–60
Constant	3.4884**	4.4255**	4.281**	0.5871**	0.6538**	0.6115**	1.0833*
	(10.11)	(12.96)	(12.55)	(8.50)	(9.72)	(8.90)	(15.16)
E	0.5396**	0.4295**	0.4146**	0.0182*	0.0138	0.0120	0.0046
	(9.75)	(7.91)	(7.66)	(1.76)	(1.37)	(1.19)	(0.45)
E^2	-0.0133**	-0.0103**	-0.0099**	0.0020**	0.0021**	0.0022**	0.0027**
	(-6.01)	(-4.74)	(-4.57)	(4.76)	(5.06)	(5.30)	(6.25)
X	0.0905**	0.0404**	0.0388**	0.0281**	0.0180**	0.0188**	0.0216**
	(8.80)	(3.94)	(3.79)	(9.73)	(6.14)	(6.42)	(6.71)
X^2	-0.0014**	-0.0007**	0.0007**	-0.0004**	-0.0003**	-0.0003**	-0.0004**
	(-6.64)	(-3.48)	(-3.52)	(-6.97)	(-5.27)	(-5.57)	(-5.93)
T		0.0658**	0.0527**		0.0184**	0.01369**	0.0115**
		(13.54)	(9.65)		(9.98)	(6.43)	(5.25)
T^2		-0.0009**	-0.005**		-0.0003**	-0.0001**	-0.0001
		(-5.80)	(-3.39)		(-4.19)	(-2.02)	(-1.32)
C			-0.1398*			-0.0836**	-0.0855**
			(-1.59)			(-4.19)	(-3.96)
M			0.4314**			0.0875**	0.0792**
			(8.22)			(4.99)	(4.27)
U							0.0961**
							(8.21)
R^2	0.089	0.130	0.136	0.216	0.260	0.266	0.277

Note: Figures in parentheses are t values. *Significant at the 10 per cent level. **Significant at the 5 per cent level. The dependent variables is the log wage rate. E is the number of years of schooling; X is total work experience; T is tenure at the current firm; C is a dummy for a job changer; U is a dummy for a union member; M is a dummy for a married person; U is a dummy for a union member. In the Japanese data, the information of whether the worker is a union member or non-union member is not available. Year dummy variables are added to the above independent variables in US equations. These coefficients are omitted in this table.

Table A11.3   *Regressions of male separation equations in Japan and the United States*

Equation type:	Japan (1982)		United States (1977–81)		
	(A)	(B)	(A)	(B)	(C)
Age group:	15–55	15–55	18–60	18–60	18–60
Constant	0.2677**	0.2102**	0.4908**	0.4689**	0.4756**
	(6.23)	(4.90)	(7.54)	(7.43)	(7.56)
E	−0.0150**	−0.0043	0.0027	0.0075	0.0121
	(−2.31)	(−0.68)	(0.28)	(0.83)	(1.34)
E^2	0.0003	0.00002	−0.0007*	−0.0008**	−0.0011**
	(1.31)	(0.09)	(−1.89)	(−2.19)	(−2.98)
X	−0.0082**	0.0017**	−0.0194**	−0.0017	−0.0018
	(17.99)	(2.80)	(−12.51)	(−1.04)	(−1.07)
X^2	0.0002**	−0.00004**	0.0003**	−0.0000	−0.00000
	(13.03)	(−2.59)	(7.48)	(−0.13)	(−0.14)
T		−0.0156**		−0.0377**	−0.0361**
		(−26.07)		(−22.99)	(−21.95)
T^2		0.00037**		0.0010**	0.0010*
		(21.25)		(17.30)	(16.66)
M		−0.0177**		−0.0588**	−0.0565**
		(−4.35)		(−4.89)	(−4.73)
NUR			−0.0101	−0.0070**	−0.0088
			(−1.28)	(−0.93)	(−1.16)
U					−0.0708**
					(−7.85)
R^2	0.020	0.050	0.063	0.137	0.142
F val. on E	50.63**	12.58**	71.47**	47.06**	48.86**

Table A11.3   *Regressions of male separation equations in Japan and the United States continued*

	Japan (1982)		United States (1977–81)		
Equation type:	(A)	(B)	(A)	(B)	(C)
Age group:	15–30	15–30	18–30	18–30	18–30
Constant	0.5698**	0.3671**	1.0871**	0.9286**	0.9673**
	(4.54)	(2.97)	(4.96	(4.41)	(4.30)
E	−0.0504**	−0.0056	−0.0490	−0.0299	−0.0275
	(−2.83)	(−0.32)	(−1.50)	(−0.96)	(−0.82)
E^2	0.0013**	−0.00006	0.0007	0.0002	−0.0001
	(2.15)	(−0.10)	(0.55)	(0.14)	(−0.04)
X	−0.0154**	0.0081**	−0.0508**	−0.0021	0.0033
	(−7.06)	(3.24)	(−4.79)	(−0.19)	(0.28)
X^2	0.0006**	−0.0004**	0.0021**	−0.00005	−0.0004
	(2.85)	(−1.65)	(2.70)	(−0.06)	(−0.41)
T		−0.0695**		−0.1039**	−0.1057**
		(−16.22)		(−12.37)	(−10.98)
T^2		0.0037**		0.0065**	0.0071**
		(11.60)		(7.02)	(6.24)
M		0.0062		−0.0389**	−0.0447**
		(0.80)		(−2.03)	(2.24)
NUR			−0.0272*	−0.0239*	−0.0333*
			(−1.88)	(−1.73)	(−2.28)
U					−0.0901**
					(−5.10)
R^2	0.018	0.074	0.046	0.133	0.135
F val. on E	51.38**	29.08**	45.21**	30.87**	31.04**

Table A11.3   Regressions of male separation equations in Japan and the
United States concluded

Equation type:	Japan (1982)		United States (1977–81)		
	(A)	(B)	(A)	(B)	(C)
Age group:	31–55	31–55	31–60	31–60	31–60
Constant	0.2134**	0.1713*	0.3341	0.3164	0.3095
	(4.95)	(4.02)	(5.15)	(5.03)	(5.02)
E	−0.0104*	−0.0011	−0.0064	−0.0020	0.0045
	(−1.64)	(−0.17)	(−0.73)	(−0.02)	(0.53)
E^2	0.0002	−0.00003	−0.0001	−0.0001	−0.0005
	(0.89)	(−0.14)	(−0.15)	(−0.36)	(−1.42)
X	−0.0063**	0.0010	−0.0084**	0.0048*	0.0043*
	(−6.16)	(0.98)	(−3.07)	(1.81)	(1.71)
X^2	0.0001**	−0.00002	0.00008	−0.0001**	−0.0001**
	(5.58)	(−0.70)	(1.41)	(−2.24)	(−2.20)
T		−0.0118**		−0.0291**	−0.0294*
		(−21.20)		(−18.76)	(−19.01)
T^2		0.0003**		0.0007**	0.0007**
		(16.68)		(13.60)	(13.93)
M		−0.0349**		−0.0494**	−0.0438**
		(−7.15)		(−3.28)	(−2.99)
NUR			0.0022	0.2253	0.0071
			(0.25)	(0.64)	(0.87)
U					−0.0478
					(−4.93)
R^2	0.004	0.039	0.017	0.114	0.120
F val. on E	32.13**	11.06**	13.05**	11.21**	12.11**

Note
Figures in parentheses are *t* values. *Significant at the 10 per cent level. **Significant at the 5
per cent level. The dependent variable is the dummy for job separation. We exclude exits
from and entries into the labor market. Consequently, job separation is synonymous with
job change in our data. The total work experience (X) and the tenure (T) are defined on the
basis of information in the previous year of the survey period. The nationwide unemployment rate (NUR) is that of white males age 18–60 in each year.

Table A11.4 The coefficients of Industry dummy $\times$ Tenure (IND_1T) and Industry dummy (IND_1) in US and Japanese wage equations

Age group	United States						Non-union (18–60)	
	18–60		18–30		31–60			
Industry	IND_iT (a_1)	IND_i (a_2)	IND_iT (a_1)	IND_i (a_2)	IND_iT (a_1)	IND_i (a_2)	IND_iT (a_1)	IND_i (a_2)
1	0	0	0	0	0	0	0	0
2	0.0040*	0.1054**	−0.0319*	0.0585	0.0105**	−0.2476**	0.0066	−0.0424
3	−0.0130**	−0.2815**	0.0067	−0.03558**	−0.0132**	−0.3357**	−0.0137**	−0.2111**
4	−0.0004	−0.0944**	−0.0029	−0.1035**	0.0017	−0.1443**	0.0014	−0.070*
5	0.0114**	−0.2259**	−0.0091	−0.1322**	0.0159**	−0.3389**	0.0136**	−0.2210**
6	0.00003	−0.0568*	0.0024	−0.1237**	−0.0022	−0.0252	0.0070*	−0.0275
7	0.0026	−0.0942**	−0.0129	−0.0399	0.0065*	−0.1754**	0.0077*	−0.0405
8	0.0036*	−0.0582*	−0.0181	0.0255	0.0079**	−0.01466**	0.0047	0.0405
9	0.0017	0.0110	−0.0181	0.0824*	0.0073**	−0.0992	0.0052	0.0254
10	−0.0006	−0.0500	0.0062	−0.1183**	−0.0008	−0.0516	0.0020	−0.0127
11	−0.0018	−0.1870**	0.0014	−0.1820**	−0.0003	−0.2415**	−0.0004	−0.1565**
12	0.0181**	−0.1657**	0.0245*	−0.2328**	0.0163**	−0.1685**	0.0178**	−0.1107**
13	0.0035*	−0.0536*	0.0046	−0.0694	0.0065**	−0.1227**	0.0082**	−0.0605
14	0.0022	−0.0635*	−0.0057	−0.0640	0.0058*	−0.1374*	0.0051	−0.0422
15	−0.0007	−0.2417**	−0.0320**	−0.1428**	0.0036	0.3309	−0.0014	−0.1769**
16	0.061**	−0.1574**	−0.1082	−0.0831*	0.0111**	−0.2475**	0.0090**	−0.1212**

Table A11.4   The coefficients of Industry dummy × Tenure (IND_iT) and Industry dummy (IND_1) in US and Japanese wage equations concluded

Japan

Age group	15–55		15–30		31–55	
	IND_iT (a_1)	IND_i (a_2)	IND_iT (a_1)	IND_i (a_2)	IND_iT (a_1)	IND_i (a_2)
1	0	0	0	0	0	0
2	−0.0078	0.5148**	−0.1839**	0.8614**	−0.0112	0.6727*
3	−0.0064	0.5995**	−0.1846**	−0.9093**	−0.0116	0.7957**
4	−0.0001	0.2596	−0.1102*	0.4989	−0.0018	0.3536
5	−0.0063	0.6561**	−0.1186*	0.8645**	−0.0046	0.6725**
6	−0.0041	0.3418*	−0.077	0.1028	−0.0158*	0.6414**
7	−0.0053	0.3822**	−0.1212*	0.3799	−0.0148*	0.6476**
8	−0.0087	0.3235*	−0.1645**	0.4275	−0.0228*	0.7188**
9	−0.0102	0.0691	−0.1457**	0.2683	−0.0132	0.2038
10	0.0068	0.4736**	−0.1283*	0.6941*	0.0036	0.6067**
11	−0.0011	0.5378**	−0.1271*	0.6835*	−0.0082	0.7417**
12	0.0107	0.7577**	−0.1505**	1.0477**	0.0074	0.8737**
13	−0.0027	0.2867	−0.1480**	0.5436	−0.0077	0.4551*
14	−0.0038	0.6271**	−0.1263*	0.7500**	−0.0097	0.8074**
15	−0.0023	0.5845**	−0.1430**	0.7622**	−0.0111	0.8282**
16	0.0025	0.7147**	−0.0976	0.7064**	−0.0057	0.9466**

Notes: Controls included are E, E^2, X, X^2, T, T^2, M, U, and year dummy variables. Industries: 1: Mining; 2: Foods; 3: Textiles; 4: Lumber, stone, and furnitures; 5: Publishing and printing; 6: Chemicals; 7: Metal products; 8: Machinery; 9: Transportation equipment; 10: Miscellaneous manufacturing; 11: Trade; 12: Finance, insurance, and real estate; 13: Transportation and communications; 14: Utilities; 15: Services; 16: Public administration.
*Significant at the 20 per cent level. **Significant at the 10 per cent level.

Table A11.5   Productivity indexes by industry (growth over the period)

Industry	United States		Japan	
	1960–79	1970–79	1960–79	1970–79
1	− 0.46	− 0.50	0.34	0.11
2	0.00	− 0.03	− 0.18	− 0.17
3	0.33	0.16	0.27	0.10
4	− 0.01	− 0.07	− 0.35	0.04
5	0.21	0.20	0.00	− 0.11
6	0.13	− 0.03	0.45	0.05
7	0.03	− 0.02	0.30	0.08
8	0.27	0.12	0.63	0.19
9	0.13	0.05	0.21	− 0.02
10	0.05	− 0.03	0.54	0.23
11	0.19	0.06	0.28	− 0.01
12	0.08	0.08	1.19	0.43
13	0.21	0.11	0.61	0.19
14	0.00	− 0.14	0.19	− 0.01
15	− 0.05	0.02	0.00	− 0.12
16	–	–	–	–
17	− 0.13	− 0.01	− 0.13	− 0.03
18	0.25	0.18	− 0.06	0.02

Notes
1.00 = 100 per cent. Industries: see notes to Table A11.4, plus 17: Construction; 18: Agriculture.
Source: Conrad and Jorgenson (1985).

Table A11.6   Means and standard deviations of schooling, total work experience, and job tenure at the current firms of male workers in JPUS plants and American firms

	JPUS (American workers)	United States (non-union comparable firms)[a]
All ages		
School years	12.41	12.84
	(1.32)	(2.51)
Experience	14.38	17.51
	(9.87)	(10.96)
Tenure	5.25	8.31
	(4.38)	(9.02)
Under 30 years old		
School years	12.20	12.87
	(0.94)	(2.19)
Experience	7.12	6.86
	(3.10)	(2.90)
Tenure	3.28	2.95
	(2.62)	(2.78)
Over 30 years old		
School years	12.61	12.82
	(1.59)	(2.68)
Experience	21.58	23.87
	(8.96)	(8.87)
Tenure	7.20	11.52
	(4.87)	(9.90)

[a]Non-union firms in textiles, metal, machinery, and food industries.

12 Human capital responses to technological change in the labor market*

Introduction

In my view, human capital plays a dual role in the process of economic growth: (a) as a stock of skills – produced by education and training – it is a factor of production, coordinate with physical capital and with 'raw' (unimproved, unskilled labor), in producing total output; (b) as a stock of knowledge it is a source of innovation, a basic cause of economic growth.[1]

A particular elaboration of the view of human capital as a factor of production implies that the marginal contribution of human capital to output is greater the larger the volume of physical capital. This is so if physical capital is more complementary with human capital than with unskilled labor.[2] In the older analyses, physical capital accumulation was the mainspring of economic growth. In it, the complementarity hypothesis implies a differential growth of demand for skilled and unskilled labor, as capital accumulates. The resulting increase in skill-wage differentials induces increased acquisition of human capital. In turn, the increased supply of human capital limits the wage differentials to an equilibrium level, at which this investment is as profitable at the margin as other kinds of investment.

In the above analysis, the growth of human capital is a consequence of exogenous accumulation of physical capital. If so, the growth of human capital contributes to economic growth, but is not the prime cause of it. But by the same complementarity hypothesis, the growth of physical capital could analogously be a response to exogenous increases in human capital. However, theoretical and empirical economic analysis rejects the notion of exogenous investments. Instead, emerging opportunities for profit must be looked to for the source of growth creating investments: cost-reducing and product-innovating changes in technology are the engines of growth which propel all factors of production by increasing their productivity. According to this theory (Solow, 1957), growth in outputs results from growth of physical capital, growth of labor, and improvements in technology.

Whether or not technological improvements are exogenous, as scientific and practical knowledge grows, or endogenous to, for example, R&D

*This chapter is a previously unpublished paper presented at the Conference on Economic Growth, 1989, SUNY, Buffalo, New York; revised 1991.

investments, the complementarity hypothesis may be extended to include technological change. That is to say that technological change is more complementary with human capital than with raw (unskilled) labor. The implications of growth of technology for human capital remain the same as before, *mutatis mutandis*. Also, to the extent that technical change is 'embodied' in physical capital, human capital is complementary with new vintages of physical capital, a hypothesis tested by Bartel and Lichtenberg (1987) for the school education component of human capital. Indeed, the 'embodiment' of technical change in both physical and human capital, that is the improvement in their 'quality', is another way of perceiving complementarity of both capital factors with technological change.

We should note that, although we focus here on human capital as a factor of production which responds to technical change rather than as a source of the latter, this does not mean that the growth of such human capital is merely an effect rather than a cause of economic growth: even in the narrow sense of improvement in labor 'quality', the growth of human capital contributes to economic growth by raising productivity.[3]

Several implications of the complementarity or skill-bias hypothesis are explored empirically in this study.

(a) A more rapid pace of technological progress should induce increased inputs of human capital, formed at school and on the job, by making their acquisition more profitable. Both utilization and wage effects ought to be observable.

(b) To the extent that technical innovations are firm-specific, needed on-the-job investments in worker training or retraining lead to more durable attachments of workers to firms, that is to lesser job mobility. Regardless of the degree of firm specificity, increased worker investment in job training should steepen their wage profiles.

(c) The time sequence in these human capital adjustments may differ as between the hiring of workers with needed education and the training and retraining of others. Skill adjustments may first be obtained by hiring policies, and later by training as the processes become more routinized. If so, effects on labor mobility may also be different in their time sequence.

(d) The job mobility phenomena have implications for the incidence of unemployment in the relevant sectors. The much-debated and little- or partially explored question of technological unemployment can be more thoroughly explored in our empirical analysis.

All these implications are relevant to economies differing in rates of technological progress, or to the same economy in different periods, or to different sectors of the same economy in a particular time period. This study uses industry sectors for an initial analysis. Changes over time are analyzed in a separate study (Chapter 13 of this volume).

2. Measuring technical change

In this study, as in a related previous one (Mincer and Higuchi, 1988), I use multi-factor or total factor productivity growth indices for 28 US industries calculated by Conrad and Jorgenson (1985) for the period 1960–79, extended by Fraumeni and Jorgenson (pers. comm.) to 1980–85, and subperiods. Productivity growth is, of course, a consequence of technical change, not a measure of it. It may serve as a measure of or proxy for technological change if other factors affecting productivity growth are either unimportant or taken account of in the statistical applications. Among the other factors, business cycles affect productivity growth as hired inputs fluctuate less than output, reducing productivity growth in downswings and increasing it in upswings. Similarly, economies or diseconomies of scale could affect productivity in either direction, as inputs grow.

Perhaps the major problem arises from the method of calculating productivity growth as the difference between the rate of growth of output and (a weighted measure of) the rates of growth of the capital and labor inputs: different measures are produced depending on the concepts and degree of detail regarding definitions of outputs and inputs, as well as form of the production function connecting the two. Jorgenson's measures used here are the only ones that contain the more-detailed adjustments of labor inputs for their 'quality' components, such as education, age, and sex composition. The productivity growth residuals are thus largely purged of human capital components. For our purposes this insures that shifts of the production function are not attributable to human capital, that is that there is no spurious correlation in the empirical relations between productivity growth and human capital that we are exploring.

Summarizing, the multi-factor productivity growth (*PG*) indices, when used as measures of technological change, contain two kinds of errors: systematic, such as those due to business cycles and economies of scale, and errors of measurement which are absorbed in the statistical residual which is the productivity growth measure. The problem of errors and of business cycles is mitigated by use of averages over longer periods cutting across business cycles and by use of unemployment rates as 'standardizing' variables. Our results are attenuated (understated) if sizable random errors, or extraneous factors remain in the averages.

We proceed to the empirical analysis which explores the effects of productivity growth not attributable to 'embodied' human capital on the utilization of human capital in the labor market (section 3), on the wage structure (section 4), on labor mobility or turnover (section 5), and on unemployment (section 6). A summary and concluding remarks follow (section 7).

3.   Pace of productivity growth and the utilization of human capital

Does more-rapid technical change which results in more-rapid productivity growth bring about greater utilization of human capital? The proposition that more-educated labor can deal more effectively with a rapidly changing environment, or with temporary 'disequilibria' resulting from technological change, has been suggested by Nelson and Phelps (1967), and restated and empirically documented, mainly in an agricultural context, by Schultz (1975) and Welch (1970). More recently, the effects of technical change on the educational composition of employment in industrial sectors extending to manufacturing and to the whole economy have been studies by Bartel and Lichtenberg (1987) and by Gill (1988), while the effects on the incidence of job training were explored by Lillard and Tan (1986).

Using Census data on the education composition of the labor force in 61 manufacturing industries in each of the years 1960, 1970, and 1980, Bartel and Lichtenberg related the proportion of employees with more than a high school education to the mean age of capital equipment in the industry, as well as to the R&D intensity (ratio of expenditures on R&D to the value of sales). The R&D variable was interacted with age of capital on the assumption that new capital is most likely to embody new technology in R&D intensive industries. They find that more-educated workers are utilized the younger the age of equipment, and that this effect is magnified in R&D-intensive industries.[4] The results hold for workers with relatively recent vintages of education; they are not significant for workers above age 45.

Gill (1988) relates proportions of full-time workers with specified levels of education in annual pooled Current Population Survey (CPS) data (1969–84) to Jorgenson's measures of multi-factor productivity growth (*PG*) in 28 industries covering the whole economy over the periods 1960–79 and 1970–79. Positive correlations are observed for workers with more than high school, negative for high school dropouts and zero for high school graduates.

Lillard and Tan (1986) found a greater prevalence of job training in sectors in which (Jorgenson) measures of productivity growth were higher using CPS, National Longitudinal Survey (NLS), and Equal Opportunity, Pilot Project (EOPP) microdata samples between the late 1960s and early

1980s. In an unpublished paper Tan (1987) focused on the relations between job training and technical change in 1983–4 CPS data, using Jorgenson–Gollop indexes for 1947–73 and 1973–79 periods. He found that the lagged, long-term productivity growth (1947–73) had a positive effect on in-house training, reported in 1983–4 jobs, and a negative effect on outside (classroom) training. In the shorter run (1973–9) productivity growth had the opposite effect: classroom training increased, while on-the-job training was either unaffected or less frequent. It is not clear whether the 1973–9 effect represents 'short-term' as distinguished from 'long-run' effects, or whether it is due to the specific historical period in which productivity stagnated.

We now explore the available evidence in another data set. The PSID data used here is restricted to males, non-students, age 18–60. The usable sample covers about 1100 persons each year from 1968–87. The Jorgenson–Fraumeni indices for 28 industries updated to 1985 have been allocated (averaged) to the more-aggregated, hence smaller number of industries (18) in the PSID. They are shown in Table 12.1 together with growth of employment (*EG*) over the 1960–79 period.

The distribution of education and of training across the PSID industries is reported in Table 12.2, as affected by productivity growth (*PG*) and employment growth (*EG*) in these industries. Other independent variables included in the equations, but not shown in the tables, are listed in the summary statistics of Table 12.7. They are: years of work experience; marital status; race; union membership; and unemployment rates. Years of education are excluded from Panel (A) but included in (B) and (C). All tables also distinguish young workers (defined as having 12 or fewer years of work experience) from all workers.

The upper panel (A) of Table 12.2 shows the proportion of workers with more than high school education as a function of productivity growth, standardizing for the rate of employment growth in the industry. Employment growth is likely to involve more-frequent new hires, and these are progressively more-educated, given overall trends in education.[5] The estimates shown in this panel confirm findings of Bartel and Lichtenberg and of Gill to the effect that concurrently and over the longer run more technologically progressive industries tend to utilize more-educated workers – as shown by the positive coefficient on *PG*. Also, as was suggested, this is true of industries with growing employment, given productivity growth, shown by the coefficient on employment growth (*EG*) over the 1960–79 period. As might be expected, the preference for more-educated workers among the younger workers is more likely to coincide with *concurrent* technological change. This shows up in the larger and significant coefficient on *PG* among the younger workers. Though it

Table 12.1   Productivity growth indexes (percent per year)

Industry	PG1960–79	PG1970–9	PG1980–5	EG1960–79
1. Agriculture	1.18	0.64	3.51	−2.93
2. Mining	−3.19	−7.32	0.17	2.50
3. Construction	−0.73	−1.43	−0.21	2.70
4. Food, etc.	0.00	−0.33	0.63	−0.003
5. Leather, textile mill, apparel, etc.	1.27	1.57	0.87	−0.04
6. Stone, clay, glass, precision instruments, lumber, wood, furniture	0.17	−0.41	1.05	1.70
7. Printing, etc.	1.01	2.03	0.38	1.34
8. Chemicals, petroleum, rubber, plastic	0.48	−0.63	−2.97	
9. Metal industries	0.13	−0.25	−0.47	1.37
10. Machinery, incl. electrical	1.32	1.31	1.64	2.63
11. Motor vehicles and other transportation equipments	0.63	0.54	−0.04	1.34
12. Misc. manufacturing	−0.05	−1.06	−6.50	0.61
13. Trade	0.92	0.68	1.09	1.74
14. Finance, insurance	0.41	0.86	−1.65	3.51
15. Transport and communication	1.01	1.17	−0.10	1.48
16. Utilities	0.00	−1.64	−0.17	1.73
17. Services	−0.27	0.24	−1.18	3.29
18. Paper, etc.	0.45	0.00	0.45	1.11

Notes
PG = productivity growth; EG = employment growth. EG calculated from CPS data.
Other independent variables listed in Table 12.7.
Sources: Cols 1 and 2: Conrad and Jorgenson (1985), Table 1; col. 3: Jorgenson and Fraumeni (1990).

appears weak in the PSID, the preference for more-educated workers extends to older age groups in other data sets, especially when related to long-run technical change, as Gill found in the CPS data by relating PG (1960–79) to educational distributions in several age groups.

The dependent variables in the lower panel (B) of Table 12.2 is the

Table 12.2   Education levels and training in industry (PSID) males)

(A) Proportion of workers with more than 12 years of schooling (1968 to 1985 pooled)

	All	Young $x \leq 12$
PG	2.02	3.02
	(1.8)	(2.1)
EG	0.07	0.07
	(4.7)	(4.9)
R^2	0.33	0.35

	(B) Learned on the job in 1976			(C) Prior training in 1976 and 1985		
Variables	All	Younger	Older	All	Younger	Older
PG(1970–79),						
(1980–85)	n.s.	n.s.	n.s.	−0.010	n.s.	−0.012
				(2.2)		(1.9)
PG(1960–70)	0.069	0.107	n.s.	0.045	0.044	0.037
	(2.6)	(2.6)		(4.2)	(3.0)	(2.4)
EG(1960–79)	0.031	0.049	n.s.	0.022	n.s.	0.025
	(2.1)	(2.3)		(3.1)		(2.6)

Note
t-statistics in parentheses
n.s. = not significant
Other independent variables listed in Table 12.7.

incidence of training reported in 1976 when a question was asked on the presence of a learning content in the job.[6] The variable is '1' if the answer was positive, zero otherwise. The estimated coefficients show no significant effects of current productivity growth on learning on the job (panel B) but positive effects of lagged productivity growth. No significant effects apply to older workers. Apparently, training processes follow technological change with a lag, while increased utilization of educated workers is a concurrent response. With technology a decade old, training is common practice.

In panel (C) the dependent variable is whether prior training was required for the job held in 1976 and again in 1985, when this question was asked. The results are similar to those in panel (B). The negative sign of the coefficient on concurrent productivity growth may mean that training on the old job is less or not relevant to current technology in the new job.

A training variable which is most frequently utilized in research with PSID data is *RQT*, defined as average duration of training required to become fully qualified in the current job, and reported by PSID survey respondents in 1976, 1978, and 1985. This variable, though positive, lacked significance in Table 12.2 (not shown). A variable, defined '1' when *RQT* exceeded one year, and zero otherwise, so measuring the incidence of more intensive training, was positive and significant in 1985, but barely so in 1978, when regressed among other variables on *PG* (1970–9) and *PG* (1980–5), respectively. Since the evidence of Lillard and Tan and of panels (B) and (C) here refer to incidence of training, a possible explanation, aside from severe measurement errors in *RQT*, is that, although faster technological change requires more workers to be trained and perhaps more frequently, the duration of training need not be longer.

Shares of educated workers are larger in industries where employment is expanding. As shown by the positive coefficients on *EG*, in such industries training expands also, mainly for younger workers. This is consistent with a positive correlation between education and training, found in many microdata sets,[7] and which may reflect a complementarity between the two forms of skill acquisition.

In sum, sectoral utilization of educated workers is greater in technologically progressive and in expanding industries. Although they may lag behind educational utilization, training activities are more frequent when productivity growth is faster. They are also more common in faster-growing industries.

The claim that more-rapidly growing technology increases demand for education and training is generally consistent with the present findings on their utilization in Table 12.2 and in other studies. If so, wages or payoffs to human capital should also be higher in progressive sectors, at least for some time. We look at such wage effects in the next section.

4.   Effects of productivity growth on wage structures

In studying the effects of sectoral productivity growth on the wage structure, it is important to distinguish its effects on the demand for labor, given its human capital composition, from effects on the demand for human capital. The analysis assumes that relevant supply curves of labor and of human capital are upward-sloping, but less steeply in the longer than in the shorter run.

The short-run effect of a productivity change on the demand for labor depends on the elasticity of demand for the product. If the increase in (marginal) productivity is neutral with respect to labor and capital, demand for labor increases if the product price elasticity is greater than unity, and falls otherwise. If productivity growth is labor-saving, demand for labor is reduced even with a more-elastic product demand function. In the long run, the adverse employment effect is reduced or reversed because demand elasticities increase. If productivity growth is widespread, income growth also increases the overall derived demand for labor. Thus, in the short run, relative wages may rise or fall in sectors with more-rapid productivity growth. In the longer run, income growth and labor mobility spread the real wage gains to all sectors.

The effects on the demand for human capital are more predictable as complementarity between technology and human capital attracts educated workers as well as encourages training in the newer technologies. The bias of technological change toward human capital, therefore, means that in the short run wages of more-educated workers increase more or are reduced less in sectors with more-rapid productivity growth. Empirically, even if education is held constant in our microdata, the interaction of education and productivity growth in wage functions ought to be positive, at least in the short run.

To the extent that trained workers bear some of the costs of investments in training, their wages grow during training as their productivity is raised. As training and experience become more profitable in the short run and expand in the longer run, wage profiles ought to steepen.

We may summarize the empirical implications as follows:

(a) In the short run, relative sectoral wages of labor of given 'quality' (given the human capital composition) may increase or decrease in sectors with more-rapid productivity growth.

(b) The demand for educated workers should increase relative to demand for less-educated workers in these sectors, so wages of the former should rise relative to those of the latter.

(c) In the longer run, the average sectoral advantage should erode as educated workers migrate to 'progressive' sectors and firms within sectors and as young labor-force entrants are hired in these sectors.

(d) The profitability of training should increase following the initially increased demand for educated workers. As training spreads, wage profiles in progressive sectors should steepen.

Table 12.3 shows estimates of pooled wage functions over the years 1976–87 in the PSID.[8] The dependent variable is the logarithm of wages. A rich set of independent variables (listed in Table 12.9) is chosen to provide the information to verify or contradict the implications described above.

Table 12.3 indicates that:

Table 12.3   Wage functions with interactions (1976–87)

Variables	All	Young	Variables	All	Young
PG (1970–9)	6.50	4.68	PG (1970–9) × RQT	n.s.	0.044
	(15.4)	(8.2)			(2.1)
PG (1980–5)	−8.28)	−5.96	PG (1980–5) × RQT	0.027	2.05
	(7.7)	(3.3)		(2.8)	(9.6)
EG (1960–79)	0.011	0.012	PG (1970–9) × X	0.054	n.s.
	(1.7)	(2.4)		(2.6)	
RQT[a]	0.011	0.030	PG (1980–5) × X	0.075	n.s.
	(10.5)	(11.7)		(3.8)	
PG (1970–79) × Ed[b]	n.s.	n.s.			
PG (1980–5) × Ed	0.52	0.35			
	(6.8)	(2.7)			

Notes
[a] 1976 *RQT* in 1976 job, 1978 *RQT* in 1978 job, and 1985 *RQT* in 1985 job.
All other years indexed by dummy = 1, if in other jobs.
[b] Interactions with Education (*Ed*), Training (*RQT*), and Experience (*X*) are estimated in separate equations.
Other independent variables listed in Table 12.7.

(a)   In the short run, higher productivity growth reduces wages in the sector *relative* to wages in other sectors. But in the longer run, this effect reverses: the coefficient on *PG* (1980–5) is negative, but positive on *PG* (1970–9).

(b)   Sectors with more-rapid productivity growth show higher wages of more-educated workers *relative* to those of less-educated workers, suggesting higher rates of return to education in these sectors: the coefficients on the interaction variable *Ed* × *PG* are positive and significant in concurrent growth, but not significant in longer run or lagged *PG*. Interestingly, Gill's findings in the CPS data suggest that fast *PG* growth was associated with *higher* wages of workers with education above high school and *lower* wages of workers with high school or below.

(c)   Greater short-run profitability of human capital in progressive sectors shows up also in the greater profitability of accumulated experience and training. This is observed in Table 12.3 in terms of significant positive coefficients of the interaction variable *PG* × *RQT* and *PG* × *X*. The coefficients for younger workers are larger

Table 12.4   *Selectivity of industry movers: males, PSID (1971–85), hourly earnings before moving related to PG at destination*

Alternatives	All Gross	Net*	Young workers ($X \leq 12$) Gross	Net
PG (1960–79)	3.40	3.03	3.05	1.49
	(3.4)	(2.0)	(2.6)	(1.5)
PG (1970–9)	2.63	1.10	2.33	0.96
	(3.8)	(1.8)	(2.8)	(1.4)
PG (1980–5)	n.s.	n.s.	n.s.	n.s.

Notes
Other variables: *Ed, X, X², Mar, Union, Race, Unemployment*

> than for older workers, as might be expected. Effects on growth of wages with experience (coefficients of interaction $PG \times X$) are significant for all workers, but not for younger workers.

The greater profitability of human capital in the more (technologically) progressive sectors was documented here as evidence of higher levels of demand for human capital in such sectors. The greater profitability is the incentive which leads more-able, skilled, and educated workers into these sectors. Table 12.2 shows the outcome of this selectivity but not the labor mobility that leads to it. The positive selectivity of better-educated younger workers does suggest that new labor-force entrants with more schooling are more likely to move to progressive sectors. Is this also true of job changers with higher levels of measured or unmeasured human capital? To some extent, panel (C) of Table 12.2 also answers this question positively, as prior training is more likely to be required of job movers into the more-progressive sectors.

Table 12.4 uses the wage equations to detect both measured and unmeasured selectivity of job movers. Their wage *prior to moving* was regressed on the *PG* of the industry of destination. The 'gross effect' is the coefficient of *PG*, when it is the sole independent variable (col. 1). It is the 'net effect' (col. 2), when additional variables such as education, experience and other variables listed earlier are included or 'standardized for'. The gross effect is positive and significant. It is clearly attributable to higher levels of human capital which is, in part, measured by the left-out variables: the coefficients in col. (2) are cut in half and less significant as the measured variables are added. But they are not zero in col. (2). The 'net effect' here obviously captures the unmeasured dimensions of human capital: greater skills acquired by training or due to ability. Measured by prior wages, workers who are selected into the firms in the higher *PG* sectors are more-productive to begin with, even at given levels of education, experience and so on. This selectivity may well explain also why it is that initially negative effects of *PG* on sectoral wages, at given levels of measured human capital, become positive, instead of vanishing in the longer run. Selectivity in terms of unmeasured 'quality' of workers may well be the answer,[9] in addition to the greater elasticity of demand in the longer run.

5.   Effects of productivity growth on labor turnover

Training received on the job increases productivity and therefore wages. It is likely that such training contains some elements of specificity, that is, that the training is somewhat (or much) more valuable in the firm in which it was received than in other firms: the greatest opportunities for training are likely to exist in firms in which training processes are closely related to and integrated with their production processes. If so, workers trained in the firm are less likely to leave the firm than those trained elsewhere or not trained because they risk a loss in wages. Similarly, employers are more reluctant to lay off such workers, since they invested in their training and would therefore suffer a capital loss.

In a recent study based on the PSID (Mincer, 1988a), I found that workers trained on the job stay longer in the firm and that the more-educated are also likely to be more permanently attached to firms, partly because they are more likely to obtain training. Theoretically, some degree of specificity in training is required for these results to hold.

We found in section 3 that training is more prevalent where productivity growth is more rapid: the technological changes in production processes that underlie productivity growth require training and retraining of workers. This proposition may be questioned: if skills acquired in training become rapidly obsolete, the incentives of workers to invest in training would be reduced. However, if obsolescence is gradual or partial, successive training or retraining would add to skills, and incentives would not be impaired, especially if employers share the training costs.

Although the threat of even partial obsolescence may deter workers from investing in training, firms must persist in technological adaptation to remain competitive, employing workforces with complementary and changing skills. The latter may be achieved either by training workers for flexibility (by rotation) and by retraining, or by greater turnover to replace workers without the new skills with workers who are already knowledge-able, perhaps as a result of recent education. However, if technological adaptation or changes are in some degree firm-specific, the firm will tend to train its workers after initially hiring more-adaptable and -educated workers who, in turn, serve as the 'teachers'. Human-capital management

Table 12.5   Effects of PG on labor turnover (1968–87)

All workers	Separations	Layoffs	Quits
PG (1960–79)	−2.22	−1.20	−0.66
	(6.9)	(6.6)	(2.6)
PG (1980–5)	1.37	0.70	n.s.
	(3.9)	(3.6)	
EG (1960–79)	0.016	0.005	0.008
	(5.5)	(3.2)	(3.3)
Young workers			
PG (1960–79)	−1.92	−1.22	n.s.
	(3.5)	(3.8)	
PG (1980–5)	n.s.	0.43	n.s.
		(1.4)	
EG (1960–79)	0.011	n.s.	0.007
	(2.3)		(1.8)

Notes
Other variables: *Educ, X, X^2, Married, Union, Race, Nat'l unemployment.*
n.s. = not significant.

in Japanese firms illustrates these responses under conditions of most-rapid productivity growth in recent times.[10] Qualitatively similar adjustments characterize high productivity growth sectors in the US. To the extent that educational upgrading is the initial response in US firms, turnover may even increase as productivity growth accelerates, but with persistent progress and established training processes, turnover should decline.

We have seen in Table 12.2 that the response to faster productivity growth is an increase in the proportion of educated workers, while the longer-run response is an increase in training. Table 12.5 shows that turnover (separation) rates behave correspondingly. They decline in the sectors with long-run high rates of productivity growth, and increase in the sectors with concurrently accelerating productivity growth. This short-run effect is mainly due to greater layoffs. In the long run, both quits and especially layoffs are lower in the progressive sectors.

An interpretation of these findings is that, in the short run, rapid technological changes increase layoffs of less-qualified and corresponding hiring of better-qualified workers. Some of the new hires may have come

Table 12.6   Incidence of unemployment (1968–87)

	All	Young	All movers	Young movers
PG (1970–9)	−3.32	−2.91	−2.11	−1.72
	(16.0)	(7.7)	(4.0)	(2.8)
PG (1980–5)	−0.58	−0.94	n.s.	n.s.
	(1.5)	(1.4)		
EG (1960–79)	−0.012	−0.014	−0.015	n.s.
	(5.2)	(3.4)	(1.9)	

Note
Other independent variables listed in Table 12.7.

from other firms within the sector, which shows up in increased quits of the more-educated and otherwise qualified workers in the sector. Other new hires of more-qualified workers came from labor-force entrants and other better-qualified movers into sectors with higher rates of productivity growth, as was indicated in Tables 12.2 and 12.4. In the longer run, when training activities increase in high productivity growth sectors, separation rates in them decrease. Even then, layoffs are reduced more than quits. The asymmetry in effects on quits and layoffs which appears here is not observed in effects of training which is not linked to technological change.[11] The likely reason, already stated, is that firms adopting technological innovations tend to finance much of the training of workers, who may be more reluctant to invest in such training in view of looming obsolescence. The larger share of investments by firms deters layoffs more than quits.

6.   Effects on unemployment

The reduction in turnover, and especially in layoffs, implies that the incidence of (permanent) unemployment[12] is also likely to decline among experienced workers, at least in the longer run. This is because the probability of encountering unemployment $P(u)$ is a product of the probability of separating from a job $P(s)$ and of the conditional probability of becoming unemployed when separated $P(u/s)$. Table 12.5 showed that $P(s)$ declines in the longer run but increases in the short run, especially among older workers. Thus, unless $P(u/s)$ increases as much as or more than $P(s)$ declines, $P(u)$ must decline.

Table 12.6 shows the predicted effect: unemployment incidence $P(u)$ declines in sectors with rapidly growing productivity in the long run among all workers, including job movers $P(u/s)$, but not in the short run. These findings hold for unemployment which includes temporary layoffs.

The probability or incidence of unemployment $P(u)$ is not the same thing as the unemployment rate (u). Does productivity growth affect the latter as well? To answer this we must observe the effects of *PG* on the *duration* $d(u)$ of unemployment, since – ignoring periods of non-participation in the labor force – the unemployment rate is the product of $P(u)$ and $d(u)$.[13] *A priori*, there is little reason to expect any effects on duration since *PG* increases the demand for labor in some sectors and reduces it in others. Indeed, no effects on duration were observed. Consequently, the unemployment rate behaves very much like the incidence of unemployment.

The right-hand panel of Table 12.6 shows that the incidence of unemployment $P(u)$ is lower in high *PG* sectors in the longer run, though not significantly in the short run. The incidence here is that of experiencing some unemployment during the year, which necessarily includes recall unemployment. The right-hand panel is an imperfect portrayal of conditional unemployment $P(u/s)$ using unemployment during the year in which a job change occurred. This was negatively related to *PG* in the longer run; positively, but not significantly in the short run. Although $P(u)$ here is not quite commensurate with $P(u/s)$, as the former includes recall unemployment and the latter does not, the findings of the effects of *PG* on unemployment are consistent with those on separations: unemployment *declines* in progressive sectors after a few initial years during which it is either unaffected or perhaps increasing.

Unemployment declines also in consequence of growth in capital intensity but the extent to which this effect is confounded with (*PG*) effects is not quite clear.

The findings that, except for a few initial years, technological change *tends to reduce* unemployment in technologically progressive sectors runs counter to the widely held fear of the 'specter of technological unemployment'. Economic theorists from Ricardo to Hicks held 'technological unemployment' to be likely in the short run though less likely in the longer run. Because workers' fear of technological displacement is not uncommon, our finding that, *on average*, unemployment in progressive sectors is lower in the longer run and *not significantly higher*, if at all, in the short run may seem surprising. Yet what previous analyses overlooked is that two processes are set off by technological changes: a waning series of job displacements and a waxing process of worker adaptation which makes their attachments to the firm more durable. Our data suggest that the two forces almost cancel in the short run, and that the second – due to human capital responses – dominates in the long run.[14]

Table 12.7

A.   Dependent variables: sample sizes, means, and standard deviations (PSID, 1968–85, pooled)

Variables	All	Young
Ed-Dum 1 if EDUCI > 12	0.43	0.510
	(0.49)	(0.50)
Learn76	0.54	0.57
	(0.49)	(0.49)
Prior training 76–78–85 combined	10.18	4.29
	(9.45)	(3.25)
Logwage	1.44	1.34
	(0.44)	(0.42)
Sepn	0.16	0.25
	(0.37)	(0.43)
Quit	0.09	0.14
	(0.29)	(0.35)
Layf	0.07	0.09
	(0.24)	(0.29)
Conditional quit	0.54	0.56
	(0.50)	(0.50)
Conditional unemployment	0.48	0.48
	(0.50)	(0.50)
Incidence of unemployment (recall excl)	0.08	0.12
Incidence of unemployment (recall incl)	0.17	0.22
	(0.37)	(0.41)
Duration of unempl in wks	11.86	11.35
	(0.50)	(0.50)
Incidence of unemployment (recall excl)	0.08	0.12
	(0.27)	(0.33)
Duration of unempl in wks	11.86	11.35
	(11.72)	(10.99)

B.   Independent variables: sample sizes, means and standard deviations

Variables	All	Young
Educ yrs of education	12.75	13.33
	(2.78)	(2.35)
Exp yrs of experience	16.80	6.85
	(10.90)	(3.29)
Ten tenure	7.78	2.98
	(8.36)	(2.91)
Preexp Exp-ten	9.35	4.181
	(8.64)	(3.17)
Marital status	0.87	0.80
	(0.33)	(0.40)
Race 1 = Black 0 = White	0.07	0.07
	(0.25)	(0.25)
Union membership	0.28	0.24
	(0.45)	(0.43)
National unemp rate	6.84	6.89
	(1.68)	(1.61)
RQT	2.32	1.72
	(5.41)	(4.60)
EG	2.00	2.01
	(1.22)	(1.31)
PG(1970–9)	0.53	0.48
	(1.18)	(1.20)
PG(1980–5)	0.37	0.39
	(1.22)	(1.20)
PG(1970–9)*Ed*	6.76	6.17
	(14.88)	(15.21)
PG(1980–5)*Ed*	3.97	4.42
	(15.78)	(15.53)
PG(1970–9)*RQT*	1.15	0.83
	(7.32)	(6.10)
PG(1980–5)*RQT*	0.74	0.53
	(9.30)	(8.69)
PG(1970–9)*X*	9.57	3.44
	(24.80)	(9.85)
PG(1980–5)*X*	6.34	2.62
	(27.38)	(9.39)

Note
Sample size was 1279 in 1979, of which 576 had 12 or less years of experience, 703 had more than 12 years. The average number of job changers was 260 per year.

7.   Summary of findings

The hypothesis that recent technological change is biased toward human capital is tested on 18 US industrial sectors using annual PSID data on the male labor force in 1968–87 and Jorgenson–Fraumeni productivity growth indexes for the period 1960–85.

Consistent with this hypothesis, the PSID data show that a more rapid pace of technology (indexed by *PG*) in a sector generates an increased demand for education and training of the sectoral workforce:

(a)   The share of educated workers is raised concurrently without much of an initial effect on training. In the longer run the use of training increases.

(b)   Relative wages rise for more-educated workers within sectors with rapid productivity growth concurrently.

(c)   Mobility of educated, especially young, workers into these sectors is observable and appears to erode much of the educational wage gains a decade later.

(d)   Wage profiles are steeper in progressive sectors as profitability of training and experience increase.

(e)   Separation rates increase slightly in the short run. They decline in the longer run, presumably because training intensifies.

(f)   The probability of unemployment and unemployment rates are unaffected in the short run, but decline rather soon.

All these findings can be viewed as responses of firms to skill-biased technological change. This is true of the utilization and wage effects and, with an additional assumption, of the turnover and unemployment effects. The additional assumption is a degree of firm specificity in training investments necessitated by changing technology or, more precisely, significant employer investments in such training.

Not shown in the tables are some previous attempts to explore effects of the capital–skill complementarity, *given the rate of productivity growth.*[15] These yielded some positive and some ambiguous results: capital intensity growth was measured by growth of the sectoral capital–labor ratio. It showed positive effects on utilization of educated labor, but effects on training and on wages were not visible. Effects on turnover and on unemployment were negative. All these effects were weaker in revised data. It is in any case problematic whether the capital–skill complementarity does not really reflect the technological bias, as new capital is likely to embody new technology.

We should note that the sectoral effects are relative to other sectors, and do not imply similar aggregate effects. Thus higher wages or lower unemployment in progressive sectors are observed *relative* to wages and unemployment in lagging sectors, and the latter may dominate the aggregate. But this is surely not the sense in which 'the specter of technological unemployment' has been perceived or analyzed. Indeed, with the growth of the 'open' economy, that is of world trade, these perceptions are changing, and the specter of technological unemployment is now more likely to be seen to threaten technologically lagging rather than leading sectors or countries. This is clearly exemplified by what would be a paradox under the old perception, namely that Japan, the country that experienced the most rapid productivity growth in recent decades, also had the lowest unemployment rates.

Some applications

(a)   The remarkably low labor turnover rate (and related unemployment rate) in Japan has attracted a great deal of attention. Often exaggerated as 'life-time employment' it is frequently described as a reflection of a culture which puts great emphasis on loyalty. Yet, in the same culture, turnover rates were a great deal higher prior to the Second World War. The difference is the remarkably rapid technological progress in Japan since 1950. The technological catch-up required sizable investments in human capital in schools and in enterprises. The phenomenal growth of educational attainment in Japan in the recent decades is well known. The even more intense effort to adapt, train, and retrain workers for continuous rapid technological changes is not directly visible in available data. However, effects of training on wage growth and turnover are visible in a negative relation between the two within industrial sectors observed in Japan and in the US. This was shown in a study by Mincer and Higuchi (1988). The same study showed that industries with more-rapid productivity growth had both steeper individual wage profiles and lesser turnover rates. Indeed, using the parameters of those relations, a four-fold rate of productivity growth in Japan compared to the US in the 1960–80 period predicted rather well the over three-fold steeper wage profiles and the less than one-third frequency of firm separations in Japan.

(b)   Current research suggests that technological change produces market demands for human capital. More research across sectors, periods and countries is needed for more-complete verification of the hypothesis. Even at this stage, the evidence suggests a resolution of a long-standing puzzle, that of no secular decline in rates of return to education[16] in the face of continuous upward trends in education: without growing demands by industry for educated and skilled workers, increasing supplies of such workers would depress educational differentials in wages to the point where rates of return to educational investments would fall to zero or below. But, if growing demands by industry are a major factor in inducing increasing supplies of educated labor, the profitability of education can be maintained in the long run at levels roughly comparable to that of other investments.[17]

Notes

1. An exposition of this view is contained in Mincer (1984). (Chapter 10 in this volume.)
2. Griliches (1969).
3. According to Jorgenson (1989), the contribution of labor quality over the period 1947–85 to annual growth of output per hour worked in the US was about two-thirds of the contribution of the (physical) capital stock per hour worked.
4. Griliches and Lichtenberg (1984) found that R&D intensities are positively correlated with productivity growth (*PG*) across industries. This lends support to the use of *PG* measures in the present study.
5. Here the data are grouped by industry averages for 1970–9 pooled with averages for 1980–5. Each variable therefore contains $2 \times 18 = 36$ observations. Panels (B) and (C) of Table 12.2 and all subsequent tables contain ungrouped individual observations.
6. The question was: 'Are you learning on the job, so that you could be promoted, or get a better job?'
7. For evidence see Lillard and Tan (1986), and Mincer (1988a).
8. Prior to 1976 wage rates at the point of the survey are not available. An inferior proxy, average hourly earnings in the preceding year, is used in Table 12.4.
9. Tables 12.3 and 12.4 suggest that in studying inter-industry wage differentials, technical change and training activities should be explored, explicitly if feasible. One attempt to do just that is unpublished work by Eng-Seng-Loh (1991).
10. See Mincer and Higuchi (1988). For additional evidence, see Mincer and Jovanovic (Chapter 5 of this volume), and Topel (1990).
11. Mincer (1988a).
12. 'Permanent' unemployment is defined as one which results in job change.
13. Mincer (1988b).
14. Training and retraining responses appear to be quicker in Japan where productivity growth has been much more rapid than in the US in the recent (post-1950) decades. In Japan all the 'longer-run' effects show up in the concurrent decade (Mincer and Higuchi, 1988).
15. These findings were included in a previous version which appeared as an NBER Working Paper.
16. In the short run rates fluctuate a great deal, as swings in the past decade indicate.
17. Based on data for 60 countries, Psacharapoulos (1985) finds that rates of return to education are somewhat higher than rates of return to physical capital in LDCs and only slightly lower in advanced countries.

References

Bartel, A. and F. Lichtenberg (1987), 'The Comparative Advantage of Educated Workers in Implementing New Technology', *Review of Economics and Statistics*, February.

Becker, G. S. (1975), *Human Capital*, 2nd edn, Chicago: University of Chicago Press.

Conrad, K. and D. W. Jorgenson (1985), *Sectoral Productivity Gaps, 1960–1979*, Department of Economics, Harvard University Reprint.

Eng Seng Loh (1991), 'Technological Changes, Training, and the Inter-industry Wage Structure', Kent State University.

Gill, I. (1988), 'Technological Change, Education and Obsolescence of Human Capital', University of Chicago, paper prepared for NBER Summer Institute.

Griliches, Z. (1969), 'Capital–Skill Complementarity', *Review of Economics and Statistics*.

Griliches, Z. and F. Lichtenberg (1984), 'Interindustry Technology Flows and Productivity Growth', *Review of Economics and Statistics*, May.

Jorgenson, D. (1989), 'Comment', at Conference on Economic Growth, SUNT Buffalo.

Jorgenson, D., F. Gollop and B. Fraumeni (1987), *Productivity and U.S. Economic Growth*, Cambridge, Mass.: Harvard University Press, updated series, 1990.

Jorgenson, D., M. Kuroda and M. Nishimizu (1986), *Japan–US Industry Level Comparisons, 1960–1979*, Harvard University, Economics Department Discussion Paper no. 1254.

Lillard, L. and H. Tan (1986), 'Training: Who Gets It and What Are Its Effects', Rand Corp. R-3331-DOL, March.

Mincer, J. (1984), 'Human Capital and Economic Growth', *Economics of Education Review*, vol. 3, no. 3. (Chapter 10 of this volume.)

Mincer, J. (1986), 'Wage Changes in Job Changes', in *Research in Labor Economics*, ed. R. Ehrenberg, Greenwich, CT: JAI Press. (Chapter 6 of this volume.)

Mincer, J. (1988a), 'Job Training, Wage Growth, and Labor Turnover', NBER Working Paper no. 2690. (Chapter 8 of this volume.)

Mincer, J. (1988b), 'Education and Unemployment', NCEE Paper. (Chapter 7 of this volume.)

Mincer, J. and Higuchi, Y. (1988), 'Wage Structures and Labor Turnover in the U.S. and in Japan', *Journal of the Japanese and International Economics*, June. (Chapter 11 of this volume.)

Nelson, R. and E. Phelps (1967), 'Investment in Humans, Technological Diffusion, and Economic Growth', *American Economic Review*, May.

Psacharopoulos, G. (1985), 'Returns to Education: an International Update', *Journal of Human Resources*, Fall.

Schultz, T. W. (1975), 'The Value of the Ability to Deal with Disequilibria', *Journal of Economic Literature*.

Solow, R. M. (1957), 'Technical Change and the Aggregate Production Function', *Review of Economics and Statistics*, August.

Tan, H. (1987), 'Technical Change and its Consequences for Training and Earnings', Rand Corp., *mimeo*.

Topel, R. (1990), 'Specific Capital, Mobility, and Wages', NBER Working Paper no. 3294 March.

Welch, F. (1970), 'Education in Production', *Journal of Political Economy*.

13 Human capital, technology, and the wage structure: what do time series show?*

1. Long-term stability and short-term changes in the profitability of education

The effect of education on earnings was the initial and continues to be the central subject of research in the economic analysis of education. The gain in earnings associated with an additional year of education is viewed as a return on the investment costs of the additional year. This return, expressed as a percent gain in wages obtainable without the investment, is the educational (relative) wage differential or the 'educational premium'. The same annual return, expressed as a ratio to the investment costs, is the (marginal) rate of return to education, a measure of education's profitability.

In competitive labor markets, higher wages associated with a higher level of education correspond to the greater productivity of that labor. However, with no other changes, increased supplies of educated labor reduce its marginal product, therefore the educational wage differential. Thus rapid growth of education relative to demand for it reduces its profitability while slow or no growth increases it. Changing profitabilities in turn represent incentives for subsequent changes in supply: enrollments decrease when profitability declines, and once the market experiences a significant decline in the relative supply of educated labor, educational wage differentials return back to a normal or equilibrium[1] level of profitability. Rates of return to education can also increase with unchanging supplies, when demand for educated labor increases, either because demand for its services or products increases or because its productivity grows as a result of technological changes. Again, supply adjustment is induced as described before, pushing profitability rates back to equilibrium. The time lag between the impulse of high or low profitabilities and their return to normal involves a supply adjustment which tends to be lengthy: for example, in response to an increased profitability of college education more high school graduates enter college. It takes at least four years to graduate and several more years until the increased supply of

*This chapter is a previously unpublished paper presented at the Conference on Research and Development, 1991, Jerusalem; National Bureau of Economic Research (NBER) Working Paper no. 3581; revised 1991.

college graduates reduces the wage differential to a level at which relative supplies stabilize if no further impulses intervene.

The usual estimates of rates of return to an additional year of education run between 5–10 per cent. These magnitudes are consistent with the investment interpretation, as they are comparable to rates on alternative capital investments. Sporadic estimates of rates of return to education in the US, based mainly on data in the late 1950s and the 1960s, left an impression of temporal stability. However, the decline in the educational wage premia in the mid- to late 1970s (Freeman, 1976) and even greater rebound in the 1980s (Murphy and Welch, 1989) led to intensive ongoing research on what seem to be unprecedented changes in the past two decades in the US.

Data on long-run changes here and abroad (Becker, 1975; Psacharopoulos, 1985) indicate relatively small reductions in the rates of return to education over many decades of growth in educational attainment.

Two questions are posed by these facts on educational wage premia: (a) what explains the absence of a significant downward long-term trend in the profitability of education, given massive increases in supplies of educated workers?; and (b) what explains the rather dramatic swing in the wage premium in the US during the past two decades?

The economists' answer to the first question is a conjecture based on a generally accepted hypothesis that downward pressures on profitability due to increase in supply of educated labor are counteracted by long-term growth in the demand for educated labor. In this view, the massive growth of educational attainment represents, in large measure, a continuous response to growth in profitability of education engendered by growing demand. Profitability is kept in check – near equilibrium levels – as an outcome of these private and social supply responses. Unfortunately, empirical work on factors generating long-term trends in the demand for educated workers and on documenting the supply responses is only in its infancy. More work has been done on shorter-term fluctuations in demand and on supply responses in particular occupations (mainly by Freeman).

It is generally acknowledged that the basic reason for the secular growth of education is economic growth. That education, conversely, contributes to economic growth is not a contradiction – the relation is partly reciprocal. The positive effects of economic growth on educational attainment are due to growth of income which leads to increases in private and public expenditures on education, as it does to an increase in consumption expenditures on most other goods and services. This is so whether education is viewed as skill- or culture-enhancing. This income effect obviously results in an increase in the supply of educated workers with consequent downward pressure on profitability. The counteracting growth of industrial demands for educated workers originates from the production side: (a) the growth of quantity and quality of physical capital (machines and equipment) per worker; and (b) improvements in technology which can increase output without changes in inputs, that is increase total (or multi-) factor productivity. Both are mainsprings of economic growth and each one generates increases in demand for human capital under plausible conditions: (a) for growth of physical capital to have this effect it must be less substitutable (or more complementary) for educated (skilled) than for less-skilled labor. Econometric studies by Griliches (1969), and by Hamermesh and Grant (1979) appear to support this hypothesis of a positive skill bias of physical capital accumulation; (b) for new technology to have a similar effect, it must be skill-biased. A growing body of recent economic research is consistent with the older proposition that more-schooled (Nelson and Phelps, 1966; Welch, 1970; and Schultz, 1975) and -trained workers more readily muster the new technologies. Thus, Bartel and Lichtenberg (1987) using Census data report that relatively more-educated workers are employed in those manufacturing industries (in 1960, 1970, and 1980) where capital equipment was newer and R&D (research and development) expenditures were more intensive.

That this is due to a greater demand for educated workers is confirmed by findings of higher relative wages of better-educated workers in such industries, compared to other industries.

These findings were reported in my recent study (Mincer, 1989a) of PSID data in which I related indices of demand for educated workers, such as their utilization, relative wages, wage growth with tenure, turnover, and unemployment, to decade-long averages of the pace of technology. For the latter I used Jorgenson's total factor productivity (TFP) indexes.[2] The cross-industry findings showed higher levels of demand for human capital in progressive sectors in the 1960s and 1970s. Similar results concerning effects on relative educational wage differentials within industries were found in Census data by Gill (1989).

In order to explore the effects of capital–skill complementarily I used the sectoral (decade-long) growth of capital intensity as a variable, in addition to the productivity-growth variable. The effects on utilization of educated labor were positive, but no relative educational wage effects were visible within sectors. The effects may be confounded, as newer vintages of capital contain new technology. Consequently, the skill bias of technology may to some extent reflect the skill bias of capital and conversely.

In a previous study (Mincer and Higuchi, 1988) we have shown that differences between the US and Japan in rates of technological change (measured by national and sectoral TFP indexes) can explain why wage structures (and turnover rates) differ in and between the two countries.

All the studies cited are sectoral (industry) cross-sections. While they are strongly suggestive in showing a positive association between the pace of technology in a sector (measured by various proxies) and indices of relative demand for educated workers in the sector, they do not – by themselves – establish a causal relation nor the direction of causality. For the interpretation to be more compelling, the analysis must be cast in a time-series format to determine whether changes in the pace of technology are followed by corresponding changes in educational differentials, and whether inferences based on sectors hold up in the aggregate – a notion that is often misleading.

The cross-section studies point to technology-induced demand for human capital as a likely answer to the question about long-term stability of as well as changes in the rate of return to education. With currently available data a time-series approach appears to be feasible and promising for verifying these hypotheses and for estimating the effects of changing demand for human capital.

The question concerning causes of the pronounced shorter term swings in educational wage premia during the past two or three decades requires attention to fluctuations in supply and demand for educated labor, rather than to trends in them. Demand or supply impulses can generate such fluctuations. These can be relatively lengthy, as adjustments proceeding through the educational pipeline take time. If the pace of technology varies over time, its effects as demand 'shifters' ought to be discernible in the time-series of the past 25 years.

Several exogenous events ('shocks') are likely to have caused the gyrations in supply and demand and consequently in rates of return to education in the recent period: (a) on the supply side: influx of the baby boom cohorts into the labor market during the 1970s, and especially of college graduates. Above-trend growth of income and of public subsidies to higher education in the 1960s are basic to the increased supply of college graduates, which was additionally accelerated by the Vietnam War draft exemptions; (b) on the demand side: productivity growth which was substantial in the 1950s and 1960s collapsed to low levels in the 1970s, partly as a result of the emergence of oil cartels and the oil price shocks, but largely for reasons not yet well understood. A partial recovery was evident in the 1980s, but its course or measurement seems uncertain. The suggestion that the pace of technology is implicated in the short as it is in the long run, is a major motivation of the present study; (c) another possible factor on the demand side, first pointed out by Murphy and Welch (1989), is the growth of world trade, hence of international competition, which became pronounced in the 1980s. This resulted in losses of US exports and growth of imports which substituted for domestic production (automobiles and electronics being the most visible examples). The reduced demand for labor put downward pressures on wages and employment in the affected sectors, which are generally less education-intensive than other sectors (such as services, finance and insurance; and so on). The decline in union density which was probably induced by these developments, is another, but not independent, reason for the relative decline in wages of less-educated (high school or below) workers.

It is clear that in order to test the relation between technological change and the demand for education in a time series of wage differentials, it is also necessary to take into account changes in demography and in relative educational supplies. In other words, although the major purpose of this work is to ascertain the reality of technological skill bias in historical changes rather than in cross-sections, empirical research necessitates an investigation of the major forces at play including technological change in the recent changes in the wage structure.

2.   Skill differentials in education and experience, and changes in them: some hypotheses

Since labor-market skills are acquired by learning at school and by learning on the job, changes in demand for skills should affect both wage differentials by education as well as those by labor market experience: increases in the latter need not, however, be of the same size at different levels of education. For example, if technology is biased toward newer vintages of higher education, the experience differential may be smaller at college than at high school levels. Similarly, reductions in demand for less-educated workers resulting from international competition would affect primarily employment and wages of younger workers, with lesser skill and seniority. As a result the experience differential at lower (high school or less) levels would increase relative to the experience differential at college (or above) levels.

The influx of 'baby boomers', and especially of college graduates, into the labor markets of the 1970s, stimulated a research focus on effects of changes in relative supplies on relative wage differentials. The growth of numbers of college graduates relative to numbers of less-educated workers in the 1970s narrowed the (percent) wage differential between college and high school graduates. With the apparent excess supply of college graduates, the US labor force appeared to be 'overeducated'. At the same time, the pronounced increase in the number of young relative to older workers, the 'baby boom' effect, was to widen the experience differentials in wages at all levels of education, and especially at the college level.

The bigger increase of young relative to older workers at the college level was mainly a result of the more rapid increases of numbers of college graduates compared to high school graduates. In other words, changes in relative educational supplies which mainly (initially) affected young cohorts automatically affected relative age distributions differentially in the two groups.

The greater 'youthening' of the college group compared to the high school group is, of course, a result of accelerated college enrollments. Entry of large young cohorts tends to reduce wages of young workers relative to wages of older workers only if substitution in production between older and younger workers is imperfect. No experience differential would arise (though wages of all would be reduced somewhat) if substitution were perfect. If substitution between younger and older workers is weaker among those educated, this could be an additional reason for the greater widening of the age differential in wages ('steepening of the experience profile') of college than of high school graduates in the 1970s – simply as a result of demography and not of 'overeducation'. And this purely demographic effect would at the same time reduce the educational wage differential or the college 'wage premium' among young workers.

As 'baby bust' cohorts entered the labor market in the 1980s and relative supplies of college graduates stopped growing or even decreased, opposite implications should have emerged. Wage profiles should have flattened – more so at college than at high school levels, while the college premium should have risen.

On the demand side, decline of the pace of technology in the 1970s would intensify the decline in rates of return of college graduates already attributed in part to increased supply. Renewed growth of demand for educated workers based on skill-biased technology in the 80s coupled with declines in demand for less-educated workers due to international competition would produce a reversal (growth) in the college wage premium.

The hypotheses spelled out here are not new. They are partly based on findings of current research of a number of labor economists[3] and partly on conjectures which have not as yet been verified. In particular, the role of technology has not been empirically estimated – a major motivation here – nor have analyses been framed in a continuous (year-to-year) time series which is attempted here.

Before I proceed to the empirical analysis, a closer look at the meaning of experience differentials in wages is helpful. The growth of wages with experience as a result of learning on the job is the major factor affecting working age differentials in wages (the 'wage profile') according to human capital theory. The ratio of wages of older to those of younger workers which we study here does not describe wage progress over time within a cohort (a longitudinal concept) but wage differences across different cohorts at a given time (a cross-sectional concept). Differences between the longitudinal and cross-sectional constructs are due to (a) economic growth, and (b) changes in age distributions over time. Economic growth makes the longitudinal profile slope upward even if no learning takes place. Consequently, with stable age distributions, the cross-sectional profile may best reflect the expected wage payoff to learning on the job.[4]

This payoff increases with experience, that is the slope of the cross-sectional profile is steeper in one period than another because more learning (training) takes place, or because the acquired learning has become more profitable. Consequently, once relative demographic supplies are held constant, the experience-wage differentials should move in the same direction as the profitability of education, assuming that the demand for human capital affects both that acquired at school and on the job. In the empirical analysis, therefore, both relative supply variables and demand variables which affect profitability should play a role in creating changes in experience wage differentials.

In this connection there is a question of subsidiary interest: does the demographic change affect learning processes, that is investments in training, and in what direction? Two different theories predict opposite effects: one holds that the opportunity costs of training were reduced by the reduction in wages of the young 'baby boom' workers in the 1970s. The consequent increase in training should have increased longitudinal wage growth in addition to the cross-sectional steepening due to the demographic effect (Welch, 1979). The opposite theory maintains that a decrease in the ratio of teachers (trainers, older workers) to students (trainees, young workers) results in less training per worker (Berger, 1985) and so a flatter longitudinal profile is possible despite the steeper cross-section profile due to the baby boom. The empirical analysis should shed some light on this matter as well.

3. Empirical analysis: data and dependent variables

As already explained, casting the link between technology and human capital in a time-series framework involves an investigation of the changes in the US wage structure in the recent decades for which annual data are available. The changes which continue to attract attention of economists and of others were summarized as: (a) a near-cessation of growth of real wages since the 1970s, coupled with (b) large, decade-long swings in wage differentials among skill groups in the workforce. In particular, the near-cessation of average wage growth was accompanied by declines in real wages of workers with below average skill and education, especially in the

1980s; and (c) wage differentials by age appear to have risen throughout most of the period. Other changes which are not analyzed in this paper are: the switch from a stable sex-differential in wages prior to the mid-1970s to a subsequent narrowing of it; and the exact opposite in the black–white wage differentials. These issues are excluded by restricting the data to white male workers. The current report utilizes data from the March issues of the Current Population Survey (CPS). The data are in the form of averages of logarithms of hourly wages of white, male workers in each single year of experience, with 40 such years in each of the six education groups, in each calendar year from 1963 to 1987.[5]

The wage structure to be analyzed is represented by differences in logarithms of wages across education and experience (age) groups. Such education and experience differentials in wages could be represented as continuous variables which enter non-linearly into the 'human capital' wage function. The coefficients of schooling and of experience in such a function fitted to the data in which logarithms of wages are the dependent variable would indicate both educational and experience (relative) wage differentials, or wage premia of an additional year of each. Time changes in these coefficients would provide time series of the changes to be explained.

However, such a procedure is too restrictive and can distort the measurement of wage differentials and, especially, of their time pattern, if the shapes of the experience-wage profiles of the different education groups are different and change differentially over time, which is the case. A preferred non-parametric approach is to measure the educational-wage differentials by (logs of) ratios of wages of higher to lower education levels in the 6–10 years of experience groups. This (log) ratio or wage premium per year is the best approximation of the rate of return to education, as it is measured roughly at the 'overtaking stage' of the working life.[6] The cross-section (log) ratios of older to younger workers within an education group, in turn, represent the experience differentials, in wages. I use wages of workers with 21–25 years of experience in the numerator and wages of those with 1–5 years of experience in the denominator. Basically, this ratio (in logs) labeled (Dif 51) measures the cross-sectional increase from starting wages in a given education group to the level at which further increases are rather small. As mentioned before, this cross-sectional increase does not correspond to the actual growth of wages within a given cohort, unless the age distribution is fixed and the level of wages does not change over time differentially at the various experience levels. Some attempt is, therefore, made also to explore the within-cohort wage growth of young workers over several years of their actual experience.

Although our complete analysis utilized information on six education

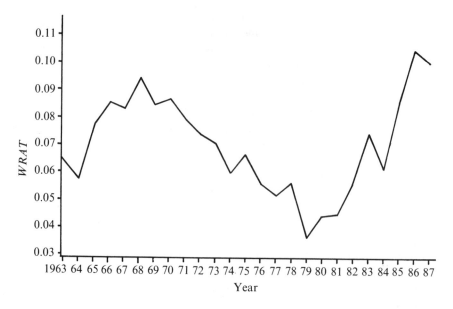

Figure 13.1   Educational wage differentials (college–high school)

groups (years of school < 8, 8–11, 12, 13–15, 16, 17+), we focus primarily on the wage differential between college and high school graduates. The average education level within all other groups changed over time and this would blur the analysis. At any rate, the big differences and changes appear in the dichotomy between lower levels (12 or less) and post-secondary education, and the bulk of that is most clearly captured in comparing graduates of precisely 12 years (high school graduates) with those of 16 years of schooling (college graduates). Indeed, most of the recent studies focus mainly on this comparison for analyses of educational differentials and age (or experience) differentials.

The changing structure of educational and age (experience) wage differentials is portrayed in Figures 13.1 and 13.2. Figure 13.1 shows the changing (per cent) wage differential (per year) between college and high school graduates who had 6–10 years of work experience. This differential rose between 1963 and 1968, it then declined to about half size by 1979 and rose steeply thereafter, more than recovering lost ground by 1986.

Figure 13.2 shows the changing experience differential in wages (difference in log-wages between older and younger workers) for high school graduates in graph marked H and for college graduates in graph marked C. Among high school graduates, this experience 'premium' rises about 25 per cent from the 1960s to the 1970s and continues to rise about twice as

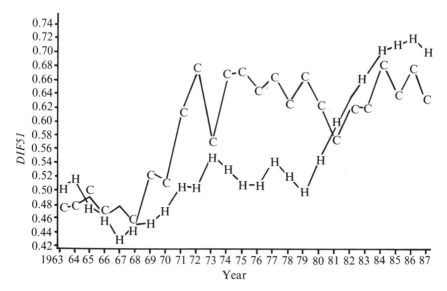

Figure 13.2   Experience wage differentials (college, C. and high school, H)

rapidly in the 1980s. Among college graduates, the pattern is of a steep (about 50 per cent) rise from the late 1960s to the early or mid 1970s, and a rough plateau (slight decline followed by slight increase) thereafter.

It is important to keep in mind the components of the (log) ratios shown in Figures 13.1 and 13.2: these are average levels of wages for groups with 1–5, 6–10, and 21–25 years of labor market experience of male high school and college graduates. All these wages rose in real terms before 1973, though a bit faster for college graduates. After 1973 they declined among young high school graduates, ceased rising for older high school graduates but continued to rise for college graduates.[7] Thus when increases in rates of return to college graduates are attributed to increases in *relative* demand, the latter consists both of increases in demand for college graduates and decreases in demand for high school graduates.

4.   Independent variables: concepts and data
To the extent that workers differing in education and in age (experience) are imperfect substitutes in production, relative supplies exert a negative effect on relative wages. Relative numbers of all college graduates among all males in the population aged 18–64 or of young college graduates among all young people (young defined here as 20–29 years of age) are used as measures of relative supply.[8] Figure 13.3 shows that the relative supply of young college graduates just about doubled between the early

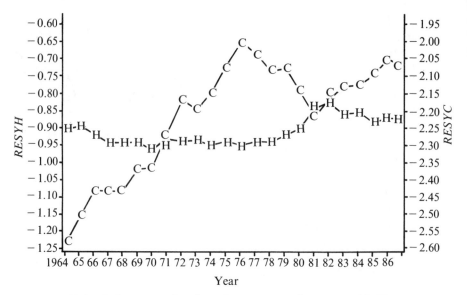

Figure 13.3   Relative supply of graduates in population, age 20–29

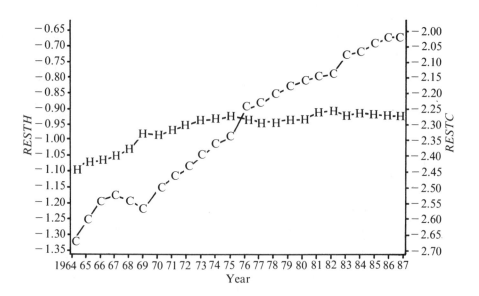

Figure 13.3A   Relative supply of graduates in total population, age 18–64

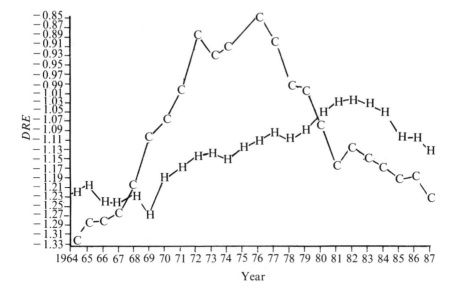

Figure 13.4   Relative cohort sizes

1960s and mid-1970s accelerating between 1968 and 1976. Growth of supply stopped subsequently; indeed the supply of college graduates declined somewhat from 1976 to 1981 and rose mildly thereafter. In contrast, the relative supply of high school graduates declined mildly until the mid-1970s, rose subsequently (as fewer students proceeded to college) and stabilized since about 1982. These changes are consistent with the changes in the wage differentials between college and high school graduates (Figure 13.1) but only partially explain the latter, as the regression analysis shows.

Relative supplies of young and older workers, among high school and college graduates respectively, are shown in Figure 13.4. These are ratios of numbers of young (age 20–29) to all graduates with the same educational level. The growth of young (relative) to all college graduates is rapid (about 50 per cent) between 1964 and 1974. The subsequent relative decline is equally steep and continuous after 1977. Clearly, a steepening of the college cross-section wage profile down to the mid or later 1970s is expected on this account, and is indeed observed. But instead of declining, the ratios of wages of older to younger college graduates subsequently stabilize (Figure 13.2). Changes in relative supplies of young high school graduates are milder: after a slight decline in the 1960s, the proportion increases mildly until about 1980, and declines mildly subsequently.

Again, the corresponding changes in the wage profile by age (Figure 13.2) are consistent up to the late 1970s, but the continued and strong steepening of the profile thereafter is inconsistent with the expected effects of relative supplies.

Of primary interest among variables affecting relative demands for skills is a measure of the pace of technology. This factor, according to previous work,[9] is skill-biased. It widens the educational wage differentials when the pace quickens. In the study of the effects of technological change on the demand for human capital (skills) across industrial sectors I utilized indexes of growth of multi-factor productivity (*PG*) constructed by Jorgenson *et al.* (1987). Their major merit for the purpose at hand was that they represent changes in productivity, given quality-adjusted labor and capital inputs. This means that the residual which measures growth in productivity is not attributable to human capital thus avoiding a spurious correlation between the two variables. To the extent that the residually measured productivity growth is affected by technology, it may serve as a proxy variable in relating technology to changes in demand for human capital. The well-known problem with the productivity growth indexes is that they reflect other factors than technology, such as economies and diseconomies of scale, business cycles in capacity utilization, and labor hoarding. Perhaps worst of all is the pronounced year-to-year volatility, reflecting errors of measurement due to the residual nature (differences between output and input growth) of this statistic.

For decade-long cross-sections, averaging the productivity indexes over a decade alleviated both the volatility and the business cycle distortions, leaving a usable, albeit imperfect, empirical variable. However, the problem is more acute for annual time series analysis in the present study. A partial and unsatisfactory (arbitrary) solution is the use of subperiod averages or moving averages of the Jorgenson residual. Subperiod averages provide by Jorgenson and Fraumeni are shown in Figure 13.5. A preferred alternative index of the pace of technology in the current study is based on annual aggregated expenditures on R&D (research and development). The Bartel and Lichtenberg cross-section study (1987) showed that sectoral (industry) R&D intensity (ratio of R&D expenditures to sales) could serve as an index of demand for educated labor – affecting its utilization and wages in the industry cross-section.

The conceptual advantage of R&D measures is that they more directly represent sources and application of new technology to productive processes, rather than their partial reflection in productivity growth, even if the latter were measured without error. As many studies have shown, effects of R&D on productivity growth are substantial. About one-third of multi-factor productivity growth is attributable to R&D, according to a

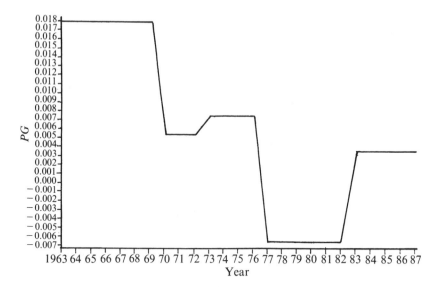

Figure 13.5 Total factor productivity growth

recent Bureau of Labour Statistics (BLS) review (1989). The impact, however, is likely to vary over time and across industries, especially as between privately and government-sponsored R&D. A weakness of the R&D index at the sectoral level is that it leaves out interindustry spillovers which augment the R&D effects in the aggregate. For the purpose of the present study, conducted on the aggregate level, sectoral differences and spillovers cause no problems. Neither does the distinction between privately and government-sponsored R&D create problems, since the effects on demand for educated labor – if the innovations are skill biased – does not depend much on the particular application of the new technology: in all cases various sources of demand compete for the same supply of, say, engineers and scientists. Figure 13.6 shows the time series of real annual expenditures per worker[10] on R&D from all sources, based on the BLS (1989) data.

The time series of R&D per worker shown in Figure 13.6 has some similarity to the step function of the *PG* index (Figure 13.5), mainly in the decline from the late 1960s to about 1980. But the rise thereafter is much smaller for *PG* than for R&D, suggesting a weakening effect of the latter on measured productivity growth, but not necessarily on the *relative* demand for educated labor. Indeed, the time pattern of R&D (Figure 13.6) is strikingly closer to the pattern of educational wage differentials shown in Figure 13.1, than to the *PG* series in Figure 13.5.

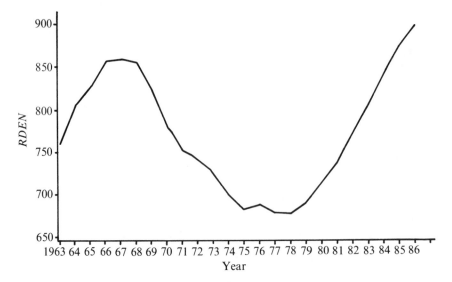

*Figure 13.6   Research and development expenditures per worker
(1982 dollars)*

Two other indexes of relative demand for educated workers are: a measure of the impact of the growth of international trade; the net balance of merchandise trade as proportion of total output (*RNE*), shown in Figure 13.7. Here losses of exports and replacement of domestic production by import reduced demand for labor, mainly in goods producing (manufacturing) industries. The affected sectors are less education-intensive than service producing industries. The decline in unionism, especially important in manufacturing industries, is likely to have been a result of declining demand for labor in them, contributing to the widening of the educational-wage differential in the 1980s. It is not used here as a variable because of its suspected endogeneity. Another variable that is used, despite its partial endogeneity, is the ratio of service to goods employment (*RSG*), shown in Figure 13.8: service industries are the major employer of educated workers. Growth of service relative to goods employment is a longer-term trend which appears to reflect demand more than supply trends, as is partly evidenced by the differential growth in real wages in the two sectors.

The growing demand for skills in service jobs is partly driven by the growth of information technologies. This is best illustrated by the growing use of computers. The number of computer workstations has increased from less than 1 million in 1976 to 28 million in 1986, or from 15 to 450 per

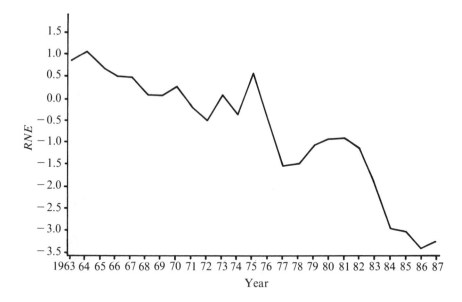

Figure 13.7   Balance of merchandise trade (ratio to GNP)

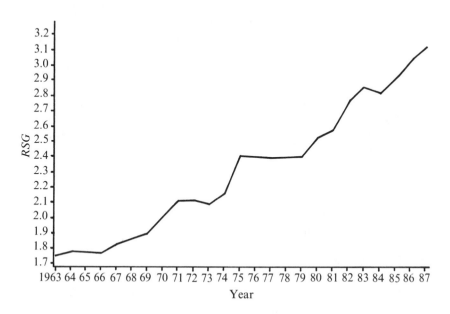

Figure 13.8   Ratio of service to goods employment

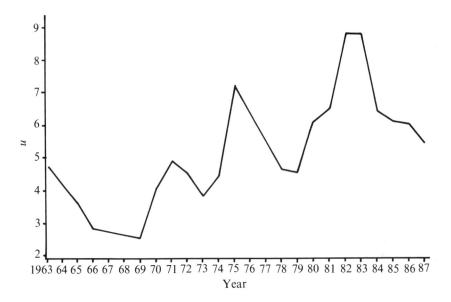

Figure 13.9   Aggregate unemployment rates

thousand white-collar workers – roughly doubling the use per worker every two years (Cyert and Mowery, 1987).

The negative export balance was small prior to the 1980s, but grew rapidly in the past decade. The ratio of service to goods employment, however, shows mainly a continuous upward trend over the whole period (and before).

Note that the relative supply variables are different in the analysis of the educational wage structure and in the experience wage structure. But the relevant demand variables are likely to be the same as they affect the profitability of human capital acquired at school and on the job, especially if their impact is stronger among younger than among older workers. One demand index, as yet not mentioned, which may affect the experience differentials and the educational differentials in wages is the business cycle. As indexes of the latter I tried to utilize unemployment rates (figure 13.9) or capacity utilization rates.

5.   Regression analysis
Table 13.1 lists the variables employed in the regressions, their abbreviated symbols, as well as their means and standard deviations. Their construction and sources are indicated in Table 13.1A. We now turn to the description of findings, showing the 'effects' (regression coefficients) of the

Table 13.1   Descriptive statistics

Variable	Label	Mean	Standard deviation
WRAT	Ratio of C to HS wages	0.0699986	0.0179855
DIF51H	Ratio of wages of older to young for H	0.5480032	0.0901616
DIF51C	Ratio of wages of older to young for C	0.5903232	0.0803022
LNWYH	Log wages of young HS graduates	2.0174320	0.1148710
LNWOH	Log wages of older HS graduates	2.4925520	0.0619754
LNWYC	Log wages of young C graduates	2.3145088	0.0627982
LNWOC	Log wages of older C graduates	2.8766680	0.0799420
W3GH	3-year wage growth, young HS	0.0363590	0.0231209
W3GC	3-year wage growth, young C	0.0463413	0.0271777
RESYH	Ratio of yng HS grads to tot. yng pop.	-0.9122227	0.0395294
RESYC	Ratio of yng C grads to tot. yng pop.	-2.2172216	0.1675379
RESTH	Ratio of all HS grads to tot. pop.	-0.9625125	0.0581968
RESTC	Ratio of all C grads to tot. pop.	-2.3146855	0.2097672
DREH	Ratio of yng HS grads to tot. HS grads	-1.1380589	0.0722243
DREC	Ratio of yng C grads to tot. C grads	-1.0908849	0.1506778
DR	Ratio of young to total population	-1.1883487	0.1092755
PG	Total factor productivity growth	0.0059040	0.0091330
RDE	Expenditures on R&D per employee	771.9550087	70.2909693
RNE	Ratio of net exports to GNP	-0.7573694	1.3391780
RSG	Ratio of emp in serv. to gds. industries	2.3088832	0.4377514
U	Unemployment rate	5.0760000	1.7325992

Note
All ratios expressed as differences in logarithms

hypothesized explanatory variables on (a) educational wage premia, and (b) experience wage differentials, over the 25-year period for which data were collected.

Table 13.2   Educational wage differentials (college – high school)

Variables	Coefficients				
	(1)	(2)	(3)	(4)	(5)
Intercept	−0.09	−0.59	−0.41	0.06	−0.14
	(1.4)	(3.4)	(4.6)	(1.0)	(3.5)
$RESY_{-2}$	−0.065				
	(2.2)				
$REST_{-3}$		−0.086	−0.080	0.081	0.002
		(1.9)	(3.0)	(1.1)	(0.2)
DR_{-2}		−0.20		−0.14	
		(4.6)		(2.7)	
PG	1.12	0.45		0.88	
	(2.2)	(1.00)		(1.9)	
$R\&D_{-2}$			0.00024		0.00025
			(12.3)		(9.0)
RNE	−0.011				
	(4.5)				
RSG		0.088	0.044		
		(4.1)	(3.5)		
EQ				0.000064	0.000028
				(3.4)	(2.1)
R^2	0.69	0.80	0.91	0.75	0.89
D.W.	1.67	1.61	2.35	1.89	2.45

Notes
t-values in parentheses. Excluded variables not significant. Subscripts $_{-2}$ and $_{-3}$ denote a 2-year and 3-year lag.
D.W. = Durbin–Watson statistics.

Educational wage premia
Table 13.2 presents the regression coefficients for the college wage premium ($WRAT$), the percentage wage gain per year of college, at the 'overtaking stage' (6–10 years) of work experience. More precisely, the dependent variable is the difference in the average logarithms of wage rates per hour of college and high school graduates, based on March surveys of the CPS.

Equation 1 (col. 1) features the effects of the relative educational supply variable ($RESY$) (fraction of population age 20–29 who are college graduates), the Jorgenson productivity index (PG), and (RNE), the net export balance (as a fraction of GNP). The explanatory power, measured by the adjusted R^2, increases from 0.69 to 0.80 in equation 2 (col. 2) in which the relative supply variable (*RESY*) is replaced by two components: the demographic variable (*DR*), measuring the numbers of young people (ages 20–29), and (*REST*), the number of college graduates, both as fractions of all (ages 18–64) in all education groups combined. An added variable is a relative demand index (*RSG*), the ratio of employment in service producing to goods producing industries.

The relative supply of college graduates (*RES*) does indeed exert a negative effect on the wage gains to college education, holding demand variables fixed. The demand variables, in turn, also exert the theoretically expected effect. Thus in equation (1) the (Jorgenson) productivity growth variable has a positive effect presumably by increasing the demand for college graduates and so does the export deficit, by reducing wages of high school graduates.

In equation (1) the relative supply variable (*RES*), the fraction of young college graduates among all young people, does not take into account the context of baby boom, bust, or of a steady aggregate age distribution. In equation (2) the additional demographic variable (*DR*) representing the aggregate age distribution does, indeed, have a negative effect on the wage differential, at 6–10 years of experience, consistent with the hypothesis that there is less substitutability between young and experienced college graduates than between young and older high school graduates. The additional relative demand variable in (2) is the ratio of service employment to goods employment (*RSG*). It shows a positive effect on the college wage premium, reflecting a skill bias in the growing demand for services as well as the depressing effect of international competition on employment and wages of less-educated workers in manufacturing. Inclusion of this variable in equation (2), therefore, appears to replace (eliminate) the net export variable and weaken the productivity growth variable.

Although the explanatory power is significantly increased in equation (2) compared to equation (1), we should not reject the validity of the technological (*PG*) and international trade (*RNE*) demand factors, especially as they may, in part, represent the background influences affecting the employment ratio (*RSG*).

In equation (3) an alternative (to *PG*) measure of the pace of technology affecting the demand for human capital is provided by the (*R&D*) research and development expenditures per worker.[11] This is a sum of private and of government expenditures on R&D. Although studies indicate that government expenditures have a lesser effect on aggregate productivity growth than private expenditures do (BLS, 1989), the effect on demand for higher-level workers does not depend on the source of demand. Indeed, when the two components are put separately into the regression, their coefficients are quite close. The time pattern of the (combined) R&D variable is remarkably similar to the time-pattern of the college wage premium, when the former is lagged two or three years.[12] Consequently, this variable dominates (equation 3), and jointly with the relative supply (*REST*) and the relative employment variable (*RSG*) which remain significant, yields the strongest explanatory power for equation (3) compared to the preceding ones ($R^2 = 0.91$).

In cols (4) and (5) I replaced the *RSG* variable, which is to some extent suspected of endogeneity, by another variable which serves also to explore the applicability of the capital–skill complementarity hypothesis proposed by Griliches (1969). For the growth of capital intensity per worker I used expenditures on capital equipment per worker (*EQ*). I used equipment rather than all capital investments for obvious reasons: necessary skills apply to handling of equipment rather than to working inside particular structures (buildings). The *EQ* variable is positive and significant in cols (4) and (5), even when it is put alongside the productivity (*PG*) or research and development (R&D) variables. Both technology–skill and capital–skill complementarities appear to be at work, as measured. Still, as new technology is likely to be built into new equipment, the skill bias of technology may be revealed through both imperfectly correlated variables.[13] The explanatory power of regressions (4) and (5) is slightly weaker than of regressions (2) and (3). There is no strong evidence of serial correlation in any of the regressions.

The (aggregate) unemployment rate variable (*u*) was not significant[14] in any of the equations. Neither was a union density variable (membership as a proportion of the work force). Declining union membership may have been expected to help widen the wage differential in the 1980s and to partially counteract its narrowing in the 1970s. Union decline is very likely a consequence of declining demand for low-skilled labor in both periods, captured by the other variables. That equation (3) tracks the time pattern of the profitability of college education quite closely is shown in Figure 13.10, where the broken lines are the values predicted by the three variables in regression (3). Some of the 'saw-tooth' fluctuations in the actual value of college wage premia (solid line) are due to measurement errors, so the predictive power of the equation is likely to be even stronger than appears.

Additional insights on the way variables in Table 13.2 affect college (relative to high school) wage premia are provided by considering the effects of these variables on the components of the comparison, that is on *levels* of wages of high school and of college graduates, separately. This is done in Table 13.3 both at starting levels (1–5 years) and advanced levels (21–25 years) of experience of the two education groups. The skill bias of

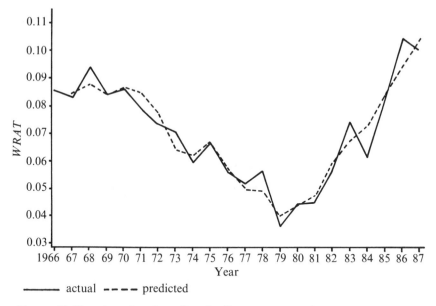

Figure 13.10   Actual and predicted college wage premia

the demand indexes of technology is quite apparent in their negative effect on wage levels of high school graduates, both young and old, and positive effects on wages of college graduates. Specifically, equations (1) and (2) of Table 13.3 show a negative effect of the Jorgenson productivity growth index (*PG*) on wage levels of young and of older high school graduates, but a positive effect on wages of young college graduates, and no significant effect on wages of older college graduates. Equations (3) and (4) show a negative effect of the research and development variable (*R&D*) on wages of young and older high school graduates, but a positive effect on wages of college graduates at both levels of experience.

The international trade deficit (*RNE*) reduced wages of young high school graduates, but not of older ones, and had a weak but, if anything, an opposite effect on wage levels of college graduates. Finally, the ratio of service to goods employment (*RSG*) had a negative effect on wages of young, and less so of older high school graduates and a positive effect on wages of young (less clearly), and of old college graduates (more clearly).

As was expected, the *RNE* and *RSG* variables tend to substitute for one another, so their effects are attenuated when both are included in the regressions (2) and (4) of Table 13.3.

Table 13.3 *Wage-level regressions*

	Experience 1–5 years				Experience 21–25 years			
	(1)	(2)	(3)	(4)	(1)	(2)	(3)	(4)
	High school							
Intercept	1.70 (6.0)	2.40 (8.3)	1.57 (6.8)	2.23 (7.3)	2.35 Z(13.9)	2.47 (10.8)	2.36 (15.2)	2.38 (9.5)
DRE_{-2}	0.48 (1.8)	0.66 (3.1)	-0.21 (0.5)	0.20 (0.6)	0.34 (2.1)	0.37 (2.2)	0.075 (0.3)	0.085 (0.3)
RES_{-2}	-1.39 (3.7)	-1.41 (5.00)	-0.95 (2.50)	-1.16 (3.6)	-0.85 (3.8)	-0.86 (3.8)	-0.71 (2.8)	-0.71 (2.7)
$R\&D_{-2}$			-.001 (2.8)	-0.0007 (2.4)			-0.0005 (2.1)	-0.0005 (1.9)
RNE	0.054 (4.7)	n.s.	0.024 (1.8)	n.s.	n.s.	n.s.	-0.019 (2.2)	-0.02 (1.6)
PG	-2.75 (1.4)	-3.30 (2.1)			-2.23 (1.8)	-2.32 (1.9)		
RSG		-0.183 (3.7)		-0.140 (2.8)		n.s.		n.s.
R^2	0.83	0.90	0.87	0.91	0.59	0.58	0.61	0.59

College

	(1)	(2)	(3)	(4)	(5)	(6)	(7)	(8)
Intercept	2.51	3.00	2.04	2.32	2.21	1.06	2.18	1.61
	(8.8)	(8.0)	(12.2)	(8.4)	(6.4)	(1.6)	(9.1)	(4.4)
DRE_{-2}	0.049	-0.12	0.20	0.11	0.60	0.86	0.74	0.86
	(0.3)	(0.6)	(1.9)	(0.8)	(3.8)	(4.4)	(5.3)	(5.7)
RES_{-2}	0.037	0.25	-0.036	0.072	-0.58	-0.98	-0.46	-0.64
	(0.2)	(1.1)	(0.3)	(0.5)	(2.8)	(3.5)	(2.8)	(3.4)
$R\&D_{-2}$			0.0008	0.0007			0.0007	0.0007
			(6.7)	(5.5)			(2.8)	(3.1)
RNE	n.s.		0.021	0.014	-0.051	n.s.	-0.034	-0.021
			(1.8)	(1.0)	(3.1)		(2.3)	(1.3)
PG	4.14	2.96			n.s.	n.s.		
	(2.6)	(1.8)						
RSG		0.126	n.s.			2.85		0.092
		(1.8)				(2.0)		(1.8)
R^2	0.45	0.52	0.79	0.80	0.34	0.42	0.55	0.59

Note
Excluded variables not significant.
t-values in parentheses.
n.s. = not significant.

389

Experience wage premia: age differentials in wages

The cross-sectional experience wage profile reflects (working) age differentials in wages. In a large literature, growth of older to younger wage ratios between the 1960s and 1970s has been attributed to the entry of the baby boom cohorts into the labor market.[15] With increased supplies of young workers relative to older workers, relative wages for the young declined, steepening the wage profiles in all education groups. Relative supplies (ratio of numbers of younger to all workers in the education group) were shown in Figure 13.4. Until the mid 1970s relative growth in young cohorts characterized all education groups, but was especially pronounced for post-secondary graduates. As a result Figure 13.2 shows that (log) wage ratios of older (those with 21–25 years of experience) to younger workers (with 1–5 years of experience) increased, more steeply for college than for high school graduates. Subsequently, however, the relative supply of young college graduates declined almost as steeply as it rose before, while the proportion of young high school graduates entering the market continued to increase until the mid-1980s. Figure 13.2 shows a continued steepening of the high school wage profile, accelerated in the 1980s. In contrast, the college wage profile stabilizes in the 1970s and 1980s. While the difference between the two education age profiles of wages is to some extent consistent with the differential growth of relative numbers, we might have expected a flattening of the college profile, given the relative decline in its young cohorts. The much steeper growth of the high school wage profile in the 1980s than in the 1970s is also out of line with the milder (compared to the college profile) and not-accelerating increase in relative numbers of young high school graduates.

Additional factors must have been at play in preventing the college profile from flattening and in accelerating the growth of the high school profile in the 1980s. A growing demand for skilled and experienced workers and a declining demand for unskilled and inexperienced workers would be consistent with the data in the face of the fading and reversal of the 'baby boom'.

A cursory look at differential effects of the demand variable (*R&D*, *PG*, *RSG*, and *RNE*) on levels of wages in Table 13.3 shows consistently stronger effects on wages of younger than older high school graduates. This is clear in the *negative* effects of high school wages and less clearly in *positive* effects on college wages. The relative skill bias of demand for labor thus contributes to the understanding of the differential changes in the slope of wages profiles in the high school and college groups.

A hypothesis which interprets these findings is that the changing profitability of human capital is reflected in age differentials in wages which are due to acquisitions of human capital at work, as it was in educational

Table 13.4 Cross-section experience profiles

Variables	High school			College		
	(1)	(2)	(3)	(1)	(2)	(3)
Intercept	0.65	1.77	1.51	0.60	1.00	0.72
	(2.8)	(15.1)	(6.5)	(4.6)	(10.3)	(7.8)
DRE_{-2}	0.48	1.21	0.90	0.44	0.48	
	(2.3)	(11.3)	(5.1)	(4.7)	(3.5)	(2.4)
RNE	−0.033			−0.019		
	(3.4)			(2.6)		
$R\&D_{-2}$	0.0004			0.0005		
	(3.5)			(2.1)		
u	0.016			0.015		
	(3.1)			(2.6)		
$W\hat{R}AT$		2.3			1.85	
		(5.3)			(1.7)	
$WRAT(A)$						1.23
						(3.7)
$WRAT(B)$			0.98			
			(1.6)			
R^2	0.92	0.88	0.71	0.78	0.41	0.65
D.W.	1.69	1.69	0.71	2.30	1.11	1.71

Notes
$W\hat{R}AT$: College-high school wage differential, estimated by equation 3 in Table 13.2.
$WRAT(A)$: Wage differential between postgraduates and college.
$WRAT(B)$: Wage differential between high school graduates and dropouts.
D.W. Durbin–Watson statistics.

differentials resulting from differences in human capital acquired at school. Although relative supply factors differ by school and age, the same demand factors must be at work. This hypothesis permits two alternative specifications of the wage profile regressions in Table 13.4. One, shown in col. 1 of Table 13.4, is to include, in addition to the cohort variable of the education group, the demand variables which were utilized in the educational premia regressions in Table 13.2. Alternatively, as shown in cols 2 and 3 of Table 13.4, the profitability variable itself (or its estimated value by the Table 13.2 regression 3) can be used for the same purpose.

Wage disadvantages for younger workers and wage advantages for older cohorts steepen the profile. Among the disadvantages of younger workers are the growth of their cohort in the education group (variable

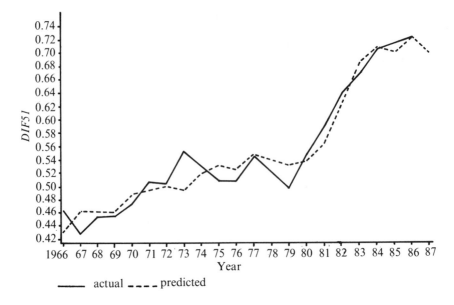

Figure 13.11   Actual and predicted experience wage ratios (high school)

DRE), growth of net imports for the less-educated, especially younger workers (*RNE*), and business cycle declines which tend to affect the young, low-tenured workers disproportionately, here measured by the unemployment rate (*u*). Relative wage advantages accruing to experienced (older) workers in both education groups are captured by the research and development (*R&D*) variable. All these variables were included in equation (1).

As col. 1 in Table 13.4 shows, each of the variables is significant[16] in explaining the changing wage profile of high school graduates of the past 25 years. Jointly they explain 92 per cent of the time variance of the wage profile. The college profile is affected by the same variables, but the joint explanatory power of the regression is weaker than in the high school group. Here $R^2 = 78$.

The wage profiles predicted by these regressions are indicated by broken lines in Figures 13.11 and 13.12, for high school and college respectively.

In the alternative specification (cols 2 and 3 of Table 13.4) the educational wage premium is substituted for the demand variables of col. 1. The reasoning, spelled out before, was that, if human capital becomes more profitable, both educational and experience wage premia should increase.

The estimated value of the college wage premium, based on equation 3 of Table 13.2 and shown in the broken line of Figure 13.10, has a stronger

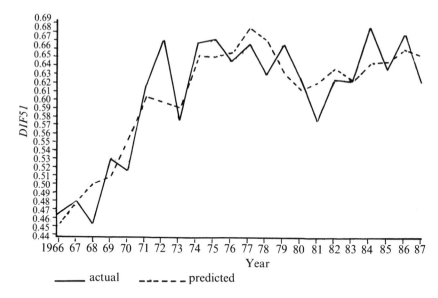

Figure 13.12   Actual and predicted experience wage ratios (college)

effect on the wage profiles of high school graduates than on that of college graduates. Also, equation (2), which uses the estimated college premium in the high school wage profile regressions, yields an $R^2 = 0.88$, close to the explanatory power of equation (1).

The explanatory power of the college–high school wage premium in the college wage profile regression is much lower ($R^2 = 0.41$ in col. 2). Although the profitability of experience moves in the same direction as the profitability of education, changes in the wage profile of the lower education group appear to be more closely tied to changes in profitability of the higher education group, rather than conversely. This impression is strengthened when the use of the post-graduate wage premium (relative to college) in the college experience regression yields a stronger explanatory power ($R^2 = 0.65$ compared to 0.41 in col. 3) for college; while the high school educational premium (relative to dropouts) yields only a weak effect in the high school regression (with $R^2 = 0.71$ compared to 0.88 in col. 3).

Since the college premium was estimated by regression, while the high school (relative to dropouts) and postgraduate (relative to graduate) premium are observed values (not regression estimated), the comparisons may be misleading. Table 13.5 therefore shows these comparisons in terms of observed premia: here *WRAT* (*A*) is the premium relative to the next higher educational group; *WRAT* (*B*) is relative to the next lower. The

Table 13.5   *Cross section experience profiles and observed educational profitabilities*

Education (years)	8–11		12		16		17+
Intercept	0.93	1.13	1.89	1.51	0.72	0.99	0.71
	(4.6)	(8.6)	(12.4)	(6.5)	(7.8)	(12.0)	(8.0)
DRE_{-2}	0.28	0.35	1.25	0.90	0.18	0.46	0.155
	(2.5)	(4.3)	(8.7)	(5.1)	(2.4)	(4.6)	(2.6)
WRAT(A)	0.72		1.71		1.23		
	(0.9)		(3.0)		(3.7)		
WRAT(B)		−0.82		0.98		1.22	0.70
		(0.9)		(1.6)		(2.0)	(2.3)
R^2	0.44	0.46	0.78	0.71	0.65	0.51	0.35

Notes
WRAT(A): Wage differential between education group and next above.
WRAT(B): Wage differential between education group and next below.
Neither was significant in the 13–15 years of education group.

results for the high school profile (cols 3 and 4) are confirmed: it is the rise in the college premium *WRAT* (*A*) that makes experience of high school more valuable, rather than the high school premium *WRAT* (*B*): the latter is smaller, and barely significant. At the college level (cols 5 and 6), the effects (in terms of regression coefficients) appear to be equal for *WRAT* (*B*) and *WRAT* (*A*), though the explanatory power is greater for the latter. Finally, the slope of the high school dropout group (cols 1 and 2) shows no effects of educational premia below or above, while the educational premium *WRAT* (*B*), (the only possible) is positive and significant for the slope of the postgraduate group.

In sum, a growing educational premium (best visible in the college–high school differential) raises the slopes of all education groups, high school and above.[17] The effects are, on balance, stronger when the profitability of the next higher groups changes. It is difficult, however, to say, at this point, whether this means that on-the-job skills of high school graduates rather than of college graduates substitute more for the scarcity of numbers of college graduates.

Another insight into this question may be obtained by looking at progress over time rather than cross-sections. This is done for groups of young workers in Table 13.6. Here the dependent variable is growth of

Table 13.6 Wage growth of young workers over 3 years of calendar time

	High school	College
Intercept	−0.054	−0.060
	(0.9)	(3.4)
DRE_{-2}	−0.028	−0.144
	(0.4)	(5.5)
$WRAT(A)$	0.77	
	(2.9)	
$WRAT(B)$		−0.85
		(3.4)
R^2	0.49	0.64

wages over three successive calendar years[18] of experience for the young workers (experience 3–6 and 7–10 pooled). The regression shows a positive effect of the college premium on progress of young high school workers, but not on early growth of college graduates' wages. This is perhaps clearer evidence that skill training of young high school graduates responds (at least in profitability terms) to the demand for or scarcity of college skills. However, the negative effect on early wage growth of college graduates (col. 2) is puzzling.

Table 13.6 also indicates a negative cohort (*DRE*) effect on wage progress as distinguished from cross-sectional slope, in the college group. No effect is seen in the high school group. If training effects on wages are reflected in the longitudinal findings, the results appear to indicate that effects of changes in the age distribution (teacher–trainee ratios), rather than of changes in opportunity costs, affected changes in the profitability of training. This suggests that the larger cohorts of college graduates in the 1970s received less (or less-profitable) training than before, when their numbers were larger than in the 1980s when they became scarce. Training of high school graduates, by the same interpretation, declined or became less profitable in the 1970s not because of the cohort increase (which was mild), but because of the abundance of college graduates (as reflected in the low college-wage premium); a reversal in the 1980s results, therefore, from the newly emerging scarcity of college graduates.

We may infer from this interpretation that job training is likely to have become more profitable in the 1980s compared to the 1970s, at least for high school graduates.[19]

Table 13.7   Education unemployment differentials (high school – college and above), 1968–86

Variables	Coefficients			
	(1) $N=18$	(2) $N=18$	(3) $N=18$	(4) $N=18$
Intercept	0.89	1.24	1.56	2.16
	(2.1)	(2.5)	(4.0)	(3.8)
Unemployment rate	0.046	0.045	0.035	0.031
	(3.1)	(3.1)	(2.3)	(2.0)
$RESYHS_{-2}$	1.33	1.82	1.39	2.06
	(3.9)	(3.5)	(3.7)	(3.4)
$R\&D_{-2}$	0.001	0.0012		
	(3.2)	(3.5)		
$PWRAT$			3.23	4.28
			(2.6)	(3.0)
RNE		0.033		0.043
		(1.2)		(1.4)
Adj. R^2	0.767	0.774	0.729	0.745
D.W.	1.81	2.29	1.62	2.18

Notes
t-values in parentheses.
Subscript $_{-2}$ denotes a 2-year lag.
D.W. = Durbin–Watson statistics.

A corollary: educational unemployment differentials

As is well known, the demand for unskilled labor is more volatile than that for skilled labor. This shows up in a negative relation between unemployment rates and education levels within the labor force,[20] as well as in widening unemployment differentials by education during recessions. By the same token, if the effect of technology is to increase the relative demand for more-educated labor, relative unemployment differentials should widen just as relative wages do when the pace of technology quickens.

To test this proposition, Table 13.7 relates relative unemployment differentials (logs of the ratio of unemployment rates of high school to college graduates) to aggregate unemployment (LUR), the relative supply of high school graduates ($RESYH$), the technological index ($R\&D$), the predicted wage differentials ($PWRAT$) used in col. 2 of Table 13.4, and the negative export balance (RNE). The results confirm the skill-bias in labor demand produced by technology. The significant positive coefficient on

R&D shows the widening of unemployment differentials when technology quickens. That this widening concurs with widening of wage differentials is shown by the positive and significant coefficients on (*PWRAT*) when it replaces *R&D*. Otherwise, the positive coefficients on aggregate unemployment confirm the widening due to business cycles, while relative increases of supply of high school graduates also raise their unemployment rate relative to the rate of college graduates. The significant coefficient on *RNE* confirms the negative effect of the growth of net imports on the demand for less-skilled workers.

6. Summary and concluding remarks

The empirical analysis resulted in several findings:

(a) The year-to-year educational wage differentials (between college and high school) are closely tracked by relative supplies of graduates in (roughly) their first decade of work experience, and more closely by changes in relative demand for more-educated workers which is indexed by research and development expenditures per worker (*RDE*), as well as by relative trends in service employment (*RSG*). Of these, *RDE* accounts for most of the explanatory power. Both Jorgenson-type multi-factor productivity growth (*PG*) indexes and net growth of goods imports were significant as alternatives, but showed weaker explanatory power.

(b) The skill-biased changes in demand appear to originate both from technology–skill and capital–skill complementarity; as indicated by the significance of the research and development variable as well as of the investment in equipment variable. However, the conceptual distinction may well be false, as new equipment embodies new technology.

(c) Neither unemployment fluctuations nor changes in union density appeared to play a role in the swings of the wage differentials. However, skill differentials in unemployment moved together with skill differentials in wages, or with the demand variables which produced them. This represents corollary evidence on the dominance of changes in demand for human capital in creating changes in the wage structure.

(d) With the decline of average productivity growth and the near-cessation of average real wage growth, the skill-biased changes in demand took the form of *increases* in demand for workers with post-secondary education and *decreases* in demand for workers at lower education levels.

(e) Changes in age distributions (cohort effects) account, in part, for the

observed steepening of experience profiles of wages. They do not
account for the acceleration of the high school profile or for the
stabilization of the college profile between the 1970s and 1980s. An
explanation is provided by additional variables reflecting the growing profitability of human capital which extends to that acquired by
experience on the job. This is shown by the effects of the demand
factors which are both skill- and age-biased, or alternatively by the
effects of changing profitability (educational wage differentials)
which is due to the demand changes, given the relative demographic
supplies.

In the latter specification, it appears that the increased value of experience of high school graduates is related to growing profitability of additional (college) education, but not of its own (relative to high school
dropouts). Also, the increased value of experience of college graduates is
related both to the profitability of college and of postgraduate education.

Viewed longitudinally, some evidence confirms the positive effect of
profitability of college on wage growth of young high school graduates,
but not on the profile of college graduates. Also, negative cohort effects
are observed on wage growth of college graduates but none on high school
graduates. This limited evidence may suggest substitution between
(college) school education and work experience or training of high school
graduates. It also suggests that large cohorts reduce, rather than increase,
the profitability of training by increasing rather than reducing its costs.

Increased growth in college enrollments of high school graduates which
started in the 1980s may continue in the 1990s if the rates of return have
not yet stabilized. We should note that these increments do not translate
into absolute numbers, as the young cohorts declined. Growth of job
training is all the more predictable, short of a protracted recession or of
prohibitive costs due to a deteriorating quality of trainees.

The major purpose of this study was to detect effects of changes in
technology on changes in the demand for human capital. Positive effects
of the pace of technology have been observed before in decade-long cross-
sections across industrial sectors. The present study extends the analysis to
annual time series at the national, aggregate level. It explores alternative
empirical indexes of the pace of technology. Effects of changes in demand
for human capital are observed in regressions, in which the dependent
variables are the profitability of human capital acquired at school, measured by the educational wage differential, and on human capital acquired
at work, measured by the experience-wage differential. In order to observe
these effects, it was necessary to include in the analysis other factors
affecting the profitability of human capital, such as relative educational

composition and age distributions, representing educational and experience dimensions of relative supplies of human capital. As a result, this study joins a number of recent studies which analyze the changing wage structure in recent decades.

The implementation of empirical indexes or proxies for the changing pace of technology appears to be successful in verifying its role in affecting the demand for human capital and the direction of its skill bias. These findings move us closer to an understanding of the apparent paradox of an absence of long-term decline in the profitability of human capital despite the massive growth of educational attainment. It remains to be seen whether the positive skill bias of technology inferred for the past two or three decades dominated also the preceding economic history.

Shorter-term (decade-long?) fluctuations in the profitability of human capital, here seen as skill differentials in wages, generate supply (enrollment) responses which, over time, provide a corrective to changes in profitability in an equilibrating manner. The long-term tendencies toward equilibrium are apparently trendless. I do not analyze the supply response. Rather, it is its feedback effect through a long pipeline that shows up in effects on profitability in this study.

The supply responses, or change in enrollment, are sensitive both to returns and costs of educational investments. The latter include opportunity costs as well as net direct costs. Direct costs are a balance of tuition and fees and of student earnings, loans subsidies, and grants. Skill (education) differentials in wages analyzed here (and elsewhere) measure returns net of opportunity costs only. They therefore overstate the growth of profitability, if net direct cost increases. It is very likely that the decline of profitability of human capital in the 1970s, and even more so its rebound in the 1980s are somewhat overstated. The overstatement is not major, as private net direct costs are much smaller than forgone earnings at the post-secondary levels.

Fluctuations in the indexes of technology rule out assumptions of a steady pace of demand for human capital. The reality behind the turnaround in the 'pace of technology' indexes between the 1970s and 1980s may be attributed to a growing momentum in information technologies. Indeed, supply responses in particular fields, currently visible at the postgraduate level, support this view: the US Department of Education (1990) reports that the number of MAs conferred in mathematics, computer science and engineering grew 70 per cent in the 1980s, while stagnant in other fields (with the exception of MBAs which grew 25 per cent). Among doctoral degrees which grew 7 per cent since 1980, engineering degrees, which declined in the 1970s, grew 67 per cent in the 1980s. Similarly, the number of doctorates in the natural sciences, which declines sharply in the 1970s, has outpaced the growth of total doctorates since the early 1980s.

A great deal of apprehension has been generated by the perception of a deteriorating quality of high school and lower levels of education in the past two decades. Evidence of low achievement levels is found in Standardized Aptitude Test (SAT) scores, and more compellingly in international comparisons, according to which, US students (high school and below) are in bottom ranks among industrialized countries. Deterioration over time is more difficult to document. Some weak evidence consists of declines in SAT scores, which levelled off recently and increases in high school graduation equivalence diplomas and high school equivalence certificates, relative to high school graduation.[21] If quality deterioration has not (yet?) affected post-secondary education, it may have contributed to the widened educational-wage differential. If so, this is another reason for a likely overstatement of the recent growth in profitability of college education.

Acknowledgements

This paper is a product of a research program funded by the National Science Foundation and the US Department of Education via the National Center on Education and Employment at Columbia University. I am grateful to David Bloom and to Finis Welch for data and discussions, and to Lalith Munasinghe for conscientious research assistance.

Notes

1. Equilibrium is best defined as the equality of rates of return on alternative capital investments.
2. A major merit of the Jorgenson TFP indexes for the purpose at hand was their construction as residuals from quality-adjusted changes in capital and labor-growth accounting. Quality adjustment of the labor input eliminates (or, at least, minimizes) the human capital content of the residuals thereby largely eliminating a spurious correlation between the residuals and the inputs that would otherwise occur. The decade long averages also reduce much of the year-to-year error and the effects of the business cycle.
3. Aside from the initial and continuing work of Murphy and Welch (1989), a number of papers were presented at three conferences at least in 1989 at Brookings, NBER, and AEI. A special focus on less-skilled workers is provided by Blackburn, Bloom, and Freeman (1990). Informative sectoral analyses are available in recent papers by Davis and Haltwanger (1990), and by Bound and Johnson (1991). A survey of related work on the changing income distributions is provided by Levy and Murnane (1991).
4. For simplicity of exposition, I ignore possible non-neutralities of economic growth with respect to age.
5. I am grateful to Finis Welch for providing the data.
6. This is the period when the net contribution of job training to wages is close to zero, thus revealing only schooling effects on wages (Mincer, 1974). For this wage premium to equal the rate of return, the denominator of the ratio has to include direct costs in addition to the opportunity costs, represented by the lower level wage.
7. The patterns of change in average wages differ somewhat depending on the definition of the average: because dispersion (inequality) in wages increased within groups during this period, arithmetic averages show greater increases and smaller declines, while the

logarithmic averages, used here, show smaller increase and greater declines (Kosters, 1989).
8. We used *population* measures of relative educational and demographic supplies, rather than *employment* numbers of specific groups (here white males). Relative population supplies are the truly exogenous variables which affect both relative employment and wages of specific subgroups (here white). This may be an overly cautious approach.
9. As referred to by Bartel and Lichtenberg; Gill; and Mincer.
10. Intensity of R&D per worker is clearly a more appropriate variable in affecting demand for labor quality than its intensity per dollar of GNP.
11. All monetary variables are in real terms. They are deflated by the Consumer Price Index.
12. According to the literature (BLS Bull, 1989), the same lag holds for the effects of R&D on productivity growth.
13. Berndt and Morrison (1991) single out 'high-tech' equipment (which includes computer, communications, and photocopy equipment). They find that it grew from 10% of the manufacturing capital stock in 1976 to 26% in 1986, and that increases in this 'high-tech' intensity of capital within two-digit manufacturing industries were correlated with increases in the average educational attainment of workers in these industries.
14. This is somewhat surprising, as skill differentials in wages tend to widen in recessions. The widening of unemployment differentials is confirmed in Table 13.7.
15. See Welch (1979) and the references therein.
16. The (*PG*) and (*RSG*) variables were not significant. Neither was a capacity utilization variable when substituted for the unemployment rate.
17. With the exception of 'some college'.
18. Given experience level x in year t, we look at wages of $(x + 1)$ in year $(t + 1)$, and so on.
19. Scattered evidence on profitability of job training (Mincer, 1989b) yields no clear evidence on this inference.
20. For a detailed analysis, see Mincer (1990).
21. See Bishop (1991); Cameron and Heckman (1991).

References

Bartel, A. and F. Lichtenberg (1987), 'The Comparative Advantage of Educated Workers in Implementing New Technology', *Review of Economics and Statistics*, February.
Becker, G. S. (1975), *Human Capital*, 2nd edn, Chicago: Chicago University Press.
Berger, M. C. (1985) 'The Effect of Cohort Size on Earnings Growth', *Journal of Political Economy*, June.
Berndt, E. R. and C. J. Morrison (1991), 'High-tech Capital, Economic Performance and Labor Composition', Conference on Productivity, Hebrew University of Jerusalem.
Bishop, J. (1991), 'Achievement, Test Scores, and Relative Wages', American Enterprise Institute.
Blackburn, M. L., D. E. Bloom and R. B. Freeman (1990), 'The Declining Economic Position of Less-Skilled American Men', in *A Future of Lousy Jobs?*, ed. G. Burtless, Washington, D.C.: Brookings Institution.
Bound, J. and G. Johnson (1991), 'Changes in the Structure of Wages in the 1980s: an evaluation of alternative explanations', Department of Economics, University of Michigan.
BLS Bulletin 2331 (1989), *The Impact of Research and Development on Productivity Growth*, Washington, D.C., September.
Cameron, S. V. and J. Heckman (1991), 'The Nonequivalence of High School Equivalents', University of Chicago.
Cyert, R. M. and D. C. Mowery (1987), *Technology and Employment*, Washington, D.C.: National Academy Press.

Davis, S. and J. Haltiwanger (1990), 'Wage Dispersion between and within U.S. Manufacturing Plants, 1963–1987', Brookings Conference.

Freeman, R. B. (1976), *The Overeducated American*, London: Academic Press.

Freeman, R. B. (1986), 'Demand for Education', in *Handbook of Labor Economics*, vol. 1, ed. O. Ashenfelter and R. Layard, Amsterdam: North-Holland, ch. 6.

Gill, I. (1989), 'Technological Change, Education, and Obsolescence of Human Capital', PhD thesis, University of Chicago.

Griliches, Z. (1969), 'Capital-Skill Complementarity', *Review of Economics and Statistics*, November.

Hamermesh, D. and J. Grant (1979), 'Econometric Studies of Labor – Labor Substitution and their Implications for Policy', *Journal of Human Resources*, Summer.

Jorgenson, D., F. Gollop and B. Fraumeni (1987), *Productivity and U.S. Economic Growth*, Cambridge, Mass.: Harvard University Press; updated series, 1990.

Kosters, M. (1989), 'The Wage Structure', paper presented at American Enterprise Institute Conference, September.

Levy, F. and R. J. Murnane (1990), 'Earnings Levels and Inequality', unpublished review, University of Maryland.

Mincer, J. (1974), *Schooling, Experience and Earnings*, New York: Columbia University Press.

Mincer, J. (1989a), 'Human Capital Responses to Technological Change', NBER Working Paper, December.

Mincer, J. (1989b), 'Job Training, Costs, Returns, and Wage Profiles', NCEE Paper, October. (Chapter 9 of this volume.)

Mincer, J. (1990), 'Education and Unemployment', NCEE Paper. (Chapter 7 of this volume.)

Mincer, J. and Higuchi, Y. (1988), 'Wage Structures and Labor Turnover in the United States and Japan', *Journal of the Japanese and International Economics*, June. (Chapter 11 of this volume.)

Murphy, K. and F. Welch (1989), 'Wage Premiums for College Graduates', *Educational Researcher*, May.

Nelson, R. and E. Phelps (1966), 'Investment in Humans, Technological Diffusion, and Economic Growth', *American Economic Review*, May.

Psacharopoulos, G. (1985), 'Returns to Education: an International Update', *Journal of Human Resources*, Fall.

Schultz, T. W. (1975), 'The Value of the Ability to Deal with Disequilibria', *Journal of Economic Literature*.

US Department of Education, Office of Educational Research and Improvement (1990), *Conditions of Education*, NCES Report no. 681.

US Department of Labour, Bureau of Labor Statistics (1989), *The Impact of Research and Development on Productivity Growth*, Bulletin no. 2331, September.

Welch, F. (1970), 'Education in Production', *Journal of Political Economy*.

Welch, F. (1979), 'Effects of Cohort Size on Earnings', *Journal of Political Economy*, October.

Appendix

Table A13.1   Construction of variables and sources

WRAT

Construction: The difference of the means of log hourly wages for the college and high school education groups averaged at 6–10 years of experience (white males).
Source: CPS, March issues, annual 1963 to 1987. Averages of logarithmic wages for each experience year and education group.

DIF51H and DIF51C

Construction: For each education group we take the means of log wages for two experience levels – for those with 1 to 5, and 21 to 25 years of experience. *DIF51H* is the difference in these two means for those with high school level of education (12 years of schooling), and *DIF51C* is the same for those with a college level of education (16 years of schooling) (white males).
Source: CPS, March issues, annual 1963 to 1987. Averages of logarithmic wages for each experience year and education group.

LNWYH, LNWOH, LNWYC, and LNWOC

Construction: For each education group we take the means for two experience levels – for those with 1 to 5, and 21 to 25 years of experience. Then we deflate the set means of log wages by the CPI (white males).
Source: CPS, March issues, annual 1963 to 1987. Averages of logarithmic wages for each experience year and education group.

W3GH and W3GC

Construction: Difference between 3 years ahead log wages and current log wages, for workers with 3 to 10 years of experience (white males).
Source: CPS, March issues, annual 1963 to 1987. Averages of logarithmic wages for each experience year and education group.

RESYH, RESYC, RESTH, RESTC, DREH, DREC and DR

Construction: Population restricted to white males.
$RESYH = \log\{$ # of noninstitutional population in the age group of 20–29 years with high school diploma (12 years of schooling)/total # of noninstitutional population in the age group of 20–29}.

$RESYC = \log\{$ # of noninstitutional population in the age group of 20–29 years with college degree (16 years of schooling)/total # of noninstitutional population in the age group of 20–29}.

Table 13.1A   Construction of variables and sources continued

---

$RESTH = \log\{\#$ of noninstitutional population in the age group of 18–46 years with high school diploma (12 years of schooling)/total $\#$ of noninstitutional population in the age group of 18–64}.

$RESTC = \log\{\#$ of noninstitutional population in the age group of 18–64 years with college degree (16 years of schooling)/total $\#$ of noninstitutional population in the age group of 18–64}.

$DREH = \log\{\#$ of noninstitutional population in the age group of 20–29 years with high school diploma (12 years of schooling)/total $\#$ of noninstitutional population (age group of 18–64) with high school diploma (12 yers of schooling)}.

$DREC = \log\{\#$ of noninstitutional population in the age group of 20–29 years with college degree (16 years of schooling)/total $\#$ of noninstitutional population (age group of 18–64) with college degree (16 years of schooling)}.

$DR = \log\{\#$ of noninstitutional population in the age group of 20–29 years/total $\#$ of noninstitutional population (age group of 18–64)}.

Source: US Bureau of the Census, *Current Population Report*, P–20 series; *Educational Attainment in the United States*, 1964–88.

PG
Source: D. Jorgenson, F. Gallop and B. Fraumeni, *Productivity and U.S. Economic Growth*, Cambridge, Mass.: Harvard University Press, 1987; updated series, 1990.

RDE
Construction: RDE = total dollar expenditure on research and development divided by the total employed in the US labor force.
Sources: (1) Total employed in US labor force: *Economic Report of the President*, February 1990, p. 332, Table C–33, column 1; (2) R&D expenditure in private sector: *The Impact of Research and Development on Productivity Growth*, US Department of Labor, Bureau of Labor Statistics, Bulletin 2331, September 1989, p. 26, Table 10; (3) R&D expenditure in government sector: Budget authority data from the National Science Foundation (1985, 1986B), page 35 in Technology and Employment: Innovation and Growth in the U.S. Economy, p. 35.

Table 13.1A   Construction of variables and sources concluded

RNE
Construction: The ratio of net exports in dollars to GNP in dollars multiplied by 100, generating the percent figure of net exports to GNP.
Source: Economic report of the President, February 1990. Net exports: p. 410, Table C–102, column 3; GNP: p. 306, Table C–10, column 1.

RSG
Construction: Ratio of the number of employees in goods-producing industries to the number of employees in service-producing industries.
Source: Economic Report of the President, February 1990. Total number of employees in goods-producing industries: p. 342, Table C–43, column 2; number of employees in service-producing industries: p. 343, Table C–43, column 1.

U
Source: Aggregate unemployment rate for white males reported in the *Economic Report of the President,* February 1990, p. 339, Table C–40, column 3.

Index

Economists of the Twentieth Century

Monetarism and Macroeconomic Policy
Thomas Mayer

Studies in Fiscal Federalism
Wallace E. Oates

The World Economy in Perspective
Essays in International Trade and European Integration
Herbert Giersch

Towards a New Economics
Critical Essays on Ecology, Distribution and Other Themes
Kenneth E. Boulding

Studies in Positive and Normative Economics
Martin J. Bailey

The Collected Essays of Richard E. Quandt (2 volumes)
Richard E. Quandt

International Trade Theory and Policy
Selected Essays of W. Max Corden
W. Max Corden

Organization and Technology in Capitalist Development
William Lazonick

Studies in Human Capital
Collected Essays of Jacob Mincer, Volume 1
Jacob Mincer

Studies in Labor Supply
Collected Essays of Jacob Mincer, Volume 2
Jacob Mincer

Macroeconomics and Economic Policy
The Selected Essays of Assar Lindbeck, Volume 1
Assar Lindbeck

The Welfare State
The Selected Essays of Assar Lindbeck, Volume 2
Assar Lindbeck

Classical Economics, Public Expenditure and Growth
Walter Eltis

The Liberal Economic Order (2 volumes)
Gottfried Haberler
Edited by Anthony Y. C. Koo

Economic Growth and Business Cycles
Prices and the Process of Cyclical Development
Paolo Sylos Labini

Economic Theory and Market Socialism
Selected Essays of Oskar Lange
Edited by Tadeusz Kowalik